Reviewed by Sheldon Rothblatt in the *American Historical Review*, 78 (December, 1973), 1466-1467; by Eamon Duffy in the *Journal of Ecclesiastical History*, 29 (October, 1978) 499-500.

ENGLISH
ROMAN CATHOLICS
AND HIGHER
EDUCATION

1830–1903

ENGLISH ROMAN CATHOLICS AND HIGHER EDUCATION

1830–1903

BY

VINCENT ALAN McCLELLAND

PROFESSOR OF EDUCATION IN THE
NATIONAL UNIVERSITY OF IRELAND

OXFORD
AT THE CLARENDON PRESS
1973

Oxford University Press, Ely House, London W. 1

GLASGOW NEW YORK TORONTO MELBOURNE WELLINGTON
CAPE TOWN IBADAN NAIROBI DAR ES SALAAM LUSAKA ADDIS ABABA
DELHI BOMBAY CALCUTTA MADRAS KARACHI LAHORE DACCA
KUALA LUMPUR SINGAPORE HONG KONG TOKYO

*Printed in Great Britain
at the University Press, Oxford
by Vivian Ridler
Printer to the University*

FOR MARIE
AND IN MEMORY OF
MY MOTHER

PREFACE

IN 1830 there were approximately 700,000 Roman Catholics in England and Wales; by 1903 this figure had risen to something in the region of 1,500,000. For a considerable part of the second half of the nineteenth century English Catholics were divided into three broad social groupings—'Old Catholics', who had preserved their faith unsullied from penal times, and who were dominated by an exclusive titular and landed aristocracy; Irish Catholics, largely made up of refugees from the famine and persecution endemic in their native land, and constituting a large, urban, pauperized community; and converts, many of them highly cultured and educated, products of the Oxford Movement and its aftermath. Gradually these groupings were eroded, partly as a consequence of intermarriage between converts and Old Catholics and between the Irish and their social counterparts among the Protestant English, and partly as a result of the rapid industrialization of the country and the emergence of a powerful professional class.

The effort to come to terms with the larger society within which Catholics in England had to function is the main theme of this study. The problem can be seen in microcosm in the fight for the provision of higher education and in the internal tensions and turmoil to which it gave rise. There are three main phases in the contest—a period of withdrawal, isolation, and dogged self-help, characterized by efforts to provide enlightened collegiate education and by a realization of the need for professional qualifications recognized by the State; a period of compromise and modification, typified by attempts to erect denominational university institutions for English Catholics in Ireland, Oxford, and London; and thirdly, a period of gradual assimilation, combined with efforts to retain a recognizable community identity. The process of gradual absorption has not yet been fully completed.

University College, Cork   V. A. M.
1972

ACKNOWLEDGEMENTS

I WISH to thank Professor W. H. G. Armytage of the University of Sheffield for wise and friendly counsel supplied over many years. This book, a substantially abridged version of my doctoral dissertation, owes much to his stimulating and evocative criticism. A considerable debt of gratitude is due to Bishop Thomas Leo Parker, Mgr. Alfred Newman Gilbey, Abbé Alphonse Chapeau, Fr. Francis Edwards, S.J., Dom Gerard Sitwell, Dr. David Milburn, and Fr. Peadar MacSuibhne, for bringing to my notice hitherto unpublished material and for giving me leave to quote from sources in their possession. The Archbishops of Birmingham and Southwark, the Bishops of Clifton and Leeds, the Abbots of Ampleforth and Downside, the Redemptorist Provincial, and the Superior of the London Oratory have opened their archives to me and for this I am deeply grateful. I acknowledge help from Professor A. C. F. Beales, from archivists and librarians, and from others too numerous to mention by name. I wish to thank publishers and authors for permission to quote from a wide range of books; full acknowledgement will be found in the notes and Bibliography. I apologize if I have unwittingly infringed anyone's copyright.

My deepest debt of gratitude is to my father, for his tireless support and encouragement during the period this work has taken to mature.

CONTENTS

Part One

EMANCIPATION AND THE FORMATION OF THE COLLEGIATE LINK WITH LONDON UNIVERSITY

I

EARLY EXPERIMENTS

AT the beginning of the nineteenth century English Catholics were still treated as inferior citizens. Although, since 1791, they had achieved a certain measure of toleration, in that they were free to set up their own credal schools, they were yet prevented from voting at parliamentary and municipal elections, were unable to enter Parliament, and were not permitted to hold positions under the Crown or in corporations.[1] From 1 December 1678 until 28 April 1829 there was not a Roman Catholic in either House of Parliament.[2] In the years from 1800 to 1829 the only measure of substantial relief awarded to Catholics was achieved through connivance on the part of War Office and Admiralty. Certain members of the Catholic nobility were at last enabled to hold junior posts in the army and navy and in government service.[3] It is true, however, that by skilful use of patronage the Old Catholic families were able to extend their sphere of influence considerably beyond the narrow limits prescribed by law. Among the Catholic nobility, for instance, the Duke of Norfolk was patron of five livings, the Earl of Shrewsbury of eleven, and Lord Petre of three, and a similar patronage was exercised in the provision of parliamentary candidates.[4] It was a gradual willingness on the part of authority to overlook minor breaches of law that enabled members of the Catholic landed families to assume positions of social standing in county affairs.

[1] Grant Robertson, C., *Select Statutes, Cases, and Documents* (London, 1923), esp. pp. 81–4.

[2] For details see Rogers, P., 'Catholic Emancipation', in Tierney, M. (ed.), *Daniel O'Connell: Nine Centenary Essays*, pp. 115–51 and esp. p. 123.

[3] Amherst, W. J., *The History of Catholic Emancipation, 1771–1820*, vol. 2, pp. 250–69.

[4] Lilly and Wallis, *A Manual of the Law Specially Affecting Catholics* (London, 1893), pp. 43 seq.

This tentative recognition of their status made them reluctant to risk antagonizing authority by assuming the lead in the struggle for full Emancipation. Bishop Milner, a protagonist in the fight for recognition before the law, felt 'that the great body of English Catholics, the middle classes and the poor, were on his side and it was only the five hundred wealthy Catholics whom he regarded with invincible repugnance'.[5] O'Connell, too, found the fashionable Catholic families indifferent to the Emancipation fight—they remained aloof 'as they attended the routs in London and their curricles rolled along the Brighton road'. It was an attitude borne out by their reaction to the Catholic Relief Bill of 1829. They were slow to take advantage of the new fields of influence opened up to them. When the eldest son of the Duke of Norfolk, the Earl of Arundel, secured election as Member of Parliament for Horsham, he refused to concern himself with religious issues and immediately pledged his support to the entire Whig programme.

The 'emancipation' clauses of 1829 were not revolutionary, although they alarmed John Henry Newman in his concern for the ascendancy of Anglican interests at Oxford. The declaration against transubstantiation in the Acts of 1673 and 1678 was dropped, except for the offices of Regent, Lord Chancellor of England, Lord Chancellor of Ireland, Lord Lieutenant of Ireland, and High Commissioner to the General Assembly of the Church of Scotland. Catholics were enabled to sit and vote in either House of Parliament. All posts of profit or trust under the Crown were opened to them except those already prescribed. They were enabled to vote at parliamentary elections and exercise all other civil rights, a new oath being imposed which they could take with a clear conscience. In 1832 an Act was passed protecting Catholic charitable trusts, and a new Marriage Act in 1836 legalized Catholic marriages in a church registered for the purpose. What the Emancipation Act failed to do, and the failure invalidated much of what Catholics had hoped the Act would make possible, was to open the Universities of Oxford and Cambridge to Catholic youth. Although parliamentary Acts were passed for

[5] Mathew, the Revd. D., *Catholicism in England: the Portrait of a Minority, its Culture and Tradition*, pp. 172–3.

Oxford in 1854 and for Cambridge two years later, opening the bachelor's degree to Dissenters at both universities, the final abolition of the religious tests had to wait until 1871.

It is true that one or two Catholics made their way to Cambridge as undergraduates prior to the fifties, because the religious test was only exacted there upon graduation and not at matriculation as it was at Oxford. Indeed, no less a personage than Cardinal Acton pursued the entire undergraduate course at Magdalene College, Cambridge, in the early 1820s. But such examples were rare, and the general effect of Emancipation was to increase the frustration experienced by the Catholic gentry. When most doors to professional advancement had been closed, they had not felt a pressing need for university education; now that career prospects were at last before them, they were incapable of seizing the opportunity. It is this situation which brought about the first attempt since the seventeenth century to make distinct provision for the higher education of English Catholics. The man who attempted to meet the challenge was a forceful, gifted, Benedictine monk, whose activities and far-sighted plans were to dominate the Roman Catholic Church in England in the years immediately preceding and following the passing of the Emancipation Act. His name was Peter Augustine Baines; his religious home was Ampleforth.

Cardinal Wiseman in *Recollections of the Last Four Popes* has left us a graphic pen-picture of Baines. 'He had a power of fascinating all who approached, in spite of a positive tone and manner which scarcely admitted of a difference from him in opinion', he writes. 'He had sometimes original views upon a certain class of subject; but on every topic he had a command of language and a clear manner of expressing his sentiments which commanded attention, and generally won assent. Hence his acquaintances were always willing listeners, and soon became warm admirers, then warm partisans.'[6] Wiseman himself fell victim to the charm, declaring that he was 'devoted to [Baines] heart and soul, and lost favour in Rome by the manner in which I espoused his cause'.[7] Wiseman's

---

[6] Wiseman, Cardinal, *Recollections of the Last Four Popes*, p. 325.
[7] Ward, B., *Sequel to Catholic Emancipation*, vol. i, p. 70.

estimate of Baines's character finds an echo in a letter of Fr. Jean Loewenbrück, of the Institute of Charity, to his Superior, Antonio Rosmini-Serbati, in September 1837. He thought Baines was 'very distinguished in many ways, but he is a swashbuckler, a despot. He often acts on angry impulse, and is capable of suddenly conceiving and executing extreme measures that really require time to mature.'[8] It has been said that in Baines we see an example of the theorist getting the better of the practical man, and 'the experimenter ousting the one who is unwilling "to be the first on whom the new is tried"'.[9] It has to be admitted, however, that Baines possessed an insight denied to lesser men, and that he came very near to success in a venture which would have daunted many Churchmen of today.

Peter Augustine Baines, O.S.B., first came to the notice of English Catholics in 1823, when at the age of thirty-seven he was designated titular Bishop of 'Siga' and Coadjutor, *cum jure successionis*, to the sickly and ageing Franciscan, Peter Bernardine Collingridge, Vicar Apostolic of the Western District of England. Baines had enjoyed a distinguished career at Ampleforth as Director of Studies and Sub-Prior. It is not without significance for his future history, however, that he elected to be consecrated not in England but in Ireland by Dr. Daniel Murray, Archbishop of Dublin. He was to become a warm friend in particular of J. K. L., James Doyle, the fiery Augustinian who 'so far surpassed O'Connell as O'Connell surpassed other men', and who was referred to by the great Emancipator himself as the 'Lion of the Fold of Judah'[10] for his advocacy of the cause of denominational education and Irish land reform. It was his friendship with Doyle and other Irish bishops that was destined to make Baines's name anathema to many members of the English Catholic aristocracy.

When Baines arrived in the Western District he was confronted with a vast expanse of territory (the whole of Wales and the area

---

[8] Letter quoted by Leetham, the Revd. C., *Luigi Gentili: a Sower for the Second Spring*, p. 88.

[9] Roche, the Revd. J. S., *A History of Prior Park College and its Founder Bishop Baines*, p. 37.

[10] MacSuibhne, the Revd. P., *Paul Cullen and his Contemporaries, with their Letters from 1820–1902*, vol. I, p. 145.

from Gloucestershire and Wiltshire to Cornwall), a paucity of priests, a shortage of money, and an ailing Bishop. The District did not possess an ecclesiastical college and had no means of preparing candidates for the priesthood. It did, however, have a flourishing and prosperous Benedictine house—Downside— independent of the Vicar, well stocked with priests, some of them engaged exclusively in teaching. It was an institution which appeared to have no direct link with the District. It is true that the monastery served a number of rural missions close to the main house, but even these isolated pockets of activity were exempted from the Vicar's control. Baines initially proposed to solve his troubles by making the monastery the focal point of the District. He hoped that Downside would undertake the duties of educating students for the pastoral priesthood, and of providing a good education for the poorer lay boys of the District. He relied, some-what naïvely as it turned out, on the fact that the Community would not resent working in collaboration with a bishop who was a Benedictine. But the rule of a monk of Ampleforth was not viewed with equanimity by the monks of its Somerset rival.

When Downside eventually refused to have any part of Baines's plan, he tried to arrange that the Ampleforth and Downside monks should exchange their monastic buildings, for the Ample-forth Community was much more in line with the thinking of their old Sub-Prior. Again Downside resisted, not wishing to exchange the luxury of Somerset for the arid wastes of Mowbray Vale. The Bishop's attempts at coercion won him dislike at home and distrust at Rome. It is easy, of course, to judge Baines harshly, but it may be asked from whence was he to get the necessary men to serve his District, as it should be served for the good of religion, if the Community of St. Gregory's held aloof? It was a dilemma that would have taxed the patience of a much less volatile man. Baines was not seeking a prestige-symbol; a Diocesan College was necessary for the very life-blood of the District. Without such a College there would never be vocations to the pastoral clergy.

In 1826 Baines experienced a serious breakdown in health. It was diagnosed that he was suffering from cancer and had not long to live. In the winter of 1826 he journeyed to Rome, hoping that the Italian climate might help in staying the disease. Wiseman has described the Bishop's 'state of almost hopeless illness' and his 'enfeebled frame and constitution'[11] when he arrived in the city. He was destined to spend three years in Assisi, Porto di Fermo, and Rome, before, as Wiseman describes it, 'the mild climate, the interesting recreation, and perhaps, more still, the rest from the labour and excitement in which he had lived' finally effected a cure.

During his stay in Rome Baines was not idle. He acquired, for instance, a considerable reputation as a preacher. 'The church, which was nearly empty when preachers of inferior rank occupied it, was crowded when Bishop Baines was announced as the orator', writes Wiseman, for 'the flow of his words was easy and copious, his imagery was often very elegant, and his discourses were replete with thought and solid matter. But his great power was in his delivery, in voice, in tone, in look, and gesture. His whole manner was full of pathos, sometimes more even than the matter justified.'[12] It was probably their joint interest in the art of pulpit oratory which brought together Baines and Wiseman. The latter was Rector of the English College in Rome, and shared with Baines the duty of giving the English sermon instituted by Leo XII. When Leo, attracted by the personality of the young English Benedictine, offered him the Red Hat, Baines declined, not wishing to pass the remainder of his life in the Papal Curia. It is ironic that the Hat, so cavalierly rejected, should eventually be placed on the head of his young companion, the Rector of the English College.

In January 1827, shortly after his arrival in Rome, a plan began to form in Baines's mind concerning the provision of a house of higher studies in the Eternal City. This institution, formally affiliated to the Roman University, would work in collaboration with the seminary-college he dreamed of establishing in the Western District. There was no shortage of talent in Rome, and students, both clerical and lay, could pass automatically from the college at home to the house of higher studies. The academic course would be capped by the award of a degree. Baines wrote

---

[11] Fothergill, B., *Nicholas Wiseman*, p. 53.
[12] Wiseman, *Recollections of the Last Four Popes*, pp. 205–6.

to Prior Burgess of Ampleforth in 1828 that a plan for the opening of a college in Rome to cater for lay students had been put before the Pope, who had approved it in principle. Shortly after his return to England the Bishop drew up a prospectus for the 'Establishment for Completing the Education of Catholic Gentlemen at Rome Under the Direction of Revd. Thomas Rooker of Prior Park College, near Bath'.[13] It opened with the statement: 'this establishment is intended to supply to a limited number of Catholic Young Gentlemen the benefit of a University education, which the existing laws do not allow them to secure at home, as well as to supersede the necessity of an expensive, dangerous, and often ill-directed, inefficient course of travels.'

The curriculum to be followed at Rome included the Italian Language; Moral, Natural, and Experimental Philosophy; Roman and other Antiquities; History, Doctrine, and Ceremonial of the Catholic Church; Higher branches of Classical Literature in general; Music, Drawing, and Painting. It was stated that students must be ready to travel to Rome with the Revd. Mr. Rooker in August 1830.

In March 1829 Bishop Collingridge had died and Baines had succeeded to full control of the Western District. He was successful in persuading a number of the Ampleforth Community to accompany him to Bath to commence the project of establishing a Catholic College and Seminary in the Western District. The Prior of Ampleforth Thomas Burgess, the Sub-Prior Thomas Rooker, and the Procurator Edward Metcalfe, together with another monk, Thomas Brindle, and three novices, Leonard Calderbank, Moses Furlong, and Peter Hutton, all agreed to join the Bishop. The monks were released from vows.

In November 1829 Baines sought the approval of his fellow bishops for the purchase of Prior Park mansion. They not only sanctioned the venture but promised to set up a special subscription in every chapel in the kingdom to provide the necessary money, and they agreed to recommend the purchase in an episcopal letter. From Dom Ralph William Cooper, Prior of St. Laurence's in 1867, we learn that Baines 'gave the sum of £22,500

[13] Cited in Roche, dated 14 Apr. 1830, and addressed to Burgess.

in the original purchase', and Cooper asserts that 'a good deal of that came from the funds and property' of the District.[14] Baines himself claimed, however, that only £5,000 of the original purchase money was taken from District funds, and that the collection promised by his fellow bishops raised about £6,000. The remainder was obtained from private benefactors and the property was mortgaged for £11,500. The estate itself encompassed more than 187 acres of land and was situated on a hilly site two miles from Bath. The grounds were magnificent and the buildings of architectural splendour. It was in such surroundings that Baines determined to make a start on his educational venture. Many of the first students accompanied their old masters from Ampleforth, or were relatives of Baines or of the staff. Two of them were Wiseman's nephews. With the opening of Prior Park it was inevitable that the Roman scheme should fall into abeyance. It was to die a natural death once Baines decided it would be more practicable to locate the house of higher studies in a wing of the Prior Park building.

In October 1834 Baines wrote to the Bishop of Liège concerning the plan of founding a Catholic university at Prior Park. In the previous January he had journeyed to Rome to enlist the aid of Wiseman in the foundation and to secure Papal approval. Wiseman records the outcome: 'His Holiness the Pope has been pleased most highly to commend and encourage this undertaking, and has promised to erect the Establishment into a University as soon as all things shall be organised for that purpose.'[15] He added that he himself 'in conformity with the wishes of H.H. the Pope had undertaken to order and organise the new Establishment on behalf of the Rt. Reverend Bishop Baines'. There was, however, to be a *quid pro quo*. In return for Wiseman's help, he was to be nominated as Baines's Coadjutor with the right of succession. In a letter to Archbishop Whitefield, of Baltimore, Wiseman declared in 1834 that 'should the establishment flourish and my presence be of service to it, it is the declared intention of the bishop, Dr. Baines, to propose me for his Coadjutor. Indeed he has done so

14 Ampleforth Archives, vol. 245, no. 172. Letter dated 18 Jan. 1867.
15 Letter printed in *The Venerabile*, 4, no. 1 (1928), pp. 55–6.

already, but a delay has been proposed till some other affairs of his diocese are satisfactorily arranged. The probabilities are strong that I shall return no more to Rome to reside. At any rate my absence will be prolonged.'[16]

Although Baines returned from Rome jubilant at his success, Wiseman had been less than frank with him. The latter had other offers, and Wiseman's visit to England in 1835, ostensibly to fulfil a series of preaching engagements, was primarily to view the available openings. In 1832 Bishop Thomas Walsh of the Midland District had competed for his services: 'Come to the healthy Midland county of England', he had written, and he had flattered Wiseman, referring to him as the 'learned doctor'.[17] Furthermore, Walsh already had an ecclesiastical college, Old Oscott, and was able to offer considerable scope to a young cleric filled with glorious ideas of the conversion of England. It was hinted that Wiseman might be made Coadjutor to Walsh and be permitted to assume responsibilities for the mission at Cambridge. Piquancy was added to these temptations by Wiseman's growing acquaintance with the Cambridge converts, Ambrose Phillipps and Kenelm Digby, and by the zeal of the young convert parson, George Spencer, son of Lord Althorp, a future Chancellor of the Exchequer. Spencer had been sent to study at the English College under Wiseman, and through the acquaintance the latter became the confidant of Lord Shrewsbury. It was in the Midland District that Shrewsbury was most influential, and where, together with the genius of Pugin and the enthusiasm of Phillipps, the most spectacular achievements of the Gothic Revival were to be appreciated. Baines, on the other hand, was at odds with Shrewsbury and out of sympathy with the ideals of Gothicism. Whenever Baines was invited to be present at the opening of Pugin's churches he made a formal protest against extravagant display. In 1839 he refused to attend the opening of the church at Uttoxeter because Gothic vestments were to be used, and shortly afterwards he protested at Rome against chasubles three feet six inches wide.[18]

[16] Letter printed in *The Dublin Review* (Oct. 1918).
[17] *The Venerabile*, 4, no. 1 (1928), pp. 55–6.
[18] See Gwynn, D., *Lord Shrewsbury, Pugin, and the Catholic Revival*, pp. 54–5.

Such attitudes found no sympathy in Wiseman's heart, and Baines's growing dislike of Lord Shrewsbury, on account of the latter's antagonism to the Irish bishops, was another source of conflict. The feeling for Ireland which Baines always cherished had been enhanced by frequent visits to the Irish College in Rome during his long period of convalescence. There he had cultivated the friendship of Andrew Quinn, later to be Vicar General in Dublin, and Edmund O'Reilly, who was to become involved in Newman's university project. Wiseman became more and more attracted to Shrewsbury, and Bishop Walsh was later to admit that it was only 'after insistent pressure from Lord Shrewsbury' that he had recommended Wiseman for the Westminster See during the negotiations for the restoration of the English hierarchy.[19]

When Wiseman journeyed to Prior Park in 1835, it was with mixed feelings that he contemplated the future. By allying himself with Baines he might be sacrificing all that he ardently desired. The Western District was too remote from those centres of the Catholic Revival, Oscott and the Universities of Oxford and Cambridge, where rumour had it even now that strange developments were taking place. He would be engaged in endeavouring to establish a Catholic University *de novo*, when it would be much easier to take over the going concern of Oscott, a college favoured by his aristocratic friends. How much more good could be done in the heart of England, at the head of the movement which was going to lead the nation back into the true fold, than in the remote areas of Wales and Gloucestershire, where Catholics were few and scattered. Such thoughts must have had weight in the mind of a man who was later to request the Pope that in the event of a hierarchy's being set up he should be kept in London, because it was 'a theatre more vast and more suitable for his zeal'.[20] And what too of that momentous meeting Wiseman had experienced in 1831 with the three seminal minds of French Catholicism, the Abbé de Lamennais, the Abbé Lacordaire, and the Count de Montalembert, a meeting to be followed two years later by one even more memorable, that with John Henry Newman

[19] Leetham, *Luigi Gentili*, pp. 324–5. Letter of Gentili to Cardinal Franzoni, 8 Nov. 1847.   [20] Ibid., p. 321.

and Hurrell Froude? In 1847, looking back to this meeting, Wiseman declared: 'From the day of Newman and Froude's visit to me, never for an instant did I waver in my conviction that a new era had commenced in England . . . to this grand object I devoted myself . . . the favourite studies of former years were abandoned for the pursuit of this aim alone.'[21] Before Wiseman reached the portals of Prior Park his internal conflict had been resolved. He left within three weeks, dissociating himself further from the university scheme. But more than this, Wiseman spoke disparagingly of the entire episode to his aristocratic allies, and hinted that Baines had not dealt openly with him in the matter of the bishopric.[22] Baines was furious, for he maintained he had always been frank with Wiseman. In November 1835 he wrote a letter to Wiseman accusing him of distorting the truth.[23] It was a rebuff such 'as I had never received before, and never have since', wrote Wiseman years later.[24] Baines felt the gravity of the blow that Wiseman's defection had aimed at his infant foundation, for the latter was a man 'who would have attracted . . . the best families of England by the high opinion he had earned as a learned scholar and an active administrator'.[25]

Baines, however, did not give up easily. The establishment at Prior Park was divided into two distinct Colleges by the erection of new buildings in 1836 for the older students. St. Peter's College remained the school, while the new St. Paul's was to be a house of higher studies and to accommodate the ecclesiastical students. The Bishop himself occupied the mansion house, thus separating the two institutions from each other. He found his greatest difficulty to be that of acquiring suitable professors. In 1832 he enhanced the dignity of Rooker by securing a Papal doctorate in Divinity for him, and he parted with two members of his original team, Burgess and Metcalfe, when he realized they were not of the intellectual calibre to make a success of a university venture. He was able to attract a distinguished Cambridge convert to join him, Thomas Logan, whom he ordained at Prior

[21] Fothergill, p. 63.   [22] *The Venerabile*, 4, no. 1 (1928), pp. 55–6.
[23] Ibid.   [24] Ward, B., *Sequel to Catholic Emancipation*, vol. 1, p. 70.
[25] Leetham, C., *Rosmini: Priest, Philosopher, and Patriot* (London, 1957), p. 189.

Park in 1830. Of Logan, Wiseman wrote that 'as a Professor of Philosophy he is equal to the chair of any university, whether in metaphysics, or their application to branches of natural sciences [and] his reading besides in every department of literature is immense and quite extraordinary'.[26] Undoubtedly Baines was worried that the competition provided by Oscott (especially from 1838, when 'New Oscott' was opened), with a staff containing the names of Wiseman and Pugin, would prove too great for the success of Prior Park. He tried to negotiate for the services of Lingard, the historian, and when this failed he appointed a Dr. Dunham, on Lingard's advice, as Professor of History. Dunham's appointment proved to be disastrous when he was arrested at Prior Park for debt.

Much more successful was Baines's effort to acquire the aid of Antonio Rosmini's Institute of Charity. It had been hoped originally that Wiseman's presence at Prior Park would attract Italian and German scholars to join the staff. But Baines had his own contacts. In 1830 he had been joined by Wiseman and the Rector of the Irish College, Rome, in pressing Luigi Gentili to accept a post in the incipient university. Gentili's formation in the Institute of Charity was, however, yet to be completed, but the original contact did at last bear fruit when Rosmini promised Baines, at Domodossola in 1834, that he would send three of his men to teach at Prior Park. These left Italy in 1835 and served the Bishop loyally and generously until 1843. Gentili was the leader of the little band, and his first companions were two Frenchmen, Antonio Rey and Emilio Belisy.

When St. Paul's College was formally opened in 1836, Baines left no one in doubt of his intentions. He declared that the College had been established 'with a particular eye to the education of the Catholic Laity', and claimed that, although 'the Catholic youth of this country have long laboured under a serious disadvantage in being excluded from the public universities and in not possessing any adequate substitutes for these essential institutions', the English Catholic colleges in existence, as far as the lay students were concerned, had 'supplied the place of the school rather than the

[26] Roche, p. 113.

university'.[27] He went on to state that in the other colleges 'the elements of the learned languages, as well as of Mathematics, and some of the more useful Sciences have been ably taught, but the completion of their studies and their application to the useful purposes for which they are designed, have been, though necessarily too, generally omitted. Yet it is certain that studies mainly elementary are of little use for the improvement of the mind. They are the instruments of wisdom rather than wisdom itself, the keys which unlock the treasures rather than the treasures themselves'.

The buildings of St Paul's College were completed in the autumn of 1836, after a disastrous fire had destroyed the mansion in the central concourse of buildings in the previous May. Gentili became President of St. Paul's, which was run as a distinct and separate entity from the school (St. Peter's College). The Bishop described St. Paul's as existing 'for the prosecution of higher studies, ecclesiastical and secular, and for supplying in a certain degree the want of a Catholic University'. The building, equipped with private rooms for the senior students and the staff, was provided with library, chapel, lecture-rooms, and an exhibition room. In *The Laity's Directory* for 1837 an advertisement appeared which described the studies at St. Paul's as embracing 'the classical, scientific, and literary courses usually assigned to the University'. This Catholic 'University' had its own press, set up by Baines in 1831, from which emanated Bishop Hendren's *Translations of the Psalms* and Antonio Rey's two-volume *Dogmatic Theology*.

Although St. Peter's School continued to flourish, St. Paul's never really got off the ground. Five years before his death, in a letter to Bishop John Briggs of the Northern District, Baines gave way to the frustration he experienced. 'I wish I could make your Lordship feel as strongly as I do', he wrote, 'the vast importance of establishing in England, independently of our several episcopal seminaries, one general College in the form of a University where a considerable number of our clerical students from the different Districts might obtain a superior education on sound clerical principles and be trained in a system of discipline which never

[27] Ibid., pp. 117–18.

can exist in a small establishment.'[28] But the cry was useless; at the time Baines was writing, Briggs was attempting to suborn the Rosminians from Prior Park in favour of his establishment at Ushaw.[29] Baines died in 1843, aged fifty-seven, and although the College struggled on until 1856 it ceased to be talked of as a Catholic University. Three years before his death Baines succeeded in having the College affiliated to London University, and students were thus enabled to prepare for Matriculation and the Bachelor's degree. In this matter, however, Prior Park was in no sense unique. Similar affiliation was sought and obtained by most of the rival Catholic institutions. Prior Park College was to be reopened in 1867 by Bishop Clifford of Clifton, who immediately resurrected the idea of developing the establishment into a Catholic University,[30] but this attempt was closely followed by Archbishop Manning's own scheme in 1873 for a Catholic University College at Kensington, and yielded precedence to it.

Baines's failure cannot be ascribed entirely to the reluctance of the Catholic aristocracy to support the venture. Lord Arundell of Wardour and Lady Mary Arundell were among his keenest supporters,[31] and Lord Clifford of Chudleigh often officiated at the viva-voce examinations held in the College. The Doughty-Tichbornes respected his scholarship and integrity, the Mostyns sent their children to him, and even Ambrose Phillipps, on account of his ripening friendship with Gentili and the Rosminians, began to see considerable worth in the Bishop. But there were too many colleges, each one having its own traditions and aristocratic clientele. The moment of conception was inopportune. Emancipation was but a recent fact. The Catholic landed families had not begun to appreciate fully the need for a separate provision for higher education, and their attention was distracted by developments within the Church of England and by the revival of Gothicism within their own Church. A hierarchy was being talked of and mass conversions from the Establishment were expected in

[28] Roche, p. 118.

[29] Milburn, D., *A History of Ushaw College*, p. 175 n.

[30] See my *Cardinal Manning*, pp. 104 seq.

[31] See Hirst, J., and others, *Memoirs of Lady Mary Arundell, Moses Furlong, Angelo Rinolfi, Peter Hutton, William Lockhart*, passim.

its wake. The Vicars themselves, all sturdily independent personalities, were unused to corporate action and were suspicious of
those who urged it. They were unwilling to impoverish the Colleges of Oscott, Ushaw, and St. Edmund's for the sake of Bishop
Baines and his remote institution. There were few educated professors available to staff all the colleges and there was keen rivalry
among the Vicars for the available talent. The Old Catholic
families, too, were insular in outlook and reluctant to commit
their sons to the educational care of Italians and Frenchmen. It is
doubtful, if Wiseman and Lingard had been secured for Prior Park,
whether Baines would have been able to gather together under
one roof all the senior students from the other colleges. The
rivalry between the Religious Orders and Congregations, and
between Regulars and Seculars, was to bedevil Catholic education
at all levels throughout the nineteenth century, and to prevent
anything like a concerted policy in the matter of higher education.

Wiseman assumed the Presidency of Oscott in September 1840.
'I find everything to my hand that I could desire for furthering
my views', he wrote to John Lingard. He now ruled 'a magnificent college, with a still more magnificent library (and) professors,
some already most able, the rest qualifying themselves to raise our
education to the highest standard'. He pointed out that 'these
are certainly great advantages, which, conjointly with a central position, I could hardly have found elsewhere'.[32] Once the
embarrassment of his relations with Prior Park had been forgotten, he determined to make Oscott the leading Catholic
College in the country. There is little doubt that he nurtured the
hope that it would eventually emerge as a university institution.
That Wiseman kept this dream before him was testified to by
Newman in a letter he wrote in 1863 to Bishop Ullathorne on
the subject of university education. According to Canon Bernard
Smith, however, Wiseman's real success lay in the prestige he was
able to bring to the College. Smith relates with pride how the
College had visits 'from such men as Mr. Gladstone, Lord
Lyttelton, the Duke de Bordeaux, Daniel O'Connell, Lord
Spencer, Monckton Milnes (afterwards Lord Houghton), and

[32] Ward, B., *Sequel to Catholic Emancipation*, vol. 2, pp. 5–6.

many others'.[33] Lord Acton testified that the students 'used to see [Wiseman] with Lord Shrewsbury, with O'Connell, with Father Mathew, with a Mesopotamian patriarch, with Newman, with Pugin', and that they 'had a feeling that Oscott, next to Pekin, was a centre of the world'.[34] This indeed was Wiseman's great achievement at Oscott, and it was one made easier by the fact that hardly six months of his presidency had elapsed before the issue of Tract 90. As a consequence he found himself and his College in the very centre of controversy. He became one of the most sought-after men of his day and the recognized exponent of all that was attractive and compelling in the Roman tradition. Wiseman's vision became wider as his hopes for the future of English Catholicism soared higher. 'Often in my darkest days and hours,' he wrote in 1847, 'feeling as if alone in my hopes, have I walked in front of [the College], and casting my eyes towards it, exclaimed to myself, "No, it was not to educate a few boys that this was erected, but to be the rallying point of the yet silent but vast movement towards the Catholic Church, which has commenced and must prosper." I felt as assured of this as if the word of prophecy had spoken it.'[35] The harbouring of such great and expansive dreams was not compatible with the purpose of developing Oscott as a purely localized institution for the higher education of the sons of the traditional Catholic families. To attempt to turn Oscott at once into a Catholic University would be to dissipate its energies at the time when it was needed as a second home for the converts. Wiseman could not assume the generalship of the Oxford battalion if he were to devote himself to details of college administration and academic policy; it is not surprising, therefore, that the university-idea should begin to lose its immediacy as Wiseman's concept of his own destiny became ever more acute.

But the *need* for the provision of an institution for higher studies did *not* disappear. Once Wiseman had recovered from his over-sanguine hopes of the imminent conversion of England, and

[33] Ward, Wilfrid, *The Life and Times of Cardinal Wiseman*, vol. 1, p. 350.
[34] Quoted in Ward, W., *Life of Wiseman*, vol. 1, p. 349.
[35] Ibid., p. 348.

had outlived the extravagances of the Flaminian Gate epoch,[36] he was to turn his attention to the basic problem again. The subject of a Catholic University came under discussion between Manning and himself in 1863, when the former suggested, as a temporary expedient, the possibility that a house might be opened in Rome, 'an Accademia for young Englishmen', to serve 'till we have an University'.[37] The plan would 'only be feasible for the richer', but these were the most clamorous in their advocacy of the social argument for university education. The idea met with considerable support from Wiseman and received papal approval, although Pius IX doubted whether it would be successful in attracting young Englishmen to Rome.[38] Mgr. Edward Stonor was approached as to the possibility of his assuming the direction of 'a Catholic Accademia in Rome for laymen'; he was eminently suited for the task on account of his aristocratic pedigree and his friends among the Old Catholic families. 'The English Catholics would trust him', declared Manning.[39] Stonor, however, met with little enthusiasm.[40] The objections against sending young men to Rome were as strong now as they had been when Baines first mooted the idea. They were aptly summed up by the convert Frederick Oakeley, whom Stonor consulted. Oakeley was convinced that 'our English laity, especially of the higher classes, ought to be educated in this country', and he argued that 'their exercising a beneficial influence upon the mind of the country depends mainly upon their spending within its boundaries the most important period of their education and early training.'[41] Before anything definite could be decided fate once more took a hand. Wiseman died in February 1865.

[36] Wiseman's famous Pastoral Letter, heralding the restoration of the Roman Catholic hierarchy in England and Wales in 1850, was issued 'From Out the Flaminian Gate'. By its extravagant claims and language it was one of the chief contributory factors to Lord John Russell's Ecclesiastical Titles Bill of the following year.

[37] Manning Papers, Bayswater. Manning to Wiseman (from Rome), 19 Jan. 1864.   [38] Leslie, S., *Henry Edward Manning: his Life and Labours*, p. 145.

[39] Purcell, E. S., *Life of Cardinal Manning*, vol. 2, p. 379.

[40] Butler, C., *The Life and Times of Bishop Ullathorne, 1806–1889*, vol. 2, p. 33.

[41] Oakeley to Stonor, 12 Feb. 1864, quoted *in extenso* in Purcell's *Life of Manning*, vol. 2, pp. 379–81.

II

DEGREES WITHOUT RESIDENCE

'THANKS be to God, the Protestantism of England has shut out Catholics from Oxford, and with few exceptions indeed, from Cambridge also',[1] declared the organ of the newly converted, *The Rambler*, in 1851. 'Some two or three unhappy youths are the only victims of parental ignorance who are sent to learn vice and mathematics on the banks of the Cam', it maintained. Three years later Henry Edward Manning was writing in the *Dublin Review* on the reluctance of Catholics to avail themselves of the meagre opportunities for higher education which *were* open to them.

It is well known [he declared], that Catholics have been admitted for a long period of years to reside and study in Cambridge, but not to take degrees. Until 1854 they were absolutely excluded from Oxford. By a recent change, sanctioned by Act of Parliament, Catholics may now reside and study in the colleges and halls of Oxford, and proceed to the degree of Bachelor of Arts. In Cambridge the degree of Master of Arts is also open to them. In the course of the nine years since 1854 it is said that twenty Catholics have passed through Oxford.[2]

An average of two students a year passing through Oxford indicates how slowly Catholics were preparing themselves for public life, thirty years after Emancipation. There were, of course, other possibilities open to them apart from Oxford and Cambridge. The converts, always the most vociferous in their condemnation of the social education offered at the ancient Universities, were no less opposed to one of these alternatives, Trinity College, Dublin. It was a foundation which appeared to them to have done 'infinitely more to destroy the faith of Catholics than all the artillery that ever was fired from the batteries of the forty

---

[1] *The Rambler* (July 1851), p. 3.
[2] *The Dublin Review*, N.S. I (1863), p. 150.

colleges of Oxford and Cambridge'.[3] 'What institution can be conceived more deadly in its operations on the young intellect of Ireland', *The Rambler* indignantly inquired, 'than this "silent sister" of Oxford and Cambridge?' Because Trinity College was 'endowed with riches for its president and fellows far beyond anything that exists in the English University', and because it admitted Catholics 'to its classes and its degrees, but not to its emoluments', it had 'never ceased to combine the utmost practicable amount of seducing temptation with the utmost practicable amount of open injury'.

Catholics had begun to frequent Trinity College from 1793, and in the early years of the nineteenth century Stonyhurst College was engaged in preparing boys for Dublin. When Thomas Wyse arrived at Trinity in 1808 he found a number of his Stonyhurst acquaintances in residence. Richard Lalor Sheil, the distinguished lawyer who in 1831 became Member of Parliament for Milborne Port (then in Dorsetshire), and later occupied the offices of Judge Advocate, Master of the Mint, and British Minister at Florence, left Stonyhurst the year before Wyse, 1807, 'and like others of his companions, proceeded to Trinity College, Dublin', where 'he not only obtained and sustained a character for sound scholarship, but devoted much attention to dramatic affairs'.[4] While Master of the Mint, he issued the first florins without the letters F.D. (*Fidei Defensor*), because the inscription was contrary to his religious feelings. Destined not only to sit in Parliament and to play a leading role in the struggle for Emancipation, he was to be one of the first Catholics since the Reformation to become a Privy Councillor. Another old Stonyhurst boy who benefited from the education provided by Trinity was Stephen Woulfe, the first Catholic after Emancipation to be raised to the Irish Bench. In 1836 he was Solicitor-General and two years later Attorney-General. A contemporary of Sheil, Wyse, and Woulfe was Nicholas Ball. He too went to Trinity from Stonyhurst and in due time succeeded Woulfe as Attorney-General, becoming in 1839 a judge of the Irish Common Pleas. These three young

[3] *The Rambler* (July 1851), p. 3.
[4] Gerard, the Revd. J., *Stonyhurst College, Centenary Record*, p. 217.

men, Woulfe, Ball, and Wyse, made the Grand Tour together after the fall of Napoleon. The connection between Stonyhurst and Trinity College was cemented in 1847–8 when the entrance course of Trinity was adopted as the standard of work in Rhetoric, the highest of the seven classes in the Jesuit College. Stonyhurst also prepared boys for the Scottish universities. Richard Vaughan Barnewell left Stonyhurst for Edinburgh University to read Law, and by the time of his death in 1842 he had enjoyed a distinguished career at the Bar, practising at the Surrey Sessions and in the Home Circuit.

Stonyhurst was not unique among the Catholic colleges in preparing boys for a university education in Ireland and elsewhere. The editor of *The Oscotian* in 1888 testified to the 'very large number of Oscott boys' who had matriculated at Trinity College, Dublin.[5] In 1861 Gerard Strickland, an Oscott student, matriculated in the University of Malta, and after graduating at Cambridge, became a member of the Council of the Government of Malta and President of the Standing Committee of Maltese Privileges. Edward Mackey was prepared for Queen's College, Birmingham, and in 1873 Joseph Smith, on leaving Oscott, proceeded to Dublin, where he obtained the degree of Doctor of Music and eventually became Examiner in Music to the Royal University. The trickle of students to Dublin University dried up, however, as the Irish hierarchy hardened in its attitude to Trinity with the appointment of Paul Cullen as Roman Catholic Archbishop of Dublin in 1852. Up to that time an education at Trinity had been no bar, in fact, to episcopal promotion for Roman Catholics. Dr. Michael Slattery, who had entered Trinity in 1799, held the offices of Professor of Philosophy and Theology at Carlow College and President of Maynooth, before becoming in 1833 Archbishop of Cashel. His experiences at Trinity, however, made him 'an uncompromising and life-long opponent of undenominational education'.[6]

A Roman Catholic graduate of Trinity, Denis Cauldfield Heron, commented in 1847 upon the paucity of Catholics entering Trinity

---

5 *The Oscotian* (1888), p. 589 n.
6 MacSuibhne, vol. 1, p. 6.

since their legal admission in 1793.[7] From 1794 to 1829 he estimated that those graduating from Trinity averaged only fifteen
per annum. From 1829 to 1844 the average number of Catholics
entering the College was but thirty-two. In 1844 twenty-three
entered. He pointed out that only one seventy-fifth part of College
emoluments was open to the competition of Catholics.

With the foundation of the University of London, however,
Catholics were encouraged to consider the advantages of pursuing higher studies in order to acquire a degree recognized by
the State. The date of origin of London University is usually
given as 1825, when the poet Thomas Campbell wrote a public
letter to the future Lord Brougham. A capital sum was raised of
£160,000 for the foundation of a college in Gower Street, London,
the purpose of which has recently been succinctly stated by Herman
Ausubel as being for the benefit of middle-class Londoners, in
order that they might obtain their desire for 'a complete scientific
and literary education'.[8] To H. A. L. Fisher the movement really
found its inspiration 'in the philosophy of Jeremy Bentham and
a model in the newly-founded University of Berlin',[9] and it was
perhaps such inspiration which gave rise to a declaration in *The
Rambler* that the faith of a young Catholic 'would be more
subtly undermined at University College, London, than at
Oxford or Cambridge'.[10] Anglicans, too, looked askance at the
new institution, with its appeal to Nonconformist susceptibility
and its proscription of religious tests. An article in the *Quarterly*
declared that 'every mode of instruction which so teaches learning,
science or art, as to make them seem all in all and fails to connect
them with the higher object of all education, the fitting man for
his ultimate destiny, we consider to be both incomplete and pernicious'.[11] Led by the Duke of Wellington, 'to counter-balance the

[7] Heron, D. C., *The Constitutional History of the University of Dublin, with some
account of its present condition and suggestions for improvement*.

[8] Ausubel, H., *In Hard Times: Reformers among the Late Victorians* (New York,
1960), pp. 197–8.

[9] Fisher, H. A. L., 'Our Universities', in University of London *Centenary
Addresses* (London, 1927), p. 8.

[10] *The Rambler* (July 1851), p. 6.

[11] See also Mathieson, W. L., *English Church Reform, 1815–40* (London, 1923),
p. 209.

dangers of "Godless education"',[12] a movement was organized to establish a rival institution based on the Christian ethic. King's College was founded in the Strand in 1829.

On 26 March 1835 an Address was presented from the House of Commons to the Crown, which prayed William IV 'to confer upon the London University College [then called the London University] a Charter of Incorporation as University, by which it might be enabled to grant Degrees to its Students in all the Faculties except Divinity and Medicine'.[13] In November of the same year the Chancellor of the Exchequer, Spring Rice, declared: 'It should always be kept in mind that what is sought on the present occasion is an equality in all respects with the ancient Universities, freed from those exclusions and religious distinctions which abridge the usefulness of Oxford and Cambridge.'[14]

The organization, thus set up with the avowed intention of providing a higher education not governed by Tests, furnished a salutary shock to the ancient Universities. Such education was no longer to be the exclusive privilege of ecclesiastics and patricians. In 1834 a corpus of opinion at Oxford believed that the granting of a charter for the University of London was 'fraught with danger'[15] to the existing Universities. It is not surprising that Newman, perhaps the leading exponent of the ideals for which Oxford stood in 1835, should have viewed the London scheme askance. He who, in 1838, was very seriously considering whether democracy and anti-Christ were not closely connected,[16] and who was to add 'no one can dislike the democratic principle more than I do',[17] was to be expected to oppose an institution destined to make higher education more easily available to middle-class Nonconformists. The word 'university', applied to a mere examining body, was to Newman a misnomer. He detested

[12] McPherson, R. G., *Theory of Higher Education in Nineteenth-Century England*, p. 31.

[13] Hüber, V. A., *The English Universities* (translated from the German; edited by Francis W. Newman), vol. 2, pp. 563 seq.

[14] *University of London: Historical Record (1836–1912)*, p. 9.

[15] Mallet, *A History of the University of Oxford*, vol. 3, p. 232.

[16] Newman, J. H.: *Discussions and Arguments*, pp. 72 seq.

[17] Newman, J. H.: *Difficulties of Anglicans* (London, 1908 ed.), vol. 2, p. 268.

Benthamism and Benthamizing, and was to write of London: 'That grief, anger, cowardice, self-conceit, pride or passion, can be subdued by an examination of shells or grasses, or inhaling of gases, or chipping of rocks, or calculating the longitude, is the veriest of pretences which sophist or mountebank ever professed to a gaping auditory.'[18] That his brother Frank, Unitarian, Vegetarian, and Temperance-advocate, was later to occupy a Chair at London was not a factor to mollify his attitude, for to John 'Frank was an unprincipled renegade'.[19] Newman's behaviour was reflected in that of Dr. Arnold, who in 1838 'could not tolerate the lack of formal Christian instruction and the admission of Jews, Unitarians, and other "infidels"'[20] to the benefits of university education.

That the new University was merely to be an examining body, and that the teaching was to be undertaken in affiliated institutions, was a proposal which commended itself to the Catholic colleges. The latter would not be unduly influenced by the University. Contact would be confined to following the syllabus prescribed by London for Matriculation and Graduation, and direct relations would be concerned only in the matter of examining. Regulations prescribed that candidates could only be admitted to degrees of the University if they were students of University College, or King's College, or some other affiliated establishment. It was, therefore, incumbent on some or all of the Catholic colleges to apply for affiliation, and the opportunity was at once eagerly seized. The wise course of action would have been for one or two colleges only to have applied, and then, once affiliation had been secured, to confine all the students wishing to engage upon university courses in those colleges. This would have ensured the development of one or two Catholic institutions concerned exclusively with higher scholarship, but such co-operation was too much to expect when each college possessed a fierce spirit of independence.

[18] Newman, J. H., *Discussions and Arguments*, p. 268.
[19] Faber, G., *Oxford Apostles: A Character Study of the Oxford Movement* (London, 1933), p. 347.
[20] See Robbins, W., *The Newman Brothers*, p. 96.

V. A. Hüber publishes a map of the affiliated colleges in 1842.[21] The English Catholic colleges which had received recognition from the University by that date are listed as being Ushaw, Stonyhurst, Prior Park, Downside, Oscott, and St. Edmund's College, Ware. The first of the colleges to apply for affiliation was Downside. The possibility was eagerly taken up by the other colleges, 'who recognised in its adoption a means to keep up the level of their studies through the open competition it afforded, and the possibility of comparing their own work with that going on in other educational centres'. Dom Norbert Birt informs us that it was appreciated that 'here was afforded an opportunity of supplying in some degree the long-felt want of a university course.'[22]

In 1838 George Errington warned the President of Ushaw, Mgr. Newsham, that both Stonyhurst and Oscott were preparing to adjust their studies in order to apply to London for affiliation, and this knowledge transformed Ushaw into a hive of reform. When the latter formally applied to London in March 1839, it based its claim to be heard 'on the grounds of the new University's aim of advancing religion and morality and of promoting general knowledge among all classes of the Queen's subjects without distinction'.[23] The effect of affiliation, the President of Oscott wrote, was 'to place Catholic education, from its first elements to its highest honours, entirely in our own hands.'[24] He went on to add in a letter addressed to the parents of those children already at Oscott that 'henceforth the studies necessary for obtaining these honours may be pursued *here*; and students, on receiving from us a certificate of competency, will be entitled to present themselves in London for examination for degrees, honours, exhibitions, and scholarships, granted by the Senate of the said University'. It was directed that 'parents who wish their children to avail themselves of these privileges should give due notice of their intentions, in order that the studies of these young gentlemen may be shaped accordingly'.

---

[21] Hüber, p. 564.   [22] Birt, H. N., *Downside*, p. 215.   [23] Milburn, p. 168.
[24] Oscott College Archives. From 'Records of St. Mary's College, Oscott' (bound MS.), begun 26 May 1830, to 1900, by Henry Weedall, D.D.

A major realignment of the studies within the affiliated Catholic colleges was effected as a result of the connection with London. It was not to be lessened by the fact that a new Charter for the University issued in 1858 effectively abolished the scheme of affiliation, and in the case of candidates for degrees in the Faculties of Arts and Laws no longer required that they be educated in any specific institution. Certificates of proficiency were abolished and the sole test of ability and training was to be the examination. The change was a minor one in reality, for from the very beginning under the process of affiliation 'the sole means possessed by the Senate whereby the efficiency of the Colleges could be tested was the examination of their students, and its sole means of influencing the courses and character of the teaching was to be found in its schemes and regulations for examination'.[25]

[25] *University of London: Historical Record (1836–1912)*, p. 12.

III

HIGHER STUDIES AT STONYHURST

'IT has been our happiness to live under a government so liberal as the present; who, despising the prejudices of religious dissensions, have boldly and generously granted to their less fortunate country-men all the advantages a university can bestow', wrote a corre-spondent, A...P..., in the *Weekly Orthodox Journal* in May 1840. He expressed the jubilation of the Catholic colleges on their affiliation to London University by writing that at last Catholics felt themselves to be 'the subjects of a free land'. They were 'liberated and disenthralled by the irresistible genius of universal emancipation'. Henceforward 'all Catholics, as well as Protestants and Dissenters, are indiscriminately admitted to stand for the re-wards which science holds forth to the successful candidates'.

But were the Colleges themselves fitted to take immediate advantage of their new-found opportunity? Percy Fitzgerald, a senior student at Stonyhurst in the 1840s, pinpoints the condi-tions as he found them. He describes the boys in the highest class, Rhetoric, as patricians of seventeen or eighteen years old, many of whom were Patagonian in stature, displayed whiskers, and stalked about with 'a haughty dignity'.[1] They all wore the tradi-tional blue tail-coat with gilt buttons. The academic staff con-sisted of a few priests, occupying such posts as Rector, Prefect of Studies, and Chaplain, a number of young Jesuits in minor orders ('Scholastics'), engaged in teaching, and a few lay masters, such as the music master, John Beresford, who 'was as submissive to the Superiors as one of themselves could be', and was thus 'just the man for Stonyhurst'.[2]

The Higher Studies in the College were confined to the class of 'Philosophers', that is, those who had completed the normal

[1] Fitzgerald, P., *Stonyhurst Memories; or, Six Years at School*, p. 11.
[2] Ibid., p. 290.

school course and who remained on for an indefinite period to perfect their education. Fitzgerald, a Rhetorician in 1847, asserts that only three of his own original class of forty pupils opted to remain for the Philosophers' course. To this group it was intended to add those about to prepare for London examinations. In 1847 the total number of Philosophers was about twenty, many of them 'foolish, riotous, and restive', sons of rich parents 'sent by their families to fill up the intermediate time in an easy and enjoyable way'.[3] They paid 'a hundred a year, lived pleasantly at the Seminary, a spacious mansion standing in its own fair grounds and gardens, a few minutes' walk from the College, had a good table, dressed as they liked, and were allowed to smoke when and where they pleased'. They were provided with billiard-room and library. Their *dégagé* style of dress particularly impressed the young Rhetorician, 'especially their seeming such an odd set of fellows, some of them over five and twenty, and some with great black moustaches'. Sauntering among the grounds in shooting-jackets and wide-awakes, they assumed the appearance of '"fast" men who spent the day smoking and lounging about'. When Fitzgerald joined the Philosophy class in 1847 he found life extremely pleasant, 'nothing but amusement thought of', and he spent the days at St. Mary's Hall 'lounging about' or in the library, in which he occasionally rummaged. At night there was the dissipation of the racquet court, and diversion could be found in the pastime of sparrow-shooting or in indulging in intermittent bouts of drunkenness. In 1848 the Philosophers were lodged in a wing of the main College, where they enjoyed their own rooms and continued to form an entity distinct from the rest of the establishment. They were enabled to keep dogs and to stable horses. Shooting over the College preserves was permitted and animals were trained for the hunt. Yet in the 1840s truly aristocratic names were not in evidence among the Philosophers. Among those listed by Fitzgerald as his contemporaries were 'Edward Berkeley, a dashing sort of fellow; Cuzel, a Belgian, in spectacles; Belay, another Belgian, a nice fellow; John Lawson, my own class-fellow; [and] Lafoutant, a black, six feet high, from

---

[3] Ibid., pp. 353–4.

St. Domingo'.[4] Berkeley, who attempted the London B.A. degree, spent four years among the Philosophers, 'a very wild dashing fellow', before entering the Life Guards. Lafoutant, the Haytian, was relentlessly persecuted, until he retaliated by drawing a knife on his attackers. The only formal instruction which Fitzgerald admits to having received were a few simple Philosophy lectures delivered in Latin.

The paucity of numbers in the Philosophy course was a direct outcome of the decline in college numbers at Stonyhurst in the thirties. In 1815 there were 214 boys on roll, including one in Philosophy, but so rapid was the decline that in 1829 there were only 120 students at the College.[5] This falling-off was on account of the competition provided by other colleges, and a dislike on the part of the Catholic aristocracy for the niceties of Jesuit discipline. But it was also influenced by the pernicious practice carried on from the period of exile, whereby a master 'went up with his boys from Elements or Figures to Rhetoric'.[6] This was, no doubt, a stimulating experience if the master was an expert pedagogue, but a disastrous one if he was of poor intellectual calibre.

Fitzgerald's testimony of the manner in which the Philosophers dissipated their energies can be verified from other sources. The institution itself came in for its greatest notoriety at the time of the Tichborne trial. Roger Tichborne had been sent to Stonyhurst in 1845 at the age of sixteen, totally ignorant from the want of formal schooling, and yet too old to be placed in the normal school course. He was to remain among the Philosophers for three years, although he 'showed little aptitude for study of any kind',[7] and at the time of the trial in 1870 the claimant was subjected to searching questions on the nature of the Philosophers' course. Edward Vaughan Kenealy, Q.C., in a highly colourful speech described the education provided as being made up of 'smoking, snuffing, . . . dissecting birds and stuffing them'.[8] The

[4] Fitzgerald, P., *Stonyhurst Memories; or Six Years at School*, pp. 363–4.
[5] Gerard, pp. 141 n., 142.   [6] Ibid., p. 101 n.
[7] Woodruff, D., *The Tichborne Claimant: a Victorian Mystery* (London, 1957), pp. 8–9.   [8] Ibid., p. 287.

claimant, Kenealy emphasized, 'was taught nothing, but allowed to grow up like a weed, perpetually hiding behind shrubberies with that lamentable and detestable habit of unlimited smoking to which he surrendered himself'. Lord Bellew, Tichborne's fellow Philosopher at Stonyhurst, testified that the latter had passed his time in showing him how to practise the art of tattooing. Much of the vitriol expended against the College at the trial cannot, of course, be accepted at face value, but it is interesting to note that another Philosopher, Walter Strickland Mannock, a contemporary of Tichborne, was in 1873, like the claimant, unable to elucidate the meaning of the Jesuits' motto, A.M.D.G., and thought he had never actually ventured across the *Pons Asinorum*!

At a considerably later date Colonel Raleigh Chichester, while entirely sympathetic to the Stonyhurst regimen, felt constrained to criticize 'the class of parlour boarders, miscalled Philosophers', who, he alleged, 'are allowed to keep horses, to ride about the country, to fish and shoot, just as if they were Oxford undergraduates, although some of these young men are twenty-two years of age, and many of them are foreigners, who come merely to pick up the language'.[9] In the same year, 1882, Bishop John Cuthbert Hedley informed Rome that 'many of our best Catholic young men . . . attach themselves informally to our colleges of young boys, where they in great measure lose their time'.[10] Three years later Fr. R. F. Clarke, S.J., took up the Bishop's point in *The Month*, only to find that his Jesuit Superiors censored his article on account of its criticism of Stonyhurst. Although Clarke admitted that life in town had its perils for young men, he felt that 'life in the country has no sufficient opportunities of culture, and many a bright intelligence has become rusty and many a life which might have achieved great things for God and for his country has been lounged away, because it had no definite direction given to it at the critical period when permanent habits are formed and tastes developed, and the character is moulded for weal or woe'.[11] He felt that the Philosophy classes at Stonyhurst

9 Chichester, C., Raleigh, *Schools*, pp. 81–2, 104.
10 Hedley's *votum* is given in Wilson, J. A., *The Life of Bishop Hedley*, pp. 231 seq. 11 Clarke, R. F., unpublished article in Farm Street Archives.

were in the nature of an 'accidental appendage' rather than 'a class which ought to be their pride and glory and the enrolment in which is to be the crowning object of ambition to every boy in the school'. In 1872, thirteen years before Clarke made his criticism, the Jesuit Provincial was bemoaning the fate of 'the secular philosophers', and declaring sadly, that 'the name of Jesuit is no longer a talisman to conjure with'.[12]

Fr. E. J. Purbrick, himself a Rector of Stonyhurst, testified to the hierarchy in 1872 that, excluding the studies of those students specifically engaged on London B.A. work, 'Stonyhurst provided a three year course of Logic, Metaphysics, and Ethics, with Natural Science', and that students could learn Italian and German or stay on to perfect their knowledge of French. They would be trained to read essays before a literary society, and a debating club was provided, but, he added ruefully, 'only about six stay on to follow the course',[13] and these were swamped by youths whose earlier education had been deficient or by foreign youths engaged in perfecting their English. In 1872 only twelve students in all were pursuing Higher Studies, and to make matters worse, Purbrick added, 'we do not come near Eton, Rugby, Cheltenham, Wellington . . . in scholarship (Greek verse is utterly unknown to us) . . . in expansion of mind, earnestness of purpose, definiteness of aim'. The presence of many boys from the lower classes of society, he felt, gave rise to 'the *vis inertiae* of comfortable, self-satisfied, mediocre, inambitious traditions'. Among the aristocracy, too, he claimed there was 'a pretty universal sense of intellectual inferiority, by some acquiesced in, by some resented, by all deplored'.[14] The few who did pursue Higher Studies were 'either in some danger of lounging away their time, or of fretting under the yoke of a discipline which, because of their being under the same roof with boys, is necessarily stricter than suits their age'. He thought that 'a certain number work conscientiously, but without that collision of mind with mind, that eager contest with

[12] Farm Street Archives. Manuscript note by Provincial, 1872, based on the Revd. E. J. Purbrick's report to the Sub-Commission on Higher Education of that year.

[13] Southwark Archdiocesan Archives. Report of E. J. Purbrick, S.J., 1872.

[14] Brompton Oratory Archives. Purbrick's report to the hierarchy, 1872.

the flower of English youth in the race for University honours, that looking forward to public life and professional careers, that "esprit de corps", that manly sense of a glorious necessity, which alone can fully awaken the dormant faculties and breed high aspirations and large views of their own destiny in life'.

In the light of Purbrick's criticism it is of interest to compare Fitzgerald's description of life among the Philosophers in the 1840s with that given by Francis Fortescue Urquhart forty years later. Urquhart entered the Philosophy group in 1886 from Beaumont, with the intention of reading for the London degree. He took his B.A. in 1889 with Honours in Latin and Greek, and carried off from Stonyhurst a number of prizes in Classics, Modern Languages, English, and Religious Instruction, and he eventually became the College's Senior Philosopher. He was, therefore, one of the conscientious students referred to by Purbrick. He had a room to himself, was able to divide up the day in accordance with his own wishes, and was examined in his work from time to time. Clearly this was a considerable improvement on what had been taking place in the forties. For amusement, Urquhart and his companions read *Oliver Twist* and *Martin Chuzzlewit* to each other, they played whist, tennis, and hockey, and occasionally shot pheasants, hares, and rabbits. They entertained their guests in a civilized manner.[15] Urquhart's industry ultimately led him to an exhibition in Modern History at Balliol in 1890.

The improvement in the conditions of life among the Philosophers can be attributed to London University courses. Fr. Purbrick declared in 1872 that the connection with London had 'an undoubtedly beneficial influence on the state of the studies', and that 'the hope of obtaining a degree has attracted a certain number of young men who, without this definite object proposed to them, would in all probability never have gone beyond the school course'.[16] He divined a still greater benefit 'from the stimulus given to boys in their earlier studies, from the partial removal of the sense of isolation, and from the effect of an external test to the proficiency of our boys'. Fr. John Gerard, S.J., writing some

---

[15] For details see Bailey, C., *Francis Fortesque Urquhart: a Memoir*, pp. 12–13, 14–15.   [16] Report of E. J. Purbrick.

twenty years after Purbrick, felt that 'the foundation, in 1838, of the University of London, the examinations and degrees of which were open to all, was welcomed with enthusiasm as the beginning of a new era', and he claimed that an entire reorganization of the studies was effected at Stonyhurst 'in the fervour of the moment'.[17] This reorganization consisted in the appointment, in September 1840, of specialists to teach Latin, Greek, and Mathematics to those preparing for London examinations. A Professor of Rhetoric and Poetry was designated to teach the remaining subjects, but subsequently his duties were lessened by the appointment of specialist teachers for French and History. This marked a considerable break with tradition, but unfortunately old traditions die hard. Once the initial flurry of reform relaxed, more reactionary counsels prevailed, and six years later a new Rector removed the specialists and rejuvenated the old class-master system.

The connection with London led to a renewed interest in the teaching of Science, typified by the foundation of an Observatory at the College in 1838–9. Within twenty years the Board of Trade had selected Stonyhurst as one of its primary meteorological stations. The money thus obtained proved a decided asset in the further development of the Observatory, and its real heyday began in 1868 with the appointment as director of Fr. Stephen Perry. Magnetic surveys were made in France and Belgium, and Fr. Perry was in charge of the British Expedition which observed the Transit of Venus in 1874 in Kerguelen Island. He served on Government Expeditions in Madagascar (1882), Carriacon in the West Indies (1886), Pogost on the Volga (1887), and the Isle du Salut (1889). A Botanic Garden was established at Stonyhurst in 1839, and in 1840 mathematical prizes were instituted in the College, the criterion of success being the London Matriculation and B.A. examinations.

One of the most alarming aspects of the London examinations, however, was the wide variety of subjects in which proficiency was tested. Many of these subjects found but a minor place in the curricula of Catholic colleges, and at Stonyhurst, in particular, very little attention before 1840 was devoted to Science. The

[17] Gerard, pp. 175–6.

Registrar of London University, Dr. W. E. Carpenter, in his evidence before the Schools Inquiry Commission in 1865, gave details of the range of subjects required for success in the examinations. For Matriculation the list was formidable. The examination was not to be taken by a candidate until he had completed his sixteenth year, but the subjects to be tested were

Classics, both Latin and Greek, with the grammar of those languages, and some amount of history; then a modern language, either French or German; English, the grammatical structure of the language, and the power of writing correctly from dictation; a moderate knowledge of English History and Modern Geography . . . ; Mathematics, including the first four books of Euclid, Arithmetic up to fractions, Algebra up to simple equations; and an elementary knowledge, such as might be acquired by attending a good class of experimental lectures, of Natural Philosophy, and Inorganic Chemistry as far as the non-metallic bodies are concerned.[18]

When he was asked if it was necessary for a candidate for Matriculation to be acquainted to some extent with all the subjects he had quoted, Carpenter replied: 'There is only an option between French and German, otherwise the candidate is required to pass to the satisfaction of the Examiners in all those subjects.' Before 1859 candidates for the degree of B.A. were required to pass only two examinations, the Matriculation examination and a final examination taken two years later. After 1859 an Intermediate examination in Arts was introduced, by which 'the candidate for the degree of B.A. was . . . required to pass two examinations'[19] after Matriculation, and this of necessity lengthened the course and created hardship for the Catholic colleges. The subjects for the Intermediate Examination (or 1st B.A.) were Arithmetic, Algebra, Geometry, Plane Trigonometry; the Latin language— with two subjects, one in prose, the other in verse; Roman History; the English Language, Literature, and History, with special subjects set for each year; and the French or German language. In each of these areas of study separate examinations

[18] Minutes of Evidence taken before the Schools Inquiry Commission, 1865, *Report* of the Commission, 735.

[19] *University of London: the Historical Record (1836–1912)*, p. 15.

were held for Honours candidates. The second (or final) B.A. examination required a knowledge of Mechanical and Natural Philosophy; Animal Physiology; the Greek and Latin Languages (one Greek subject and one Latin prose subject); Grecian History; and Logic and Moral Philosophy. Candidates could be examined separately for Honours in any branch of this examination. What such regulations meant in terms of college reorganization for the Catholic institutions does not require much imagination. In spite of the difficulties, however, Stonyhurst early earned a reputation for successful preparation for these examinations. William Smith, the industrious author of a whole series of students' histories in the forties and fifties, and from 1867 editor of the *Quarterly*, informed Lord Taunton of the Schools Inquiry Commission that

there is at present a most excellent College in the North of England, called Stonyhurst College, conducted by the Jesuits; when the University was founded, and the College was affiliated, I heard from my colleague Mr. Burcham (I was not then examiner) that the candidates they sent up came very ill-prepared, so much so that they were frequently rejected. They were withdrawn for a year or two, and then were sent up exceedingly well prepared—so well prepared that I do not believe any of the boys from the sixth forms of our public schools are better prepared. I do not think it possible that they could have a better education given to them than Stonyhurst gives, and I attribute that very much to the influence of the University of London.[20]

It was an opinion reinforced by the Registrar, as far as Classics were concerned. Carpenter told Lord Taunton 'we know perfectly well that the candidates who come up from Stonyhurst would be thoroughly well grounded in Classics; in other schools we know that the candidates will probably show a very imperfect knowledge of Grammar'.

Carpenter's evidence is well supported by statistics. Immediately after the College had obtained its charter of affiliation in 1840 it presented candidates for Matriculation. Three of these first candidates took Honours in Zoology and one in Chemistry, but the

----

[20] *Report* of Schools Inquiry Commission.

initial success was not followed up, and it was some years before the College was again able to figure its pupils among the success- ful candidates. If we pursue the University lists for the names of undergraduates who obtained Honours in the Intermediate Examination after its introduction in 1859 until 1899, when the College ceased to enter its students, we discover that emphasis upon Classics indicated in Dr. Carpenter's evidence of 1865. Between 1859 and 1899 eighty-three students from Stonyhurst were successful in gaining Honours in the Intermediate examina- tion. Of these eighty-three, sixty-five did so in Latin, and of this number thirty-four were placed in Class I, twenty-four in Class II, and seven in Class III. The remaining number divided up as follows: French, eleven candidates (seven in Class I, three in Class II, and one in Class III); German, two candidates (one in Class I and one in Class II); Mathematics, three candidates (one in Class II, two in Class III); English, two candidates (one in Class II, one in Class III). When we consider the candidates from Stonyhurst who finally emerged with a B.A. degree with Honours a similar pattern presents itself. In the period from 1840 to 1899 six candidates obtained the degree before the introduction of the system of classifying the Honours in 1863, and seventy-six obtained Honours after that date. Of the first six successful candidates, four attained Honours in Classics, one in Mathematics, and one in Animal Physiology. It is interesting to note that Stony- hurst did not obtain its first Honours graduate until 1853, four years after Oscott, three years after Downside, and a year after Prior Park. Of the seventy-seven graduates from Stonyhurst after 1863, sixty-one received their Honours for Classics (seven- teen in Class I; thirty-two in Class II, and twelve in Class III). Seven awards were made in Mental and Moral Science (three in Class I, one in Class II, and three in Class III), five in French (four in Class II and one in Class III), two in German (one in Class I and one in Class II), and two in Mathematics (one in Class II and one in Class III). Only two Stonyhurst men went on to obtain the Master's degree with Honours, one in 1869 in Classics, and Herbert Lucas in 1878 in Classics, Mental and Moral Science, and Philosophy and Economics. In 1880 a Stonyhurst boy obtained a Class I Bachelor of Laws degree. The College did not figure highly in the competition for exhibitions and prizes, although in 1862 Joseph Rickaby, and the following year Stephen Hayes, won the £30 Exhibition at the Matriculation examination of those years. One of the most important factors emerging from a perusal of the Honours class-lists is the total absence of the names of members of the Catholic aristocracy. The successful candidates were those middle-class boys of whom Fr. Purbrick spoke so disparagingly in 1872. This fact helps to substantiate Cardinal Manning's claim in 1888 that the old families were seeking 'to have latch-keys to Grosvenor Square'. London degrees were, therefore, unattractive.

The class-lists indicate the limited resources of the College in the Mechanical and Natural Sciences and in Mathematics. Fr. G. R. Kingdon, Prefect of Studies at Stonyhurst, protested in 1868 against the content of these courses as prescribed by the University, 'especially when it is remembered', he said, 'that natural philosophy includes statics, dynamics, hydrostatics, hydraulics, pneumatics, geometrical and physical optics, acoustics, and astronomy'.[21] He maintained that it was 'in the "ologies"' that the examiners seemed to revel, 'the natural philosophy papers being long and difficult, and that on animal physiology remarkable for the varied and comprehensive character of the questions'. But six years later Fr. Alfred Weld, the Jesuits' Assistant in Rome, in a letter to the English Provincial, indicated that the inadequacy of Stonyhurst's performance in these fields was a direct outcome of misguided Jesuit policy. There was a distinct failure on the part of Superiors to appreciate the need for Science. Weld was particularly concerned about the failure to train up good men in Chemistry. 'I think you will never form any really learned men in it who will do credit as professors', he wrote, 'without sending them to study in London with nothing else to do, so as to let them make acquaintances of scientific men and see what is being done.'[22] If they were to have 'a thoroughly good man at Stonyhurst, acquainted with scientific men, and

---

[21] *The Month* (Oct. 1868), p. 393.
[22] Farm Street Archives. The Revd. A. Weld, S.J., to Provincial, 16 Aug. 1874.

knowing what was done by others, and in correspondence with them', they could easily train up other members of the Society under his direction. Fr. Weld commented on the then occupant of the Science post at Stonyhurst as being 'not half-educated in science'. He objected to the complaints which used to be made 'if anyone was applied to science that was fit for anything else'. Until then it had been 'necessary for peace sake to be content with people . . . who were entirely uneducated'. 'Under this system it was impossible ever to form a professor', he added, and tendered the advice that the Provincial should 'choose a good man (in all respects) in the Juniorate and put him to science in spite of everybody, if he himself takes to it', and that such a man 'should have nothing else to do'. He added ruefully: 'To make a young man Prefect of Philosophers, as I was, is to ruin him for science.' He declared that they failed in Mathematics, too, 'because our standard in the various classes is not high enough', and because 'we have not competent teachers' for them. Fr. Weld was critical of the policy of employing Scholastics as fixed masters in charge of the senior classes of Poetry and Rhetoric. These posts should be given to experienced and successful priests. If this were done it would 'remedy two great evils. 1st. You will get your young men sooner to their theology, and 2nd. you will give a better tone of study and manliness to the whole College, and so improve the race of candidates of the Society.' Want of this remedy, he added, was 'the reason why so few real *bookmen* have entered the Society out of Stonyhurst for many years until lately', and he concluded that he thought that 'choice men teaching Rhetoric and Poetry' would effect a remedy. The London Matriculation was normally taken in Rhetoric. Weld was realistic enough to appreciate that the Catholic aristocracy would never be the main-stay of the College. If Stonyhurst was to flourish as an educational establishment, it would only be by concentrating upon the middle classes. The sooner the older Jesuits abandoned aristocratic predi-lections the more the Society would prosper, especially now that the rich and titled preferred Oscott and the Oratory School as more suited to their needs. Many regretted this latter fact, sharing the views of Purbrick. Others felt with Fr. John Morris, S.J., that had the boys from the lower walks of life been eliminated 'the London University Examiners would never have had the opportunity of passing compliments on the classical attainments of youths from Stonyhurst', because those 'with £10,000 a year, no matter what their Religion is, exempt themselves from the tedium of study'.[23] If the Society was to concentrate upon educating the middle classes, however, it must not offer them an exclusively classical course. The middle classes could only be captured by greater emphasis upon, and greater proficiency in, Science. If Stonyhurst was unfit for this, then the Society might do well to concentrate upon their Derbyshire college instead. In 1874 Fr. Weld was advising the Provincial to allocate his best resources in Science upon Mount St. Mary's College, Spinkhill. This advice elicited specific proposals which Fr. Weld placed before the Jesuit General. Weld urged the Provincial to advertise the school 'for the Middle-Classes, with plenty of science (Chemistry and Physics) instead of Greek—except for Church boys'.[24] He declared that 'there is nothing of the kind in England, and nothing would do so much good to the Catholic body', for 'boys with knowledge of Chemistry and Physics can get any employment and if they know Latin they will push themselves on'. The Society could easily get 300 boys if this policy was adopted. But to make Mount St. Mary's into a little Stonyhurst would make it good 'only for Church boys'. The students ought to have 'a school of practical Chemistry like at University College, London'.

But there were difficulties in the way of developing Mount St. Mary's along these lines. For one thing, there was the depressingly bleak and uninteresting countryside around the College. There was, too, an inadequate water supply. 'The deepening of a mine in the neighbourhood took away half the supply of water from the brook which supplies the tanks', Weld pointed out, 'and it was said, that a similar cause might any day take away the other half.' One consequence of this was that 'the boys used often to go

[23] Farm Street Archives. Manuscript notes by Fr. J. Morris, S.J., on Fr. Purbrick's report to the hierarchy, 1872.

[24] Farm Street Archives. Letter of Fr. A. Weld, S.J., to English Provincial, 21 Aug. 1874.

without second washing for want of water—not a nice thing to be said of a College'. A great deal of money needed to be expended on the dilapidated property. Weld felt that the Mount would never become a satisfactory school 'without rebuilding a great deal of it'. A slow effort to enhance the reputation of Mount St. Mary's was set on foot in 1875, and six years later the College boasted of its first Honours in the London Intermediate Examination. From 1881 until 1891 (when the last candidate was presented for Honours), the College was successful on nineteen occasions, but the lists of successes indicate how ineffectual had been the advice of Weld. Seventeen of them were for Honours in Latin (five in Class I, ten in Class II, and two in Class III), and the remaining two were one in French (Class II) and one in English (Class II). No candidate graduated B.A. while at the College; those who showed any likelihood of doing so were transferred to Stonyhurst. This factor in itself was sufficient to prevent the growth of the College's reputation. It was branded as an inferior institution, as indeed was the third Jesuit boarding school, Beaumont. This school, situated at Old Windsor, had an even shorter association with London examinations. It obtained its first Honours result in 1869 at the Intermediate Examination of that year and its last ten years later. Honours were awarded in all on seven occasions (five times in Latin, once in French, and once in German), although no fewer than six of the seven awards were made in Class I. In fact more candidates were presented for the Intermediate Examination from the Jesuits' middle-class school in Liverpool (St. Francis Xavier's) from 1878 until 1894, an institution which always had a steady stream of good results in Latin. The Jesuit college at Clongoeswood in Ireland prepared candidates for the London examinations in 1874, and in 1894 the Society's college in Preston presented its first Honours candidates.

The Jesuits at Stonyhurst were not concerned with the specific needs of the middle classes. Instead of adopting Weld's advice, they refused to adapt their curriculum to contemporary needs. The rigidity of the *Ratio Studiorum* was clung to with profound intensity, especially in its practical application in the teaching of the Classics. Fr. Purbrick in 1874 gave utterance to the feeling of the Stonyhurst Community when he endorsed the opinion of F. R. Ward that 'the London examinations press very hardly on young men who have no taste for the physical sciences',[25] and that this was a clear reason why Catholics should agitate for what would really be a great boon—the abandonment of London in favour of the power of obtaining degrees at Oxford or Cambridge without residence. If such a revolution were to take place the Society would, perhaps, be able to regain the allegiance of the aristocracy. This viewpoint was succinctly stated by Fr. G. R. Kingdon, S.J., in *The Month* in 1868. Writing on the London Matriculation examination in particular he declared:

The character of our higher education is essentially classical and literary, like that of the public schools, and the Matriculation Examination of London is essentially non-Classical and non-literary. Its tendency consequently is to lower the aim of our education, and to swamp the liberal element in it by a multitude of details, each of which has an exaggerated importance attributed to it by the obligatory character of the examination. Looked upon as a test of what a boy's attainments should be at the close of his school course, the standard for classics is a great deal too low, while the standard in all other subjects, except perhaps mathematics and French, is a great deal too high.[26]

The teaching offered in Philosophy at Stonyhurst was also in need of drastic overhaul. The method of the scholastic disputation, with its emphasis on formal syllogistic argument, was more at home in the seminary than the university. Although the London examiners had no objection to reading the work of candidates nurtured on Aquinas and Suarez, the papers must have provided a strange contrast to those submitted by candidates who had concentrated upon Martineau and Bain, Mill and Sir William Hamilton. In 1868 Bain himself was the examiner. The non-Catholic candidates were taught by the historico-critical method, which according to Urquhart was 'the wrong order'.[27] Fr. John Morris, S.J., in 1872 complained bitterly against the way Philosophy was taught at Stonyhurst. Philosophy *should* have been

---

[25] *Report* of the Sub-Commission on Higher Education, 1872, p. 24, para. II.
[26] *The Month* (July 1868), p. 6.   [27] Bailey, p. 14.

studied from the viewpoint of its historical development, he felt, and if this had taken place, better efforts in the London examinations would have resulted. 'And why was not this boldly done at Stonyhurst', he questioned, 'for the last twenty years and more instead of sighing for a Hall at Oxford which is utterly unattainable?' 'Had we made ourselves a power in London University,' he went on, 'they could not have afforded to despise us, as I fear they now do.'[28]

London University and its examinations were looked upon by many at Stonyhurst 'as a radical invention for giving degrees to tag-rag and bob-tail', for 'the "jeunesse dorée" of the aristocracy of letters would have nothing to do with such a republican device'.[29] To make too much of the London connection would be to brand Stonyhurst as a second-rate educational establishment and one doomed to catering for a middle-class clientele. General evidence of the social boycotting of London first appeared in Dr. Carpenter's testimony to the Schools Inquiry Commission in 1868. He was asked: 'With regard to the nine schools that were under the previous commission,[30] can you tell us what proportion of your candidates have come from those nine schools?' He answered 'very few indeed: it was quite an exception to have any from the great public schools'. When he was further asked if he had ever had one from Eton, he replied: 'Yes, one or two; only one or two. That was where there was a special object in coming up, as for instance the medical profession.' When the Prefect of Studies at Stonyhurst, Fr. G. R. Kingdon, was examined before the Commission the point received further emphasis. He was told by Lord Lyttelton: 'We have evidence with regard to the Matriculation Examination of the London University, that your boys come up better prepared than perhaps any school in England with regard to Classics.' Fr. Kingdon immediately replied: 'I should not myself lay great stress on that fact, because you are no doubt aware that the first public schools of the country do not

[28] Farm Street Archives. Morris's Manuscript comments on the *Report* of the Sub-Commission on Higher Education, 1872, p. 39.

[29] *The Month* (July, 1868), p. 3.

[30] The Clarendon Commission, 1864.

send their candidates to the London University; therefore it is
not a competition against the whole of England, but it is mainly
against second-class schools.' Lord Lyttelton rejoined that he did
not speak 'only relatively to other schools. What we are told is
that they come up remarkably well prepared and have done so
for some time.'[31] Fr. Kingdon gave further expression to his viewpoint in the columns of *The Month* in the same year. He felt that
'the very object with which the London University was established, to give an opportunity of gaining degrees to those who
were still excluded from Oxford and Cambridge, that is to
Dissenters of all denominations, was of itself enough to make the
institution stink in the nostrils of those schools of orthodoxy (the
great Protestant public schools) and all connected with them'.[32]
A further reason why the Public Schools despised the London
examinations could be found in the nature of those examinations
themselves, for 'an examination in which Classics are put on a
level with seven other subjects (at Matriculation) is one which
will not suit their studies, and will always be repugnant to their
style of education'. 'There is no chance', he declared, 'of the
public schools ever sending their boys to undergo them; and the
question recurs, do these examinations answer the purpose of our
higher Catholic colleges any more than they do that of the Protestant public schools?' He argued that the purpose 'of measuring
ourselves with the best educated youth of the country is not
answered at all, for the best educated never meets us on this ground'.
Stonyhurst boys met in London youths from 'middle-class schools,
Dissenting schools, and second-rate proprietary schools'. On the
other hand, Fr. Joseph Rickaby, S.J., held a different opinion. At
the end of his long and distinguished life he wrote that his memory
carried him back to the year 1866, 'when I sat for my B.A. degree
in the University of London', and he expressed gratitude 'to the
potentates who then ruled at Burlington House and Savile Row',
for 'they took me down to the depths of things, they made me
think'.[33] To Fr. Henry Tristram of the Birmingham Oratory it

---

[31] *Report* of Schools Inquiry Commission, 1865, 842, 843.
[32] *The Month* (July 1868), p. 2.
[33] See *The Dublin Review* (Oct. 1936), pp. 277-8.

was the London Matriculation Examination more than anything else which 'forcibly revolutionized the character of the education given in the Catholic colleges'.[34] It was a revolution both far-reaching and profound.

[34] Ibid., p. 276.

IV

HIGHER STUDIES AT USHAW

STONYHURST's closest rival in the London University stakes was St. Cuthbert's College, Ushaw. It was also the most intellectually alive of the Catholic foundations. Established at Ushaw (whence it had migrated from Crook Hall, Durham) in 1808, with its course of studies and mode of teaching 'nearly on the same plan as were pursued at the celebrated parent establishment at Doway',[1] it flourished to such a degree that within twenty years it could lay claim to the most fully developed curriculum to be found in any Catholic College. In 1827 the *Catholic Miscellany* outlined the course of studies: 'Five years are devoted to the study of Latin, Greek, English and French languages, history sacred and profane, geography, writing, arithmetic, and elocution. The study of poetry occupies one year more, and rhetoric another.[2] Then follows two years of philosophy, and lastly, three years assigned to theology and the Sacred Scriptures complete the course.'[3]

The credit for this early organization must be given to John Lingard, Prefect of Studies from 1808 until 1811, a post he combined with those of Vice-President and Procurator. It was his determination which secured for Ushaw the rights belonging to a pontifical university, with the power to confer the degree of Doctor of Divinity.[4] Lingard was also responsible for the development of courses in Fencing, Dancing, and Navigation in order to attract to the College the sons of Catholic gentlemen. An eagerness to keep abreast of current changes of taste in the field of

---

[1] *The Catholic Miscellany and Monthly Repository of Information*, Ushaw Archives 7 (1827), p. 19.

[2] Poetry and Rhetoric were, as at Stonyhurst, the two highest classes in the school.

[3] For those proceeding to Holy Orders. The College was not a Tridentine seminary but provided the 'shared' education characteristic of Oscott and St. Edmund's, Ware. [4] *Ushaw Magazine*, no. 168 (1946), p. 75.

secular education was indeed one of the chief characteristics of these early years at Ushaw. In 1821–2, for instance, Charles Newsham, Prefect of Studies since 1817, left for Edinburgh to attend a course of lectures at the University 'in order to transport to Ushaw whatever he can collect there'.[5] Shortly after this Nicholas Wiseman, who had been a boy at the College from 1810 until 1818, received a letter from a correspondent who spoke of the 'excellent course of Maths.' and the 'extensive and rational course of Natural Philosophy, Chemistry, etc.' which had started to flourish under Newsham's direction.[6] In 1841 the latter's example was followed by William Wrennall, who entered the College of St. Stanislaus in Paris in order that he might study the latest developments in Mathematics, with a view to imparting the new knowledge at Ushaw.

In 1837 Newsham was appointed President of the College, at a time when the air was filled with talk of the benefits which were shortly to be made available to Catholics in connection with the new University of London. By 1838 he had learned from George Errington that both Stonyhurst and Oscott were occupied in preparing their students for Matriculation, and he was aware that if Ushaw was to compete with its Catholic rivals it was essential to commence a scheme of reform at once. In November 1837 he had already appealed for funds for the erection of a new museum, 'suitably furnished with specimens, apparatus and models, for the purpose of illustrating the explanation of the professors and facilitating the progress of the students in the various branches of natural history, chemistry, and experimental philosophy'.[7] In 1842 the College could boast of possessing brass levers, pulleys, air-pumps, globes, and a microscope, extensive apparatus for ordinary Electricity, a good Gregorian telescope, a barometer, hydrometer, Hadley's sextant, theodolite, goniometer, and apparatus for Acoustics and Electro-magnetism. Chemistry was introduced seriously into the school in 1838, when Joseph Cottam Fisher, Prefect of Studies from 1833 to 1837, began to experiment

[5] Carson, Mgr. Liam: 'Studies in the Early Days at Ushaw', *Ushaw Magazine* (Dec. 1946), p. 71.

[6] Ibid., pp. 71–2.   [7] *Ushaw Magazine*, no. 169 (1947), p. 10.

'with caloric on the reflector, canister and diff. thermometer', produced oxygen gas and hydrogen, and 'burnt sulphur in oxygen and made of it sulphuric acid'.[8] Later he conducted experiments in Electricity, and his boys were encouraged to perform 'some experiments at leisure'.[9]

In 1839 Newsham produced his masterpiece, a total reorganization of Ushaw's curriculum. Advancing on the somewhat casual way in which Stonyhurst and Oscott had approached the authorities of London University, Ushaw determined to show that she took the new challenge seriously. Three distinct courses were to be provided. In the first of these Newsham produced a direct response to the needs of the middle classes. There was to be a Commercial Course comprising 'writing, arithmetic, and book-keeping; the English, Latin, French, German, and Italian languages; history, antiquities, geography, and the use of the globes; elementary algebra and geometry, with the practical branches of mathematics; reading and public speaking, and the grounds of natural and revealed religion'.[10] There was to be a second course directed at 'those who are intended for any of the learned professions' or 'who are born to independence'. This would include, in addition to the subjects available to the commercial students, 'the Greek language, and complete classical education; poetry, rhetoric, the philosophy of the human mind, metaphysics and ethics; ecclesiastical history; the higher branches of mathematics, natural philosophy, astronomy, chemistry, and natural history'. Finally, there was the Ecclesiastical Course for those preparing for the priesthood, partaking of subjects prescribed for the other two courses, in addition to 'the Hebrew language, and the several departments of sacred learning'. The scheme was to be flexible, because, 'as these three courses enter into the general plan of education, any one of them, or any portion of them, may be selected, according to the profession, or state of life, for which the student is intended'. There is embodied in the Prospectus, announcing the changes,

---

[8] *Ushaw Magazine*, no. 169 (1947), p. 11.   [9] Ibid.

[10] Ushaw Archives. Newsham's General Plan of Education, in *The Course of Studies with the Theses and Examination Papers, July 1839* (London, MDCCCXXXIX), pp. 1–2.

reference to two unique institutions. If Ushaw was to engage seriously in university studies, then the general culture of its undergraduates ought not to be restricted to particular courses. A series of public lectures was to be instituted in the College, open to all students, and embracing 'chemistry, mineralogy, geology, botany, zoology, astronomy, and the different branches of natural philosophy; literature and the fine arts; and the principles and history of architecture'. Instruction was immediately provided in Architecture, in the Liturgy, and in Languages.

The second unique institution was that of the pedagogues. The plan declared: 'Each student below the class of Poetry is placed under the care of a private tutor, who prepares him for the lessons of his Professor.' This scheme of individual tuition was still in use in the College in 1882, as we learn from Raleigh Chichester's visit to Ushaw at that time, but by 1892 the last vestiges of the system were withering away. Chichester describes the pedagogue system as an extra educational agent: 'Divines and philosophers have each a room, and it has been the custom for the prefect of studies to assign to these young men from three to five boys in the three lower classes of the college, who, during play-hours, were allowed to go to their room for teaching, assistance, and advice.'[11] But the pedagogue was also 'a counsellor, a friend, a helper, and sometimes even a protector'.[12] The system had many advantages. Dr. Milburn points out that 'it encouraged study in the young students, it developed in the pedagogue a sense of responsibility and self-reliance, it relieved the professor of much preparation and all the work of revision'.[13] He might also have added that the system encouraged enduring friendships, especially between clerics and laymen, that it helped to overcome embarrassment and reticence in backward or awkward boys, and that it nurtured a spirit of camaraderie often lacking in more sophisticated institutions.

Newsham's Plan contained reference to the religious training the College intended to supply. After claiming that 'the religious and moral instruction and conduct of all, are attended to with

[11] Chichester, C. Raleigh, p. 78.   [12] Milburn, p. 139.
[13] Ibid., p. 140.

watchful and anxious care', it asserted that 'besides the usual course of catechetical instructions, public lectures are delivered on the liturgies and ceremonies of the Church; our English version of the Sacred Scriptures is explained at stated hours every week; and the whole of the Greek Testament is read in class'. A booklet of some fifty pages accompanied Newsham's scheme, in which were specified details of, and textbooks for, the courses. Prizes and silver medals were introduced to stimulate effort. Wiseman's advice that the old Douay names for studies in the lower classes—Rudiments, Grammar, and Syntax—should be abolished in favour of *literae humaniores* was adopted, the title being anglicized to Classes of Humanity.

A reform in the studies pursued at Ushaw was, however, not the only consequence of the London connection. If the College was to make the most of its new status it ought to resemble a university externally. In 1839 a beginning was made by the adoption of the university cap, designed after the Cambridge model, and worn by the professors. The practice did not die out until about 1848. An improvement and development of physical amenities in the College was also initiated in 1839. Gas lighting was introduced into the main buildings, and Newsham 'opened a Library and Museum for the use of the boys'.[14] Dormitories were extended, playing fields developed, and new ball places and racket courts constructed. In 1844 a start was made on a new chapel and two years later 'the Refectory was gothicised and adorned by A. W. Pugin'. Much of the enthusiasm for these developments was generated by the Revd. John Gillow, who devoted his time to the construction of large reservoirs, sewage-disposal units, and the design and laying-out of the five acres of gardens and orchard. Lingard had feared at the outset that this external activity and the radical reorganization in studies might be viewed as 'all a puff' by those sceptical of Newsham's earnestness of purpose. But, for himself, Lingard considered that the academic changes were 'more than I ever expected and as much as I could even wish'.[15]

---

[14] An Old Alumnus, *Records and Recollections of St. Cuthbert's College, Ushaw*; with introductory Poem, pp. 173 seq.

[15] *Ushaw Magazine* (1941), p. 236.

The Hon. Charles Langdale, M.P., presented Ushaw's petition for affiliation to London University in March 1839, and in the following February the petition was granted. Within three months of the event Ushaw offered her first students for the degree of B.A. The two candidates worked extremely hard, rising daily for study at 4 a.m. Francis Wilkinson and Richard Wilson were not only successful in the examination but received 'high encomiums from the first examiner of London and Cambridge Universities',[16] who pointed out that the French composition of Wilson had 'surpassed all others out-and-out'. A writer in the *Weekly Orthodox Journal* in May 1840, himself educated 'by the best talent of Stonyhurst', was the first to acclaim the spectacular achievement of Ushaw in leading the way for other Catholic colleges to follow. Ushaw had obtained the unique privilege of producing the first Catholic students since the Reformation to be trained entirely in an English Catholic institution, and to have their merit rewarded by the conferring of a degree recognized by the State. Both Wilkinson and Wilson were placed in the first division of the degree, and received a triumphal welcome on their return to the College.

In the following year, when Oscott gained its first success in the degree examination, Ushaw presented six candidates and all six were successful. The candidates from St. Edmund's, Ware, and from Downside were failed. All seemed set for a splendid future for Ushaw. It is, therefore, with no little surprise that we read in the class-lists of the University that the College during the next twenty-two years obtained only two degrees and an occasional Matriculation. The change in attitude is indicated in a letter of Newsham to Dr. Weedall of Oscott, dated 24 January 1859. In this he declares that, unless a degree is absolutely necessary for a young man, 'the time required to prepare for the examination is far less usefully spent than it would be in pursuing our own course of education'.[17] The letter goes on:

For some time past, our practice has been neither to encourage our students to take degrees in London, nor to dissuade them from it, but

---

[16] *The Weekly Orthodox Journal* (May 1840), p. 394.
[17] Oscott Archives. Letter of President Newsham to Dr. Weedall, 24 Jan. 1859.

simply to leave the matter to the wishes of their parents. Of parents who expressly require it, we give the students facilities for preparing themselves. The cases, therefore, are now so few that we do not find much practical inconvenience. On the other hand, we are convinced from past experience that a system of preparing any number of students annually for London would be a most serious detriment to our course of studies: and that no advantage would be gained that could in any way counterbalance the injurious effects we should feel from it.

The volte-face was complete by 1859, and for an explanation of its origins we have to turn to the years 1839–42. The early successes in the London examinations had encouraged the Prefect of Studies at the College, Ralph Platt, to proceed with a number of rapid changes. In 1842, for instance, a *Professor Litterarum Latinarum* and a *Professor Litterarum Graecarum* were named. These appointments, a logical development in Platt's policy of introducing academic specialists fully responsible for their own subjects, militated against the older Douay tradition of the class-master. Under Platt's new arrangements certain classes were to be fused (Grammar and Syntax, Poetry and Rhetoric) and the Classics course was to be extended into Philosophy. New text-books were introduced, including annotated editions, and (from 1839) flogging was abolished. The changes were radical. They presented too startling a break with tradition and offended the loyalties of many of the alumni and of the professors. It seemed, too, that the College was laying great stress upon academic and worldly renown, when it should be concentrating primarily upon its ecclesiastical function of providing competent priests for the mission. Discipline in the College was weak—in twenty-two years from 1820 to 1842 there had been no fewer than ten prefects of discipline, many of them incompetent. The President himself had been lax and willing to delegate overmuch to the Prefect of Studies. The students resented constant changes in established tradition, and this, together with increased academic pressure, led to open revolt in November 1842. A state of anarchy prevailed for the better part of a week, before the bewildered professors could restore the house to tranquillity. It was an eventful time, during which one member of staff had a poker thrown at him and others had been threatened by a student armed with a pistol. Many of the older alumni were only too ready to point out that this was a direct result of the foolhardy attempt to abandon Douay tradition, and Newsham, timid by nature, decided that the cause of reform had gone too far. He retracted his support, and withdrew Platt's plans for greater co-operation between the studies pursued at Ushaw and the schemes of the London examiners. Platt resigned and proceeded *in vineam Domini*; with his departure the connection with London gradually fell into desuetude. Ironically, Platt was to be succeeded as Prefect of Studies in 1843 by that same Francis Wilkinson who had graduated B.A. from London in 1840. Newsham remained President until 1863 and no further efforts were made during his time to pursue the London connection seriously. But for this fallow period, Ushaw would undoubtedly have outstripped Stonyhurst in its number of London graduates. The original stimulus had, however, greatly invigorated the College and it was the progenitor of the renewed educational vigour of the sixties.

Robert Tate assumed the Presidency of Ushaw in 1863, and was followed thirteen years later, in rapid succession, by Francis Wilkinson, B.A. (1876–7), James Chadwick (1877–8), and William Wrennall, B.A., D.D. (1878–85). Tate made preparation for the London B.A. degree an integral part of the college curriculum. Since 1858 the process of affiliation had disappeared, and this, in a sense, made it easier for Tate to effect the reorganization. He could not be accused of subjecting the interests of the College to an outside body. Now the arrangement was an entirely internal affair, and the Matriculation examination was held, from 1863, in the College itself. The plan which Tate arrived at was that all students in the class of Poetry would be prepared for Matriculation, selected students in Rhetoric for the Intermediate Examination (or first B.A.), and those in High Philosophy for the final B.A. Examination. In 1887 *The Tablet* was able to proclaim that since 1863 Ushaw had 'sent up a continuous stream of students to the examinations held by the London University, and now proudly claims a greater number of achieved successes than any other

Catholic institution can point to in the same period'.[18] By 1896 she had lost the lead to Stonyhurst, but could still vaunt of having obtained sixty degrees (eight with Honours) and 354 successes at Matriculation. Seven Ushaw students proceeded M.A., and the gold medal in Classics, which, writes The Old Alumnus in 1889, 'has been awarded only fourteen times since the foundation of the University in 1837', was won twice by candidates from Ushaw.

In 1896 the first complete and formal break with the London Matriculation took place, to be followed by Ushaw's subsequent adoption of the Oxford Local Examinations and those of the Oxford and Cambridge Examination Board. The real occasion of the break, however, can be attributed to Ushaw's growing attraction to the University of Durham, situated as it was only a few miles distant from the College. The responsibility for developing the new connection belonged to Thomas W. Wilkinson, who in 1888 became Auxiliary Bishop of the Diocese of Hexham and Newcastle, and who succeeded to full control of the see in the following year. Wilkinson, a convert parson and old Harrovian, was of wealthy yeoman stock, and had expended the greater part of his energies as a priest in the capacity of a retired country farmer rearing a fine herd of Durham shorthorns. He himself had graduated at Durham in 1845 prior to taking orders in the Church of England, and he always possessed a predeliction for his Alma Mater. As Bishop of the Diocese, Wilkinson decided to reside at Ushaw, and in 1890 assumed, in addition to his other duties, the Presidency of the College. During the nine years he held this position he concentrated his energies on furthering Ushaw's relations with Durham.

The University of Durham had been established in 1832, as primarily an Anglican foundation, but the basically tolerant attitude of the University authorities had led to friendly contacts being established with Ushaw, and these were preserved over a number of years, until in 1896 Wilkinson persuaded his fellow bishops to allow him to send selected students to Durham University for advanced courses in Mathematics, Science, and

18 *The Tablet*, 19 Nov. 1887.

Classics. Three years later the University permitted Ushaw men to take its degrees while they resided at St. Cuthbert's, and the close relationship remained until the advent of the Modernist scare brought it to an end sixteen years later. By that time Ushaw students had headed the class lists of the University in Classics and Literature and had carried off the University Classical Scholarship five times. Over a dozen gained Arts degrees. The London connection was resumed yet again in 1906 and survived until 1939. London University itself had been reorganized in 1900 to distinguish Internal and External Students, and from 1906 until the outbreak of the Second World War Ushaw could claim 279 successful candidates at the London Matriculation, twelve Honours B.A. degrees, and two Master's degrees. In 1936 the College turned for a second time to the Oxford and Cambridge examinations, chiefly because after 1924 London ceased to provide Honours in the Intermediate Arts examination, and after the Second World War the Durham School Certificate and Higher School Certificate were introduced at Ushaw. One of the most recent Presidents of St. Cuthbert's, Mgr. Paul Grant, has further developed the contact with Durham University.[19]

[19] See my article, 'The Athens of the North: Ushaw in the Nineteenth Century', in *The Tablet*, 218, no. 6478, 18 July 1964, pp. 798–9.

V

HIGHER STUDIES AT OSCOTT, WARE DOWNSIDE, AND OTHER CATHOLIC COLLEGES

In 1888, the final year of Oscott's existence as a college for the education of laymen as well as clerics, Fr. William J. Amherst, S.J., reviewed the contribution it had made to the development of Catholic life in England. 'There is one matter', he wrote, 'in which St. Mary's has not shown itself so prominently as it might have done. I mean in the records of the London University. On the question whether it is or is not beneficial to our Colleges to be in connection with the above institution I do not wish to express any opinion whatever. . . . But the mere fact that Oscott has not through its course sent young men to London in anything like the proportion of other Colleges has, I think, been somewhat detrimental to the College.'[1] As a consequence of such a policy 'the name of Oscott has dropped out of the list of Colleges the names of which most frequently meet the public eye'.

The editor of *The Oscotian* added a note to Fr. Amherst's article, explaining why it was 'that Oscott has not in the past presented as many candidates for the examinations of the London University as other colleges'. The fact was that Oscott was debarred, 'by the class of boys that go to make it up', from proving a formidable rival in this respect. The Catholic aristocracy had developed the College primarily as their own institution, and they were uninterested in their sons, matriculating at London, 'which will be of little or no advantage to them'. London examinations were for middle-class boys, whereas the youths at Oscott were to be prepared for the Army or Navy, for Diplomacy or the Foreign Office, for the Law, or for the management of the family estates.

[1] *The Oscotian* (1888), pp. 56–7.

Oscott was one of the first of the Catholic colleges to become affiliated to London University, and in 1839 Dr. Henry Weedall, the then President of the College, presented Queen Victoria with a gold medal to commemorate the event which he had announced to the parents of his boys as a milestone in the history of the College and of Catholic life in England. That the original promise was not immediately fulfilled can be attributed in large measure to force of circumstances. Dr. Weedall had been effectively in charge of the College since 1826 and he regarded the securing of London recognition as the climax of his work of consolidation and expansion. He was responsible for the purchase of the new site for the College in 1833, and the design and magnificence of the new building, opened in 1835 at the height of the Gothic revival, was itself indicative of the President's high aspirations.

Tragedy struck for Weedall in 1840, immediately after he had negotiated the London affiliation successfully. On 3 July 1840 Pope Gregory XVI raised the number of Vicariates in England from four to eight, as a preliminary step leading to the restoration of a formal hierarchy ten years later. In the new organization the President of Oscott was to be raised to the episcopate as Vicar Apostolic of the Northern District. Weedall suspected sinister motives at work. His bishop was Thomas Walsh, who for some time had been trying to deflect Nicholas Wiseman from collaborating with Bishop Baines in establishing a Catholic University at Prior Park. One of the ways to secure Wiseman's services, and to offset the potential danger to Oscott from Prior Park, was for Walsh to arrange that Wiseman should be named as his own Coadjutor, with the right of succession. This he obtained in June 1840. It was necessary, however, that Wiseman should be found a position of importance in the District. The promise of the Presidency of Oscott had been a chief attraction in persuading Wiseman to abandon the Prior Park project. Wiseman's influence with the Catholic aristocracy and the Oxford reformers made it easier to dispense with the services of Weedall. Although forced to leave Oscott to make room for Wiseman, Weedall resolutely refused to accept episcopal preferment, and he urged the clergy in the North—through Fr. William Hogarth, later to be first Bishop of

Hexham—to protest at having him for their bishop. Weedall journeyed to Rome and made a direct appeal to the Pope. Maintaining that he had spent the whole of his life in the service of Oscott, he pointed out that the break would be too great a rupture. Gregory XVI heeded his plea and the appointment was cancelled. The outcome was embarrassing for Wiseman, who was, by 1841, the effective President of Oscott. The Vice-President of the College, the Revd. William Wareing, had been removed at the same time as Weedall by securing his appointment as Vicar Apostolic of the new Eastern District. In his place Wiseman had installed a Cambridge convert, the Revd. H. F. C. Logan. Weedall's return from Rome in victorious mood presented, therefore, a serious problem. He could not be given a subordinate post at Oscott and public opinion had to be considered. The difficulty was circumvented temporarily by naming Weedall head of the preparatory school at Old Oscott. There he remained, until in 1843 he escaped from the indignity by accepting the rectorship of the mission at Leamington Spa.

The turmoil consequent upon these events prevented a coherent policy from being adopted at Oscott in regard to the London examinations. Before Weedall's removal candidates had been entered for the London Matriculation, however, and in 1841 Oscott gained its first graduates, John Coupe, Thomas Donohoe, John Kennedy, and Thomas Longman. The victors were awarded a tumultuous reception at the College and were dragged in triumph from the College lodge to the main entrance. The years of Wiseman's presidency, however, were not distinguished in the annals of London University. The College did not obtain a B.A. degree with Honours until 1848, when Edward Gilpin Bagshawe headed the Honours list in Classics, some months after Wiseman's appointment as Pro-Vicar-Apostolic of the London District. Bagshawe, who was to join the Oratory, became third Bishop of Nottingham in 1874, and earned a considerable reputation as a social thinker. There were two other Bagshawes who were to graduate while at Oscott—John (Matriculation 1844, B.A. 1846), who later became Canon Penitentiary of Southwark, and William Henry Gunning Bagshawe, brother of John (Matriculation 1841,

B.A. 1843), who became one of H.M. County Court Judges and Examiner in Equity to London University.

Wiseman was not, in the words of Mgr. Barnes, 'a schoolmaster by temperament or training',[2] and a greater interest in the examinations and awards of London University had to await the return of Dr. Weedall from Leamington in 1853. He was to remain six years as President, glad to be back, but exhausted in mind and body after five years as Vicar-General of the District. These final years were, nevertheless, years of solid achievement for Oscott, turning the College into 'a world as lively as it was varied, cosmopolitan to a high degree, and singularly unlike what English opinion conceives a mere school must be'.[3] It was this 'world' that Weedall bequeathed in 1859 to James Spencer Northcote.

Northcote, a member of an old Devonshire family, had taken a 'double first' at Corpus Christi College, Oxford. He was ordained to the curacy of Ilfracombe and was converted to Roman Catholicism in 1845. During the years he held the Presidency of Oscott, 1860–76, Northcote concentrated on increasing the lay element in the College. It was imperative that Oscott should draw its pupils 'from the best Catholic families'.[4] He rapidly became the spokesman for aristocratic interests, and advocated, after the removal of the Tests, the setting up of a Catholic Hall at Oxford, preferably under Newman's control, or if needs be, in the hands of the Jesuits.[5] With 'Howards, and Stourtons, and Cliffords, and Petres, and Scropes, and Mostyns'[6] he felt such a Hall could succeed. University education must be provided primarily for the Catholic nobility and gentry, for the families 'bearing great historical names'.[7] In the 1840s a spirit of friendly rivalry had existed between Oscott and Ushaw in the race for London honours; by the 1860s Northcote had effectively killed it. The rivalry had been initiated in 1841, as is indicated by a note preserved at Ushaw. This reads: 'Mr. Bagshawe bets Mr. Platt that Oscott will be

---

[2] Barnes, A. S., *The Catholic Schools of England* (London, 1926), p. 148.

[3] Barry, W., *Memories and Opinions*, pp. 46–7.

[4] Barnes, p. 149.

[5] Brompton Oratory Archives. Report of Northcote to the Sub-Commission on Higher Education, *passim*.

[6] Ibid., p. 7.   [7] Ibid.

first to obtain M.A. Three half-crowns a side. Mr. Pagliano to be holder of the Stakes. Monday, 7 June, 1841. First Meeting of Bachelors.'[8]

The bet was won by Ushaw, the successful candidate being Mr. Valentine Browne, who proceeded M.A. in 1874. Unimportant as the episode is, in itself, it is indicative of the healthy stimulation of friendly rivalry introduced by the London examinations. Such competition was frowned upon by Northcote, although he did not prevent his charges from attempting the London examinations if parents particularly expressed a desire to have their sons compete.

If we peruse the list of noble and titled students at Oscott we are able to discover just how few of them were anxious for academic honours. The Hon. Thomas Edward Stonor, son of the third Lord Camoys, matriculated at London in 1842. William Joseph Fitzherbert-Brockholes matriculated in 1868. Robert Valentine Berkeley matriculated in 1874, becoming in due time a captain in the Worcester Militia. The Hon. Ranulph Mostyn, grandson of the sixth Lord Vaux of Harrowden, matriculated at London in 1877 before assuming a commission in the Army. Osmund de Lisle, son of Ambrose Phillipps de Lisle, matriculated in 1865, as also did David Fitzgerald, the son of one of Her Majesty's Lords of Appeal. David Fitzgerald subsequently graduated at Cambridge. Charles du Moulin-Browne matriculated in 1868, at the same time as Francis Loraine Petre (nephew of the twelfth baron), who eventually took the Intermediate Arts examination before becoming a barrister and in due course a Judge in India. Ralph William Petre (another nephew of the twelfth baron) matriculated in 1873 and obtained the Intermediate Arts in 1876. He later became an attaché at the English Embassy in Brussels. Richard Sheil, son of General Sir Justin Sheil, matriculated in 1876, and was followed five years later by Edgar Durup de Balaine. Finally, in 1883 Hugh Charles Fairfax-Cholmeley's name is recorded among those who successfully passed the London Matriculation examination. It is difficult to find a single

---

[8] See *Ushaw Magazine* (1941), pp. 235 seq., and my article in *The Tablet*, 218, no. 6478, p. 798.

London graduate from among the greater families, apart from Henry John Scrope, who obtained the B.A. in 1847, as did Edward Acton in 1858. What successes there were came from clerical students or middle-class youths. In all, in the forty-eight years from 1841 to 1888 Oscott obtained twenty-one B.A. degrees and one LL.B. degree. Eight went as far as the first B.A. (Intermediate) examination and ninety-seven were successful at Matriculation.

Of the remaining Catholic colleges presenting candidates for the London examinations, perhaps the most enthusiastic was St. Edmund's College, Ware. By 1893, the year in which it began to consider seriously the possibility of sending divines to Cambridge, 113 candidates had matriculated at London from St. Edmund's and fifty-five had obtained either the first or second B.A. degree examination. The College was affiliated to the University in 1840, and in that year it sent up James Danell and Henry Rymer to attempt the Matriculation examination. They were both successful. Danell in 1871 became the second Bishop of Southwark, and Rymer was to be a Canon of the same diocese. The College did not obtain its first B.A. until 1844, when Lawrence Dolan graduated. In 1847 the Revd. George Pringle, a Classics Professor at St. Edmund's, took the first Exhibition in Classics at the Matriculation examination, and in 1883 Arthur Doubleday, destined to be second Bishop of Brentwood, took seventh place in the General Honours London Matriculation of that year. Bernard Ward points out, however, that the best year for the College was 1885, when five Edmundians obtained B.A. degrees, five passed the Intermediate Arts examination, and ten matriculated.[9]

When Raleigh Chichester visited Downside in 1882, he found only 105 boys in residence, divided up as follows: Philosophy, 4; Rhetoric, 10; Poetry, 10; Higher Syntax, 15; Lower Syntax, 16; Higher Grammar, 17; Middle Grammar, 16; Lower Grammar, 17. With numbers such as these it is clear that Downside's successes in the London examinations could not be many. Dom Peter Wilson, Prior of Downside in 1840, sought affiliation for the College in his first year in office, and throughout the second half of the

[9] Ward, B., *History of St. Edmund's College Old Hall*, pp. 255–6.

century a small but significant number of young men figure in the lists of the University.[10] Of especial importance, perhaps, were two successes; one in 1845, when John Charles Day graduated, and the other four years later, when George Decimus Davis obtained the B.A. degree with Honours in Chemistry. Day was called to the Bar and became Q.C. in 1872, a Bencher in 1873, and a Judge in 1882, when he was knighted. Davis's achievement did much to improve the teaching of Science in the school.

In 1882 Chichester observed that the Benedictines employed two lay teachers, who were themselves London graduates and whose duties were to teach the four undergraduates in the class of Philosophy.[11] Preparation for Matriculation was undertaken in the class of Rhetoric, and here a lay master was in charge of Greek. One of the consequences of the policy of entering youths for the examinations of London was the establishment at Downside of a series of academic boards. There was 'a classical board with six professors, the English board with six more, and the mathematical board with four'.[12] These boards met together from time to time, under the direction of the Prefect of Studies, to discuss academic policy. The system of academic specialists, the attempted introduction of which had caused so much trouble at both Stonyhurst and Ushaw, was early adopted at Downside and flourished.

Prior Park was affiliated to London in 1840 and from time to time presented candidates for Matriculation. In 1852 Edward Williams obtained an Honours B.A. in Classics, and in 1880 Joseph John Bisgood took a second-class Honours degree in French. Woburn Park also engaged in preparing the occasional candidate, and on the time-table of the school for 1881 special provision was made for university work in Form VI of the Classical side, although in the same year the school magazine criticized Stonyhurst for its 'burning thirst for the *immediate* prizes of talent'.[13]

The University influenced the courses at Ampleforth and the lesser colleges, such as St. Edward's, Liverpool, and the Oratory

[10] For further details see Birt, H. N., p. 215.
[11] Chichester, C. Raleigh, p. 55.   [12] Ibid., p. 56.
[13] *The Amoeba*, 21 June 1881, no. 3, pp. 11 seq.

School. Candidates from the Oratory School appear from time to time in the London Pass lists, and its most distinguished successes were those of Francis Ince Anderton, who took a first-class B.A. in Classics in 1877, and John Hungerford Pollen, who obtained a second-class in Latin in the Intermediate Examination in 1880. In 1868 Newman, who claimed 'I have never recognised, I have never endured, the London University', swallowed his principles in order to prepare, personally, the sons of Mr. Serjeant Bellasis for the London University Matriculation examination.[14] Newman also coached Bellasis's elder boy for the London B.A., and turned a blind eye to the fact that boys were regularly prepared for the examinations at the Oratory School.

The opening of the Oratory School so close to Oscott had presented the latter establishment with a formidable rival. It was an institution which, on account of Newman's reputation among the Old Catholic aristocracy and many of the affluent converts, was bent on tapping Oscott's own source of recruitment. It was a major contributory factor to Oscott's demise as a lay school in 1888.[15]

[14] For a fuller treatment of this episode see my article in *The Month* entitled 'The Kensington Scheme', N.S. 33, no. 3, pp. 172–82, and esp. p. 180.

[15] Barnes, p. 150.

VI

INFLUENTIAL CATHOLIC OPINION
AND THE LONDON EXAMINATIONS

IN a letter to *The Tablet* in December 1848 Bishop Ullathorne, rejoicing that two of the first Greek medals to be won at the London University 'were borne away by students whose chief studies had been at Downside', claimed that up to that date 'the history of the London University examinations is decisive as to the state of our college training'. Youths undergoing the discipline of those examinations in Catholic colleges had been constrained to remark upon 'the limited range of Oxford acquirements' in comparison with their own. Two months later W. G. Ward challenged Ullathorne's statements. In a long letter in *The Rambler* he claimed that the Catholic colleges were 'mainly adapted . . . for those lay students who, at the age of sixteen or thereabouts, expect to be called into active life in the way of commercial or other pursuits'.[1] Although 'several stay till a later age, say nineteen or twenty, and take, perhaps, their B.A. degree at the London University', he maintained that there was no endeavour to cater for the wealthier classes, adding 'no parent among the leisured classes would be content with his son's education closing at that age'. Ward suggested as one possible remedy, 'until some Catholic organisation for the purpose be completed', that 'it would be a very great advantage if some priest in London were to take boarders, who might profit by the admirable instruction of University College, and so prepare for their M.A. degree'. He had more respect for Oxford acquirements than Ullathorne, for he considered the examination for the London M.A. corresponded pretty accurately with Oxford's B.A. examination. Of course he realized that a number of the sons of the Catholic landed families went into residence at Cambridge

[1] *The Rambler* (Feb. 1849), p. 449.

for a time after leaving school, but he felt sure it would be recognized that if his recommendation were followed 'those fearful snares and perils which, under all conceivable circumstances must beset the Catholic youth at Cambridge' would be avoided. At University College 'no intimacies whatever are formed with the companions of their studies, who are hardly so much as seen out of the lecture-room: the student does but leave in the morning the house which is as his home to attend the college-lecture; and the lecture being over, he straightway returns'. Such a plan, he felt, would be more acceptable than that outlined by Frederick Oakeley in 1848. Oakeley, a prominent Tractarian, had been Chaplain-Fellow of Balliol and Student of Christ Church before his conversion to Roman Catholicism in 1845. In 1848 he could see virtue in the shared, clerical–lay, education characteristic of the Catholic colleges. Joining the debate in *The Rambler* in that year, he gave his opinion that 'the difference between the existing English Catholic idea of education and that to which we [converts] were accustomed at Oxford is, as you know, a fundamental one; the one making the formation of [mental] *character* its great aim, the other, the storing of the mind with a certain amount of valuable facts. Hence *our* requirements seem to Catholics "limited" and *their* intellectual character and habits seem to us shallow and desultory'.[2] Ward was less complacent. The education provided in the existing Catholic colleges, as a consequence of the regulations governing the London Matriculation and B.A. examinations, was geared more and more to the task of acquiring factual information and perfecting primary academic skills. What was lacking was real *scholarship*. A house in London, where Catholic youths could prepare for the Master's degree and from whence they could attend lectures at University College, would provide a remedy. This was vitally necessary, Ward argued, for 'mathematical habits, no less than classical, are felt by him who attains them to convey something quite different in *kind* from mere knowledge and information; a new *faculty*, as it were, which gives him a sort of dominion over the various fields of science, such as nothing else can possibly confer'.[3] In acquiring this new faculty 'much assistance

---

[2] Ibid. Letter dated 11 Dec. 1848.   [3] Ibid. (Feb. 1849), p. 449.

may be derived from non-Catholic institutions, during the unfortunate absence of Catholic ones'.

Ward's attack on the superficial quality of the London Matriculation and B.A. examinations gained powerful support from the
editor of *The Rambler* himself, John Moore Capes, in September
1849. The root of London's ineffectuality lay in its belief that
it was possible 'to educate the mind without touching upon
theological questions'.[4] This brought much trouble in its wake.
'The examiners of candidates for degrees in Arts,' he wrote, 'if
honest, either dare not ask the questions they ought to ask, lest
they lead to a theological reply; or they so modify what they ask,
as to deprive the whole procedure of all spirit, influence, and
vitality. . . . They are driven to take refuge in verbal niceties,
trivial criticisms, unimportant historical events, uninfluential
biographies, sham philosophy, stiff logic, cold and hollow
metaphysics.' To this cause could be attributed 'the true secret
of the slow progress of the London University examinations'.
But lest it be imagined that Capes was contrasting unfavourably
the education which London represented with that offered at the
ancient Universities, it must be added that he followed up his
attack a year later with an equally scathing one upon Oxford and
Cambridge. The education given to the upper classes 'at the
public schools, at all large private schools, and at Oxford and
Cambridge' in the 1840s 'was *at the least* as non-religious as that
which is now expected by the University of London . . . '.[5] The
theme was taken up again in 1851 by the *Dublin Review*, which
attacked unnecessary proliferation of academic subjects. 'Geography, geology, mineralogy, botany, and every branch of natural
philosophy: jurisprudence, and political economy, trade manufactures, and statistics' were the fertile progeny of the *novum
organon*, 'not to mention a host of modern languages' which now
'burst upon our bewildered youth, and threaten to exhaust, or to
dissipate on variety of subjects, the energies of a life, under the
claim to train an education'.[6]

---

[4] *The Rambler* (Sept. 1849), pp. 305 seq.
[5] Ibid. (Aug. 1850), p. 91.
[6] *The Dublin Review* (Mar. 1851), p. 225.

In July 1851 *The Rambler* presumed to comment that such a scheme as that propounded by Ward for a close tie with University College, London, would cause the faith of a young Catholic to be '*more* subtlely undermined'[7] than it would be at Oxford or Cambridge. In the following month Capes[8] exposed the real weakness in Catholic higher education, the diversity of interests and multiplication of resources. 'Each separate college', he wrote, 'is too small, its resources too limited, and its professors too overburdened with work, to form a nucleus of Catholic learning.' The number of students in any one college who were engaged in advanced courses of study was too small to support a staff of competent teachers, 'not to speak of the difficulty of some score or more of colleges, utterly unendowed, being each able to secure first-class teachers of all the multiform subjects which should be comprised in such an education'. To this difficulty must be added the heterogeneous nature of the students, middle-class youths preparing for London degrees and the professions, clerical students, and 'a small remnant of the sons of men of property'. This 'landed' element 'consists wholly of those who feel that there is no necessity for their applying themselves to the acquisition of knowledge', and they found ecclesiastical discipline irksome. The sons of the opulent, therefore, very rarely remained in the Catholic colleges after the age of sixteen or eighteen, and 'those who do might very generally as well have left at that age, as far as any advancement in learning is concerned'. Capes pointedly reinforced his remarks by stating that 'since the opening of the London University to the Catholic colleges, not more than a dozen sons of the gentry have graduated from them'.

Capes urged the Catholic colleges to subordinate their individual interests to the general good. All those intending to pursue higher studies should be gathered together in one institution. Only with the effecting of such a reform would there be adequate academic resources available for university studies. The relationship with London University ought not to be viewed as anything more than a temporary expedient. Capes reminded his readers in

---

[7] *The Rambler* (July 1851), p. 6.
[8] In the period 1848–52 Capes and *The Rambler* are practically synonymous.

1854 that London University 'is no more a place of education than the College of Physicians, or any board of examiners, is a place of education; it is a corporation, with a power of granting certificates of merit'. Far from the possibility of the Catholic colleges' agreeing to establish all their advanced students in one centre, by 1859 a number of them were considering abandoning the London connection altogether. The reason for this can be discovered in the University Charter of 1858, which led to the relinquishment of the system of affiliation, by empowering the University Senate to dispense with certificates of studentship in the Faculties of Arts and Laws. The awards of the University were henceforth 'to be obtained solely on the ground of proficiency as shown in examination'.[9] This system was to persist until the end of the century, when the classification into Internal and External students was evolved. With the removal of the condition of collegiate attendance in 1858, the new Intermediate Examination in Arts was introduced in the following year as a guarantee of continuous study. Along with this latter innovation came a further one that candidates for the degree were to be examined in Mental and Moral Science.

As early as 1842 the Revd. Ralph Platt of Ushaw had been in correspondence with Dr. J. H. Jerrard, tutor of Caius College, Cambridge, concerning a possible protest to the Home Secretary against the preponderance of scientists, medical men, atheists, and free-thinkers, in the Senate of London University. It was desirable that more classicists and arts graduates should join the Senate, and Jerrard suggested a deputation to Lord Burlington, Chancellor of the University.[10] Now that Mental and Moral Science was to become matter for examination for the senior students, serious doubts were felt, and Fr. E. J. Purbick, S.J., presented a Memorial in 1858 to the responsible committee of the Senate protesting against its introduction. In January 1859 Purbick informed Weedall, President of Oscott, that 'the answer of the Committee of the Senate to our Memorial is not by any means satisfactory. In fact no concession would fully meet the case short of simple

9 *University of London: Historical Record (1836–1912)*, p. 12.
10 *Ushaw Magazine* (1941), p. 243.

elimination of the examination in Philosophy'.[11] He claimed that 'it is impossible to make the Senate understand that a question of method in Philosophy may be a matter of principle', adding, 'one of them who was here the other day admitted to me almost every point which we have urged, but Grote carries all before him in the Senate, and he is our most determined opponent'. George Grote was 'a clever man and first rate historian [but] he thinks himself competent for any task of reform'. In educational matters 'his views are extremely raw and mostly second hand and therefore valueless', yet 'his energy and determination of will carry the day against his more sober colleagues'. F. W. Newman describes the philosophical thinking prevalent in the University at the time as 'predominantly negative, critical, sceptical',[12] and it was a fear that this attitude would influence the behaviour of examiners that worried the Catholic Superiors. One victory Purbrick succeeded in obtaining, in that the Senate 'have now pledged themselves not to trespass on the province of the History of Philosophy'.[13] He advised other colleges not to make any decision concerning a possible break with London until 1861, by which date 'we reckon that we shall have time to judge of the Philosophical Examination Papers before finally deciding upon abandonment of the University'. Perhaps, too, by then Convocation would have come to the rescue, for its committee had already entered fully into the spirit of Purbrick's protest and 'recommended the elimination of Philosophy, and the leaving of some branches as optional'. Purbrick also regretted the introduction of the new Intermediate Examination, which would impose serious academic and administrative problems for Stonyhurst. The B.A. Honours examinations were an undoubted stimulus, he felt, to the Stonyhurst youths, but he had little good to say about the Pass examinations.

Newsham of Ushaw thought that if the new requirement 'tends to diminish the number of candidates amongst us we shall

[11] Oscott Archives. Letter of Purbrick to Weedall, dated Stonyhurst, 24 Jan. 1859.

[12] Note by F. W. Newman in V. A. Hüber, *The English Universities*, vol. 2, part 1, p. 371.

[13] Oscott Archives. Purbrick's letter of 24 Jan. 1859.

be rather glad than otherwise'.[14] Prior Sweeney of Downside was less pessimistic. 'With regard to the degree of B.A. in the London University,' he wrote to Weedall, 'we do attach considerable importance to it. In many instances we have known the degree to be of real service to those who have gone to the Bar: and to the College in general the preparing for it, and the stimulus it has given to the studies has been of great advantage. The course required for it we consider to be very useful, and calculated to give a good amount of learning to those who go through it.'[15] But he too had doubts concerning the Philosophy examinations, objecting to having young Catholics examined in Philosophy 'by those who are in reality only Sophists and Sceptics'. Despite the fact that Convocation supported the Catholic claim, the Senate 'did not like to undo what they had too precipitately committed themselves to'. Sweeney had accompanied three Jesuits, Fathers A. Weld, P. Gallwey, and E. J. Purbrick, when they appeared before the Senate to present their case that Mental and Moral Philosophy should be struck out of the B.A. course, and that independent degrees in Philosophy should be instituted for those who particularly desired such courses. The examiners were 'surprised to see that we had so much to say in favour of our opposition', writes Sweeney, and they were 'utterly unable to answer our objections'. They did, however, give an assurance 'that nothing objectionable to us' should ever be required in the examinations themselves, and Sweeney for his part was willing to give the system a year's trial. The University agreed to drop 'Logic, Mental and Moral Philosophy' for examination purposes, in deference to Catholics, and to substitute 'Logic, and Moral Philosophy'. Sweeney was particularly pleased that the examinations could now be held within the walls of the Catholic colleges (in the presence of a London examiner), and he was prepared to take advantage of the concession at Downside. St. Edmund's particularly had feared that the introduction of Mental Philosophy into the matter for examination—as originally planned in 1859— would create insuperable difficulties for Catholics. The College

[14] Oscott Archives. Newsham to Weedall, 24 Jan 1859.
[15] Ibid. Sweeney to Weedall, 28 Jan. 1859.

viewed with pain 'the extreme freedom of the German School of Philosophy in the investigation of subjects included under Mental Philosophy', and regarded their systems 'as irreconcileable with revealed truth'.[16] The problem was overcome by the conciliatory attitude of the University authorities.

Grumbles were still heard from Catholics, however, from time to time. Fr. H. J. Coleridge, S.J., declared in *The Month* in 1869 that a Catholic would have no reason for complaint against the London examinations 'if London will give him his degree for Classics and Mathematics, without Philosophy', even though 'the examination may be encumbered by a few of the "ologies" for which, as an instrument of education, he has not much respect'.[17] *The Tablet* commented on the campaign conducted throughout the early part of 1869 in *The Month* against 'the tyranny practised on Catholics by the philosophical examinations of the London University and the grievous religious injury which they must inflict on the more thoughtful Catholic student'.[18] But the solution which *The Month* advocated—that Catholics should agitate for the admission of non-residents to the examinations of Oxford and Cambridge—would be hardly less objectionable, because of the 'shallow unbelief' and 'infidel philosophy' in the Literae Humaniores examinations. *The Tablet*, in an article on London University and its examinations in the same year, pointed out that six hours out of twenty-four in the final London B.A. examination were devoted to philosophical subjects. 'Any philosophical system', it declared, 'which is inconsistent with revelation is condemned thereby as false. Thus the philosopher who has the Faith possesses a touchstone by which to detect error. A light shines upon him in his researches which, without teaching him how to speculate or supplying him with the premises from which to reason, will save him from many a wandering among the by-paths of erroneous philosophy.'[19] In this regard, London University placed Catholics in a difficult position, 'The University must limit and define for [the student] the subjects to be studied. It must therefore adopt

---

[16] Ibid. Correspondence of 1859. The letter has no date.
[17] *The Month* (July 1869), p. 17.   [18] *The Tablet*, 10 Apr. 1869.
[19] Ibid., 10 July 1869.

one of the philosophical schools for its own, and make its examinations turn upon a thorough acquaintance with the principles and theories of this school. It cannot found its preference on the agreement of the school selected with revelation, for it professes to know nothing of religious belief, and it aims at stimulating intellectual culture without reference to supernatural truth.' But if all this were allowed, the journal was disturbed to find that the University 'has not only adopted a philosophy, but a philosopher, and made success in its examination depend on intimate acquaintance with the writings of one of its own examiners, Professor Bain'. The paper urged Catholics to consider 'how far it is justifiable to expose the more intellectual and promising portion of our youth to the perilous study of such anti-Christian and materialistic philosophy', and recommended the Catholic colleges to hold aloof from the examinations.

Dr. John Gillow, Vice-President of Ushaw, joined the battle in 1869, and pointed out in *The Dublin Review* that at his College 'our ordinary course for laymen does not end with the London University course: for after they have gone through the work required at London, the lay students have still an academical year, from October to August, devoted exclusively to sound Christian moral philosophy in all its branches',[20] and this he maintained was sufficient to offset any evils which might accrue from following the London course of Philosophy. Francis Wilkinson, who in 1876 was to become President of Ushaw, finally demolished the arguments of the opponents of the examinations by informing the hierarchy in 1872 that London, 'not being a teaching body . . . , can teach no system, and so far from professing to adopt any special system in its examinations, the Senate through the Registrar has repeatedly declared that the Authorities of the University purposely abstain from naming any special treatise to be studied, and all that is required is a knowledge of the subject. Provided this be shown, an examiner is bound to pass a candidate who endeavours to refute his theories equally with one who adopts them'.[21] The mathematical master at the Oratory School,

---

[20] *The Dublin Review* (Apr. 1869), p. 522.
[21] Brompton Oratory Archives. Wilkinson's Report, 3 Apr. 1872.

Pope, who (to Newman's pain) advocated closer ties with London University, pointed out that, 'as to the Philosophy, I can testify that, when I took my degree there, the books I read in that subject were M'Cosh, and a pamphlet, the name of which I forget, by a Jesuit, and no exception was taken to my answers'. Pope took his degree in 1864 and Bain was the examiner. Wilkinson commented that 'M'Cosh, whatever else may be said of him, holds views the most antagonistic to those of both Mill and Bain', and he submitted to the bishops copies of all the examination questions set since 1865, to show their Lordships 'that they contain no question which a Catholic need object to'.

The volume of criticism against the London examinations was greatest from those not directly concerned in the presentation of candidates, or who lacked first-hand experience of the kind possessed by Wilkinson and Pope. Much of it was the outcome of ingrained prejudice against the University itself, more was artificially engineered in the fight to gain access to examinations of the ancient Universities. But whatever the motives, the criticism of the London Philosophy examination had become so insistent by 1873 that Archbishop Manning, himself sympathetic to what the University was doing for the middle classes, felt constrained to object to the Philosophy papers. He had a personal interview with Dr. Carpenter, the Registrar, and the latter agreed to put his views in writing so that they could be considered by the assembled hierarchy in Low Week, 1876. In a letter, dated 21 April 1876, Carpenter stated that the examination at London was in the *subject* rather than in *books* (as was the case at Oxford and Cambridge). He then quoted many Catholics who had obtained degrees at London and attempted the Logic and Moral Philosophy papers. None had been failed because their views did not agree with those of the examiners. Carpenter cited, in particular, V. S. Browne (Ushaw, 1874), D. N. O'Conor (Downside, 1861), T. A. Snow (Downside, 1867), and Henry Worsley (Ushaw, 1873), who had all done remarkably well in the papers under discussion, and he concluded: 'it is not within [my] knowledge that any candidate from a Catholic college has *failed* at this examination.'

Manning proposed to the bishops the following resolution, which was approved: 'On these explicit assurances the Bishops are unanimous in believing that, as Catholics have no other means of obtaining a degree, and as our Catholic youth will be more exposed to danger if they be not prepared by Catholic Teachers to see the fallacy of modern systems, it is neither possible nor prudent to hinder their presenting themselves for the Examinations of the London University.' With the adoption of this resolution, the agitation against the London Philosophy examinations failed to gain the support of the bishops, and did not, therefore, assume the proportions of a major threat for the future of Catholic higher education.

But other objections had to be considered. In 1864 a pamphlet published by 'A Catholic Layman' indicated the true extent of the antagonism to London. It was addressed to Newman. 'The University of London does not, and from its constitution cannot, satisfy our present wants',[22] the author declared. 'Let us not be ungrateful for what it has done for us', he went on, for 'it has admitted the students of our colleges to examinations for matriculation and academical degrees in which they have to compete with students from all parts of England, and has thus helped to keep the standard of instruction in our colleges on a level with that in a great number of the Protestant schools.' But 'we are in need of a University education and the London University does not give us this. It is not a University at all in the old and strict sense of the term—the only sense in which we need a University. As far as we are concerned, it is a mere examining board for students of our colleges. . . . Education is not to be tested by the amount of information possessed at a given moment, but by the mode in which it is possessed and by which it has been acquired.' Bishop Ullathorne represented the hierarchy's opinion when, in a pastoral letter, he expressed suspicion of this viewpoint. 'It is not so much a course of studies that is sought for,' he wrote, 'as a certain social atmosphere'. It was 'precisely from this atmosphere that we would wish to shelter Catholic youth until their character

[22] Brompton Oratory Archives. *University Education for English Catholics: A Letter to the Very Rev. J. H. Newman, D.D.*, by 'a Catholic Layman', pp. 11–12.

and principles are formed'.[23] Newman disagreed with Ullathorne. In public he referred to London University as a 'bazaar or pantechnicon'; in private it was 'Stinkomalee'. He never retracted from his early scornful condemnation of the institution as one made up of 'utilitarians, political economists, useful knowledge people', governed by enmity to religion. 'A University', he wrote, 'which is scarcely more than a Board of Examiners and an apparatus for degrees, and a College which is but a collection of lecture-halls, open to young men who need never see each other or their professors elsewhere, in no way rises to the height of the ancient idea, of which they usurp the title.'[24]

The debate concerning the respective merits and disadvantages of the London commitment continued throughout the sixties and seventies with considerable vehemence. According to Dr. John Gillow, the connection with London University ensured that Catholic youths would not associate with 'that large body of men of weak abilities or negligent habits who are found, certainly not less in the colleges of the universities [of Oxford and Cambridge] than in other colleges', of men who at the ancient Universities spent the great portion of their time 'in hunting, boating, riding, wine parties, etc.', and very little at their books.[25] Such were 'wholly eliminated from the London examinations', along with those equally undesirable elements 'who are attracted to the universities rather by the prestige of the name, or the society to be there found, than by any desire of learning', and 'who never could be qualified to "pass" at any respectable examination'. He maintained that 'if all the men who graduate at Oxford or Cambridge were subjected to the London test, the number of B.A.'s would be marvellously diminished'.

Oakeley considered that Gillow placed emphasis in the wrong place. 'We were always taught to consider', he wrote in 1869, 'that the great end of a liberal education was not so much to store the mind with a certain amount of knowledge, as to form its character

[23] Birmingham Archdiocesan Archives. Ullathorne's Pastoral Letter of 13 Oct. 1867, p. 13.

[24] In a paper by Newman in *The Catholic University Gazette*, 3 May 1855. entitled 'University and King's Colleges in London'.

[25] *The Dublin Review* (April 1869), p. 520.

by subjecting it to a certain salutary discipline, and laying the foundation of those habits of accurate thought, adequate expression, discriminative judgment, and cultivated taste, which constitute the true difference between a more and [a] less highly educated man.'[26] London did not educate along these lines and its concentration upon academic prowess was positively harmful. The debate among Catholics rapidly developed into one concerned with the old arguments as to what did or did not constitute a liberal education. 'A well-educated man', in Oakeley's opinion, is one 'whose education not merely provides him with an abundance of rational resources, but enables him to set forth his knowledge to the best advantage, imparts to him the power of critical discernment and selection, the keen perception of the truly beautiful, and those especial qualities which, whether comprehended under the αἴσθησις of the Greeks, *judicium* of the Romans, or our English word "taste", is one of the fruits of education which no amount of mere knowledge can supply or secure.' Gillow's criticism of the Oxford student was, to Oakeley, as unfair as that made recently by Mark Pattison, for 'many an Oxford man, who would find it a hard matter in his later years to extricate the meaning of a crabbed passage in the *Agamemnon* or the eighth book of Thucydides from the meshes of a corrupted text, will yet give unquestionable proof in his public appearances of the mental cultivation that has followed upon the academical studies in the retrospect of which those processes do not constitute one of the most attractive features'. Those Catholics, like Gillow, who were enamoured of the London examinations were warned by Oakeley that 'if students be taught to aim as an object of ambition at success in examinations which are conducted not only without reference to religion but with an avowed exclusion of it', he could not but fear 'that even the safeguards of a Catholic college will hardly avail, against the power of this habitual temptation, to impress them with the great truth, that religion is not a mere professional matter, but the informing principle of all conduct, and the ultimate test of all true knowledge'.

The *Dublin's* support was given to Gillow's views, and although

[26] *The Dublin Review* (July/Oct. 1869), p. 248.

the review was prepared to admit with *The Month* that idleness, frivolity, gambling, and sensuality were not defects exclusive to any one class in society, it claimed that a boy educated in a Catholic college would not be tempted, except in the rarest cases, 'to that which (in the Catholic view) is an immeasurably greater calamity than any of these or all put together, viz. deliberate doubt on the truth of his religion'.[27] The indisputable truth remained also, that 'a youth stamped with the credit of London honours would enter life with much greater prestige than could be obtained from any merely Catholic distinction'. By 1874 Stonyhurst's rivalry with Ushaw was at its most intense, and was marked by an acrimonious correspondence, dealing with Stonyhurst's contribution to higher studies, which broke out in *The Weekly Register and Catholic Standard* during July and August of that year. League tables of the University stakes were drawn up and disedifying comparisons made.

In 1884 the demand for the establishment of a teaching university in London achieved formal expression, an Association being set up to promote that object. It was desired 'that the Colleges (King's and University) should once more become, but in a truer sense than at first, constituent parts of the academic body, and that London should possess a teaching University with power to regulate higher education'.[28] There were three major points of view as to the form this reorganization ought to assume. All of them were aired in Convocation in 1885. There were those who desired a second university for the City, made up of colleges only and residential. Only resident students would be eligible for its degrees. There were the supporters of University College and King's College who felt that these two institutions contained in themselves all that was necessary for a residential university. Finally, there were advocates of such establishments as the Roman Catholic colleges, anxious to preserve existing opportunities for their students.

Convocation submitted a draft scheme to the Senate of the University, attempting to reconcile the conflicting interests. King's College and University College refused to compromise

---

[27] Ibid. (Jan. 1874), p. 192.
[28] *University of London: Historical Record (1836–1912)*, p. 18.

and applied to the Privy Council for a charter to establish them as an independent university. The College of Physicians and the College of Surgeons followed their example as far as medical qualifications were in question. The outcome was the setting up of two Royal Commissions; the first, under Lord Selborne, reported in 1888, and the second, under Earl Cowper, in 1894. The latter disapproved of two universities for the City and recommended the reorganization of the existing University to cater for all needs. The University of London Act of 1898, 'while preserving the corporate continuity of the University, provided for its complete re-constitution in general harmony with the recommendations of the Commission of 1892'.[29] In 1905 University College, London, and in 1908 King's College, London, were transferred to the University, and the system of internal and external students which we know today emerged.

The Catholic colleges had led considerable opposition at the time of Selborne's Commission, for they feared their students would be placed on an unequal footing with those of the London colleges. Once the immediate danger passed they decided to concentrate, while reform was in the air, on securing radical changes in the nature of the Matriculation examination. It would be apparent what a boon such changes would constitute, the *Downside Review* urged, because 'complaints about the London Matriculation syllabus have been long-standing and widespread'.[30] It maintained that 'conservative educationalists have all along deplored the manner in which traditional literary and mathematical education is sacrificed at the London Matriculation to the modern rage for smatterings of many things'. Strong Catholic pressure upon Convocation was urged, but for this to be effective it was necessary that the Catholic colleges should speak with one voice. An impetus to this end was given in 1886 by Louis Charles Casartelli, headmaster of St. Bede's College in Manchester, who seventeen years later was to become fourth Bishop of Salford. Casartelli had taken his B.A. degree in 1872 while a student at Ushaw, and in 1837 had been one of the few Catholic students

[29] *University of London: Historical Record* (1836–1912), p. 19.
[30] *Downside Review*, 9 (1890), pp. 213–16.

to obtain the London M.A. He was to follow up his academic distinction by obtaining a doctorate in Oriental Languages at Louvain, a qualification which led to his appointment in 1903 as lecturer in Iranian Languages at Owen's College, Manchester. Casartelli, who after the introduction of the London external-degree system was to describe it as a 'tyrannous fetish',[31] was in 1886 instrumental in suggesting the calling together of a Catholic headmasters' meeting. It was time for Catholics to speak out 'with no uncertain note, and to urge . . . the adoption of such changes as would put the Matriculation in full harmony with that old-fashioned literary education, which seems to enjoy the confidence of the majority of sound educators'.[32] He named three chief areas in which, it was maintained, intercollegiate action was imperative. One of these involved 'the question of *more uniformity in the syllabus* of instruction given in the different classes, forms or schools of our numerous colleges'. The second concerned the force of events which 'must make us recognise, whether we like it or not, that it is necessary to provide for a *modern side* of education, as well as for the "humanitarian" or "classical" side, to which we have so long been accustomed. The great public schools have had to do it; and our colleges must follow suit.' The third area calling for intercollegiate study was that involved in the need for the greater uniformity of textbooks for use in Catholic schools. Although Casartelli declared he was not a worshipper of London University, the latter was the sole resource for academic distinction as far as Catholics were concerned. This being so, he felt it to be 'of some considerable importance that Catholic colleges should have some chance of exercising a legitimate influence on the system of examinations, such as the authorities of the University are always ready enough to admit'. In order to exercise the desiderated influence it was necessary to provide for 'some kind of a Union, representative of our secondary and higher educational establishments', for *l'union fait la force*. Perhaps it would be possible to commence an intercollegiate journal, nor was it inconceivable that intercollegiate pedagogic debates could be

---

[31] Evennett, H. O., in *The English Catholics, 1850–1950*, p. 308 n.
[32] *The Downside Review*, 5 (1886), pp. 9 seq.

held. Casartelli was eagerly supported by the Prior of Downside, Hugh Edmund Ford.

In 1886 the Jesuits were advocating that Catholics should go to Oxford for examination, 'seeing that residence is not necessary for passing, but only for the ceremony of taking the degree'.[33] They suggested that 'for the London Matriculation [Catholics] should substitute the Certificate Examination, familiarly called ... the leaving examination; and as this examination is generally accepted at Oxford in lieu of Matriculation that all desiring to continue their higher studies should enter, but without residence, for the various degree-examinations at Oxford'. This latter course would bring Catholic youths 'into comparison with the public school boys', although they would not possess the necessary qualification for graduation—residence.

Casartelli's suggestion for an Association of Catholic head teachers did not eventualize for ten years, chiefly because the Jesuits were unwilling to participate in an organization which might develop in such a way that their freedom of unilateral action would be curtailed. There was, also, considerable jealousy of Ushaw's success in the London examinations. If Ushaw, along with the other seminary colleges, could be excluded from such an Association there would be little difficulty in convincing the other colleges of the unsuitability of London examinations. Downside, in particular, prided itself upon the quality of its teaching of the Classics, and sensed that its success in this field was receiving inadequate recognition from the London examiners. In the event, Jesuit schools were the first to abandon London examinations, and with their desertion 'the fictitious importance for Catholics of the London degrees' was lost. The year 1896 proved to be the last one in which Stonyhurst and Beaumont entered candidates. Downside ceased after 1897 to send sixth-form boys up for Matriculation. The reason for this action was stated to lie in the fact that at London 'the literary aspect is entirely neglected'. It would 'scarcely be credited by Public School men that no Latin or Greek Prose is required, no French or German writing or dictation, and but little stress is laid on ability to translate

<hr>

[33] *The Downside Review*, 5 (1886), pp. 9 seq.

unprepared passages from Latin and Greek'. For Matriculation 'no English author is set, nor is an English essay asked for', and the standard of the marking was too high, because 'those who fail to pass averages fifty per cent'. In the judgement of Downside 'the Matriculation Examination, and also the Intermediate Examination in Arts, fail to give many Catholic schools satisfaction, as they do not seem to recognise that all-important aspect of the study of the classics and of the modern languages from which their chief educative power and influence are drawn'. The Higher School Certificate examination of the Oxford and Cambridge Schools Examination Board made it possible for candidates to be successful who had little or no aptitude for Science. Subjects were divided for the purpose of this examination into four groups. In the first of these were placed Latin, Greek, French, and Spanish, and in the second Mathematics. The third group provided for Scripture Knowledge, English, and History, and the fourth for Natural Philosophy, Physical Geography, and Biology. Candidates had to offer a minimum of four subjects selected from at least three groups. But those who offered a subject from the second group or the last were permitted to choose all their remaining subjects, if they so desired, from the first group. The Downside boys, like those of Stonyhurst, were to offer Latin, Greek, French, Mathematics, and either History or Geography. For Downside the principal change involved in abandoning London was that 'more time and attention [would] be devoted to Latin writing, and the "continuous prose" [would] be commenced in the Fourth Form'. Science teaching was to suffer an immediate decline in the Catholic colleges as a consequence of the change.

Dr. Casartelli resurrected the idea of a permanent Association of Catholic headmasters in 1896, and he had more success than in the attempt of a decade earlier. There were a number of reasons for this. The Universities of Oxford and Cambridge were no longer under papal prohibition for Catholic students and the London Matriculation examinations had been rejected by the colleges. Hence, two possible sources of friction were obviated. Furthermore, Casartelli now had the backing of Cardinal Herbert Vaughan, who was persuaded to assume the initiative and use his prestige to bring about the preliminary meeting. The gathering, held under Vaughan's presidency on 3 January 1896, was to develop into the Standing Committee of Catholic Colleges. The initial meeting, however, was not without incident. Vaughan seized the occasion to lecture the headmasters on 'the importance of giving systematic training to the teachers of our secondary schools' and on his desire that the colleges 'should offer Scholarships, burses, or by whatever name they are called, to children from elementary schools who are endowed with special abilities'.[34] He bemoaned the fact that in the colleges 'there was no opening for the clever children of the poor, unless they were prepared to embrace the clerical state'. Mr. Scott Coward, Senior Inspector of Training Colleges, addressed the meeting on the importance of teacher-training for secondary schoolmasters. But the lecture was coolly received, the assembled clerics merely expressing a generally unanimous opinion 'that a University training would make up to our teachers for much of that in which they are at present most deficient'.[35]

A Standing Committee was formed, and care was taken to prevent the appointment of priests who had been strong suppor-ters of the London examinations. Fr. E. J. Purbrick, S.J., and Fr. C. Galton, S.J., joined the head of the Oratory School (Fr. John Norris) and two Benedictines on this Committee. Other members included Dr. Casartelli and Mgr. Bernard Ward of St. Edmund's (who at this time was busily contemplating the possibility of sending Old Hall students to Cambridge). Care was taken to exclude Ushaw's membership. By May, Ushaw had left the organization, in disgust at the chicanery which had been employed in the attempt to muzzle her views, and the College continued, as we have seen, in virtual isolation to enter her students (albeit somewhat fitfully) for London examinations until 1939. Ushaw's withdrawal from the Conference was accompanied by an attack on London University which emanated from Fr. John Norris. Prior Burge, in his account of the meeting, relates that Norris's

[34] See Prior T. A. Burge's eyewitness account of the meeting in *The Ampleforth Journal* 2, Part 1 (July 1896), pp. 39 seq.
[35] Ibid.

denunciations of London examinations 'were very severe, but apparently none too severe for the taste of his audience'. Father John Gerard, S.J., seeing the way events were moving, pursued a similar theme, and defended Norris after Canon Banks had taken exception to his remarks. The Jesuit criticized meetings of Convocation 'which consisted mostly of a number of business men, whose whole idea seemed to be to keep up the prestige of their examinations for difficulty'. The struggle was over; London University stood condemned.

Part Two

NEWMAN'S
IMPERIAL UNIVERSITY
IN IRELAND

I

A CATHOLIC UNIVERSITY
FOR IRELAND

WHEN, on 9 October 1847, a rescript from Rome arrived in
Ireland condemning the establishment of the Queen's Colleges in
Belfast, Cork, and Galway, it seemed evident that *Propaganda*
had acted from specifically religious motives. The rescript,
issued in response to a request for a definitive decision on the
Colleges sent to Rome by the Irish bishops in November 1845,
was in keeping with similar decisions of *Propaganda* in regard to
Russia (1747) and Egypt (1791). The Queen's Colleges were
condemned because they were 'godless', and because they were
bastions of 'mixed' education. The document admonished the
archbishops and bishops of Ireland to take no part in the Colleges,
and it declared that, 'having considered maturely this issue from
every point of view, the Sacred Congregation does not venture
to promise itself any well-being for Religion in Ireland from this
establishment of Queen's Colleges. Rather does it fear that grave
peril for the Catholic Faith will come from that source. In one
word it holds this form of education an injury to Religion.'[1]
Furthermore, the Rescript added, 'The Sacred Congregation
would consider it in the highest degree opportune, if by united
efforts the Bishops of Ireland would take steps to have erected in
Ireland a Catholic University on the model of that established
by the Bishops of Belgium in the city of Louvain.' The proposal
to establish a Catholic University in Ireland, then, emanated
from Rome as a specific measure to counteract the influence of
the Queen's Colleges. There is no suggestion in the Rescript or,
indeed, in any of the later documents from Rome on the subject

[1] Rescript of 1847, given in Corcoran, T., *Newman: Selected Discourses on
Liberal Knowledge*, with an Introduction, pp. 127 seq. Also *The Rambler* (Dec.
1849), pp. 460 seq.

(contrary to what Dwight Culler has recently alleged), that such a university was to be 'a place of resort for all Catholics who spoke the English tongue'.[2] On 11 October 1848 a second rescript from *Propaganda* reinforced the earlier decision, referring to 'the grave intrinsic dangers'[3] of the Queen's Colleges. The foundation of a Catholic University was yet again urged upon the bishops.

The Rambler, in January 1849, directed the attention of English Catholics to the affair, and its comments are of some importance in view of Newman's claim that the establishment of a Catholic University in Ireland was meant for English as well as Irish Catholics. After commenting on the fact that the Queen's Colleges, recently condemned by the Pope, were about to commence operations 'and to be furnished with a large staff of well-paid professors', it went on:

> There is no doubt that many Catholics, both in England and Ireland. intend to uphold them, notwithstanding the condemnation of the Holy See, and notwithstanding the frightful perils, both to faith and morals which will inevitably environ the young men who will there be thrown together—their own master at a time of life when all the passions of youth boil up with most vehement fierceness. . . . What was the advice which came from Rome to the Irish prelates, as to the best mode of counteracting the pernicious influence of these Government seminaries? *It was the very same as that which we have ourselves ventured to commend as suitable to English wants,*—the establishment of a system which should combine the peculiar advantages of these Irish establishments with the doctrine and discipline of the Catholic Church.[4]

It is clear that *The Rambler* approved the idea of a Catholic University for Ireland because it was a similar solution to that which the journal had been propounding for England. But it is also evident that it did not suggest that the papacy had in mind an Imperial University, located in Ireland. In the same month as the above passage appeared in print, a Provincial Synod of Tuam,

---

[2] Culler, A. Dwight, *The Imperial Intellect: A Study of Newman's Educational Ideal*, p. 168.

[3] Corcoran, *Newman: Selected Discourses, etc.*, pp. 127 seq.

[4] *The Rambler* (Jan. 1849), p. 326.

presided over by Archbishop John MacHale, issued the following statement: 'We the undersigned Prelates of the Province of Tuam, after having concluded our synodical meeting, of which the decrees are reserved for their proper time, feel that nothing can be more desirable than to express our full concurrence in the recommendation of his Holiness to found a Catholic University, and to proffer our cheerful co-operation towards its establishment.'[5] The document was signed by the Archbishop of Tuam, and by Bishops French of Kilmacduagh and Kilfenora, Browne of Elphin, Feeny of Killala, O'Donnell of Galway, and Derry of Clonfert.

Before 1849 was out Paul Cullen had been nominated Archbishop of Armagh and Primate of All Ireland, and in February 1850 he issued his first pastoral charge 'from without the Salarian Gate'. Before his arrival in Ireland in May 1850 he had also received the appointment of Apostolic Delegate, giving him complete authority over the Irish episcopacy as the Pope's personal representative. Rome had long been worried at the divisions which existed among the bishops, especially on the Queen's Colleges issue. Cullen's special brief was to restore unity and harmony among them. As the Roman agent of the hierarchy for sixteen crucial years, he had enjoyed unrivalled opportunities for getting to know the prelates and their peculiar problems, and yet, residing in Rome, he had been sufficiently removed from the immediate scene of those problems to avoid the accusations of party spirit. In charging Cullen, too, with the task of organizing and establishing a Catholic University for Ireland the papacy hoped to provide a field of work in which all the bishops could co-operate with one accord. They would have a constructive task facing them of considerable magnitude, and if they applied themselves to it with vigour they might forget the party differences of recent years. The state of the Irish episcopacy, however, was a parlous one. In 1851 Cullen wrote to *Propaganda* to report on what he had found. He complained of 'the old Bishop of Raphoe' who 'speaks without much judgement in many cases'. He reported

[5] Statement printed in full in *The Rambler* (Mar. 1849), p. 545.

that 'the Bishop of Ardagh, Monsignor Higgins, shuts himself up in his house for months on end and receives nobody, neither priests nor laymen. I believe that he is letting himself be conquered by wine and his diocese is much neglected. He would need a good coadjutor.' He pointed out that 'the Bishop of Down and Connor has not visited his parishes for seven years and has only four priests in the city of Belfast, where there are at least fifty thousand Catholics who complain to me repeatedly of their state of abandonment. This bishop has need of a coadjutor.' The Bishop of Achonry 'for three or four years has been quite ill and I believe also a little mentally affected at intervals. He is about eighty years of age.' The Bishop of Kilmacduagh is 'also very old and infirm. He has scruples about his baptism. He comes of a Protestant family and after his conversion was ordained priest and then consecrated bishop without receiving conditional baptism in the Catholic Church. I have been assured that he has not visited his diocese for fifteen years. During this summer, however, he asked the Bishop of Clonfert to make the visit for him and that worthy prelate did so with immense effort and confirmed almost half the entire population of the diocese.' The Bishop of Galway was old and inactive. 'In that diocese there have been many apostates. In the parish of Oughterard alone there has been at least 400. That parish is vacant for more than two years.'[6] During the years from 1850 to 1878 forty-four new Irish bishops were appointed. All but three of these indicate Cullen's direct influence. J. H. Whyte has recently shown that the quality of men nominated was considerably enhanced.[7] They were better educated, less insular, younger, and more vigorous than those selected in the years before 1850. 'The presence in Ireland', Whyte writes, 'of a prelate whose judgment inspired complete trust at Rome enabled the Holy See to take a much more active part in the process of selection than it had done before.'

[6] A copy of this letter to *Propaganda*, along with a number of other Cullen letters, is in the possession of the parish priest of Kildare and was shown to me there. The letter is dated 28 Sept. 1851, and headed 'Drogheda'. The *Propaganda* reference is SCR. Irlanda, vol. 30-712-13-14.

[7] Whyte, J. H., 'The Appointment of Catholic Bishops in Nineteenth-century Ireland', *The Catholic Historical Review* (1962), *passim*.

On 6 November 1849, before Cullen had received his own episcopal appointment, the Irish bishops met to decide what they should do when the Queen's Colleges were formally opened, and what action they should take concerning the two recent rescripts from Rome. They elected to place the question before a Plenary Synod of all Ireland to be held in June 1850. Because of the ill health of the Archbishop of Cashel it was agreed to hold the Synod in his cathedral town of Thurles. If such a synod was to be canonical it was necessary for a delegate, named by the Pope, to preside over it; the honour fell to Paul Cullen. The Synod was solemnly opened on 22 August 1850, and the four archbishops were present, twenty bishops, three delegates of sick bishops, and the mitred Abbot of Mount Melleray. All these, a total of twenty-eight, were allowed a vote. On most general issues there was no disagreement, but on those connected with the Queen's Colleges there was dispute. Nine decrees concerning the Colleges were put to the vote; six passed unanimously. All the prelates admitted the dangers of the Colleges; all accepted the decrees of Rome; all agreed that no bishop should take part in running the Colleges. The remaining three decrees, however, were contested. They were chiefly concerned with the prohibition of priests from administering the Colleges *sub poena suspensionis ipso facto incurrendae*. Archbishop Murray and eleven members of the Synod did not wish the threat of 'immediate suspension' to be imposed and they were against strong-arm tactics. The other three archbishops and thirteen members of the Synod voted for strict prohibitions. On each of these decrees the voting was sixteen in favour and twelve against.[8] At the end of the Synod all the members signed the pastoral letter declaring the Colleges dangerous to the Catholic faith, and all the bishops eventually promulgated the decrees after the Pope had confirmed them. The settlement was definitive. The resolutions of the Synod were a serious setback for Lords John Russell and Clarendon. It was this condemnation of the Queen's Colleges rather than Wiseman's pretentious pastoral which was the real inspiration of Russell's Ecclesiastical Titles

[8] Details taken from Cullen's account, copy seen in possession of parish priest, Kildare, dated 15 Mar. 1868.

Bill, 1851. Disraeli saw through the pretext, declaring: 'I find the noble Lord seeking as the basis of his Bill, not the visit of Dr. Wiseman to England, but the Synod of Thurles.'

The Synodical Address declared that it was 'by the sternest sense of duty—by a painful but irresistible feeling of necessity—that we are compelled, dearly beloved, to announce to you, that a system of education fraught with grievous and intrinsic dangers has, within the last twelve months, been brought to your own doors. It is presented to you, we deplore to say, in those collegiate institutions which have been established in this country, and associated with the name of our august, most gracious, and beloved Sovereign.' It went on:

> Those institutions, which would have called for our profound and lasting gratitude, had they been framed in accordance with our religious tenets and principles, must now be considered as an evil of a formidable kind, against which it is our imperative duty to warn you with all the energy of our zeal and all the weight of our authority. That a system of Education, the dangers of which have been publicly and solemnly pointed out by the Church which is the Pillar and the Ground of Truth—a system against the dangers of which the history of modern Europe bears witness—will meet with your marked reprobation; that you will not yield it encouragement or patronage of any kind, but that you will save your children from its influence—is an assurance supplied to us by your uniform and devoted obedience to the voice of that Church, and attested by every page of your history, and by every act of your lives.[9]

The 'undenominational' Queen's Colleges opened in December 1849, and in 1850 the Queen's University was incorporated to grant degrees in Arts, Law, and Medicine to the students of the three constituent Colleges. The experiment was costly. The initial outlay on buildings and equipment was in the nature of £100,000, and a further £25,257 were spent in the first decade. Originally the endowment was £18,000 per annum, but in 1849 a further grant of £12,000 was made, and after 1854 an annual

---

[9] Synodical Address of the Archbishops and Bishops of Ireland, assembled in National Synod at Thurles, 9 Sept. 1850, printed *in extenso* in Moran, P. F. (ed.), *The Pastoral Letters and other Writings of Cardinal Cullen*, vol. 1, pp. 26–50.

additional grant of £4,800. More than £375,000 were spent on these Colleges in the first ten years. In 1859 the staff numbered 260 and the total number of students was in the region of 1,209.[10] There were, about 134 students per annum in each of the three Colleges. The Synod of Thurles performed its work thoroughly. In 1859 *The Rambler*[11] recorded that the Dean of Law at Cork was advocating the abolition of his Faculty because 'he had found no students', and the Professor of Metaphysics at the same college, who had seven students in 1851, had been reduced to four by 1859. Other statistics are equally revealing. In 1859 the Professor of English Literature in Cork had five students, the Professor of Jurisprudence at Galway, two. The Professor of Medicine at Galway had five students, the Professor of Law, three. *The Rambler* added that 'the total number of graduates in Law in ten years does not equal the number of professors and examiners in that Faculty in one year'. In the year the Colleges opened forty-five students at Belfast competed for the award of forty-three scholarships. To the government the Colleges must have appeared a colossal and expensive failure.

The Synod of Thurles had taken up the recommendations of the two papal rescripts; it would not do, after all, to prohibit and provide nothing. The Synodical Address declared: 'We have determined to make every effort in our power to establish a sound and comprehensive system of University Education, that will combine all that is practically useful in the present system with all that is pure and edifying in religious doctrine. A Committee has been appointed by this Synod to examine into the details of this most important project, and to carry it into execution.'[12] The Irish scattered abroad were called upon to assist with their learning, talent, and money.

A Committee of eight prelates, eight priests, and eight laymen had been set up by the Synod to examine ways of establishing a Catholic University for Ireland. On the same day as the Synodical

[10] Pope Hennessy, John, *The Failure of the Queen's Colleges and Mixed Education in Ireland* (London, 1859), *passim*.

[11] *The Rambler* (May 1859), pp. 114–15.

[12] Synodical Address of the Archbishops and Bishops of Ireland, assembled in National Synod at Thurles, 9 Sept. 1850.

Address was issued this Committee published a letter declaring that the intention behind the scheme was 'to provide a superior university education for the youth of Ireland'.[13] The faithful were bidden to remember 'that in Ireland secular learning and religion were always linked together'. The Committee wished to provide 'for the Catholic youth of Ireland education of a high order, every way commensurate with the intellectual wants of the time', and 'a system of Academical education as extensive and diversified as any to be found in the most distinguished Universities of Europe'. It declared that 'one of the greatest calamities of modern times is the separation of religion from science, whereas the perfection of knowledge is the union of both, which produces the most perfect form of civilized society by making men not only learned but also good Christians'. 'We are a Catholic people', the document went on, and 'as such, ought we not to have a great Catholic institution, in which the aspiring youth of the country may enjoy all the advantages of a superior University education, and at the same time be imbued with a thoroughly Catholic spirit? Many of them being destined to be our future magistrates, lawyers, statesmen, it is of great importance in an age distinguished for judicial, forensic, and senatorial talent, to provide every facility for the development of Catholic genius; but it is of immeasurably greater importance that our rising youth, the hope of the country, shall be, not bigots, but enlightened Catholics. . . .' An annual collection was prescribed, and the Committee expressed the hope that Catholics in England, Scotland, the Continent of Europe, America, India, and Australia would be generous with money in aiding the new venture.

A number of things become clear from a careful study of this document. The Catholic University was to cater for *the youth of Ireland*. It was to provide for the daily professional needs of Irish society. Although financial help was to be solicited from abroad to inaugurate the venture, the greater bulk of the funds would of necessity be gathered in Ireland. The grand aim of the University

---

[13] The letter is printed *in extenso* in Moran (ed.), *The Pastoral Letters, etc.*, vol. 1, pp. 51–67, and all quotations are taken from this source.

would be to exemplify the union of science—in its broadest meaning—and theology, a theme followed by Newman in the *University Discourses*. As specified in the Rescript of 1847, the University was to be modelled on that of Louvain.

In November 1850 Cullen issued a pastoral letter to the Archdiocese of Armagh dealing at some length with the necessity for a Catholic University. He maintained that unsectarian education was repugnant to sincere Protestants as well as to Catholics, and he pointed out that already in the Queen's College at Cork the Professor of French Literature (Vericour) had been reprimanded for publishing an anti-Catholic book (*Historical Analysis of Christian Civilisation*), and that lectures had been given by another professor attacking Catholic beliefs. The Dean of the Belfast College had given a long lecture on the aggressions of popery, and nineteen out of twenty professors at the Belfast College were Protestant. And what of the Prime Minister in whose hands academic appointments remained? He had recently informed the world (Russell's 'Durham Letter') that Catholic practices were 'nothing but the "mummeries of superstition" and that the teaching of the Catholic Church tends "to confine the intellect and to enslave the mind" '. Cullen argued 'that whilst they are so decidedly and sincerely opposed to our doctrines, they cannot expect us to commit to them the guardianship of our faith'. His argument seemed irresistible, and he claimed that in the facts he had quoted there were tangible proofs of the need for a Catholic University.

In 1851 the Catholic University Committee issued appeals to the United States and to England as well as to Ireland for financial assistance in establishing the University. In the address 'To Their Brethren in America' the members of the Committee asserted that 'Ireland is not without some claim on the sympathy of nations', and they declared that the work could not be successful 'unless other countries come to the aid of poor, afflicted, and persecuted Ireland'.[14] Throughout the letter it is stressed that

[14] Address of the Committee of the Catholic University of Ireland to their Brethren in America, 8th July 1851, in Moran (ed.), *The Pastoral Letters, etc.*, pp. 138–44.

the appeal is being made to provide for the higher education of the people of Ireland. The Address to the Catholic clergy and laity of England pointed out that the new University 'will seek to diffuse its blessings as extensively as possible'.[15] The benefits emanating from its tone and spirit would be widespread. To the clergy of Ireland it was declared that 'the founding of the University is, above all things, the great duty of Catholic Ireland at the present day'.

The years 1852 and 1854 saw the arrival of further letters from Rome urging action on the University project, in which *Propaganda* declared its intention was 'to ask of you again and again to put aside all delay whatever, and hasten to set up this Catholic University'.[16] In 1854 Cullen was able to report that the Synod of Oscott had praised the Irish prelates for 'aiming higher than we can dare, at the providing of an unmixed education of the very highest order'.[17] Cardinal Wiseman preached for the University in St. George's Cathedral, Southwark, in 1852, although his sermon made it clear that the University could be of little *direct* concern to England. 'It is but just', he declared, 'that we should all concur in giving a helping hand to that which may be useful to our neighbours, to whom the Catholics of England owe such a debt of gratitude, not only for so many past benefits, but still more especially for the warm and kind-hearted sympathy with which they have bound themselves to us in our trials.'[18] The financial contributions from England were extremely poor. By 1851 the funds from Ireland alone had amounted to a total of £22,840—all of which had been gathered in a single collection in one year.[19] By 1854 the *total* contributions from England had

---

[15] Address of The Catholic University Committee to the Catholic Clergy and Laity of England, Feast of St. James the Apostle, 1851, in Moran (ed.), *The Pastoral Letters, etc.*, pp. 144–7.

[16] Full details of this letter of 20 Mar. 1854, and of earlier ones, are to be found in Corcoran, *Newman: Selected Discourses, etc.*, pp. 127 seq.

[17] See *Report of the Committee of the Catholic University of Ireland to the Archbishops and Bishops of Ireland Assembled in Council, on the 18th of May, 1854*, in Moran (ed.), *The Pastoral Letters, etc.*, pp. 302–11, and esp. p. 307.

[18] *Sermon* preached at St. George's Cathedral, Southwark, Sunday, 27 June 1852, on behalf of the Catholic University of Ireland (16 pp., London, 1852).

[19] Culler, p. 130.

not reached £4,000.[20] The disparity in the effort expended is not difficult to explain. English Catholics were little concerned to contribute to a fund to secure for the Irish the benefits of a university education which they did not possess themselves, and English Catholics of wealth and substance at no time viewed the Irish venture seriously as one from which their own children could even remotely benefit. As late as 1859 the Irish bishops were still speaking of 'the desire of Irish Catholics to have a Catholic University';[21] English Catholics regarded the experiment as laudable, but in no way a venture in which they could have direct interest. No convincing documentary evidence has ever been produced to support the oft-repeated statement that Cullen led Newman to believe in the possibility of an Imperial university. To Dwight Culler, Cullen appears 'sometimes devious in his ways and conspiratorial in his mentality', but even this unsympathetic scholar has to admit that 'he was never ungenerous or selfish, and he really believed in the project of a Catholic university'.[22] This is a view recently endorsed by E. R. Norman[23] who quotes with approval Archbishop Walsh's testimonial of 1902 that to Cullen 'the credit is due that there is a university question, alive and clamouring for settlement on the line of absolute equality for Catholics'.[24] Norman adds: 'so importantly did Cullen and the bishops regard educational matters that from the very beginning of the National Association they were prepared to sap much of its authority by dealing directly with the Government and without reference to it whenever the opportunity was presented.'[25]

[20] See Cullen's complaint in *Report of the Committee of the Catholic University of Ireland* of 18 May 1854, p. 308.

[21] Pastoral Address of the Roman Catholic Archbishops and Bishops to the Clergy and People of Ireland on the Catholic University, 1859, in Moran (ed.), *The Pastoral Letters, etc.*, pp. 701–9, and esp. p. 706.   [22] Culler, p. 129.

[23] Norman, E. R., *The Catholic Church and Ireland in the Age of Rebellion, 1859–1873*, p. 192.

[24] Walsh, W. J., *Trinity College and the University of Dublin*, p. 2.

[25] Norman, p. 193. The National Association of Ireland (founded 1864–5) was one of the happier results of Fenian organization, for it was established to provide an alternative, safe, and constitutional means of securing the redress of Irish grievances (Norman, p. 135).

II

NEWMAN'S IDEA

LOOKING back in 1925 on the selection of the first Rector for the Catholic University, Bertram Newman found it difficult to believe that the Irish bishops were in earnest. If it had been intended by the promoters to be much more than a demonstration, he wrote, 'it is difficult to believe that they would have chosen Newman to preside over it'. 'They must have known', he declared, 'that admirable as would have been the services which Newman could have rendered to an established university he had not the driving force necessary to make a success of a struggling institution.'[1] Archbishop Cullen thought differently. In his Report on the Catholic University in 1854 he gave reasons for the choice. Newman was not only eminent as a scholar, with experience of academic work, and able to attract talent, but 'his zeal and sacrifices for the Church of God left no doubt on the minds of the committee that he was admirably fitted, indeed that he was fitted beyond all others of whom they had knowledge, to mould into shape, to govern, and give character to the future University'.[2] The Committee had resolved 'to imitate the Bishops of Belgium in seeking out one man eminent for talents, piety, and learning to whom they would depute the vitally important duty of organising and governing the future University'.

Cullen had visited the Birmingham Oratory on 8 July 1851, and after a discussion with Monsell, Manning, and Hope, an invitation was conveyed to Newman asking him to accept the Rectorship. By 12 November the Irish bishops had confirmed the nomination. The episcopacy was to possess the fullness of power

---

[1] Newman, B., *Cardinal Newman: a Biographical and Literary Study*, p. 128.

[2] *Report of the Committee of the Catholic University of Ireland to the Archbishops and Bishops of Ireland assembled in Council on the 18th of May, 1854*, published in full in Moran (ed.), *The Pastoral Letters, etc.*, vol. I, pp. 302–11, and esp. p. 309.

in regard to the nascent institution, but Newman, as their delegate, was to have acting discretion. Cullen wrote, 'no other
appointment was made as the selection of other persons is to be
made with the concurrence, or on the recommendation of the
[Rector]'.[3] Newman accepted the post on the terms laid down,
although he was later to be resentful when the bishops exercised
their rights in the matter of appointments. The Vice-Rector,
Leahy, and the Secretary, Taylor, in whose appointments Newman concurred but did not take the initiative, were both regarded
by the Rector in more hypersensitive moments as merely the
watchdogs of the hierarchy.[4]

On 3 May 1852 Dr. Cullen was translated to the Metropolitan
see of Dublin, following the death of Archbishop Murray. By
virtue of his lifelong appointment as Apostolic Delegate he
remained effective head of the Irish hierarchy. Seven days later
Newman began his Dublin lectures on university education.
Two years were to elapse before he was formally installed as
Rector of the University. The delay is easy to explain. Sufficient
financial provision had to be ensured before an irrevocable step
was taken. Prudence above all was needed. It would not do to
start in a blaze of glory and end soon afterwards with a damp
squib. Furthermore, the years from 1851 to 1853 were given over
in great part to the Achilli trial, and Newman was in a constant fit
of agitation, dreading the thought of imprisonment. Reminiscing
in bitter mood many years later, Newman claimed that he regarded
himself as being in the position of one conferring a favour on
others by going to Dublin.[5] Psychologically, however, he needed
the distinction which the University would provide. In one
effort he hoped to regain the public position he had occupied
before 1845, and the infinite care which he lavished on the
University Discourses is sufficient evidence of his eagerness.
When he heard a report that he might be allocated to a diocesan
bishopric in the unfashionable areas of Liverpool or Nottingham
it was like the threat of a life-sentence to obscurity. 'If I am taken
from the University', he wrote, 'I am taken from a position

---

[3] Ward, W., *The Life of John Henry, Cardinal Newman*, vol. 1, pp. 311–12.
[4] Ibid., p. 323.   [5] Ibid., p. 327.

where I can do something to an office where I can do little or nothing. . . . I trust it will not please them at Rome to throw me away when they might turn me to account.'[6] There was little attraction in spending the remainder of his days confirming the ignorant Irish poor in such a city as Liverpool, when he might spend some years at the head of a Catholic University, especially if the latter could be transformed into an Imperial University, and be adapted to attract the sons of the Catholic aristocracy of England. He did not object to receiving the trappings of episcopal rank *per se*, for he was almost embarrassingly eager to be made a bishop *in partibus* when Wiseman suggested it later. Such rank would considerably enhance the personal importance of the head of a Catholic University. And so the glittering dream began to take shape. Perhaps he could take up again in Dublin work of the very nature of that which he had perforce abandoned in Oxford? Perhaps he could turn back the clock and reach again the happiness he had formerly experienced? 'Curious it will be,' he mused in October 1851, 'if Oxford is imported into Ireland, not in its members only, but in its principles, methods, ways, and arguments.'[7] The Irish bishops did not, however, give Oxford a thought; they set their sights, as they had been bidden to do in the papal rescripts, upon the recently revived University of Louvain. But Newman had a model before his eyes very different from that of Louvain, and he had conceived of a univeristy for Ireland bearing little resemblance to that for which the Irish bishops had solicited his aid.

Professor Owen Chadwick has recently referred to Newman's days at Oxford as 'the happiest of his life from the human point of view',[8] and in support of this contention he has quoted Newman himself from the *Apologia*: 'I was truly at home. . . . It was the time of plenty.'[9] In the novel, *Loss and Gain*, written in 1847, Newman provides an even more poignant picture of his own feelings on breaking with the university of his youth. Seeing

[6] Ward, W., *Life of Newman*, vol. 1, p. 326.

[7] Corcoran, *Newman: Selected Discourses, etc.*, p. xv.

[8] Chadwick, Owen, *The Victorian Church: Part One* (O.U.P., New York, 1966), p. 169.

[9] Newman, J. H., *Apologia pro Vita Sua*, p. 88.

himself in the character of Charles Reding, he describes the final parting from Oxford: 'There was no one to see him: he threw his arms round the willows so dear to him and kissed them; he tore off their black leaves and put them in his bosom.'[10] As late as 1855 the sentimentality was still to the fore. John Hungerford Pollen was present at dinner in Newman's Dublin house. Renouf and Laprimaudaye were also in attendance. Newman, we are told, was 'so fond of his old Oxford recollections' as they 'cosed over some port wine and biscuits for an hour'.[11] Pollen told Wilfrid Ward later that while in Dublin Newman often returned to his Oxford memories, 'and the halo of Oxford came back to him very strongly at this time'.[12] It was never far away from his thoughts. After all, he would declare with a wistful look in his eyes, 'Catholics did not make us Catholics: Oxford made us Catholics.'[13]

In October 1851, before he was formally appointed as Rector of the Catholic University, Newman wrote to Mrs. William Froude in confidential mood:

The battle there (in Dublin) will be what it was in Oxford twenty years ago. Curious too that there I shall be opposed to the Whigs, having Lord Clarendon instead of Lord Melbourne,—that Whately will be there *in propria persona*, and that while I found my tools breaking under me in Oxford, for Protestantism is not susceptible of so high a temper, I am renewing the struggle in Dublin with the Catholic Church to support me. It is very wonderful—Keble, Pusey, Maurice, Sewell, etc., who have been able to do so little against Liberalism in Oxford will be renewing the fight, although not in their persons, in Ireland.[14]

[10] For a very interesting, although sketchy, account of the effect of the Oxford Movement in literature see Sir Shane Leslie's *The Oxford Movement, 1833–1933* (London, 1933), Appendix V, pp. 134–45.

[11] Pollen, Anne, *John Hungerford Pollen*, p. 253.

[12] Ward, W., *Life of Newman*, vol. I, pp. 354–5.

[13] See John Coulson's account of this in Coulson (ed.), *Theology and the University, an Ecumenical Investigation*, Ch. on 'Newman's Idea of an Educated Laity—The Two Versions', p. 61. Coulson differs from the interpretation given here. He has, it seems to me, misunderstood the aims of Cullen and the nature of the Irish University venture (pp. 47–8). On p. 54 he quotes a passage out of context on clerical–lay education, and places an interpretation upon it which the original document will not bear.

[14] Ward, W., *Life of Newman*, vol. I, p. 312.

Such views were hardly compatible with the task he had undertaken. The Irish hierarchy were not anxious about the niceties of academic theory; they were concerned with the severely practical task of equipping young Irishmen to be lawyers, doctors, and teachers. Coulson holds that Newman's aim was simple: 'in his own words, it was "to import Oxford into Ireland".'[15] But Oxford in Döllinger's more objective view was not 'adapted for the training of public servants', nor was it intended 'to produce lawyers, or physicians, or men of science'.[16] Some little time before Newman was busily engaged in preparing his University Discourses the *Dublin* had criticized the narrowness of the education provided at the Universities of Oxford and Cambridge. The 'higher faculties of Theology, Law, and Medicine' had become a mere name, and the real education given consisted of 'a limited course of the Faculty of Arts, comprising in Oxford the Greek and Latin languages, and the Aristotelian philosophy in some small degree: and in Cambridge the mathematical sciences'.[17] One of the criticisms to be heard most frequently in Ireland, after the Discourses had been delivered, was that Newman seemed to be offering the Irish little more than a truncated Faculty of Arts dignified by the name of a university, when they desperately needed professional schools.

On the 10th of May 1852 Newman began the Discourses in Dublin. He told his listeners at the outset: 'I have lived the greater part of my life in a place which has all that time been occupied in a series of controversies both domestic and with strangers, and of measures, experimental or definitive, bearing upon [the subject of liberal education].'[18] He added that 'while an argument originating in the controversies to which I have referred, may be serviceable at this season to that great cause in which we are here

[15] Coulson, p. 48.

[16] Comments on Döllinger's view of the English universities are to be found in *The Dublin Review* (Oct. 1867), pp. 381 seq., and esp. pp. 407 and 411.

[17] Ibid. (Mar. 1851), p. 225.

[18] Newman, J. H., *The Idea of a University: Defined and Illustrated, I, in Nine Discourses Delivered to the Catholics of Dublin; II, in Occasional Lectures and Essays Addressed to the Members of the Catholic University* (London, 1912 edn.), Discourse I, p. 1.

so especially interested, to me personally it will afford satisfaction of a peculiar kind'.[19]

It would concern me, Gentlemen, were I supposed to have got up my opinions for the occasion, [he declared,[20] for] the views to which I have referred have grown into my whole system of thought, and are, as it were, part of myself. Many changes has my mind gone through; here it has known no variation or vacillation of opinion, and though this by itself is no proof of the truth of my principles, it puts a seal upon conviction and is a justification of earnestness and zeal. Those principles, which I am now to set forth under the sanction of the Catholic Church, were my profession at that early period of my life, when religion was to me more a matter of feeling and experience than of faith.[21]

The debate was to be on the principles of the Oxford of 1816 to 1845, and it was a debate capable of only one outcome, because the only protagonist was 'the advocate and the minister of a certain great principle'.[22] Yet Newman declared he was

not merely advocate and minister, else had I not been here at all, [for] it has been my previous keen sense and hearty reception of that principle, that has been at once the reason, as I must suppose, of my being selected for this office, and is the cause of my accepting it.[23]

In his Preface to the printed Discourses, written on 21 November 1852, Newman disclaimed that it was his intention in the lectures to have devised a university capable of producing nothing better or higher than 'that antiquated variety of human nature and remnant of feudalism' called 'a gentleman'.[24] Nor would he have recognized *The Dublin Review*'s description of what 'gentlemanliness' meant for Oxford in 1851: 'The end of the *first class* is honour, distinction, and advantage: the end of the boat-race, the revel, and the chase, is pleasure: the end of the mass between, who neither gain classes nor commit dissipation, is gentlemanliness.'[25] And yet some of this quality of safe ineffectuality, resulting from the avoidance of extremes, seemed to be but a natural consequence of Newman's ideal. To traditional Catholic views it was

---

[19] Ibid., p. 3.   [20] Ibid.   [21] Ibid., p. 4.
[22] Ibid., p. 8.   [23] Ibid.   [24] Ibid., p. x.
[25] *The Dublin Review* (Mar. 1851), p. 230.

particularly obnoxious, for 'honour, pleasure, and gentlemanliness are equally secular'.[26] At Oxford the 'liberal' idea meant that 'youth is seduced and seducing: rank and fashion are attractive: study is engrossing, and honour absorbing'.[27] To Bishop Hedley, writing as late as 1880, the peculiar ends of liberal education pointed to an Oxford in which the young men are able to 'form friendships which endure for life', and where 'the whole genius of the place . . . unites to give to the English gentleman that tone or character which his class easily recognise'.[28] The primary end of Newman's concept was, indeed, the 'culture of the intellect',[29] necessary for 'the man of the world, the statesman, the land-holder, or the opulent gentleman'. The time for the moral disability to be removed, under which such men, who were also Catholics, had laboured, had now arrived. The education of such 'gentlemen' was concerned not simply with manners and habits but entailed the acquisition of deeper qualities—'the force, the steadiness, the comprehensiveness and the versatility of intellect, the command over our own powers, [and] the instinctive just estimate of things as they pass before us'.[30] But Newman significantly added: 'I do not deny that the characteristic excellences of a gentleman are included in it.'[31] A liberal education did concern itself with 'a courtesy, propriety, and polish of word and action, which is beautiful in itself, and acceptable to others'.[32] But it also 'brings the mind into form'.[33] Put simply, such an education formed both mind and character, and its outward manifestations were to be seen in part in the social attributes of 'the gentleman'. For the liberally educated man would also possess 'a faculty of entering with comparative ease into any subject of thought, and of taking up with aptitude any science or profession'.[34] Such a concept of education would, of course, have little meaning for the poorer classes of the community, for as Newman remarked in the first Discourse in another context, their 'secular acquirements ever must be limited'.[35]

---

[26] *The Dublin Review* (Mar. 1851), p. 230.   [27] Ibid.
[28] Hedley's views are taken from Wilson, J. Anselm, D.D., *The Life of Bishop Hedley*, pp. 333–4.
[29] Newman, J. H., *Idea of a University*, p. xv.   [30] Ibid., p. xvi.
[31] Ibid.   [32] Ibid.   [33] Ibid.   [34] Ibid.   [35] Ibid., p. 9.

Newman was, of course, not the only convert to Roman Catholicism who had been involved in the Oxford controversies over the scope and content of a liberal education. Neither was he the only one to give expression to decided views on the topic after his conversion. Frederick Oakeley, for instance, approached the subject from an angle significantly different from that adopted by Newman.

Let us endeavour to form the perfect Christian layman [Oakeley wrote in 1864],[36] and we may then safely leave the 'gentleman' to take care of himself. The true courtesy which is dictated by consideration and respect, the spirit of generous forbearance which is too conscious of its own faults to be severe against those of another, the tenderness and refinement of feeling, the truthfulness, the simplicity, the noble-heartedness, the sincere and provident sympathy,—these and suchlike qualities, in which the spirit of the real gentleman consists—or that spirit worth caring for—are the natural and necessary fruits of a right Catholic moral education, and may exist, and do exist, among those to whom the term 'English gentleman' presents no practical idea distinct from its accidental inclusion in that which is habitual to them.

Newman would have acknowledged with approbation much of what Oakeley had to say, but the latter's definition lacked the obvious class-exclusiveness which ran like a thread throughout the Dublin Discourses.

John Moore Capes in 1848 had spoken scathingly of the education of the gentleman. If one is to insist that the end of university education is to produce 'the gentleman', then young men will go up to university with the idea that they are to receive the treatment accorded to gentlemen in the narrowest sense. This is what was happening at Oxford, he claimed, in the middle years of the nineteenth century. 'Young men go up to Oxford and Cambridge with an idea that they are to be treated *as gentlemen*', he wrote.[37]

Any interference with their conduct beyond the enforcement of a few

[36] Oakeley, F., *The Question of University Education for English Catholics, considered principally in its moral and Religious Bearings, in a Letter to the Right Rev. the Bishop of Birmingham*, p. 397.

[37] Capes in *The Rambler*, 22 Jan. 1848, pp. 59 seq.

rules respecting Chapel, lectures, and college-hours, they deem an infraction of their rights, to be resented and resisted to the uttermost. And this preposterous notion is unquestionably the recognised theory of the Universities. The undergraduate is his own master. He spends his time as he pleases. He reads what he likes, when he likes, and as much or as little as he likes. . . . In short he is literally almost 'a gentleman at large'. He furnishes his rooms, lays his pictures, orders in his wine, scolds his scout, and keeps his own hours; and is perhaps less bound down and hemmed in by the restraints of the circumstances in which he is placed than any other member of any class of men in England . . .[38]

Capes was uncompromising in his recommendations:

Let them be treated as gentlemen, but also as young men *in a state of pupilage*. . . . Let them learn to understand that they go to Oxford and Cambridge for the especial purpose of study, and for no other purpose whatsoever; and that every amusement, every occupation, every friendship, must be regulated in a most entire subservience to this one grand object.

To a certain extent, Newman would have found himself more in agreement with Manning than he would have found himself appreciating the polemic of Capes. To Manning, however, liberal education was simply 'the formation of the whole man—intellect, heart, will, character, mind, and soul', and he declared that 'whether it be the poor child in the parish school, or the son of the rich man in the university, it is all the same'.[39] Mark Pattison, writing in his *Memoirs* in 1854 of the Oxford of the 1830s, when Newman was tutor of Oriel, maintained—albeit with some exaggeration—that 70 per cent of the Oxford undergraduates were in no sense students at all. It was understood that the degrees they obtained 'denote no grade of intellectual cultivation, but have a merely social value. They are an evidence that a youth has been able to afford not only the money, but, what is impossible to so many, the time to live three years among gentlemen, doing nothing, as a gentleman should.'[40]

[38] Capes in *The Rambler*, 22 Jan. 1848, pp. 59 seq.

[39] Lilly, W. S. (ed.), *Characteristics, Political, Philosophical, and Religious from the Writings of Henry Edward, Cardinal Archbishop of Westminster* (London, 1885). The quotation is taken from Manning's 'Internal Mission of the Holy Ghost', p. 377.   [40] Pattison, Mark, *Memoirs*, p. 408, See also pp. 25–9.

Recent writers on Newman's concept of university education have differed widely in their understanding of his aims. Dwight Culler sees in Newman's 'gentleman', or 'man of philosophic habit', an intellectual exercise, a mere figment of the imagination. 'He is an aspiration,' he writes, 'an object of desire, an idealized type, and his value is the inspirational value of any unattainable ideal.'[41] But he adds that 'to say that it is an ideal is not to justify it, for there is no point in a *quantitative* ideal—in an adjuration merely to do more abundantly that which we already know we ought to do as abundantly as we can'. He goes further and asserts 'if Newman was fined a hundred pounds for those lectures (on the *Present Position of Catholics*) . . . he should have been fined a thousand for the *Idea of a University*, for the wrong which he did to Achilli was as nothing compared with the wrong which he did to the average Englishman in supposing that he would ever allow his son to be made into anything so useless as a man of philosophic habit.' R. G. McPherson has pointed out that 'in laying down the ideal conditions under which knowledge is to be attained, Newman indirectly endorses the aristocratic theory of governance';[42] that he was making a direct appeal to the English Catholic aristocratic families became ever more obvious as his academic policy evolved.

In 1851, in the Preface to the Discourses, Newman subtly introduced the idea that he did not intend to develop the University for the exclusive advantage of Irish interests. He purported to examine the sort of benefit 'which the Holy See has intended to confer on Catholics *who speak the English tongue* [my stress] by recommending to the Irish hierarchy the establishment of a University'.[43] It was a skilled use of language, distorting at the very outset the meaning of the papal rescripts. At no time did any of the Roman documents refer to the Irish University as if it were for those 'who speak the English tongue'. By concentrating his entire energies on the idea of an Imperial University, Newman hoped to attract the sons of the aristocracy to him in Dublin.

---

[41] Culler, p. 189.
[42] McPherson, R. G., *Theory of Higher Education*, p. 61.
[43] *Idea of a University*, p. xiv.

Hence, it was as necessary to eliminate the utilitarian concept as it was to stress that the knowledge which was the object of his University was not to be 'a means to something beyond it, or the preliminary of certain arts into which it naturally resolves, but an end sufficient to rest in and to pursue for its own sake'.[44] But perhaps even for 'the man of philosophic habit' this might remain a somewhat too ethereal concept in which to rest. 'If then a practical end must be assigned to a University course,' Newman grudgingly states at the end of the seventh Discourse, 'I say it is that of training good members of society. Its art is the art of social life, and its end is fitness for the world. It neither confines its views to particular professions on the one hand, nor creates heroes or inspires genius on the other.'[45] The conclusion is banal; the end-product of a liberal education is neither skilled professionalism nor the cultivation of brilliance, but a kind of planned mediocrity. In reaching the conclusion, Newman succeeded in contradicting himself; as Culler puts it, 'where before he had rejected utility as a criterion for evaluating knowledge, he now accepts that criterion and merely claims that liberal knowledge is useful too'.[46] The reason for the distortion can be found in the statement he made to Ornsby some weeks before the first Discourse was read, and it was partly a political reason. Newman's audience was largely made up of 'the English party' in Dublin, 'the Dublin barristers',[47] and a university education which resulted in the production of good and loyal citizens would be calculated to make an especial appeal, particularly to those among them who had been keen supporters of the Queen's Colleges. Newman was eager to attract the sons of such men to his foundation, for they could be expected to have identity of interest with those English aristocrats for whom he was most anxious to provide. In angling for their support he was, however, in danger of alienating the bishops. Newman's intellectual volte-face in favour of a utilitarian end for liberal education may also have been partly due to a realization—albeit a belated one—of what William E. Buckler has recently described as 'a devastating indictment of the educated

[44] *Idea of a University*, p. 103.   [45] Ibid., p. 177.
[46] Culler, p. 222.   [47] Corcoran, *Newman: Selected Discourses, etc.*, p. lv.

man'.[48] Newman's 'gentleman', he writes, which is education's
best end-product, 'is a figure with which no man of truly imagina-
tive vision would allow himself willingly to be identified'.[49]
Dublin barristers, in particular, would find some difficulty in
conceiving of an education which 'professes to exercise the mind
neither in art nor in duty', and the function of which is a nebulous
'intellectual culture'.[50]

In September 1851, almost a year before the lectures were to
be delivered, Archbishop Cullen had written to Newman to
indicate the subject upon which he thought the Discourses should
be centred. 'What we want in Ireland', he wrote, 'is to persuade
the people that education should be religious. The whole tendency
of our new systems is to make it believed that education may be
so conducted as to have nothing at all to do with religion.' What
the bishops required was an attestation of the reasons for the
establishment of a Catholic University for Ireland, and an indication as to why the education provided in the 'godless' colleges
was condemned by the Church. Newman's lectures not only
failed to fulfil episcopal hopes but they set out to destroy the very
bases of the bishops' arguments. Fr. Cormican, in a brilliant
article in *Thought* in 1926, illustrated this point admirably when he
wrote that 'Newman's "brave idea" of a university repels all
possibility of the university's becoming an instrument of the
Church at all, save at the cost of a transformation or annihilation
of what he defines to be the scope of a university. That scope is
liberal knowledge; and liberal knowledge, as he says, must lose
its liberalism when it ministers to something beyond itself, when
it is used, even by the Church.'[51] Towards the end of the fifth
Discourse Newman had declared: 'Liberal Education makes not
the Christian, not the Catholic, but the gentleman.'[52] The pursuit
of knowledge must be independent of religious motives, as it
must be stripped of the strictly utilitarian motive. In Newman's
separation of the man of intellect and the man of virtue John
Triffin has seen theories 'dangerously close to various passages in

[48] *Thought* (Spring 1964), p. 78. [49] Ibid.
[50] *Idea of a University*, p. 125. [51] *Thought* (Spring 1926), p. 68.
[52] *Idea of a University*, p. 120.

Thomas Huxley'.[53] He asserts that 'there can be little doubt that Newman was positing a wordly ideal ("a transitory possession") in the Discourses, and in so doing he is well outside the tradition of Christian humanism represented in figures like St. Thomas More, John Milton, or Matthew Arnold'.[54] The Irish bishops would have been better served, they must have felt, by a forthright statement such as that of a writer in the *Quarterly*, who, apropos of London University, had declared that 'every mode of instruction which so teaches learning, science or art, as to make them seem all in all and fails to connect them with the higher object of all education, the fitting man for his ultimate destiny, we consider to be both incomplete and pernicious'.[55] Newman, of course, believed that religion should be at the basis of fundamental education, and preached at great length on the necessity for theology to be taught in a university, if the latter was to be a true university teaching all knowledge. But his insistence that a liberal education was and ought to be an end in itself was not traditional Catholic teaching. In 1869 *The Dublin Review* gave expression to the more orthodox viewpoint by declaring that 'it is the business of education, not merely to impart mental cultivation and *power*, but far more emphatically to impart speculative and practical *truth*',[56] and the *Review* ventured to consider it 'a most serious defect in a work, otherwise so unusually powerful as F. Newman's volume on "the scope and nature of University Education", that the author lays so little stress on this particular function of universities'.[57] In October 1873, on the occasion of the reissue of *The Idea of a University*,[58] *The Dublin Review* devoted itself to a lengthy analysis of the Discourses. The reason for this was that the first appearance 'took place at the most critical moment of Catholic higher education in Ireland, and its reissue

[53] Triffin, John, 'In Defence of Newman's "Gentleman"', in *The Dublin Review* (Autumn 1965), pp. 245–54, and esp. p. 249.

[54] Ibid., p. 252.

[55] See Mathieson, W. L., *English Church Reform, 1815–40*, p. 209.

[56] *The Dublin Review* (Jan.–Apr. 1869), p. 89.

[57] Ibid.

[58] *The Idea of a University Defined and Illustrated*, by John Henry Newman, D.D., of the Oratory (Pickering, London, 1873 edn.).

takes place at the most critical moment of Catholic higher education in England'.[59] The article must have given Newman considerable pain, for it used the chief arguments of the Discourses to
justify the policy of the English hierarchy in the matter of higher
education, and in particular to point to the need for the establishment of a Catholic University in England. There was nothing
sinister or distorting in the *Dublin*'s presentation, for Newman's
arguments in favour of such a university for Ireland in the 1850s
applied with even greater force to England in the 1870s. One can
hardly blame the *Dublin*, therefore, for taking the opportunity of
Newman's reissue of the Discourses in 1873 to promote its own
campaign for a Catholic University, and this in spite of the fact
that Newman himself, after his personal failure in Dublin, was
unsympathetic to the idea of a Catholic University for England.

After giving a résumé of Newman's chief arguments, the journal developed the criticism which had been voiced in Ireland in
the fifties. Newman's language, the *Review* declared, 'would
convey an impression to the superficial reader (1) that he regards
the giving of intellectual culture as by far the principal and paramount work of higher education; and (2) that he does not
include, under the head of "giving intellectual culture", the
inculcating pervasively, and penetrating the mind with, moral
and religious truth. . . . We do not for a moment believe that
F. Newman holds this doctrine; but we do think that he has not
sufficiently guarded himself against the *imputation* of holding it.'[60]
Higher education to be really a good 'must not only impart a due
measure of intellectual culture, but no less prominently a due
measure of architectonic—that is, of moral and religious—knowledge'. It had not been sufficiently emphasized that there were
'two principal and absolutely indispensable constituents of good
Catholic higher education', and these were 'the imparting of
adequate intellectual culture, and of adequate doctrinal knowledge'. *The Dublin Review* made bold, even, to criticize the content
of that liberal education so beloved in Newman's thesis. 'We
still doubt whether [Fr. Newman] does not adhere too exclusively
to what was the recognized Oxford intellectual discipline of his

[59] *The Dublin Review* (Oct. 1873), pp. 403 seq.   [60] Ibid., pp. 415–16.

own time, the study of classics and mathematics. We certainly incline to think, that a certain not very scant admixture of physical and other studies—over and above their practical value, which is not here in question—would very importantly conduce to intellectual power and enlargement.'[61]

Then comes a subtle attack upon what is best described as the 'rubbing-off' theory of education. Newman maintained that although all students could not pursue 'every subject which is open to them', nevertheless, 'they will be the gainers by living among those and under those who represent the whole circle'.[62] He developed the point: 'An assemblage of learned men, zealous for their own sciences, and rivals of each other, are brought, by familiar intercourse and for the sake of intellectual peace, to adjust together the claims and relations of their respective subjects of investigation.' In this mutual adjustment were to be discovered the seeds of liberal education. The *Dublin's* caustic comment was that surely 'no one will maintain that Catholic students could acquire due knowledge of their religion by the mere fact of studying classics and mathematics in the same institution where others are studying theology', even if one granted that there might be 'habitual intercourse between the lay and the theological student'.[63]

In the Discourses Newman had been especially careful to point out that high intellectual culture, such as he was positing to be the true end of a liberal education, was especially necessary for the sons of the aristocracy and for the leisured classes in general. The discipline by which it was necessary to gain intellectual culture was so exacting and required so much labour that it provided sufficient occupation of mind to prevent the evils incumbent upon idleness and leisure. The mind would acquire 'an indisposition, simply natural, yet real, nay more than this, a disgust and abhorrence towards excesses and enormities of evil'.[64] He remarked: 'Scarcely can we exaggerate the value, in its place, of a safeguard such as this.' The *Dublin* concluded its examination of *The Idea of a University* with a scathing review of this concept.

61 *The Dublin Review* (Oct. 1873), p. 423.   62 *Idea of a University*, p. 101.
63 *The Dublin Review* (Oct. 1873), p. 424.   64 *Idea of a University*, p. 187.

F. Newman seems to say [it declared] that, unless they possess [intellectual culture], their interests will be so unoccupied, that those of them who are not visited with exceptional sorrow, sickness, or care, will almost infallibly (be they Catholics or non-Catholics) fall into frequent mortal sin. Now we will not deny that regular habits of application may often be of excellent service, towards assisting the struggles against mortal sin; whether in the case of bankers' clerks or of philosophical students: much more however in the former case than in the latter because in the former case regularity of habit is *compulsory*. . . . Yet surely a vigorous devotion to their duties, as magistrates and country gentlemen; or to yachting, or billiards, or chess, or whist, or the sports of the field; will do for them the very same service, which F. Newman claims as peculiar to high intellectual culture. Or they may try experiments in farming, which will at once provide them with constant interesting occupation, and also confer much benefit on the nation. Or they may follow the example of a late baronet, and take office as drivers of some four-in-hand daily coach. Or they may busy themselves in the organisation and practical working of benevolent schemes; or enrol themselves as members of a mercantile house. But even were all this otherwise, a taste for miscellaneous, desultory, ill-digested reading has no tendency whatever—as F. Newman will himself be eager in professing—to the acquirement of high intellectual culture: yet it will be every bit as useful as the latter in filling up unoccupied moments, and in 'staving off the approach of our spiritual enemy'.[65]

The irony of the article was heavy and cruel, but it did highlight both an absurd quality in the Discourses and Newman's over-eager solicitude to attract the leisured class to the University. Even *The Rambler*, in 1857, after quoting Newman on the task of the University to 'fit men for the world' and 'prepare them against what is inevitable', could not restrain itself from commenting that 'the same fundamental principle presides over the education of the peer and the peasant'.[66]

Perhaps the most sober judgement on Newman's view of a liberal education has been pronounced by Sir Walter Moberly. In discussing in recent years the modern crisis in the concept of university education, he has pointed out that in substance what

[65] *The Dublin Review* (Oct. 1873), p. 424.
[66] *The Rambler* (Jan. 1857), p. 51.

Newman depicts in *The Idea of a University* 'is Jowett's ideal of Oxford quite as much as it is his own'.[67] Jowett, according to Mark Pattison, had been responsible for attacking the concept which regarded the university as a 'home of higher research and advanced learning'.[68] To Jowett, as to Newman, the University was to be a sort of 'super public school, with all its more unpleasing characteristics', such as 'its juvenilia' and 'its newly-established-old-traditions'.[69] Newman merely gave expression to a series of ideas which had long been part and parcel of academic thought. They were to be detected in the thought of Whewell at Cambridge as they were to be found in J. S. Mill's Rectorial Address at St. Andrews. Newman's statement of the liberal ideal is 'by no means peculiar to Newman, and there is nothing about it that is specifically Catholic'.[70] He was simply 'drawing on his recollections of Oxford' and 'painting its characteristic excellences'.[71]

The first matter which led to a disagreement with Cullen immediately stemmed from Newman's insistence that the University ought to be established on the Oxford pattern, and established and organized on a collegiate basis. Cullen, with a shrewder grasp of reality, contended that it would be wiser to begin the University in one central building. In effect, a compromise was arrived at, whereby the teaching would take place in a central locale, but the students would live in smaller houses of residence which Newman organized on the basis of social status and nationality. Fergal McGrath has indicated that the compromise was a bitter pill for Newman to swallow, and comments that 'it was clearly Newman's belief that nothing could take the place of a formally constituted college'.[72] What Newman had set himself to do in Dublin in 1852, according to T. Corcoran, was to formulate a philosophy of education which held up the University of Oxford 'as being in itself an exemplar of academic perfection,

---

[67] Moberly, Sir Walter, *The Crisis in the University* (London, 1949), pp. 30–1.

[68] See Green, V. H. H., *Oxford Common Room: A Study of Lincoln College and Mark Pattison*, p. 260.

[69] Ibid.

[70] Moberly, *The Crisis in the University*, p. 30.   [71] Ibid.

[72] See McGrath, Fergal, S.J., *Newman's University, Idea and Reality*, and *The Tablet*, 15 Aug. 1964.

a model of "Liberal Education" and of the principles on which it *must* be conducted'.[73] And that meant upholding the collegiate system as far as humanly possible in all its integrity. The proposals of 1852 were 'well adapted to the leisured aristocracy, the sons of noblemen and of gentlemen who had an assurance of easily-attained financial independence',[74] but the Irish bishops, on the other hand, wanted the professional schools to be the major ingredients of their University, and stood out for 'specific outlets of academic discipline in study and in skilled scientific training, ready for action in social, national and individual service, and inspired for, animated by zeal for, such activities as the resultants of general and professional culture'.[75]

A full year before Newman actually entered upon his office as Rector of the Catholic University, *The Rambler* was already beginning to follow the suggestion contained within *The Idea of a University* that the new foundation was meant for all those Catholics who speak the English tongue. 'The University is needed as much by England as by Ireland,' it declared, 'for England is as destitute of such an institution as the sister isle.'[76] But Capes ignored the central thesis of Newman's lectures and the latter's predilections for those young men capable of profiting by his concept of 'intellectual excellence', for the journal hammered away at the theme that the new University should direct its attention to the professional classes. 'None of the Catholic colleges' in England, Capes declared, 'afford any professional teaching; hence the young Catholic physicians, surgeons, barristers, engineers,—in a word, the great bulk of the learned classes,—must complete their education elsewhere.'[77] The Catholic University in Dublin would therefore not merely direct its attention to 'those gentlemen of independent means who, having no obligation to earn their bread, are expected to acquire a more extensive education than the laborious classes' but would also provide for 'those who are intended for the learned professions and a purely literary life'. The English colleges were too small, their resources

[73] Corcoran, *Newman: Selected Discourses, etc.*, Introductory, *ad init.*
[74] Ibid., p. xxxxv.   [75] Ibid.
[76] *The Rambler* (Aug. 1853), pp. 112–27.   [77] Ibid., pp. 114–15.

too limited, and their professors too overburdened with work to enable them to provide university education. Newman was horrified at the assumption that the English Catholic colleges would supply as students for the University 'lads of sixteen intended for the liberal professions, who have already achieved a sound foundation in classics and other branches of study', together with 'younger lads desirous to share in the benefits of the education offered'. Capes also looked ahead at the part the English Catholic colleges would eventually play in the new organization:

> It is clear, that the university will draw from them the more advanced pupils who now remain there to complete their education. But it must not be thought that they will be weakened by this; rather we consider that they will be strengthened, by their energies being concentrated on special classes. Some may become preparatory schools for those intending to enter the university, like the college 'de la haute colline' at Louvain, and Eton and Rugby in England; others will devote themselves exclusively to those who require a commercial education; others will become colleges of special studies, like the Engineering College of Putney and the Agricultural College of Cirencester, and that of Esher; others, again, may supply the pressing want of Catholic normal and training schools for teachers; and thus every branch of education will gain by being at once separated and concentrated.[78]

The article caused dismay among the Irish episcopacy. It was bad enough that the idea had already been misconstrued into one alien from Irish intentions, but now English Catholics were about to demand that the Irish bishops should totally surrender the institution into English hands. The Dublin establishment was to be merely the apex of a whole new system of secondary and higher education for *English* Catholics. *The Rambler* did not even consider the needs of Ireland! But who was footing the bill? In 1853 of the £36,000 which had initially been collected for the University, £22,000 had come from Ireland, £7,750 from Irish Catholics in the United States, and £993 from other parts of the world. Only £3,568 had been collected in England. *The Rambler*'s claim was preposterous; it could only be a joke.

[78] *The Rambler* (Aug. 1853), pp. 126–7.

The following year, however, *The Rambler* turned its attention to Newman himself, and pointed to him as *a guarantee* that English interests would be safeguarded. 'We might fairly have expected', it claimed, 'that the character and principles of the individual whom [the University's] founders have appointed as its first rector, would have been a sufficient guarantee that they had no scheme on hand for setting up a hot-bed of revolutionism and political agitation. . . . What could party-spirit, exclusive nationalism, or political propagandism, have to do with the appointment of Dr. Newman?'[79] But at the same time a distinct warning was issued to Newman against allowing the University to develop into 'a nursery of Catholic gentlemen' whose main object it would be 'to reduce the power of the Pope to the lowest practicable limits, and to control the action of the Catholic Church in these kingdoms by intrigue and worldly influence'. The journal issued a warning, too, against those 'who will think it a nobler thing to be an Englishman or an Irishman than simply a Catholic'. It concluded that 'the spirit which has placed Dr. Newman in his rectorship is no more disposed to set up imagined rights of any national section of the Church against the living supremacy of Rome, than to foster dissensions among Englishmen and Irishmen, or to inculcate a taste for insubordination against lawful authority of any kind'. This statement was tantamount to accusing the old families of Gallicanism and the Irish of sedition.

In 1857 *The Rambler* had taken up what it considered to be Newman's cause in Ireland. Unfortunately it succeeded in offering him a disservice by highlighting and publicizing aims he had hoped to achieve gradually and secretly. It is not without significance that the following year, in November 1858, Newman quit Ireland and the University for good. The policy of regarding the University as an Imperial foundation was then given great prominence in the paper. 'Being in Ireland, it has been placed under the Irish episcopacy as its supreme authority', but 'the University is specially intended for all Catholics who speak the English tongue and for as many Continental Catholics as have an

[79] Ibid. (Sept. 1854), p. 199.

inclination for education under the spirit of national British ideas.'[80] The journal argued:

> It was *not* designed to be a local or provincial institution. . . . It is a violation of the first principle of its existence to nail up the cry of 'Ireland for the Irish' as a motto over its portals. It is not the 'Irish Catholic University' at all; it is the Catholic 'University of Dublin'. The fact that Dublin is in Ireland no more proves that the University is meant to be specially Irish, than the fact that Oxford is in Oxfordshire proves that it is not designed for people born in Yorkshire or Middlesex. It is founded in Dublin, rather than elsewhere, not because Dublin is in Ireland, but because it is the most convenient *Catholic* centre.

In September 1857 *The Rambler* took the leisured classes to task for pining for Oxford and Cambridge and for failing to support the Catholic University. It remarked that 'the grand aim of the new University in Dublin is the infusion into the upper classes of Irish society that spirit of loyalty to the Church and of refined intellectual culture' which were of such importance for Catholic well-being, but, the journal added woefully, 'the money has been contributed by the middle classes and the poor; and among the clergy have been found, practically speaking, the only supporters of an undertaking by which they themselves, as a class, will only indirectly benefit'.[81]

In the first two editions of *The Idea of a University* Newman, in the Dedication, thanked all those who had helped him at the time of the Achilli trial, and in doing so he mentioned Ireland first and Great Britain second. In the edition of 1873 he changed the order, putting Great Britain first. This simple indication of Newman's bitterness is also a measure of his failure. If he had attempted to fulfil his commission of erecting an Irish university as a counterpart to the Queen's Colleges he might—just possibly —have succeeded. In his efforts, however, to produce an Imperial university he was let down by his closest friends among the English landed families. They would give him neither their money nor their sons. And yet Newman sadly murmured: 'What is

---

[80] *The Rambler* (Feb. 1857), pp. 92–3.
[81] Ibid. (Sept. 1857), p. 169.

Ireland to me, except the University here is a University for England, as well as for Ireland? I have left England for what I consider to be a great English interest. . . . I would far rather do good to English Catholics in Oxford than in Dublin.'[82]

[82] Letter of Newman, dated 7 Mar. 1856, from 6 Harcourt Street, Dublin (reproduced in Corcoran, p. lv).

I

III

THE EDUCATION OF YOUTHS OF RANK, FORTUNE, AND EXPECTATION

In 1850 political power among English Catholics was wielded by the representatives of eleven major Old Catholic families—the Duke of Norfolk, Lord Shrewsbury, Lord Arundell of Wardour, Lord Beaumont, Lord Camoys, Lord Clifford, Lord Dormer, Lord Petre, Lord Stafford, Lord Stourton, and Lord Vaux of Harrowden. They were supported by a squirearchy of hereditary Catholics whose political principles made them, according to Altholz, 'indistinguishable from the class which had customarily governed England since the Glorious Revolution'.[1] Firm supporters of the principles of the Revolution (except in strictly religious matters), they were particularly anxious to demonstrate on every occasion their unbounded loyalty to Queen and Constitution. They were anti-Irish, and anti-Jesuit. The Duke of Norfolk ceased to be a practising Catholic after the restoration of the Roman Catholic hierarchy in 1850, which he regarded as the apotheosis of 'papal aggression'. They welcomed only those converts, such as Newman and Bellasis, who worshipped from afar and who were prepared to tolerate Gallican attitudes in matters of ecclesiastical government. Keen supporters of the British government in its attempts to subdue the Church in Ireland—a Church of peasants ruled by peasants—they intrigued at Rome throughout the nineteenth century to try to secure safe and ineffectual prelates for Irish sees. The English Catholic peers to a man had supported the Charitable Bequests Bill with which Peel in 1844 was busily engaged. Lord Beaumont and Lord Camoys were particularly vigorous advocates of the Bill, which

[1] *Journal of British Studies*, no. 1 (1964), pp. 90–1.

declared that no donation or bequest to any religious order or congregation or monastic establishment, or to any individual member of such, would be lawful. Beaumont dubbed it 'an excellent measure',[2] and even Lord Arundell and Surrey, heir to the Duke of Norfolk and generally sympathetic to Irish problems, deemed it 'a fair Bill'. Throughout 1844 Petre was employed at Rome, in an unofficial capacity, to offset Irish opposition.[3]

In 1848 both Wiseman and Lord Shrewsbury exerted pressure at Rome in favour of the Queen's Colleges. Both openly espoused the minority view among the Irish bishops, and Shrewsbury published a series of attacks on Archbishop MacHale and the fifteen prelates opposed to the 'godless colleges'. Wiseman, preparing for the hierarchy's restoration, was anxious to make himself acceptable to the government. As early as 1842 he urged that the minority bishops under the leadership of Archbishop Murray of Dublin should work for the appointment of an English ambassador in Rome. The English Catholic peers considered that the establishment of diplomatic relations with the Papacy would lead directly to the pacification of Ireland. The Queen's Colleges, for their part, would wean the youth of Ireland from episcopal dominance. With an Old Catholic lodged in Rome as British ambassador, the success of the Colleges would be ensured. Petre's name was openly canvassed for the post.

The anxiety of the Old Catholic families to be *seen* to be liberal and enlightened, and their eagerness not to be identified as an alien faction in English life, influenced their attitude to the Papacy. The Duke of Norfolk, for instance, was opposed to a declaration of sympathy for the Pope which was being organized among Catholics in 1860, because 'every *unnecessary* declaration we make that is not understood by our Protestant countrymen is interpreted by them as a proof of how little we are fit to be members of a reasonable and Enlightened Society: and they revenge themselves by contempt for, and slighting conduct towards those in their power'.[4] The attitude portrayed here,

---

² O'Reilly, B., *Life of John MacHale, Archbishop of Tuam*, vol. 1, p. 552.
³ MacSuibhne, vol. 1, pp. 251-2, 256-8.
⁴ Herries Papers, Beverley Record Office, 29 Dec. 1859.

coupled with an inherent dislike of the Irish, was characteristic of the English Catholic aristocracy throughout the sixties and seventies. It would be untrue to assert, however, that there was *total* antipathy between Irish prelates and English peers in the middle years of the nineteenth century. The attitude of Lord Clifford in attempting to prevent the appointment of MacHale to the see of Tuam and his later opposition to that prelate over the national system of education were eventually forgiven after MacHale received a letter of apology from Clifford in 1846. Six years later Cullen expressed in writing his own 'respect and esteem' for Lord Arundell and Surrey.[5] Similarly the attitude of the Irish bishops to some of the more affluent among the converts was not antagonistic. The Hon. and the Revd. George Spencer, whose crusade of prayer for the conversion of England earned Wiseman's lasting antipathy,[6] was a friend of both MacHale and Cullen.

Newman's dream of erecting in Ireland a university institution with an especial appeal for the sons of the Old Catholic aristocracy and squirearchy and for those of influential English converts was destined to fail at the outset. In 1852 Ambrose Phillipps de Lisle pinpointed the fundamental weakness of Newman's conception in a letter he sent to Lord Shrewsbury. 'As for the Irish University,' he wrote, 'I wish it well, but I have very scanty hopes of its success. It may creep gradually into life as a purely Irish institution, though even that is doubtful—but it will never become what its greatest friends desire—an Imperial University for all British Catholics. I never thought that for a moment. Who in his senses would send his children to a province at a distance for the completion of education when Stonyhurst and Oscott and Ushaw surely fully answer the purpose or might be made to do so, at home?'[7] Cruelly, he declared Newman's scheme to be 'a joke': 'An Imperial University in Ireland is a pure absurdity.' He declared that 'they may indeed do what the

---

[5] MacSuibhne, vol. 2, p. 117.

[6] Ward Papers. Letter of Robert Whitty to Wilfrid Ward, 28 Feb. 1895, from St. Beuno's College, Tremeirchion.

[7] Letter given in full in Purcell, E. S., *The Life and Letters of Ambrose Phillipps de Lisle*, ed. Edwin de Lisle, vol. 2, p. 3.

Pope advised, get up a University for Ireland, and that was my reason for contributing my mite towards the undertaking, but I do not at all believe in the wisdom of making it a mixed affair for England and Ireland. Such an attempt will only weaken it, excite jealousy and even opposition in the end.' De Lisle was also severely critical of Newman's appointment as Rector. 'I am astonished at their putting Father Newman at the head, or rather I am surprised at his accepting such a position, if at least he means to remain Superior of the Oratorians in England. I cannot see how the two things are compatible. Then again Newman, though a man of extraordinary ability and prodigious learning, never had anything to do with the management of a University: his position at Oxford was always a subordinate one, and his great repute was rather that of a Preacher and a Theologian than of a scholar or a teacher in the literary acceptation of the term.' With Shrewsbury, he believed that the Irish bishops ought to have made the best of the Queen's Colleges, but, de Lisle added, this view did not prevent him from wishing the new venture all success. The letter summarized, in 1852, what were to be the chief causes of Newman's failure six years later—his attempt to distort the University from it original purpose, his eagerness to attract the sons of the English well-to-do, his reluctance to yield the office of Superior of the English Oratory to another, and his own innate experience and inability in practical affairs.

Geoffrey Faber has written that Newman had not 'the smallest understanding of social problems', for 'his interest in the lower orders was confined to their souls',[8] and Terence Kenny has pointed out that Newman's vision of society was that 'of a stable class structure' united to 'a strong sense of the interdependence of social ranks and classes'.[9] Newman 'did not seem to envisage the possibility that it was as important to keep the poor in the Church as the rich', and 'he conceived that he had a mission to the gentlemen of the country, because they formed the educated classes'.[10]

---

[8] Faber, Geoffrey, *Oxford Apostles: A Character Study of the Oxford Movement*, p. 251.

[9] Kenny, Terence, *The Political Thought of John Henry Newman*, p. 35.

[10] Ibid., p. 169.

But this does not fully explain why Newman was to be so antagonistic to Manning's plans for improving the education of the poor,[11] or why in his objection to the work of the Society for the Diffusion of Useful Knowledge he should claim that knowledge was not a commodity which could be distributed from stock to all who wished to apply for it.[12] Perhaps his true position can be seen in a remark he made to his brother Frank: 'Everyone has his place in society—there is a difference of duties and of persons fitted to them.'[13] Newman would claim that such difference need have little more than hereditary justification. Kenny sums up the position by claiming that Newman 'assumed complacently a rigidity of class structure which did not exist, and he wanted to influence the upper and educated classes to which he would like himself thought to belong'.[14] In an address to the evening classes at Dublin, entitled 'Discipline of Mind', Newman praised 'the condescension' of his lecturers in deeming it worth their while to address such a humble audience, and he spoke of the 'public spirit' and 'noble free devotion' of the men who had thus so condescended.[15] For the great and rising middle classes and those desiring purely professional education he had little concern. At one time he considered that democracy and anti-Christ were in league.[16]

Newman's attitude contrasts with that of Manning. Writing in 1885 on 'The Office of the Church in Higher Catholic Education', Manning declared: 'Poverty is no doubt a hindrance, but the highest intellectual culture has been, and may still be found in poverty, and a dead level of mediocrity may be found endowed with abundant wealth. Study is not a craft or a mystery, and the fields of knowledge are open to all. The intellectual inequalities among men depend on two things—unequal gifts of intellectual power, and the unequal energies of the will in study. . . . There are no privileges nor monopolies in the realms of learning. The

[11] Kenny, p. 169.
[12] Newman, B., *Cardinal Newman: a Biographical and Literary Study*, p. 136.
[13] Ward, M., *The Young Mr. Newman*, p. 268.
[14] Kenny, pp. 170–1.
[15] Newman, J. H., *The Idea of a University* (1912 edn.), pp. 487, 503.
[16] Newman, J. H., *Discussions and Arguments*, pp. 72 seq.

records of knowledge are legible to all.'[17] Manning saw in the Irish University scheme 'the broad assertion that a Catholic people have a right to Catholic education'.[18] It was Newman's concept of 'wholeness' that led him further into a class-structured theory of education. Only the rich and the well-born could be truly 'whole'. Miss Trevor points out that it was the gentry for whom Newman wished the University to provide.[19] Newman stated his own conviction quite clearly to Capes in 1857—'you cannot have a University till the gentlemen take it up'[20]—and in his retrospective notes he added, 'I wished the gentry whose sons were to be taught by us to have the financial matters of the institution in their hands'.[21] His policy was based on a belief which ran directly counter to that held by the Irish hierarchy. In their joint Pastoral of 1860 on the Catholic University, written after Newman's departure, they were at last free to make their feelings known. 'The advantages arising from the University', they declared, 'are open not only to the more wealthy, but to many, also, in whom the absence of wealth is abundantly compensated by the presence of industry, energy, and talent.'[22]

Newman became entrenched in his attitude as a result of a familiarity which grew up between himself and Lord Shrewsbury in the 1850s.[23] In 1854 he was a guest at Alton Towers and succeeded in getting Shrewsbury's name for the books of the University. His acquaintance with Howard, Arundell, Petre, Camoys, Stourton, Stafford, Dormer, Langdale, Clifford, and Herries developed apace; by 1867 *The Guardian* could write sarcastically, 'we congratulate Dr. Newman on his alliance with the Barons'.[24] Furthermore, there was nothing to offset

[17] Manning, H. E., *The Office of the Church in Higher Catholic Education*, Pastoral Letter, 1885, p. 17.

[18] Manning, H. E., *Miscellanies*, vol. 1, p. 377.

[19] Trevor, Meriol, *Light in Winter*, pp. 49, 146.

[20] Letter quoted *in extenso* in W. Ward, *Life of Newman*, vol. 1, p. 373.

[21] Ibid., p. 381.

[22] Moran, P. F., op. cit., vol. 1, p. 702.

[23] Dessain, Charles Stephen, and Blehl, V. F. (eds.), *The Letters and Diaries of John Henry Newman*, vol. 16, pp. 208 seq. The documents in this volume will in future be referred to simply as *Newman Letters*.

[24] *The Guardian*, 24 Apr. 1867.

this influence in the Oratory, for the only born-Catholic and Irishman in the Birmingham house in 1855 was Stanislas Flanagan, and even this isolated figure before his ordination 'had led a gay social life and was well known in the hunting field'.[25]

Meriol Trevor maintains that 'Newman's attitude to laymen was one of the principal causes of the suspicion with which Cullen regarded him', and that in this suspicion Cullen 'had the support of his fellow-bishops'.[26] But what she fails to notice is that the Irish episcopacy was not united against lay influence *per se*, but only against that special type of layman which Newman was so anxious to associate with himself, a type willing to carry further the policy of developing the University for English interests. When we examine the nature of Newman's appointments to professorships and lecturerships we see concrete evidence of the process at work. Even David Moriarty, Bishop of Kerry and lifelong friend of Newman, was totally opposed to his anglicizing policy. Long after Newman had severed his connection with Dublin, Moriarty felt free to speak. In Synod in Killarney he declared that the Irish people had been called upon 'to contribute to the foundation and support of a Catholic University', and, he went on, 'if such an institution will be useful only to the small number of Catholic youth who belong to the upper classes of society, we shall then have the anomaly of the poor providing for the education of the rich'.[27] They ought instead to make education more widely available 'to the people at large', and then 'we shall have sown the seed that will fructify into a University; and that University, representing the genius of the people, will benefit and belong to those who have founded it'.[28]

If we examine what Newman meant by lay co-operation, the Rector does not appear quite so enlightened as Miss Trevor would have us believe. In a letter to James More O'Farrell of May 1854[29] he indicated that the laymen who were to have 'a direct part in the management of the university' were indeed the men whom Newman had hand-picked for professorial appoint-

---

[25] Trevor, *Light in Winter*, p. 79.   [26] Ibid., p. 50.
[27] Quoted in Corcoran, *Newman: Selected Discourses, etc.*   [28] Ibid.
[29] *Newman Letters*, Newman to James More O'Farrell, 12 May 1854 (not sent).

ments, many of them Englishmen and converts chosen for their attachment to himself. In its early years 'the whole power must be vested in one person, that is, the Rector', Newman declared, and this provisional state was not to end for three or seven years. In other words, Newman was ensuring that he would possess autocratic control of the establishment as long as he was Rector, if we are to believe his later contention that he had never contemplated remaining in Dublin longer than six years. Then, after the provisional state was ended, 'the laity, holding a good number of professorships and being members of the University, must necessarily secure their due weight in the ordinary government'. The promise was shadowy and the 'democratic principle' would be left to others to implement. In 1855 Newman, beginning to realize that he was not succeeding in his efforts to get the support of the Irish gentry, put it down to the fact—as he told Cullen— 'that they are allowed so little share in the management of the money matters of the University'. Because of this 'the educated and upper class' was sore.[30] Newman put the worst connotation upon Cullen's distrust of the Irish aristocracy; the Archbishop, he believed, merely wished to turn the University into 'a seminary'.[31] The Irish aristocracy, however, was out of touch with the aspirations of the middle and professional classes and antagonistic to the Irish episcopacy; hence, as Newman himself was at length to realize, the bishops had little contact with the members of such a class. Furthermore, the bulk of the money collected for the University emanated from the poor.

Newman, at the outset of his campaign, tried to avoid Irish episcopal control by securing Wiseman as first Chancellor of the University. The Irish bishops regarded the move as a studied insult, and, as Bertram Newman has maintained, its result was that 'relations between Newman and the Irish Archbishop [Cullen] became strained'.[32] With Wiseman as titular head of the new University and living at a distance, Newman's policies would be guaranteed. The University would be permitted to develop along Imperial lines, and the prestige of Wiseman's

[30] Ibid., Newman to Cullen, 26 July 1855.
[31] Ward, W., *Life of Newman*, vol. 1, pp. 368–9.   [32] Newman, B., p. 126.

name, together with his influence with the gentry, would attract a supply of students of the desired social background. Direct control by Irish prelates would be negatived and Archbishop Cullen kept firmly in the place where Newman wanted him. In return for the compliment, Wiseman tried to secure a titular bishopric for Newman, to aid him further in his dealings with the Irish episcopate. He would then be dealing with equals on equal terms; he would be less the instrument of the hierarchy and much more able to pursue his own peculiar policy. Cullen has been sharply criticized because he prevented the episcopal dignity from descending upon Newman. But Cullen did not so much object to the honour as to the source from whence it was to come. After informing the Secretary of the Congregation of *Propaganda* in 1854 that Wiseman had written to him to say he was suggesting Newman be raised to the episcopacy, Cullen remarked: 'if word got around that the English cardinal was proposing plans for regulating our ecclesiastical affairs it would ruin any project no matter how good in itself.' He added: 'In reply to his Eminence [Wiseman], I expressed my feeling that while I would have the greatest pleasure in seeing a man so learned and saintly as Mr. Newman raised to the highest dignities, nevertheless I thought that perhaps it would be better to wait a little until things are in better shape.' If this were done, then 'with a little delay the thing will come naturally and there will be no opposition to it'.[33] The beginning of the University ought to be unostentatious. Cullen was 'very well aware that Cardinal Wiseman has grandiose ideas and that he would like to see things spring up in a moment', but Wiseman was 'not well informed about our situation'.[34] The danger was avoided only just in time, for the wealthy had flocked around Newman's standard when the news got about. Presents showered upon him—the Duke of Norfolk sent 'a massive gold chain'; Mrs. Bowden, 'a cross and chain of Maltese filagree work'; Hope-Scott, 'a morse for a cope, ornamented with his wife's jewels'; and Monsell sent a cross.[35]

[33] MacSuibhne, vol. 2, pp. 155–6. Cullen to Barnabo, 21 Feb. 1854.
[34] Ibid.
[35] Details in Stanton's account, W. Ward, *Life of Newman*, vol. 1, p. 332.

In 1852 Wiseman was preparing himself for his future role by defining the nature and scope of a Catholic University. 'A Catholic University', he said, 'is to give learning; it is to give science; it is to diffuse education; but it is to do more. It is to bestow Wisdom; it is to make all these grow up and ripen unto true Wisdom, by diffusing through all instruction and all knowledge that highest of sciences, the knowledge of God, of His Laws, and of our duties towards Him.'[36] With its implications of doctrinal teaching, this view would sooner or later have come into conflict with that of Newman. Although the latter agreed that Wiseman should consecrate him when the expected preferment arrived, by 1854 Newman had grown suspicious of Wiseman's meddling at Rome in the matter of the University, and had even contemplated a journey to the Eternal City to offset the cardinal's influence. What Newman feared above all was the possibility that he himself might lose the initiative. 'I fear the Cardinal will do too much,' he wrote; '. . . at all events, that something would be done *different* from what is wanted.'[37]

In Newman's 'Memorandum on the Objects of the University and Means for Attaining them' of 29 April 1854, written for submission to the Irish bishops, he placed 'the education of young men of rank, fortune or expectations' in the first place, above the education of the mercantile class and those interested in the professions, and above that 'of promising youths in the lower classes'. Keeping his primary aim in mind, he decided to organize 'several houses for different classes of students',[38] and he began with three collegiate houses—St. Patrick's at 88 St. Stephen's Green, St. Laurence's at 18 and 19 Harcourt Street, and his own house, St. Mary's at 6 Harcourt Street. These were later to be joined by University House. In August 1854 he informed William Dodsworth that he intended to keep the nationalities (i.e. the English and Irish) apart. 'We shall have, I suppose, "the Nations" in distinct houses . . . and I am beginning at once an

[36] Wiseman, N., *Sermon*, preached at St. George's Cathedral, Southwark, 27 June 1852, p. 8.
[37] Ward, W., *Life of Newman*, vol. 1, p. 329.
[38] *Newman Letters*, Newman to Henry Wilberforce, 5 July 1854.

English house of *my own friends* [Newman's stress]. That is the sort of excuse, I make, for the sake of drawing a line.'[39] He was preparing to place the fees for residence higher in his own house than in the others, because, as he told George Ryder, 'I shall have no means of avoiding taking anyone, unless I name a high sum.'[40]

In November 1854 Newman was able to inform Miss M. R. Giberne, with evident relish, that he had secured a French viscount (Louis de Vaulchier) for his house. The latter was seventeen years of age and intended to follow the University course. His tutor, Peter le Page Renouf, accompanied the young Frenchman to Dublin and was made Professor of French. Shortly afterwards Newman was busy advising Lord Henry Kerr to send his son, Frank, to him, for 'I am now in my own house and I have set apart a room for Frank who is very popular at Edgbaston'.[41] By mid November 1854 he could inform Mrs. J. W. Bowden that six of seven bedrooms in his house were taken. It was a disappointment when Harry Bowden decided not to accept the seventh place, but Newman told Manning that he was hoping Francis Scawen Blunt would take it. Blunt's mother was a rich convert of 1852 and her two boys had recently been at Stonyhurst and Oscott. In the event the elder Blunt was unable to take up the place at Dublin. Of the boys in Newman's house only one was an Irishman—Sir Reginald Barnewell. In December 1854 Newman was preparing to accommodate yet another member of the aristocracy, the fifteen-year-old son of the Countess de la Pasture, a cousin of Lisle Phillipps. In the same month he had to decline to take Arthur Wilberforce because his house was then full up, and he added 'he may well wait at Ushaw some time. I am to have in my house 2 English, 2 Scotch, 2 Irish, and 2 French.'[42] The English youths were Henry Ryder and Victor Duke, the Scots were Lord Ralph Kerr and Francis Kerr, the Irish were Sir Reginald Barnewell and Ernest O'Meagher (whose father had Spanish connections

[39] *Newman Letters*, Newman to William Dodsworth, 18 Aug. 1854.
[40] Ibid., Newman to George Ryder, 17 Aug. 1854.
[41] Ibid., Newman to Lord Henry Kerr, 8 Nov. 1854.
[42] Ibid., Newman to Henry Wilberforce, 20 Dec. 1854.

and lived in Paris), and the French youths were Charles de la Pasture and Vicomte Louis de Vaulchier. In the February of the following year there was rumour that William Constable-Maxwell of Everingham (heir to Lord Herries) might be admitted to Newman's house. Newman was determined to surround himself with youths of the upper classes to whom he considered he had a special mission. 'I ought to be very thankful at the style of youths I have got', he informed Mrs. Bowden in January 1855.[43]

We are fortunate in possessing two vivid eyewitness accounts of St. Mary's, one from an inmate of the house and the other from a student at the less fashionable St. Patrick's. Vicomte Louis de Vaulchier testifies that the life he led 'under the immediate guidance of Cardinal (then Father) Newman, was as like to Oxford life as the Cardinal dared to allow, for the Irish bishops did not approve of it in the least'. He goes on: 'We were never more than ten or twelve pupils, and were rather scoffed at, being the aristocracy of the new University. The Cardinal was Dean of residence, and Sir Peter (le Page Renouf), tutor, to whom we referred all difficulties, as well in our studies as in all other matters. . . . We attended lectures pretty regularly at the University House, but were allowed to come and go according to our fancy. Leave was only asked when we missed dinner, or wanted to go out at night. The two other houses then belonging to the Catholic University did not enjoy much liberty, and consequently we were not very well spoken of. Some of us went out hunting, almost all rowing, in the day.'[44]

John Augustus O'Shea was at St. Patrick's House. Among the houses, he writes, 'were St. Patrick's or the parent house on St. Stephen's Green, and St. Mary's House, No. 6, Harcourt Street, presided over by the Rector of the University, Dr. Newman. St. Mary's was the swell house, a sort of fellow-commoners' preserve. The personages were there, and it was quite a thing for us, St. Patrick's men, to be noticed by them. It was Dr. Newman's idea to frame the new Academy as nearly as he could on the model

[43] Ibid., Newman to Mrs. J. W. Bowden, 11 Jan. 1855.

[44] Rylands, W. H., Maspero, G., and Neville, E. (eds.), *The Life Work of Sir Peter le Page Renouf*, First Series, vol. 4, pp. 1–11.

of that English University of which he had been so distinguished
an ornament.'[45] O'Shea remembered 'the pure-minded, high-
spirited array of youths' who 'bore the gentleman's escutcheon
aloft and unstained'.

But things did not always run smoothly in Newman's own
special preserve. Possessive by nature, he demanded unquestioned
and total devotion to himself. In 1855 he made it clear that his
youths were not to have a private life of their own which was not
laid open to his inspection. Francis Kerr, he complained, was
extravagant; skating was a temptation, and the youth had been
to two concerts 'under the charge of ladies he knew'.[46] He ought
to get his books and also his clothes through Newman. In April
Newman was frightened concerning four of his charges—Ralph
Kerr, who was not in good health and who must be idle, 'Francis
(Kerr) *is* idle, Frederic Thynne *wishes to be* idle, and Reginald
(Barnewell), if not idle, loves amusement.'[47] Thynne, the son of
Lord Charles Thynne, was seventeen years of age, and had been
hardly a month with Newman before the latter sent him away,
because 'he has already begun corrupting my youths, if they could
be corrupted'.[48] The charge against Thynne is vague and Newman's sentence must not be interpreted literally. It is likely that
the young man was merely a rebel against authority, disliking the
hothouse atmosphere of St. Mary's, and that he failed to succumb
to Newman's personal magnetism. Going from Dublin to the
Oratory, he was placed under the care of Fr. Nicholas Darnell for
a time, who said 'he is quite like an Eton boy and exhibits nothing
bad—no inclination to the Town or spending money'.[49] In July
of the same year Newman encouraged Francis Kerr to attend 'a
sort of fete of the Lord Lieutenant's . . . in the Lodge Gardens',[50]
a fact not unnoticed by the Irish youths of St. Patrick's.

In the summer of 1855 George Ryder quarrelled violently

[45] O'Shea, John Augustus, *War Correspondent, Roundabout Recollections*, vol.
I, pp. 92–124, and esp. pp. 95–101.
[46] *Newman Letters*, Newman to Lord Henry Kerr, 2 Mar. 1855.
[47] Ibid., Newman to F. S. Bowles, 7 Apr. 1855.
[48] Ibid., Newman to Stanislas Flanagan, 24 May 1855.
[49] Ibid., see Dessain's n. 1, p. 470.
[50] Ibid., Newman to Lady Henry Kerr, 1 July 1855.

with Newman over his two sons, accusing the Rector of coming between him and them. The incident was unpleasant and Newman was charged with duplicity. There is little doubt that a close personal affection had grown up between Henry Ryder and Newman, and that the latter encouraged the youth when he began to show a desire to enter the Oratory. Newman pointed out to him that 'personal attachment to the members of the Congregation (unlike the case of a religious vocation), is one of the marks of an Oratorian vocation'.[51] George Ryder removed both his boys from Newman's influence, not regarding it as healthy. Miss Trevor does not give the full story of the Ryder incident, assuming it was merely the outcome of a quarrel concerning the difficulties Lisle Ryder was having with prompt rising in the mornings.[52]

Newman did not take advice or reproof easily. Culler relates that 'at Oxford it was young Mr. Newman who protested to Copleston about the conduct of the gentlemen-commoners, but here it was Dr. Cullen who protested to him—and with no better avail'.[53] Cullen objected to men from St. Mary's going to plays, and hunting in full livery—it was bad example for the less-affluent students and not good publicity for a University relying for its existence upon the pennies of the poor. But Newman took no action. The cultivation of acceptable tastes and the development of polite conversation, acquired in associating with the best Irish society, led to the cultivation of the art of the drawing-room and those easily recognizable traits of the man of 'philosophic habit'.[54] One of the reasons why students of the University were not permitted to study Science until they had spent at least two years in the study of the Humanities was that Newman viewed Science as a great instrument of social change. As most students left the University after two years, Science was not needed.

Newman's personal interests in his students did not extend to the Irish middle-class youths, resident in the other houses. In January 1855 he told J. Walker of Scarborough that of the students in his own house 'all of them are gentlemen',[55] whereas

---

[51] Ibid., Newman to Henry (Ignatius) Dudley Ryder, 25 Sept. 1855.
[52] Trevor, *Light in Winter*, p. 67. [53] Culler, p. 165. [54] Ibid., p. 200.
[55] *Newman Letters*, Newman to J. Walker of Scarborough, 8 Jan. 1855.

of those 'in the University House nearly all are Irish'. 'As far as I can make out,' he wrote, 'they have a number of good youths in the University House too.' The remark contains an overtone of surprise. Two months later[56] he informed Bishop Thomas Grant of Southwark that he could speak 'with great confidence' of the students in his own house. He considered 'that of the many blessings with which we have been favoured here, the greatest is the set of youths who make up my own house . . .'. 'And it is most important,' he added, 'for, as you know, the Irish love rank and that sort of thing, and the example of youths, such as those of whom I have charge, being attentive to their duties, gentle and modest, has great influence on the whole body.' With regard to the thirty or forty students as a whole he could only say 'I do trust they are in a state of grace, and going on hopefully'. Daniel O'Connell, grandson of the great Emancipator, was a student at the Catholic University from 1854, residing at the University House; there is no record that Newman ever noticed him.[57]

56 Ibid., Newman to Bishop Thomas Grant of Southwark, 20 Mar. 1855.
57 See *Catholic University Gazette*, 1 Feb. 1855, pp. 320–3.

IV

ACADEMIC DEVELOPMENTS

NEWMAN, resolving on beginning the University with considerable publicity, occupied 1854 and 1855 in inviting prominent laymen to place their names on the University Books. In May 1854 he informed Edward Badeley that this policy would receive priority when he formally assumed the Rectorship. A month later he wrote to Sir John Acton, a student in Munich under Döllinger, asking for the use of his name, and requesting help in securing the names of Friedrich Heinrich Windischmann and George Phillipps as well as that of Döllinger himself. Hope-Scott and Badeley promised to send soon 'a number of London names, such as Lord Arundell and Surrey'.[1] George Talbot gave his name and agreed to obtain those of a variety of prominent Roman ecclesiastics and scholars.

Of greatest moment for Newman, however, were the names of English aristocrats. In June 1854, barely a month after he received the promise of Hope-Scott and Badeley that they would secure such names for him, Newman was agitated and nervous, complaining of being 'left in the lurch' by them.[2] He wrote to Manning to beg the latter's help. Manning's task was to secure the support of Lords Campden, Arundell and Surrey, Arundell of Wardour, Edward Howard, Kenmare, Castlerosse, Lovat, Stafford, Dormer, Fingall, and Vaux of Harrowden, together with that of Sir John Simeon, Maxwell of Everingham, and Stonor, as well as the support of converts like Bellasis and Bowyer. In fact Newman informs Manning that '*any* Catholic noblemen, or gentlemen of good name, will do'.[3] Manning, who permitted his own name to be inscribed, was only partially successful. Lords Kenmare, Castlerosse, Fingall, Lovat, Dormer, Vaux of Harrowden, Arundell of

---

[1] *Newman Letters*, Newman to Acton, 5 June 1854.
[2] Ibid., Newman to Manning, 13 June 1854.   [3] Ibid.

Wardour, and Edward Howard refused their support. This did not presage well for the future of the University, as Newman had conceived it.

On the same day as the Rector wrote to Manning, he wrote to Ambrose Lisle Phillipps and inquired whether the latter knew among his Catholic friends of any 'who intend to send their sons to us'.[4] Bishop Brown of Newport and Menevia was asked for 'the names of any noblemen, country gentlemen, or literary men', as well as for students.[5] Newman was particularly anxious to include Irish noblemen among his sponsors, and he informed Mgr. George Talbot that he was seeking 'the adhesion of gentlemen who have supported the Queen's Colleges'.[6] Newman's action in compiling a list of honorary members of the University was sanctioned by the Irish bishops in Synod on 18 May 1854. The scheme, however, was not viewed with complete episcopal favour, and Newman claimed that at Rome 'they gave it no countenance'.[7]

In January 1854, in a letter to Cardinal Wiseman, Newman indicated that the initial appointments in the University would be held by persons 'whom I entirely know'.[8] These would be the real university teachers. They would be aided by popular lecturers and preachers, who would provide 'an external manifestation' for the 'inward and real *formation*' of the institution. Thomas Scratton, Newman's secretary and an English convert to Rome, was later to testify that no one could work with Newman unless the latter's ideas were accepted without question, and if they were not 'he took no notice of you, being of no use to him'.[9] Professor Corcoran has maintained that by 1854 Newman had settled on having 'all the leading members of his Oxford group' in Dublin,[10] and of reconstituting a circle in which he would be focal point, inspiration, and guide. It was an idyllic dream. W. G. Ward, in 1854, was offered the Chair of the Philosophy of Religion. He

[4] *Newman Letters*, Newman to Lisle Phillipps, 23 June 1854.

[5] Ibid., Newman to Bishop Brown, 17 June 1854.

[6] Ibid., Newman to Talbot, In festo Apostolorum, 1854.

[7] Tristram, Henry (ed.), *John Henry Newman: Autobiographical Writings*, pp. 324–6. [8] *Newman Letters*, Newman to Wiseman, 23 Jan. 1854.

[9] Stockley, W. F., *Newman, Education, and Ireland*, p. 203 n.

[10] Corcoran, *Newman: Selected Discourses, etc.*, p. lv.

took a fortnight to consider, before declining. Henry William Wilberforce, fourth son of the emancipator of the slaves, was offered the Chair of Political Science. He had graduated from Oriel College, Oxford, in 1830, and had entered Lincoln's Inn, before taking Orders in the Church of England. After becoming a Roman Catholic in 1850 he engaged in religious controversy, and, in 1852, was Secretary to the Catholic Defence Association. From 1854 until 1863 he was proprietor and editor of *The Catholic Standard*. In 1854, when Newman suggested the Chair of Political Science for him, it appeared a most odd recommendation, not least to the proposed appointee himself. Wilberforce was left, however, under no illusion. The professorship was to be held 'on *my* understanding of the subject', wrote Newman, and it would embrace 'a *practical* view' of the discipline. Wilberforce played for time, and for a suitable opportunity to decline a Chair for which he had no appetite. Newman was hurt and suspected a personal insult. He wrote to Wilberforce a letter replete with wild accusations of imagined slights in the past. In the event Wilberforce declined to join the staff of the University. James Spencer Northcote and Henry Edward Manning similarly resisted Newman's overtures.[11]

Shortly after Newman was placed in possession of his office, he wrote to T. W. Allies to inquire 'if there is any way in which you can be connected with us', and he offered him as a possible province the 'Philosophy of History'.[12] In a letter to Cullen of 3 October 1854 Newman included the name of Allies as Lecturer in the Philosophy of History. In March of the following year Allies was appointed to the Chair of Modern History, a subject joined with that of the Philosophy of History for the purpose. The appointment led to Allies's writing his important work, *The Formation of Christendom*. In 1855 Allies wrote in his Journal: 'if the Philosophy of History be not exactly the subject I should have chosen, it lends itself at least to the illustration of the Church and its ἔργον in the world, the one subject of predilection to my mind.'[13]

[11] Ward, W., *Life of Newman*, vol. 1, p. 319.
[12] *Newman Letters*, Newman to T. W. Allies, 18 May 1854.
[13] Allies, Mary H., *Thomas William Allies*, p. 78.

The academic post, although soon terminated, provided the intellectual stimulus which Allies felt he desperately needed. He diagnosed his own difficulty. 'My malady', he declared, 'has been that I have a mind and education above my station. I can trace distinctly the influence of Eton on the whole character of my thoughts. If I valued birth, wealth, and station for anything, it would be for the power of choosing one's associates.'[14] Allies gave up his course shortly after it had begun, because of a dearth of students. He had found himself in a position analogous to that of the future Archbishop Croke of Cashel, who was appointed Professor of Canon Law, only to find that he had no students.

Robert Ornsby had feelings similar to those of Allies when he accepted Newman's offer of the Chair of Greek and Latin Literature in 1854. He graduated from Lincoln College, Oxford, in 1840 and three years later became a Fellow of Trinity. He eventually held the college office of Lecturer in Rhetoric and the university post of Master of the Schools. A curate for a time at St. Olave's, Chichester, he became a Roman Catholic in 1847. Thereafter he assisted Frederick Lucas with the direction of *The Tablet*. Ornsby was one of Newman's more successful appointments. After the latter's departure from Ireland he entered the service of the Duke of Norfolk, first as private tutor and then as Librarian at Arundel Castle, but in 1874 he returned to the Catholic University as Professor of Classics. In 1882, when the Senate of the Royal University was formed, Ornsby was elected Fellow and appointed Examiner in Greek. He died in Dublin in 1889. Ornsby edited the *Memoirs* of Hope-Scott in 1884, and it was on his advice that Newman desisted in his efforts to attract to a lecturership another distinguished convert, Frederick Apthorp Paley. The latter, a Cambridge convert of 1846 and renowned for an edition of Aeschylus (1844–7), was considered by both Ornsby and Newman to be recommending books for study 'exceptionable on the ground of faith and morals'.[15]

Other converts were to be accommodated. Perhaps the most

14 Allies, Mary H., *Thomas William Allies*, p. 79.

15 *Newman Letters*, Newman to Ornsby, 19 July 1854, and Ornsby to Newman, 26 July 1854.

distinguished of them was Thomas Arnold, second son of Arnold of Rugby. He had enjoyed a varied career after graduating at University College, Oxford, in 1845. In 1846 he entered Lincoln's Inn, and the following year became a clerk in the Colonial Office. He went to New Zealand in 1847 and opened a school there two years later. From 1850 to 1856 he was Inspector of Schools in Tasmania, at the end of which period he became a Roman Catholic. Newman proposed to appoint him to the Chair of English Literature in the Catholic University. Initially, Archbishop Cullen opposed the idea, because the expenses of the University seemed to be getting out of control. Once, however, he perceived Newman's determination, the Archbishop gave way to him. Arnold took up the appointment in 1856 and remained until 1862, when Newman enticed him to Edgbaston in order that he might have a good Classics master for the Oratory school.

John Hungerford Pollen was appointed in 1855 as first Professor of Fine Arts, and he built the University Church in St. Stephen's Green. Old Etonian, Student of Christ Church and Fellow of Merton, he was curate at St. Peter-le-Bailey, Oxford, and St. Saviour's, Leeds, before returning to Oxford to become Senior Proctor in 1851. The following year he was received into the Roman Church. Of a background similar to that of these men were Peter le Page Renouf and William Henry Anderdon. Renouf, of French extraction, was born on Guernsey and educated at Pembroke College, Oxford. He became a Roman Catholic in 1842, and was offered a post at Dublin chiefly in order to attract his pupil to the University, Vicomte Louis de Vaulchier. Renouf was Professor of Ancient History and Geography from 1855 until 1864, and then of Eastern Languages. He testifies that he accepted Newman's offer because the invitation 'had all the precious Oxford associations to lend it weight'.[16]

William Henry Anderdon had a more curious background. A nephew of Manning, he graduated at Oxford in 1839 and then held two curacies in the Church of England, at Withyham in Sussex, and at Reigate. In 1846 he became Vicar of St. Margaret's-with-Knighton, Leicester, and four years later was received into

[16] Rylands, W. H., Maspero, G., and Neville, E. (eds.), vol. 4, p. xlvii.

the Roman Catholic Church by Père de Ravignan, in the chapel of Notre Dame de Sion, Paris. There followed a course of theology in Rome and ordination as a Roman Catholic priest at Oscott in 1853. He was appointed to the staff of Ushaw College, where he gained a reputation as preacher and polemicist. It was this reputation which led Newman to appoint Anderdon to what he considered to be the most important post in the new University, that of permanent Chaplain of the University Church. Anderdon, who had considerable wealth, threw himself energetically into the task, and spent a substantial part of his private fortune on supplementing the deficiencies of the church. He entered into the spirit of Irish life and made numerous friends among clergy and laity. Refusing to confine his attention to University duties, he made many friends, too, among the poor, was in great demand as a preacher, and became an ardent supporter of Irish charities. Cullen at first viewed Anderdon's appointment with suspicion— surely an Irish priest could have been found for such a post! But Anderdon's genial and friendly personality and his sincerity of purpose made a strong appeal to the Irish heart and soon over- came prejudice. Unfortunately, the qualities acceptable to the Irish elicited but a sour response from Newman. Jealous of Cullen's friendship with Anderdon, he told Stanislas Flanagan of the Oratory that the Archbishop was 'hand in glove' with Anderdon. He added with some asperity: 'He can't do too much for him, asks him to dinner, does not (thank my stars) ask me.'[17] Later the animosity became more pronounced. 'Somehow [Anderdon] associates me with a bore—I don't know why', Newman wrote. 'This is no fancy. I did not tell you that on one occasion, when I dare say I *did* bore him, he was quite rude. I should think he is a petted and spoilt fellow and he is now in his element, for the ladies are all about him, filling him with sympathy and mutton chops.'[18] Unfortunately, Anderdon refused to succumb to Newman's charm; it was a sin from which he was never to be absolved.

Newman promised a Cambridge convert, Fr. Henry Johnston Marshall, a post as Dean of Residence. Marshall, a convert of

[17] Trevor, *Light in Winter*, pp. 153–4.   [18] Ibid., p. 154.

1845, had worked as a priest in Cork and Dublin. The appointment did not materialize, because of Cullen's alarm at the nomination of yet another English convert to a post which could easily be filled by an Irishman. In reviewing appointments of this kind, it must have occurred to Cullen, as it certainly did to Archbishop MacHale, that Newman was packing the University with those elements most likely to achieve the dual purpose, of effectively keeping to a minimum the Irish element in staff and students on the one hand, and of increasing the likelihood of obtaining English youths from aristocratic and affluent families on the other. There would, in addition, be little likelihood of convert Englishmen's looking for direction to what was for them an alien episcopacy. Newman would be the central figure, bound by ties too deep to be severed.

It has often been asserted by Newman's apologists that he was forced to rely on convert Englishmen and Scotsmen to staff the Irish Catholic University, because there was no adequate Irish talent readily available. Wilfrid Ward first propagated the myth that Cullen wanted a University composed of priests 'owing him strict obedience' and whose intellectual equipment 'was a matter of secondary importance'.[19] But in a letter to the Countess Granville in December 1854 Newman was compelled to admit that 'it is not wonderful, considering that Ireland has contributed, and will contribute, the greater part of the Funds, that Irishmen should be unwilling to see appointments made of Englishmen and Scotchmen', and he added that 'the only department in which the Irish are not equal, or are inferior to English, is that of classical literature'.[20] Newman reiterated these sentiments in a letter to the Earl of Shrewsbury five months later, pointing out that 'the Irish are competent on most subjects, and, *caeteris paribus*, ought to be taken'.[21] Classics, he asserted, 'are the only province in which Englishmen have a right to be located'. In spite of these remarks, however, Newman failed to appoint Irishmen, not only to positions in Classics, but also in such disciplines as the Philosophy

[19] Ward, W., *Life of Newman*, vol. 1, pp. 366–7.
[20] *Newman Letters*, Newman to the Countess Granville, 8 Dec. 1854.
[21] Ibid., Newman to the Earl of Shrewsbury, 20 Apr. 1855.

of History, Geography, Ancient History, French Language and Literature, English Literature, Italian, Spanish, and the Fine Arts.

It cannot be said that Cullen behaved autocratically towards Newman in the matter of appointments. In April 1852, when the nomination of Allies was contemplated, he gently advised caution, declaring 'we have here a set of newspaper editors and others who are trying to excite prejudices against everything English; we must avoid giving them any motive to attack us for a while longer'.[22] But in 1854 Newman indicated his real motive in appointing Englishmen. Naïvely he told Cullen that 'in preferring Englishmen I shall carry with me the very class from which we are to get our students'.[23] On 30 September 1854 Cullen cautioned Newman, quoting Hope-Scott to the effect that things ought to begin in a small way and gradually. Hope-Scott had insisted 'on the necessity of making every one understand that everything done about the University was still at a distance'.[24] The Archbishop advised against the appointment of James Stewart, a graduate of Aberdeen and Cambridge, as Lecturer in Ancient History. 'The Scotch are looked on by the people at large as their worst enemies,' Cullen wrote, 'and it is the policy of the gentry to introduce as many Scotch as possible in the country.'[25] Newman persisted in the appointment of Stewart and of two other Scotsmen, J. B. Robertson to a lecturership in Geography and E. H. Thompson as lecturer in English Literature. Although protesting that he loved and venerated his Grace, the Rector was determined that 'he who has the *responsibility*, should have the *power*'.[26]

Serious difficulty concerning appointments was avoided until Newman began to nominate Young Irelanders and, in one case, a supporter of Young Italy, to posts. The latter was Augustus Caesar Marani, who had taken a prominent part in the movement for a United Italy and who was Professor of Italian at Trinity College, Dublin. In October 1854 Marani was offered the Chair

---

[22] MacSuibhne, vol. 2, p. 126.
[23] *Newman Letters*, Newman to Cullen, 18 June 1854.
[24] Ibid., Cullen to Newman, 30 Sept. 1854.
[25] Ibid.   [26] Ibid., Newman to Cullen, 1 Oct. 1854.

of Italian and Spanish at the Catholic University. Cullen had been in Rome in 1849 when Pius IX excommunicated those members of Young Italy who had taken part in invading Church property, and he had witnessed the flight of the Pope to Gaeta. He had also been present in Rome when Count Rossi was assassinated. Yet Cullen made no formal protest against Marani's appointment in 1854. Young Italy was a thing belonging to past memories; Young Ireland was very much a present danger. Cardinal Moran, Cullen's nephew, summed up his uncle's attitude admirably. 'He condemned the Young Irelanders as sources of dissension and a source of ruin to the Irish cause', he wrote.[27] Cullen was assured that constitutional means ought to be adopted in redressing Irish grievances. Because of his attitude the Archbishop was subjected to a series of bitter attacks in *The Nation*. The Young Irelanders, especially Duffy and Lucas, spread the report that Cullen was prepared to sell the cause of Ireland for the sake of a charter for the new University. Cullen, strenuously denying the charge, urged the clergy to give no support to the Young Ireland party. On the 12th of January 1855 he declared in a letter to Newman: 'I trust you will make every exertion to keep the university free from all Young Irelandism, of which the spirit is so evident in *The Nation*.'[28] Séan O'Faoláin has found it significant of Cullen's greatness, of a man who 'stood head and shoulders above his contemporaries in Great Britain', that he was able to admire the *literary* work of the Young Irelanders while distrusting their politics and polemical spirit. In replying to Cullen's letter of the 12th of January, however, Newman made it clear that he did not feel there was any harm in employing men who had formerly been active among the Young Irelanders, adding 'I trust most earnestly that politics will not come into the university'.[29] There were six major University appointments which Newman was preparing to allocate to Young Irelanders. In two cases only was Cullen to express serious dissatisfaction. The men involved were Denis Florence McCarthy, Eugene O'Curry, John O'Hagan,

[27] Quoted in MacSuibhne, vol. 1, p. 56.
[28] Ibid., pp. 381 seq.
[29] Ibid., p. 383, Newman to Cullen, 29 Jan. 1855.

William Kirby Sullivan, John Edward Pigot, and Charles Gavan Duffy.

McCarthy, born of Roman Catholic parents, was educated at Maynooth, where he had been destined for the Church. He then studied for the Bar. In 1843 he was a vigorous supporter of the Repeal Movement and was to be a regular contributor to *The Nation*. His well-known political verse was published over the name 'Desmond'. In 1845 he was a keen advocate of the Provincial Colleges Bill, opposing in harsh language those bishops who were against the measure. When the Repeal Association, however, was disrupted in 1846, he gave his grudging allegiance to the O'Connell party and ceased to be an extreme polemicist. Seven years later Newman offered him a lecturership in Literature at the Catholic University. This he accepted, but resigned after delivering three lectures.

O'Curry was a very different man. Son of a farmer, he had worked on the paternal holding while giving his spare time to local Irish studies. His opportunity came in 1834, when he was employed by the organizers of the topographical and historical section of the Ordnance Survey of Ireland. He was given the chance of meeting a number of famous men and of gaining first-hand experience in the study of manuscripts, a study which took him to Dublin, London, and Oxford. He began next to earn his living by copying and examining such manuscripts, and in 1855 he was named Professor of Irish History and Archaeology in the Catholic University. This was a good appointment and Newman, it is said, attended all his lectures. O'Curry's work laid the foundations for a genuine study of early Irish history. Although associated with Young Ireland he was more of a romantic than a politician, and never an active member of the movement.

More involved with Young Ireland than either O'Curry or McCarthy was John O'Hagan, whom Newman appointed to a lecturership in Political Economy in 1854. Born in Ulster and educated at Trinity College, Dublin, O'Hagan was called to the Irish Bar in 1842 and worked on the Munster circuit. He was an outspoken member of the movement and, six years before Newman encountered him, he had appeared in public as one of the counsel for the defence at the trial of Gavan Duffy. He composed and wrote many patriotic songs.

William Kirby Sullivan was born near Cork in 1821 and showed an early interest in science. He studied chemistry at Giessan in Liebig's laboratory, and after his return to Ireland took up an appointment in 1846 in the Museum of Irish Industry in Dublin. Ten years later he was Newman's choice for the Chair of Chemistry. He was a supporter of Young Ireland, and in 1873 became President of the Queen's College, Cork.

Cullen did not raise any objection to the engaging of these four men. It is often implied that the Archbishop opposed the employment of *all* who had even a remote connection with Young Ireland. This was not so. In 1854 Cullen wrote to Newman from Rome, urging that the latter should engage McCarthy in writing some commemorative verse in honour of the recently proclaimed Dogma of the Immaculate Conception. He also asked that O'Curry might be employed in the task of assembling 'some old Irish documents connected with devotion to the Blessed Virgin'.[30] Cullen was friendly with both McCarthy and O'Curry; the latter frequently dined with him. According to Patrick M. Mac-Sweeney's testimony, O'Curry was 'a frequent and honoured guest' at Cullen's table, and it was the Archbishop who celebrated O'Curry's requiem Mass.[31] John O'Hagan, although early associated with the Young Irelanders, proved to be a strong supporter of Cullen on education issues, and a firm opponent of the 'godless' Colleges and of Trinity College, Dublin. He was selected by Cullen in 1876 to draw up his will. Sullivan, too, was on friendly terms with the Archbishop, although he had been a keen supporter of the 1848 rising.

When Cullen remonstrated, therefore, against the employment in the University of Young Irelanders, he was, in effect, protesting against two men. Of these two, the appointment of one, we are told, was expressly forbidden by Cullen; the other appointment by force of circumstances never materialized. The two men were Charles Gavan Duffy and John Edward Pigot.

[30] MacSuibhne, vol. 2, p. 178, Cullen to Newman, 20 Dec. 1854.
[31] Ibid., vol. 1, pp. 43, 393; vol. 2, p. 182.

Duffy was the leader of the Young Irelanders and, in the very year when Newman proposed to appoint him to the Chair of Modern History, was conducting a virulent personal campaign against Cullen. Gavan Duffy had been founder-editor of *The Nation* and perhaps the leading figure responsible for the rising of 1848. With Frederick Lucas he established the Tenant League. Duffy openly praised the work of Kossuth and Mazzini in the pages of *The Nation* in 1849 and urged Irishmen to adopt them as models. He tells the story of his appointment in *My Life in Two Hemispheres*. 'It soon leaked out', he writes,' that Dr. Newman proposed to invite me to become Professor of Modern History, but Dr. Cullen peremptorily objected.'[32] We have only Duffy's word for the fact that Cullen was responsible for the change in Newman's plan, and in view of Duffy's bitter lifelong animosity to the Archbishop it is possible that he ascribed the prohibition to the quarter from whence he felt it must have emanated. Newman himself, however, may have been nervous at putting before the assembled bishops the name of so militant a revolutionary for the Chair in Modern History, a subject which would lend itself to a more than sympathetic treatment of the continental revolutionary and anti-clerical movements at the hands of an admirer of Kossuth. Newman asserted that Cullen believed that such revolutionaries could never come right.[33] But if Cullen did so forcibly express his views he did not act upon them. In 1875, after Gavan Duffy had passed twenty years of self-imposed exile in Australia, it was Cullen who was active in the movement to set up an association on the Old Repeal principles, and who was eager to establish a daily paper as its organ. Gavan Duffy was urged to assume control of the enterprise.[34] He did not accept the proffered olive-branch.

John Edward Pigot was born in 1822, the son of Chief Baron Pigot. Called to the Bar in 1845, he early became one of the most important of the younger men in the Young Ireland movement. Newman expended considerable effort in trying to persuade him

---

[32] Duffy, Sir Charles Gavan, *My Life in Two Hemispheres* (London, 1898), vol. 2, pp. 26–7.

[33] Tristram, pp. 328–9.   [34] Duffy, vol. 2, p. 365.

to accept the Chair of Practical Law, but Pigot was suspicious of the strong English influence he could discern in the establishment. According to a letter which Scratton wrote to Newman on 1 March 1855, it was but 'after long deliberation'[35] that Pigot decided to accede to Newman's request, and even then he stipulated that he would work for the University only if it was not to be a vehicle of English domination. The offer fell through because of Newman's decision not to establish a Faculty of Law after all. Pigot, a poet busily engaged in composing lyrics for the Young Irelanders, was a personal friend of Gavan Duffy, and a keen supporter of *The Nation*. In Newman's *Memorandum about my connection with the Catholic University*, written in extreme old age, he acknowledged that Pigot 'talked like a republican' and 'was full of views', that 'he had said and done a number of wild things', and that 'he was a fanatic even then' when he was invited to participate in the University.[36] In the very month, April 1855, when Newman was seriously considering Pigot's appointment, he pointed out to Bishop David Moriarty that Pigot 'has very definite political views'.[37] It is scarcely to be wondered at, therefore, that Cullen should have been alarmed at the prospect of this appointment. It seemed incongruous to the bishops that men such as Pigot, who had been so vociferously in favour of the Queen's Colleges precisely because those establishments upheld the principle of 'mixed' education, should be appointed to Chairs and lecturerships in the Catholic University the foundation of which was specifically designed to offset the influence of the 'godless colleges'. After all, 'mixed' education was inextricably bound up with the aspirations of the chief writers in *The Nation*, because it seemed a sure way of bringing Irishmen together in the forging of a strong political entity less subject to credal division.

An integral part of Newman's academic policy was to attract to the University by the offer of professorships and lecturerships a certain number of men who would provide 'the external manifestations' of 'the inward formation' of the institution. These men would form the spectacular element of the University;

---

[35] Letter quoted in MacSuibhne, vol. 1, p. 385.   [36] Tristram, pp. 328–9.
[37] *Newman Letters*, Newman to Moriarty, 2 Apr. 1855.

they would attract English students by their name and reputation. Many would be expected to give but a short course of lectures from time to time. In his choice of such men Newman was again to be singularly unfortunate. Pride of place among them must be given to Orestes Augustus Brownson, who in 1853 was offered a lecturership in Geography. Brownson, born in Vermont in 1803, was mystic, philosopher, ecstatic, and enthusiast, and was destined to undergo no fewer than six changes of religion. In 1844 he had founded *Brownson's Quarterly Review*, a journal which soon developed into a bitterly polemical organ against all manifestations of Protestantism. By 1854 he had evinced strong anti-Irish prejudices and evoked the ire of a number of American prelates, not least Archbishop Patrick Francis Kenrick of Baltimore, Archbishop John Hughes of New York, and Dr. Michael O'Connor, Bishop of Pittsburg. Brownson, who had earlier assailed Newman's development of doctrine theory, was not enamoured of the idea of teaching geography in Dublin, and in June 1854 Newman was inclined to accommodate him. He offered Brownson the Chair of the Philosophy of Religion, which 'would open upon you the fields of logic and of history, in both of which you are so well practised'.[38] Brownson accepted the offer in July 1854, subject to the approval of the Bishop of Boston and to securing a satisfactory successor as editor of *Brownson's Quarterly Review*. Brownson eventually decided to appoint his son to edit the *Review*, and for this purpose recalled him from Munich, where he had been a fellow student of Acton. By August, however, Newman had heard disturbing accounts of Brownson's indiscretions from both Cullen (who enclosed a letter from one of the agents of the University collecting money in the United States) and Dr. James Taylor. The Rector was considerably alarmed at the episcopal and national feelings which had been outraged in America. He wrote at once a firm but polite letter asking Brownson to desist in his plan to come to Dublin, in view of the communications he had received from different places, 'which have perplexed me very much, as well as surprised me'.[39] The letter was

---

[38] *Newman Letters*, Newman to Brownson, 6 June 1854.
[39] Ibid., Newman to Brownson, 23 Aug. 1854.

courteous and talked of 'postponement', but the recipient could
have been in little doubt that this was merely a gentle way of
indicating that the appointment would now be totally inexpedient. It is not strictly accurate to make the assertion, as Miss
Trevor does, that 'it was Brownson, not Newman, who cried
off in the end'.[40] Brownson was in the act of preparing to journey
to Dublin when Newman wrote to prevent his coming. Newman
made his own position quite clear, and Brownson would have
been singularly myopic not to have read between the lines of the
letter he had received.

At the end of 1853, when Newman was first contacting
Brownson, he was also in touch with Dr. Johann Joseph Ignaz
von Döllinger, asking him to assist the University 'if only for a
time'. For much of the negotiation Newman used the services of
Döllinger's pupil, Sir John Acton, but even so, in July 1854 he
encountered a refusal. Döllinger was unable 'to discover a way,
by which, without neglecting duties nearer home, I might make
myself serviceable at Dublin'.[41] Newman persisted in hoping to
appoint Döllinger to the Chair of Ecclesiastical History, writing
'you cannot be *certain* that a little time hence, say this time two
years, you might not be able to help us'.[42] Six weeks after this
letter was written Newman was explaining to Cullen that he had
always considered Döllinger to be 'an *historian*, not a theologian',
and that he had 'not quite the circle of opinions, which would
be called Ultramontane'.[43] One of the interesting facts which
emerges from Newman's appointments is that he had a need
to surround himself with men whose theological views were
practically Gallican in tone—men such as Ornsby, Edward
Butler (whom Newman desired to make his Vice-Rector), and
Renouf. As these men were out of sympathy with the views of
by far the greater part of the Irish hierarchy, it is surprising that
the bishops showed as much tolerance as they did.

It was through the agency of Acton that Newman hoped to

---

[40] Trevor, *Light in Winter*, p. 54.
[41] Letter given in full, in *Newman Letters*, vol. 16, pp. 225–6 n. 1.
[42] *Newman Letters*, Newman to Döllinger, 18 Aug. 1854.
[43] Ibid., Newman to Cullen, 1 Oct. 1854.

attract men of the calibre of Döllinger, Brownson, Windishmann, Gratry, and Montalembert to the Irish University. Such international recognition was a vital part of his policy in counteracting the plans of the Irish hierarchy. There is little doubt that Acton, whom Cardinal Barnabo was years afterwards to refer to as the great 'birbonaccio', was a key figure in Newman's early strategy.[44] In 1854, however, Acton was but twenty years of age and time would have to elapse before the Rector could advance his name for a Chair. Dr. David Mathew has written that 'coming from the Oxford of an earlier and mellow day, Dr. Newman was incapable of taking seriously the mechanism of a University conceived in the decade of the Exhibition', and adds that 'at his age and with his background Acton could have but little patience with the bending misty Toryism and the tentative and uncompleted Oxford prejudice'.[45] In fact, there was really little in common between the youthful scholar of twenty and the ageing convert of fifty-three. By 1858 Acton was far removed from the aspirations of many of the chief converts. 'I never converse', he wrote to Richard Simpson, 'with any even of the best and cleverest converts, Dalgairns, Morris, Macmullen, Oakeley, Allies, Marshall, Wilberforce, etc., without finding them stating what I hold to be most false.' But he added: 'Hope and Manning are the only ones that I feel likely on most occasions to agree with.'[46] It was to be expected that Acton would soon reject the influence of Newman. It was not simply that the recklessness of youth and the calculated caution of late middle age were simply irreconcilable, but that Acton was always unable to become any man's disciple. It was a recognition of this trait in his character that was early divined by Newman and led to the latter's growing coolness towards his correspondent. By 1859 Acton had evolved the habit of referring to Newman as 'old Noggs',[47] and Wilfrid Ward has written that at the end of his life Acton had come to regard

[44] J. F. Hogan's review of Wilfrid Ward's *Life of Newman*, in *Irish Ecclesiastical Record* (Feb. 1912), *passim*.

[45] Mathew, David, *Acton: the Formative Years*, p. 115.

[46] Gasquet, Abbot, *Lord Acton and his Circle*, pp. 8–9.

[47] For an account of Acton's growing lack of reverence for Newman see Altholz, J., *The Liberal Catholic Movement in England*, pp. 80 seq.

Newman simply as 'a bad man';[48] he possessed no sympathy for the studiously engineered image of Newman as 'the rainswept personality'.

Acton and Aubrey de Vere were friendly and the latter was a contributor to *The Rambler* under Acton's editorship. De Vere had known 'about Newman's frustrated hopes to edit *The Rambler*'[49] and had sympathized with him. In 1854 he was offered a Chair in the Irish University, but rather surprisingly, the Chair of Political Science and not that of Poetry or Literature. On 12 August 1854 de Vere declined the offer, and pleaded ignorance of the matter he was supposed to teach. A few days later Newman wrote again, and this time switched the offer to that of the Chair of Medieval History, adding 'depend upon it, very few persons have an accurate or comprehensive knowledge of a subject, till they are called on to have it. Every year you will add to your own circle of historical attainments by the stimulus of lecturing'.[50] Manning's aid was enlisted to bring pressure to bear on de Vere. It was unavailing, until in 1856 he finally agreed to give a course of lectures on English Literature. Strongly influenced by Romanticism, de Vere was never to be classed in the first rank of poets. This fact was accounted for by the critic R. H. Hutton, when he wrote that his verse had 'an air of supreme and almost fastidious culture', and that it dealt with themes 'so remote from popular imagination'[51] that it took considerable effort to enter into them. Aubrey de Vere's name was one to be reckoned with among the Irish landed aristocracy, however, and, by means of a close association with him, Newman hoped to attract the attention of Lord Emly and the Earl of Dunraven, de Vere's near neighbours.

James Burton Robertson was offered a lecturership in Geography and Modern History in 1855. He had a considerable European reputation as the translator of Schlegel's *Philosophy of History* and Möhler's *Symbolism*, and he had cultivated the friendship of Lamennais and Gerbet. 'Death's Head' Robertson, as he was

---

[48] Ward Papers. Wilfrid Ward to Mary Drew, 14 Feb. 1903.

[49] Reilly, S. M. Paraclita, *Aubrey de Vere: the Writer and his Time* (Dublin, 1956), p. 95.

[50] *Newman Letters*, Newman to Aubrey de Vere, 21 Aug. 1854.

[51] *The Spectator*, 55 (5 Aug. 1882), p. 1023.

known to his students, belonged to the clan of the Robertsons of Strowan in Perthshire and was the son of a wealthy slave-owner in Granada.

The appointments in Science and Medicine were offered in large measure to active supporters of the Queen's Colleges, men such as Dominic Corrigan, who, at the time when Newman offered him the Chair of the Practice of Medicine, was a Senator of the Queen's University, and Henry Henessy, who was Librarian of Queen's College, Cork, when he was offered the Chair of Natural Philosophy. Edward Butler, of Trinity College, Dublin, who became Newman's Professor of Mathematics, always spoke warmly of the Queen's Colleges and the value of 'mixed' education. Butler was the father of Abbot Cuthbert Butler of Downside (1858–1934), and the latter was strongly influenced by the parental predilections, as is evidenced by his account of the Catholic University project in the *Life of Bishop Ullathorne*.[52] Edward Butler, we are told, 'was devoted to Newman', so devoted in fact that he burned the large dossier of Newman letters in his possession rather than allow Wilfrid Ward to see them.[53] When Abbot Cuthbert Butler came to write his history of the first Vatican Council he was greatly affected by the Newman tradition he had inherited.

Not all of Newman's professors came under his spell to the same extent as Edward Butler, and even he, it has to be admitted, felt that Newman's appointment was 'a misconception and mistake from the beginning'.[54] The Jesuit Edmund Joseph O'Reilly, whom Newman brought from Wales in 1857 to make Professor of Theology, had considerable qualms concerning Newman's concept of Catholic education. He gave expression to these in the columns of *The Month* in 1872. Always exceedingly friendly with the great Oratorian and very much personally influenced by him, he yet felt that Newman's interpretation of university education

[52] Butler, C., *The Life and Times of Bishop Ullathorne, 1806–1889*, vol. 2, pp. 312–13 n. 1.

[53] Ibid. See also MacSuibhne's scathing attack on Butler's judgement in *Paul Cullen and his Contemporaries*, vol. 3, p. 447 n. 18.

[54] Butler, vol. 2, p. 313 n.

was essentially Anglican and outside the main stream of Catholic thought and tradition.

A failure to make allowance for the strength of Irish suscepti-bility is shown in Newman's choice of preachers for the University Church. Not content with establishing an Oxford convert as permanent Chaplain of the Church, he drew up a list of select preachers (on the Oxford pattern) containing twenty-nine names. Of these no fewer than a third were those of converts, Old Catho-lics, and other clergymen working in England. The choice of the Hon. William Clifford and Canon William J. Vaughan was a skil-ful ploy to attract Old Catholic attention. Clifford was a young priest—barely thirty-two years old—at the time of the invitation, and had not, as yet, made a name for himself as an eloquent preacher. But he was the son of the seventh Lord Clifford and had studied at the *Accademia dei Nobili.* The Clifford family had for years been notorious for anti-Irish attitudes, and it was, to say the least, tactless for Newman to advance the name of the future Bishop of Clifton in connection with the University. Canon Vaughan, later to be Bishop of Plymouth, was a somewhat less controversial figure, but one no less acceptable to Old Catholic interests. He was a younger brother of that Vaughan of Court-field who, from among his numerous progeny, was to give to the Church a cardinal, an archbishop, a bishop, a monk, a Jesuit, a secular priest, and four nuns, and who could claim among his grandchildren a bishop in Wales and a superior of the Catholic Missionary Society.

Four of the suggested preachers were Oxford converts—Faber, Dalgairns, Lockhart, and Macmullen. The invitation to Faber and Dalgairns had an ulterior motive. The scandal of the quarrel which had arisen between the London and Birmingham Oratories had widened, and Newman wished to repair the visible crack in the Oratorian image. This action, inviting Faber to preach, must not, however, be interpreted as a peace offering from the one Superior to the other. As Ronald Chapman has pointed out, it was simply Newman's way of doing something to allay the scan-dal, a 'putting on of face' for the benefit of the faithful.[55] In the

[55] Chapman, Ronald, *Father Faber*, p. 285.

event Faber declined to participate in the hypocrisy. The invitation to Dalgairns has to be viewed in connection with the same problem. Richard Gell Macmullen was a priest of the Westminster Archdiocese and formerly Fellow of Corpus Christi College, Oxford. Like William Lockhart, he had been strongly influenced by Newman in Tractarian days. Lockhart, a Rosminian, had left Exeter College to join Newman at Littlemore in 1842. It was his reception into the Catholic Church in the following year that finally impelled the indecisive Newman to resign his own living. Considerable ill feeling existed between the men for some years, for Lockhart had stepped out of line and had pursued his own course. The invitation to preach in Dublin was the first public act of recognition Newman deigned to bestow upon his erstwhile disciple since the latter's defection. Other English priests invited to preach included two of Newman's near neighbours in Birmingham, together with a Rosminian—Fr. Moses Furlong—and Fr. James Chadwick, who in 1866 was to become Bishop of Hexham and Newcastle. In choosing a third of his preachers from outside Ireland, Newman once again gave practical expression to his belief that the Catholic University was intended to be an Imperial foundation.

V

THE RECTOR AND THE BISHOPS

ON 16 April 1851 Newman informed Cullen 'there is nothing at all which I can feel more interest in than the subject of Irish education';[1] six years later he was asking himself 'what special claim had a University, exclusively Irish, upon my time'.[2] That he had conceived of his work at the outset of the venture as a lifelong task is indicated by his desire to establish an Oratorian house in Dublin which would accommodate those of the Birmingham brethren who were nearest and dearest to him. When this proved to be financially inexpedient, he wondered whether he ought to be spending his life 'in the service of those who had not the claim upon me which my own countrymen had'.[3] The experiment in Ireland weakened his faith in papal sagacity. There is not a trace of self-examination in Newman's retrospective notes concerning the Dublin experiment. Because *he* had failed others could not have succeeded. The project had been totally misconceived. If the Pope, he declared, 'had known more of the state of things in Ireland, he would not have taken up the quarrel about the higher education which his predecessor left him, and if he could not religiously recognise the Queen's Colleges, at least would have abstained from decreeing a Catholic University'.[4] In other words, the Pope was to forbid, but was not to make any provision alternative to 'the godless colleges'. Newman thus advocated a state of affairs he was later to condemn, when papal prohibitions were made mandatory against the attendance of English Catholics at Oxford and Cambridge.[5]

When Newman embarked on the composition of the University Discourses he was fifty years of age, and could lay claim to more

[1] Culler, p. 132.

[2] From Newman's *Retrospective Notes*, quoted by Wilfrid Ward, *Life of Newman*, vol. 1, pp. 380–4, and esp. p. 384.   [3] Ibid., vol. 1, p. 384.

[4] Ibid., p. 388.   [5] Ibid., vol. 2, pp. 62–3.

than thirty years' association, as boy and man, with the University of Oxford. It is not, therefore, altogether surprising, as Professor Corcoran has shown, that Newman's philosophy of education as formulated in the Discourses of 1852 'was derived from the University of Oxford, as an institution in being, and from that University as it functioned in the first half of the nineteenth century, by its curriculum, and by its educational postulates and aims'.[6] Newman's disillusionment six years later was the outcome of the apathy he had encountered to his plan of renewing in Ireland, 'many years after its definitive collapse, a set of local controversies' which were 'Anglican in provenance, and academic or quasi-religious, or both'.[7] They were controversies 'with which neither the institution to which he was called, nor the Irish people for whom it was being established, had any connection or concern'.[8] Professional schools there were to be, but, in Newman's concept, they were merely peripheral. The real work of the University was the provision of that liberal education concerning which he waxed so eloquent in the Discourses. 'I have always had a fancy', Newman wrote in 1845, 'that I might be of use to a set of persons like the lawyers—or again I might be of use to the upper classes',[9] and his organization in Dublin was based upon rigid class divisions. He was impervious to Irish objections. 'If I am intrusted with the commencement of the University, I am to be the judge what is necessary or not for that object', he wrote in 1853.[10] The students reading Medicine he hardly regarded as his concern at all, and he had little patience with the undergraduates who were primarily interested in the Physical and Applied Sciences. Tom Mozley has testified that 'Newman as a rule—indeed I cannot remember an exception—would have nothing to say to physical science. He abstained from it much as he did from material undertakings and worldly affairs generally. He would be impatient of it, as something in the way, not worth precious time.'[11] This factor, then, led to the first great cleavage with the Irish

---

[6] Corcoran, *Newman: Selected Discourses, etc.*, p. xix.   [7] Ibid., p. xv.

[8] Ibid.   [9] Robbins, William, in *The Newman Brothers*, p. 120.

[10] Tristram, p. 305. Memorandum for 19 Dec. 1853.

[11] Seán O'Faoláin, *Newman's Way*, p. 113 n.

hierarchy. The bishops were primarily concerned with vocational schools and regarded students preparing for the professions as the nucleus of the Catholic University. Newman, on the contrary, ignored these groups and directed his attention almost exclusively to those sons of noblemen and gentlemen 'who had an assurance of easily-attained financial independence'.[12] In 1854 Newman declared to Ambrose St. John, 'all men almost tell me with one voice that nowhere in all Ireland are the youths to be found who are to fill' the University,[13] and at the same time he wrote to Mrs. W. Froude, 'there seems *no class* to afford members for a University'.[14] He informed Hungerford Pollen in 1857, 'we never had any Irish youths except one or two. Barnewell, Errington, White, I suspect are all';[15] and he declared to another friend that the Irish bishops 'have little or no influence with the classes which furnish the *students*',[16] although he acknowledged that they could command the poorer portion of the community. During the years of Newman's rectorship, from 1854 to 1858, there were over 100 Irish undergraduates in the Faculties of Arts and Science at the Catholic University. These numbers were exclusive of those in the Faculty of Medicine. Only three of these Irish youths, however, were able to measure up to the Rector's social requirement. Yet these students formed four-fifths of those in the Faculties of Arts and Science. It is little wonder that the Irish bishops grew impatient with Newman's myopic view.

The Rector had early to recognize that there was, on the part of the bishops, a University policy quite at variance with his own conception. In a letter to John Wallis, editor of *The Tablet*, written in 1856, Newman indicated his opposition to the episcopal policy.[17] The bishops were looking for the revival of an age of poor scholars, he maintained, and he objected to men like Bishop Moriarty who 'are ever looking about for poor scholars, cheap lodging houses, and schools for affiliations'. Newman

---

[12] Corcoran, *Newman: Selected Discourses, etc.*, p. xxxxiv.
[13] Ward, W., *Life of Newman*, vol. 1, p. 336.   [14] Ibid., p. 337.
[15] Ibid., p. 364.   [16] Ibid.
[17] Printed in full in the Appendix to Ch. XII of W. Ward's *Life of Newman*, vol. 1, p. 628.

declared his conviction that 'the University must look out else-where for its friends, its real friends, and must form alliances, other than that with the country and popular Irish party'. Three years later he complained that the plan of the Young Irelanders was similar to that of the bishops, it was 'to call up poor scholars in shoals, as in Scotland, whose coming will be the pledge that it is a national benefit'.[18]

In April 1854 Newman intimated to Cullen his intention of visit-ing the English colleges in order 'to stir them up in our favour',[19] the first clear sign that the University's initial appeal for students was to be directed at English rather than Irish interests. Two months later he was able to report to the Archbishop of Armagh, Joseph Dixon, that he had already visited St. Beuno's College, Tre-meirchion, St. Edmund's College, Ware, and Ushaw College, Durham, and 'found satisfaction and encouragement every-where'.[20] Tea and sympathy, however, was one thing; boys and money quite another! In the closing years of his life Newman admitted that for its very existence the University had been com-pelled 'to raise £5,000 a year from the peasantry',[21] adding that this the Irish had succeeded in doing for twenty years, and T. W. Allies informed Pope Leo XIII even as late as 1883 that 'no human inducement would be strong enough to lead English Catholics of birth and position to send their sons to an Irish University with the chance of bringing back the brogue'.[22]

In the *Retrospective Notes* Newman gave three chief reasons why he abandoned the Catholic University.[23] One of them was 'that English Catholics felt no interest at all in the University scheme, and had no intention to make use of it, should it get into shape'. He claimed that it was the express intention at the outset that the new institution should look to England as well as to Ireland, but he added significantly that even his own bishop, Dr.

[18] Appendices of W. Ward's *Life of Newman*, vol. 1, pp. 628–9. Letter of Newman to Ornsby, 19 Jan. 1859.
[19] *Newman Letters*, Newman to Cullen, 12 Apr. 1854.
[20] Ibid., Newman to Dixon, 3 June 1854.
[21] Ward, W., *Life of Newman*, vol. 2, p. 518. Letter of 24 Oct. 1881.
[22] Stockley, W. F. P., p. 70.
[23] Quoted *in extenso*, W. Ward's *Life of Newman*, vol. 1, pp. 380–4.

Ullathorne, had told him in the early days, 'as if a matter in which he acquiesced, that "the English gentlemen would never send their sons to it" '. By 1857 it had become abundantly clear that he was not to succeed in the policy of transforming the Irish University into an Imperial foundation, and all interest in the establishment drained away from him. Excuses were needed. He claimed he had been misled, misdirected, and misused. Unless the University had been 'an affair of England as well as of Ireland, I should have sympathized in so grand a conception, I should have done what I could to aid it, but I should have had no call. . . . I should have considered it presumption in me to take an active part in its execution', Newman wrote in 1872 in his *Historical Sketches*.[24] If this was so, it was a misconception of Newman's own devising, and the statement is hard to reconcile with his assertion as Cardinal that he had gone to Ireland 'with the simple aim and desire to serve a noble people who I felt had a great future'.[25]

The second reason given by Newman in the *Retrospective Notes* as to why he left the Catholic University was, he declared, the main reason: 'I could not give to the University that continuous presence which Dr. Cullen wished.' 'It was an unfortunate coincidence of untoward events, but so it was,' he wrote, 'that my residence *here* [at Birmingham] was absolutely necessary to the welfare of this Oratory.'[26] Newman was, in effect, little more than a part-time Rector of the Catholic University, and this was to prove a serious obstacle to the effective administration of the infant establishment. Newman had strong feelings concerning the evils of living out of community. 'The truth is, as you know far better than I can', he wrote to Fr. Lans the Redemptorist in 1850, 'it does not do for members of a community to live out of community. They lose their interest in the body, and moreover, losing the stimulus which it supplies to progress in the religious life, they become slothful, despondent, and tepid.'[27] It was

[24] Newman, J. H., *Historical Sketches* (3 vols., 1882), vol. 1, p. 66.
[25] Stockley, p. 46.
[26] Ward, W., *Life of Newman*, vol. 1, p. 381.
[27] Coffin Papers, Clapham, Newman to Lans, 25 Dec. 1850.

Newman's original intention to establish an Oratory in Dublin, but when this idea proved not to be a practical possibility he was left with an invidious choice. He could yield the office of Superior of the Birmingham Oratory to another, he himself remaining simply a member of the Community and giving allegiance to a new Superior, or he could withdraw from the Catholic University. It was a choice he refused to consider. He decided to retain the office of Superior of the Oratory and try to manage the University as well. To run either of these two establishments at a distance was likely to give rise to discontent, and, not surprisingly, Newman had to face discontent in both of them. From 1851 to 1858 he 'crossed St. George's Channel 56 times in the service of the University'.[28] He was frequently absent from Dublin when he was most needed, and, if decisions were taken in his absence, he bitterly resented them. Cullen's correspondence with the Rector is punctuated by appeals for Newman to devote more time to the affairs of the University. In February 1852 he was declaring 'I hope you will soon be able to devote more time to our business'.[29] Towards the end of the Achilli trial, in November 1852, Cullen declared: 'I regret that we must do without your assistance until Easter but I trust that after that period you will be able to devote yourself altogether to our good work.'[30] Three years later Cullen was still complaining of Newman's absences from Dublin. In September 1855 he told Newman, 'if you were here it would be easy to come to a better understanding about everything'.[31] He found it imperative to remind the Rector that 'it will be altogether necessary that you should be present at the meeting of the bishops or have something prepared for them'.[32] In October 1855 the Archbishop wrote to Dr. Kirby, the agent of the Irish bishops in Rome, 'with regard to the university we have done nothing. For more than three months Father Newman has been in England and has left a convert Englishman called Scratton here to take his place. To the vice-Rector he gave no instructions. I have not

---

[28] See Robbins, pp. 125–6.
[29] MacSuibhne, vol. 2, pp. 120–1. Cullen to Newman, 8 Feb. 1852.
[30] Ibid., pp. 142–3. Cullen to Newman, 29 Nov. 1852.
[31] Ibid., vol. 3, p. 210. Cullen to Newman, 16 Sept. 1855.   [32] Ibid.

therefore been able to find out how things stand, but they don't seem to be going ahead in a way that can be defended. The continued absence of the Rector cannot be defended. . . . We shall always have the difficulty that: *nemo potest duobus dominis servire* and Father Newman cannot be excepted. He cannot spend a great part of the year in England and govern a university here.'[33] Two months later, on Christmas Eve, Cullen told Cardinal Barnabo that 'if Father Newman could remain constantly in this city [Dublin] everything would proceed better, but he is so much engrossed in the affairs of his Congregation that he must spend a great part of the year in England. His absence is always injurious, since there is as yet nothing constant in the regulation of a new institute which has been in existence for just a year.'[34] In July 1858 Cullen regretted exceedingly that they had been so long deprived of Newman's presence, and expressed the wish to Newman that 'you could arrange matters to come to live among us continually'.[35] The following month Cullen wrote to Cardinal Barnabo, in one of his routine reports as Apostolic Delegate, that although Newman was still nominally in charge of the University, 'the rector had not been in Ireland at all this year and things cannot go on without someone in charge'.[36] Things were in such a state 'that they will result in collapse if some remedy is not applied'. Much of this continual absence from Dublin during the three years from 1854 to 1857 can be accounted for by the constant disturbances and ill feeling which rent the English Oratorians as a body. The influence of Faber at the London Oratory, from whence it was said that he sent people to heaven lolling on a sofa,[37] and the independence of the London house itself, were sources of continual disquiet to Newman.

Newman gave a third reason for his decision to quit Dublin. 'I confess that my relations towards Dr. Cullen', he wrote in his *Retrospective Notes*, 'had much to do with my leaving.'[38] A number

[33] Ibid., vol. 2, pp. 207–10. Report of Cullen to Kirby, Oct. 1855.
[34] Ibid., vol. 3, pp. 216–17. Cullen to Barnabo, 24 Dec. 1855.
[35] Ibid., pp. 259–60. Cullen to Newman, 20 July 1858.
[36] Ibid., vol. 2, pp. 263–5. Cullen to Barnabo, 31 Aug. 1858.
[37] Fitzgerald, Percy, op. cit., vol. 1, p. 183.
[38] Ward, W., *Life of Newman*, vol. 1, p. 383.

of sources of alienation between the two men have already been dealt with—Newman's conception of the nature of the University, his desire to place its financial administration in the hands of the gentry, his partial residence in Dublin and lack of concern for poor scholars, his organization of the establishment in rigid class divisions, and his employment of large numbers of aliens and converts in the teaching faculties of the University. Of all these developments Cullen was critical. Difficulties with the Archbishop, however, arose out of much more fundamental issues than those concerned with the organization and structure of the University itself. The University was not Cullen's private diocesan establishment; it was the Catholic University of Ireland, and as such was the responsibility of all the Irish bishops. Cullen possessed a threefold function. He was not only the middleman between Newman and the hierarchy, explaining the Rector's policies, defending them if need be, and putting the best light upon them if they were not capable of defence, but he was also the means by which the hierarchy communicated its wishes and decisions to Newman. Over and above these two duties he remained Apostolic Delegate, with a duty to report to *Propaganda* at regular and frequent intervals on the progress being made in the University. The Irish bishops were merely the agents of Rome as far as the University was concerned. Cullen, therefore, had an unenviable task. Rome wanted a University set up exactly on the pattern of the University of Louvain and, in fact, had unequivocally decreed that this was the model to be copied. The Irish bishops, while agreeing with the views of Rome as to structure, desired an effective counterpart to the Queen's Colleges, providing for the professional needs of Irish life, and concentrating upon the education of the middle classes and the intelligent but poorer sections of the community. Newman set himself at variance with these aspirations. The University was to cater for a great English interest, was to adopt the University of Oxford as its model, was to concentrate its energies upon the education of the wealthy and ennobled, many of them aliens, and was to reject 'professionalism' as a true and worthy constituent of 'liberal' education. And there was Cullen, in the midst of this welter of conflicting interests and contradictory policies, trying to keep the University financially solvent, trying to protect the Rector from the wrath of the more vigorous prelates, and trying to justify the practical organization of the University to Rome, on the one hand, and to the Irish clergy on the other, a clergy whose sympathy for the undertaking was vital if sufficient money was to be collected to subsidize the establishment. Cullen did much to assuage ruffled feelings, but was powerless to achieve more. Newman never appreciated the various roles the Archbishop was compelled to assume, and he did not make sufficient allowance for the fact that University matters were only a fraction of the duties calling for Cullen's attention. The latter was not only the occupant of the most important ecclesiastical see in Ireland but was Metropolitan of an extensive ecclesiastical province. As Apostolic Delegate he held a watching brief as effective head of the hierarchy, and it was his responsibility to keep a wary eye upon government policies. Cullen's correspondence is voluminous, not all of it concerned with weighty matters of policy. It was impossible for him to give the kind of attention to the University which it was expected that a resident Rector would be able to provide. Cullen, a great social worker, considered that one of the main tasks of a pontifex was to be a builder of social bridges. His episcopacy is noteworthy for the number of churches, schools, reformatories, orphanages, and hospitals opened. In 1856 he began the work of founding the Mater Hospital and three years later opened a new diocesan seminary at Clonliffe. This kind of activity, so necessary if the Church was to prepare itself to meet the challenge of the twentieth century, found little understanding from Newman.

Cullen's task in regard to the University became much more difficult in 1854. While the Irish bishops were assembled in Rome for the proclamation of the dogma of the Immaculate Conception, *Propaganda* announced that the Pope had approved the statutes of the new University, but that he had vested the chief responsibility for the foundation in the persons of the four Irish archbishops. The intention was good. It was felt that a small group of four men, each representing the bishops of his own Province, would be a viable body for such a delicate undertaking, and would be capable of effecting needed decisions. The difficulty, however, was what to do if the Metropolitans split two and two on any important issue. In such an event, Cullen, by virtue of his appointment as Apostolic Delegate, was to have the casting vote. This provision infuriated Dr. MacHale, Archbishop of Tuam, who was growing more and more adverse to Cullen's politics.

John MacHale was a native of the west of Ireland and devoted himself to the study of early Irish history and to the spread of the Irish language. For him the Irish University had a duty to reflect in its teaching and organization the peculiar excellences of the land of its origin. The Irish language ought to be studied, and special emphasis ought to be placed upon Irish literature, history, and archaeology. The University should be the fount from which would flow benefits to every corner of the island. Its close link with organized Catholicism was essential because the Catholic religion was as much part of an Irishman as his historical heritage or his distinctive language.

Newman, while paying lip-service to Irish studies, regarded this aspect of his work as peripheral. If he wished to attract Englishmen to study in Dublin it could not be done by emphasizing local studies and Irish national traits. Rather the contrary. Thus it was that MacHale's antagonism to Newman, and the University project as the latter had conceived of it, was first born. Cullen had to assume the role of defender of the Rector, and MacHale grew more and more to believe that Cullen and Newman were parts of a nascent conspiracy to defraud the Irish people of their birthright.

Newman's correspondence with MacHale was a constant irritant. The Archbishop of Tuam, from the beginning, was tireless in his insistence that all the Irish bishops ought to be consulted in University matters. 'The archbishops and bishops alone', he maintained, 'were to draw from the exhaustless resources of their impoverished people's generosity the necessary pecuniary means for creating and supporting this great establishment.'

Every bishop in Ireland, then, as the divinely appointed guardian of his people's faith and morals, must ever have a voice in the nomination of the men who taught and governed in the University, and who, in their teaching and governing capacity, only represented the shepherds of the flock. Moreover, as it must be on the bishop's co-operation that the University had to rely, solely or principally, for the means of support, it was natural, right, and strictly just, that every bishop in Ireland should have a voice in the administration of the University's temporalities.[39]

In this statement we have a succinct account of MacHale's attitude, and, from it, it will be seen why he objected to a small committee made up of the Metropolitans having exclusive management of the University.

The first sign of trouble occurred in August 1854, when Newman wrote to MacHale and each of the other archbishops, to state that he had purchased a medical school in Dublin for about £1,500. In the letter he inserted the following remark: 'I have not liked to conclude the transaction without having the satisfaction of feeling that I have your Grace's congratulations and blessing, though I do not expect, nor does the occasion need, that you should put yourself to the trouble of answering this.'[40] Obviously Newman regarded the task of consulting the bishops as a formality. Their permission to act in important matters, involving policy and the expenditure of considerable sums of money, was to be taken for granted. Six weeks later Newman presented a long list of academic appointments to MacHale as a formality, and in July 1855 wrote in imperious tone from the Oratory, Birmingham:

I write to your Grace and to the other archbishops to say, that I have designated and propose to present to the *Coetus Episcoporum* the following professional gentlemen of Dublin to fill chairs in the Medical Faculty of the University:

Dr. Ellis to be professor of the Practice of Surgery.
Dr. Hayden and Dr. Corrigan to be professors of Anatomy.
Dr. Lyons to be professor of Pathology.[41]

Communications of this kind seemed arrogant. MacHale informed the Rector in October 1854, 'it appears that to consult

39 O'Reilly, B., vol. 1, p. 400, and vol. 2, pp. 491–2.
40 Ibid., vol. 2, p. 504. Newman to MacHale, 17 Aug. 1854.
41 Ibid., p. 509. Newman to MacHale, 28 July 1855.

the Archbishops on the purchase of Schools or the fitness of Professors is a matter of mere courtesy'.[42] Newman produced a spirited defence of his actions. The ultimate power of ratification remained with the bishops, but, he maintained, 'the confidence their Lordships have placed in me is very full, and the powers in consequence intrusted to me are very ample: and you will have, I am sure, no difficulty in entering into my feeling when I say that, unless I have that full confidence and those ample powers, it would have been the height of presumption and folly in me to aspire to such very anxious responsibilities as I have accepted'.[43] To an extent, Newman was right. The Rector had to be in a position to take immediate decisions if the University was to flourish, and, in fact, Cullen and the bishops acknowledged this. What was wrong was Newman's manner in announcing the steps he had taken. With a little judicious tact and a somewhat less imperious tone he would have achieved his ends without antagonizing episcopal feelings. MacHale claimed that Cullen, 'by an insistence unusual in the presidents of our meetings', had compelled the bishops to accept the fact that the Rector should have exclusive right to 'present the professors to be appointed'. Such a decision had been forced 'against a majority of the bishops'.[44] When Cullen's actions are studied without the distorting view of Newman's spectacles, he appears to be much less of the tyrant, the ogre, and the fool, than Miss Trevor, for instance, would have us believe.[45] Similarly, if Cullen was as uninterested or as disappointed in the University as Ward indicates,[46] he would not have been as eager as he was to spare Newman the pain of an open breach with the bishops. Many times that breach was near, and it would have been but an easy matter for Cullen either to have joined in the general criticism or merely to have stepped aside and allowed Dr. MacHale and those who thought like him to have their way. He chose to yield to neither of these temptations, and this in spite of the fact that he too was not happy at the

[42] *Newman Letters*, MacHale to Newman, 6 Oct. 1854.
[43] Ibid., Newman to MacHale, 8 Oct. 1854.   [44] Stockley, pp. 26–7.
[45] See Trevor, *Light in Winter*, pp. 109 seq.
[46] Ward, W., *Life of Newman*, vol. 1, p. 370.

way things were going. He could not acquiesce in Newman's interpretation of the University, whereby the Irish were to be simply the holders of the plate, nor could he see any justice in relinquishing the finances of the establishment to a committee of wealthy and titled laymen. The latter would have been unrepresentative of those who provided the money and for whom the bishops had sought to establish the University.

In an article in *Studies* the late Dr. Alfred O'Rahilly wrote that 'when the evidence is examined objectively there is little or nothing to support the widespread thesis of constant interference and thwarting, especially by Cullen'.[47] There is also no evidence for Wilfrid Ward's statement that 'as a practical project, in the interests of education',[48] hardly any of the bishops took the University seriously. Moreover, it is Cullen, rather than Newman, who has to complain of being kept in the dark concerning University affairs. In July 1858, while Newman was still officially Rector of the University, Cullen wrote to him indicating that 'some persons connected with the University have informed me that the professors have signed a memorial to Mr. Disraeli asking for a charter for the University'.[49] On such an important matter concerning the status of a pontifical foundation, Newman had not thought it necessary either to consult or to inform the bishops. Cullen, who had already made tentative approaches on the matter of a charter on behalf of the bishops, wrote that he took it for granted that 'it was to the bishops the charter was to be granted and at their request'. The letter was courteous, considering the gravity of the offence, and Cullen pointed out that he wrote because he understood that Newman was to present the professors' petition (which neither the Archbishop nor any of the bishops had seen), and because he was anxious 'that as the bishops founded the University their opinions should be heard as to the terms of the charter before anything final be decided on'.[50] The letter added: 'But you will best understand what is right to be

---

[47] O'Rahilly, Alfred, 'The Irish University Question', *Studies* (Winter 1961.
[48] Ward, W., *Life of Newman*, vol. 1, p. 336.
[49] MacSuibhne, vol. 3, pp. 259–60. Cullen to Newman, 20 July 1858.
[50] Ibid.

done and I shall be perfectly satisfied with any steps you take.'
Newman's reply was curt and confined to a few lines. He did
not deny that a movement was afoot, and that he was a party to
it, but he claimed 'we are merely taking a preliminary step'.[51]
Such a step was not in any sense, he claimed, prejudicial to the
prerogatives of the bishops. But it was surely unwise to make even
a preliminary contact with government on a matter which
affected the very status of the University without first discussing
the problem with the bishops. That Cullen had heard of the
negotiation through secondary sources was in itself a humiliating
episode. The basis of the plan, moreover, was to forge a close link
with the Queen's University as the price for the power to confer
degrees. It is interesting to observe that Newman resolutely
refused to allow his students to enter for the degrees of London
University, a solution which would have resolved many difficulties without bringing him into conflict with either the government or the episcopacy. Newman was later to rationalize the
situation by claiming that the government would not treat with
an institution dominated by priests. O'Rahilly has shown that
'neither under Newman nor under Woodlock did the University
resemble a seminary',[52] and that, at Newman's final departure
from Dublin, of the thirty-two professors only five were priests.
Of these five, four professed theological subjects and the remaining one taught Modern Languages. Such an analysis of the institution's teaching strength is in itself sufficient to dispel the myth of
clerical domination in the classrooms of the University. Perhaps
the most repeated complaint of Newman's apologists, and especially of Miss Trevor, is that the Rector was not given an entirely
free hand in the matter of University appointments. In reality, as
we have seen, very few of Newman's nominees were prevented
from accepting appointment because of episcopal disapproval.
The complaint was answered long ago by John Hogan in a review
of Wilfrid Ward's *Life of Newman* in the *Irish Ecclesiastical Record*.
Concerning appointments Hogan questioned: 'Where does the
head of a university or a university college get a free hand? Has he

51 MacSuibhne, vol. 3, pp. 259–60. Newman to Cullen, 21 July 1858 (pp. 260–1).
52 *Studies* (Winter 1961).

a free hand in Louvain or in Washington? Does he get it in Oxford or Cambridge? A voice no doubt and a strong one, but a free hand is another thing.'[53] In the numerous provincial university colleges being formed in England in the second half of the nineteenth century such a claim as Newman advanced in Dublin found no place.

Newman left Ireland for good at the beginning of November 1858, and his official resignation was due to take effect a week later. For two years he had been looking for an excuse to abandon the University. One possibility would have been a row with MacHale, and the opportunity, he hoped, would present itself at the Synodal Meeting in June 1856. Writing to Ambrose St. John, he declared: 'I was up before the Bishops over an hour. I was perfectly cool; so much so that I longed to be attacked. . . . I wished the Lion to attack me, but you see I am not destined to be a Gérard.'[54] MacHale was as meek as a lamb and Newman was courteously received. His attempt to place the bishops in the wrong had failed. By 1857 Newman had fully determined to have done with an establishment for which he had lost all taste, and, in fact, he was beginning to enjoy the thought of the sensation his resignation would bring about. 'Everyone tells me my going is the only subject talked about in every society', he wrote, adding: 'I think the effect will be to increase my power wonderfully.'[55] Newman was thinking of his position *vis-à-vis* the bishops, and it is true to say that his resignation gave rise to considerable consternation. One cannot help feeling that once the decision had been made, Newman thoroughly enjoyed being complete master of the situation. There is something distasteful about his description of Cullen's discomfiture when the latter asked him to reconsider his position. Phrases such as 'I was very stiff' and 'when I spoke, I spoke with great momentum'[56] convey an unpleasant note of triumphalism in the Rector's attitude. He savoured the drama of the moment and was determined to exploit it to the full.

[53] Hogan, J. F., in *Irish Ecclesiastical Record* (Feb. 1912).

[54] Ward, W., *Life of Newman*, vol. 1, p. 371. Newman to St. John, 26 June 1856.

[55] Trevor, *Light in Winter*, p. 159.   [56] Ibid.

Despite all the expostulations of the Irish bishops and attempts to get *Propaganda* to exert its influence with Newman, the latter was adamant. He remained nominally Rector of the University, although non-resident, until the meeting of the Irish bishops on the 19th, 20th, and 21st of October 1859, when his resignatoin was formally received and the thanks and appreciation of the episcopacy duly recorded. At that meeting Cullen worked valiantly to spare the feelings of Newman and to save the infant foundation from collapse. No immediate successor was named, but the direction of the University was placed in the hands of twelve prelates, the four archbishops and two bishops from each Province. Archbishop MacHale wanted a public condemnation of Newman's administration. It took all Cullen's tact to prevent an open rupture, but gradually, by sheer patience and a willingness to swallow personal insults, he succeeded in gaining MacHale's formal acquiescence to the proceedings of the bishops. In achieving this he prevented the immediate collapse of the University, for MacHale advanced himself 'as the defender of economy in the management of public money', and 'as a lover of the rights of Ireland'.[57] MacHale was inclined to condemn 'the whole system of the same Father Newman, who wished to model everything on the pattern of Oxford and to introduce into a Catholic and far from wealthy country customs which were more suitable for a Protestant Kingdom like England and for a people of great wealth'.[58]

With Newman's severance of his association with Dublin there came to an end that policy of attempting to develop the Irish University as a school of higher studies for English Catholics. Following the episcopal meeting of 1859 a joint pastoral address, signed by all the Irish prelates, was issued, which declared: 'Some persons seem to be of opinion that a University is merely a large academical institution, designed solely for the education of the youth in the higher grades of society, and that the beneficial influence of a University is confined within a comparatively small circle. Such a notion of the nature and purposes of a Univer-

---

[57] MacSuibhne, vol. 2, pp. 300–4. Cullen to Barnabo, 11 Nov. 1859.
[58] Ibid.

sity appears to us to be not only inadequate but erroneous.'⁵⁹ To
render the University more easy of access to the poorer sections
of the community, the bishops declared they were taking certain
measures. 'The reduction of fees and the establishment of burses—
one for each diocese in Ireland—to which burse the Bishop of the
Diocese will present—are calculated to stimulate the talent and
reward the laudable industry of the Catholic youth.' 'These
regulations', they added, 'we consider to be in perfect harmony
with the spirit and practice of the Catholic Church, which loves
to befriend and develop the talent of the humble as well as of
the high.' The bishops vaguely referred to former defects of the
institution which they hoped to put right, and to ways in which
'it may have suffered from its past organization and government'.
They spoke of the contributions of Irish Catholics which had
made the University a reality, and of 'the Catholics of Great
Britain, of the Colonies, and of America, [who] mindful of the
fidelity and sufferings of the Irish people, have co-operated by
their contributions to obtain for us the advantages which flow
from a Catholic University'. The bishops dealt with the need of
a University charter: 'We contribute to the public taxes; we share
in bearing the public burdens of the country; our people shed
their blood for its defence, its honour, and its rights; and, besides
the property which was given by our fathers for religious and
educational institutions has been taken away, and appropriated to
objects widely different from the sacred purposes intended by the
charitable donors.' A charter could, surely, in justice not be withheld. But if it was, then all was not lost.

A charter cannot bestow the high literary and scientific education
which it is the function of a University to impart; and if the institution
be well sustained, its services will not be neutralised or paralysed by the
absence of a charter. If the Engineer, the Magistrate, the Member of
Parliament, and the country gentleman avail themselves successfully
of the advantages of a University no one stops to inquire whether they
obtained degrees in arts or not. The World sees, in their ability and
learning, ample proof of their useful and enlarged education, even
though this be not attested by a degree.

⁵⁹ Moran (ed.), *The Pastoral Letters and Other Writings of Cardinal Cullen,
Archbishop of Dublin*, vol. I, pp. 701–9 and esp. p. 701.

Surveying the situation as it appeared in 1859 and writing nearly thirty years later, Thomas Arnold was highly critical of Newman's 'desertion' of the University. 'He had laboured hard, preached and lectured most ably, and initiated many useful measures,' he wrote; 'still it would be too much to say that he left the University in a safe or flourishing state, and his departure was taken in many quarters as evidence that his enterprise was beset by great, if not insuperable, difficulties.'[60] Dublin was thus less happy than Louvain, 'where the first Rector, the illustrious Monsignor de Ram, bore the toils of office for thirty years, and only resigned when the institution, which at its opening had eighty students, was firmly and efficiently organized in every respect, and could point to nine hundred students on its rolls'.[60] The Irish bishops had primarily desired 'to obtain a thoroughly Catholic and thoroughly national education for their Catholic youth', and hence their object had been 'not to provide lectures and opportunities of distinction for clever young men, but to found a seat of learning'. They had wished above all, for example, 'to promote with great care the study of Celtic and Irish antiquities, so that not Irishmen only, but every Celtic scholar in any part of the world, whatever his nationality, might after a time come to know that by visiting Dublin he would have an opportunity of consulting MSS. not elsewhere to be met with, and conversing with men whose profound knowledge was racy of the soil, and corrected by the immemorial traditions of the people'.[60] These were aspirations to which Newman, in his concern for English interests, had given little more than formal recognition.

[60] Arnold, Thomas, in *The Dublin Review* (Oct. 1887), p. 352.

Part Three

THE ASSAULT ON OXFORD

I

POLEMICS COMMENCE AND
PROTAGONISTS ASSEMBLE

WRITING in 1842 on the English universities, Professor V. A. Hüber, of the University of Marburg, saw in Oxford and Cambridge 'a want of Christian faith, of intimate knowledge of fundamental truths of Christianity, or at all events a want of *lively* faith, a confusing and levelling of ideas, a dry formality, a sort of moral self-justification or negligence, a complete predominance of the material and political interests of the Church, and a reckless worldly-mindedness connected with it'.[1] Six years later *The Rambler*, in its fourth issue, devoted itself to a castigation of that 'reckless worldly-mindedness' to which Hüber referred. The undergraduates 'boat, they ride, they dress, they drink wine, they smoke cigars, they run into debt, to say nothing of those grievous excesses which can scarcely be hinted at, much less described', Capes wrote.[2] Thus was betrayed 'that startling ignorance almost of the elements of a liberal education, which too often is discovered in those who have passed three long years in a pretence of study; and all that barbarism, prejudice, and narrow-mindedness, which prevails in a certain class of University men'. When the tutors had given the undergraduate 'a certain amount of instruction, enforced obedience to a few rules, and shewn a few gentlemanly civilities' they conceived 'that their duty is done and the undergraduate must take his own course for the rest'.

In May 1848 *The Rambler* declared that 'the real abuse of Oxford and Cambridge lies in this, that they never dream of taking the youth as he is and moulding his entire moral and intellectual character by the influence of a complete system of instruction and

---

[1] Hüber, V. A., *The English Universities*, ed. Frank W. Newman, vol. 2, Part I, pp. 406–7.

[2] *The Rambler*, 22 Jan. 1848, pp. 59 seq.

discipline'.³ The Universities failed as places of both general and professional education. Unless they put their house in order, they would either be 'shelved as useless timber, or crushed before the attacks of their bitter foes'. Problems were manifold.

The ridiculous absurdities and scandalous abuses which are from time to time made public in the newspapers; the complicity of the University tradespeople with the undergraduate excesses, which at this very time the more respectable in their body are endeavouring to correct; the shameful rustications and expulsions; the never-forgotten pluckings; the astonishing ignorance of all valuable knowledge on the part of a vast number of those who obtain degrees; the incompetence of the average class of Oxford and Cambridge men to deal with the realities of actual life, and their enslavement to words, and forms, and scholastic pedantry,—all these, which at present, the popular mind believes to be the *essential* evils of the Universities, are but the results of a rotten system, the symptoms of a deadly disease at the heart itself.

To effect a salutary reform there need be 'no set of tyrannical rules, no iron frame into which the unreformed spirit is to be thrust with reckless cruelty, no mean surveillance or espionage; but a vigilant, strict, and affectionate regulation of the *whole* of the young man's daily life'.

The criticisms of *The Rambler* find an echo in the *Memoirs* of Mark Pattison, published posthumously in 1885. Gladstone considered the *Memoirs* to be 'among the most tragic and the most memorable books of the nineteenth century',⁴ and the work is important for its analysis of the Oxford of the fifties. At that time, Pattison maintained, 'very free opinions on all subjects were rife' and 'theology was totally banished from Common Rooms, and even from private conversation'.⁵ Above all, 'there was a prevailing dissatisfaction with our boasted tutorial system'. The great discoveries in chemistry and physiology 'were not even known by report' and 'science was placed under a ban by the theologians, who instinctively felt that it was fatal to their speculations'. Pattison saw 'the most permanent stamp of college reputation' as

---

³ *The Rambler*, 27 May 1848, pp. 73–4.
⁴ Sparrow, John, *Mark Pattison and the Idea of a University*, p. 23.
⁵ Pattison, Mark, *Memoirs*, pp. 244–5.

the social stamp.[6] This was to be just as true of the 1880s as it was undoubtedly true of the forties and fifties. Such a measure of worth, he maintained, 'often remains stationary under every variety of moral and intellectual change'. 'To what stratum of society the undergraduates of any college belong, what degree of connection they have with the upper ten, what social status they maintain—this is the most patent fact about any college, and one which will never cease to be influential upon the choice of parents in this country, where the vulgar estimate of people by income and position is the universal and only standard of merit.' Christ Church as late as 1883, for instance, 'is and always must be, the resort of the aristocracy'.

Pattison's reminiscences of the conditions of Oxford life in the early 1850s receive substantial confirmation when we peruse some of the opinions expressed in 1852 before the Royal Commission on Oxford. A. C. Tait, H. G. Liddell, and A. P. Stanley considered that 'the ordinary degree course is too narrow. The minimum of knowledge required is so scanty as to leave all but the dullest, or most ignorant, unoccupied. The examiners are satisfied with a very slight exhibition of knowledge as regards many of these subjects. The Latin and Greek Authors are commonly got up by the aid of translations.'[7] Archibald C. Tait had been Fellow of Balliol and in 1869 was to become Archbishop of Canterbury. Henry G. Liddell was Headmaster of Westminster School and previously tutor of Christ Church. Arthur P. Stanley was Secretary of the Commission and a former scholar of Balliol. They proclaimed that 'the education imparted at Oxford is not such as to conduce to the advancement in life of many persons, except those intended for the ministry of the Church. Few physicians are now educated at Oxford. A large proportion of those Barristers who have received an academic education are said to be Cambridge men.'[8] Bonamy Price, who had taken a double First at Oxford in 1829 and later taught under Arnold and Tait at Rugby, gave evidence before the Commission that a more strictly professional teaching was urgently required. 'It is the great

[6] Ibid., p. 17.
[7] *Report* of Royal Commission on Oxford, 1852, pp. 61–2.   [8] Ibid., p. 18.

defect of the present system', declared the future Professor of Political Economy, 'that it is limited to a purely general education; that it imparts no professional training, of any importance, for a single purpose'.

To John Moore Capes there was an even more serious objection. Writing in *The Rambler* in 1851 he asserted that 'in giving instruction on any subject in which *man* is concerned, it is literally impossible to avoid all mention of religion, and consequently . . . it is equally impossible for a non-Catholic teacher to avoid teaching that which is anti-Christian and false'. He added that 'this momentous truth has, in fact, been studiously kept out of sight by the advocates of purely secular or of mixed education both in Ireland and in England'.[9] Such decided views carried with them a blanket condemnation for Catholics of Oxford and Cambridge and of all that was taught therein. 'There is scarcely a book in existence, not treating of mere science or language, which is not more or less religious or anti-religious', Capes stated, for 'there is no such thing as a non-religious history, or non-religious moral philosophy or metaphysics, or non-religious works in general literature. They all inculcate, silently or openly *some* views respecting Almighty God and the duties of man.' Such views were easy to proclaim in 1851, when it was impossible for a Catholic to graduate at either University without subscription to the Thirty-Nine Articles. There was a conscious attempt to make a virtue out of necessity.

The evidence offered to the Oxford Commissioners in 1852 confirmed *The Rambler* in its attitude. Oxford had been shown to be a denominational institution, as truly a creature of the Established Church as was Trinity College in Dublin. What was needed was a Catholic counterpart, and it was immaterial to the journal whether such a Catholic institution were to be located in England or Ireland. 'In answer to the question, "What is meant by a Catholic University?", it might be sufficient briefly to answer we mean an establishment for the Catholic Church, such as Oxford is for the Anglican', *The Rambler* stated. 'A Catholic University is wanted for a twofold purpose: first, to supply the Catholic

[9] *The Rambler* (July 1851), p. 4.

body with what may be called superior or upper education, in contradistinction to that which is supplied by primary and middle schools, and secondly to form a fountain-head of Catholic knowledge, literature, and feeling.'[10]

The following year, 1854, saw the promulgation of the Oxford University Act; this was to be followed in 1856 by its counterpart, the Cambridge University Act. These two measures not only reformed the organization of university government but they placed the Colleges and the Universities under an obligation to reform themselves if they wished to avoid a statutory commission empowered to do it for them. But most important of all, Nonconformists were permitted to be members of colleges and to take first degrees. They were still excluded from Fellowships. The proposals brought an instant response from James Spencer Northcote in *The Rambler*:

> At Cambridge, indeed, Catholic students have long been admitted, but they have not been permitted to take a degree, and Oxford, under compulsion, is about to grant us the same 'favour'. For ourselves, however, we most heartily trust that no Catholics will be found to avail themselves of the permission thus accorded. It would be a most pernicious thing for any young Catholic to receive his education at Protestant hands, whether those hands were High Church, Low Church, Latitudinarian, Nonconformist, or Infidel. Education can no more be disservered from religion than matter from its properties of form and colour. We had better remain as we are, exiles from our natural homes till England ceases to be a Kingdom, than barter our faith, our honour, our manliness, our self-respect, our character among our fellow-countrymen, for the questionable advantages of such a teaching as Oxford and Cambridge can give, and that worldly position which the distinctions of those Universities confer on those who share them. We therefore trust that, not withstanding the 'opening' made for us by acts of the legislature or the English Universities themselves, our gentry and aristocracy will hold themselves aloof from the seducing bait, and will prefer the advantages of Catholic learning and the honours of a Catholic seminary to that fictitious knowledge and that tarnished reputation which are all that Oxford and Cambridge could confer on *us*.[11]

[10] Ibid. (Aug. 1853), pp. 114–15.   [11] Ibid. (Sept. 1854), p. 189.

Such violent language was all the more effective, representing as it did the views of converts who had first-hand experience of university life. Capes was an M.A. of Balliol and Northcote had taken a First Class in Classics at Corpus Christi College. With the close association of Richard Simpson in the policies of *The Rambler* after April 1854, however, the journal gained in him a convert with somewhat different views. He was a graduate of Newman's vintage and an Oriel man. Views on the ancient Universities were expressed in a critical manner—albeit with varying degrees of intensity—by many distinguished converts, including from Oxford Henry Danvers Clarke and John Dobrée Bernard Dalgairns of Exeter College; Robert Aston Coffin, Edward Douglas, George Sackville Frederick Lane-Fox, James Robert Hope, and Gilbert Chetwynd Talbot of Christ Church; George Wenham of Magdalen; Walter Croke-Robinson of New College; Charles Seager of Worcester; James Laird Patterson of Trinity; George Talbot of St. Mary's Hall; Frederick William Faber of University College; Charles Stanton Devas of Balliol; Frederick Oakeley of Christ Church and Balliol, and Henry Edward Manning of Balliol. From Cambridge there were Frederick Apthorp Paley of St. John's and Gordon Thompson of Sidney Sussex College. These men were strengthened in their criticisms by many other less well-known converts and by men fully conversant with conditions prevailing in the various colleges.

The views of these converts found expression in *The Rambler*:

What *can* be the moral tone, or the religious element, which is to be acquired in a place where every teacher may have his own creed; where one professor may insinuate that the Christian miracles are myths, and another, that a belief in sacramental grace was the product of mediaeval belief in magic; where one College may be Socinian, another Catholic, another Calvinist, and a fourth Deist; where youths mix together in the hours of relaxation without one of the restraints which are peculiarly necessary when the head is hot and the passions vehement, and every second companion whom the young Catholic meets may insinuate to him that there is no such thing as *sin*, after all,—the notion of the sinfulness of certain actions being an invention of superstition, which no philosopher can ever countenance. . . . The Church of

England University must have an Anglican tone; a 'no-religion' University must have an infidel tone; a Catholic University must have a Catholic tone.[12]

Such writing from the standpoint of the mid twentieth century appears narrow and bigoted, but when seen in the context of the mid nineteenth century, a period characterized by religious tests and discrimination in higher education, and one which had but recently witnessed the no-popery agitations of the fifties, it appears as the obvious expression of genuine fears, oppressions, and anxieties.

Within six years *The Rambler's* worst prognostications of evil seemed to be proved by the publication of *Essays and Reviews*. The book was a kind of nineteenth-century *Honest to God*, in which seven prominent scholars attempted to argue the point that Christianity needed rethinking in the light of modern discoveries. Six of the contributors were Anglican clergymen. Two were arraigned before an ecclesiastical court, found guilty of failing to uphold the faith of the Church of England as enunciated in the Thirty-Nine Articles, and sentenced to suspension *ab officio et beneficio* for a year. After an appeal to the Privy Council, the sentence was set aside. This act of the Privy Council ranks alongside of the Gorham Judgement, the affair of the Jerusalem bishopric, and the Colenso case, as one of the most serious threats to its spiritual integrity the Anglican Church had to endure in the nineteenth century. Most of the contributors to *Essays and Reviews* were Oxford men, and Mark Pattison's contribution, an analytical treatment of Deism, and Benjamin Jowett's attack on the popular doctrine of the Atonement particularly shocked Church feeling. *The Rambler* devoted a long article to an examination of the volume, but perhaps its main argument can be seen in one sentence of that contribution: 'It is not conceivable that the teaching of *Essays and Reviews* . . . should have emanated from Catholic Universities or been promulgated from Catholic pulpits.'[13] The publication of *Essays and Reviews* opened Wiseman's eyes to the theological condition of the Universities and to the

---

[12] *The Rambler* (Sept. 1854), p. 194.   [13] Ibid., Mar. 1861.

heterodox teachings which could with impunity be propagated there. Oxford was no longer the home of Tractarians rushing Rome-wards. Bishop Ullathorne gave expression to Roman Catholic feeling in a letter to Ambrose Phillipps de Lisle:

> Indeed we live in awful times, but I think one of the most awful things in this country just now is the spirit of downright and unblushing infidelity that is boldly manifesting itself in the Anglican Church. Have you seen the vol. of Reviews and Essays, published by Parker? The worst infidelity of France under Louis the 15th is there put forth by six beneficed clergymen, all Oxford men. They simply deny the intervention of God in the Creation; reject Creation itself, make the Bible a congeries of fictions, and reduce all truth to the inward testimony of each man's conscience. The book is a hideous nightmare, and it has produced no sensation and is now in its second edition. A greater proof of the deadness of Anglican authorities there could not be. To what is this nation coming?[14]

Early in 1863 an event of some significance for Roman Catholic education took place. In May of that year W. G. Ward suggested to his friend and spiritual adviser, Henry Edward Manning, that the latter should look back on the twelve years since his conversion and place in writing his considered view of the state of Roman Catholicism in England. Manning's antecedents were impressive. He had taken a First Class *in literis humanioribus* at Balliol College, Oxford, in 1830, and two years later had been elected Fellow of Merton. As Archdeacon of Chichester he had been involved in the doctrinal and legislative disputes which had plagued the Church of England in the forties. David Newsome has recently shown that after 1845 Manning was regarded by the Anglo-Catholic clergy as 'the one man theologically equipped to supply them with an informed account and explanation of Roman doctrine and practice'.[15] Dogmatic firmness, love of system and authority, ardent, compulsive yearning for sanctity, have been seen as the chief qualities which characterized him in the years before 1851.[16] The Gorham Judgement finally propelled him into

---

[14] *The Oscotian* (July 1886), Ullathorne to de Lisle, 30 July 1860.
[15] Newsome, David, *The Parting of Friends: A Study of the Wilberforces and Henry Manning*, p. 318.   [16] Ibid.

the Roman Church. Yet, as Fitzgerald has so perspicaciously shown, Manning retained the qualities we have enumerated after his conversion. His view of Church polity 'was surprisingly consistent, and he held it to the end'.[17] 'The wonderful thing was that he, a *new* Catholic, with hardly time to have become at all familiar with the paths and currents, should actually have been far in advance of the existing Catholic clergy and laity. . . . What he intended, which with clear vision he saw was lacking, was a system of centralisation. And before he died he saw this established in the most complete fashion. . . . He was really alone; but by education, training, refinement, discipline, immeasurably superior to all about him.'[18]

In view of Manning's experience it is, therefore, not surprising that he should have begun the task Ward had given him by attempting a definition of the Church as he saw it, and of its role and function in a society of men. The definition is remarkably simple, but it provides a searchlight which illumines the whole of Manning's social and ecclesiastical attitudes.

The Church has a two fold work to do for mankind. Its first and primary, indeed, is to save souls, to lead men to eternal life. Its second but no less true, is to ripen and to elevate the social and political life of men by its influences of morality and of law. As the Church is not a mere school of opinion for the enlightenment of the intellect, but a true kingdom for the government of the will, so its mission is not only to direct the conscience and the will of individuals as units, but of fathers as the heads of households, and of princes or governors as the rulers of peoples and of nations.[19]

It is not surprising, too, that, writing three years after the publication of *Essays and Reviews*, he should declare:

What we most fear is that Catholics may cast themselves willingly, or be drawn unconsciously, into the stream which is evidently carrying English society every year more and more decidedly and perceptibly towards worldliness and Rationalism.

[17] Fitzgerald, Percy, *Fifty Years of Catholic Life and Social Progress*, vol. 1, pp. 82–3.   [18] Ibid.

[19] Manning, H. E., 'The Work and the Wants of the Catholic Church in England', *The Dublin Review* (July 1863).

The article, published in *The Dublin Review* in July 1863, constitutes a blueprint for future policy. Manning specified five chief 'wants' for which an urgent and effective remedy had to be found. Of the five, four were concerned with education. There was needed a system of proper diocesan seminaries for the education of the priesthood according to the decrees of Trent. There was needed an adequate supply of schools for the poor and middle class. No fewer than 20,000 Catholic children in London alone were still deprived. 'To find funds sufficient for this purpose a system is needed which will not only gather or ask alms of Catholics, but so address the intellect, heart, and will of the faithful as to move them to deny themselves for the accomplishment of this great and vital work.'

The third great want was that 'of a higher literary and scientific education for our laymen—analogous in fact, to that furnished by the Protestant universities'. This was a question 'of the highest importance, a solution of which must be promptly made'. The problem was a simple one:

It is well known that Catholics have been admitted for a long period of years to reside and study in Cambridge, but not to take degrees. Until 1854 they were absolutely excluded from Oxford. By a recent change, sanctioned by Act of Parliament, Catholics may reside and study in the colleges and halls of Oxford, and proceed to the degree of Bachelor of Arts. In Cambridge the degree of Master of Arts is also open to them. In the course of the nine years since 1854 it is said that twenty Catholics have passed through Oxford, and it is likely that others will enter. Now two questions arise: first, whether it is expedient that Catholics should avail themselves of the liberty thus granted to them to study at the two Universities? and, secondly, if so, whether it be expedient that they should reside one by one within the walls of the existing Colleges and halls, or that a Catholic college and hall be founded to receive them?

After stating the problem, Manning proceeded to consider the pros and cons of the case. Nine chief reasons were advanced in favour of a close association with the Universities. It was urged that, as by the repeal of the penal laws Catholics were already admitted into the fullness of England's social and political life, 'they should re-enter also into the tradition of intellectual culture and development.' Secondly, it was undeniable that the exclusive possession of the Universities gave to the Protestant Englishman 'an advantage over his Catholic fellow-countryman'; and that, in order to cope or to compete with Protestants in public and private life, 'Catholics must be armed with their weapons, and share in the cultivation which constitutes their superiority'. Thirdly, the two Universities, and especially Oxford, 'retain in a high degree their mediaeval if not Catholic character; and it is safer for Catholics to study there than in Paris, in Pisa, or other Continental cities'. There then followed the argument that it was of great importance that Catholics should enter while young 'into relations with the men whom afterwards they must consort with in all branches of the public service, and in most of the relations of private life'. It was claimed that Catholics can 'in no other way obtain the advantages of so high a culture in literature and science', because 'the long traditional maturity and accumulated knowledge of the two Universities leave Catholics without a hope of competing with Protestants in these fields'. The sixth argument in favour of the Universities was closely allied to the earlier points. It was claimed that 'inasmuch as Catholics must be mixed up with Protestants in every walk and state of life, and that more and more as the religious animosities of the past are mitigated by the gradual fusion and blending of families and classes, there cannot be any special danger in their beginning early to learn how to carry themselves towards their Protestant fellow-citizens; or rather it would be far safer for them to acquire betimes such habits of mind as will fit them for their future contact with anti-Catholic opinions and practices in after-life'. It was urged that Catholics were already availing themselves of Oxford and Cambridge and that the fact must be accepted. Hence all that was needed were the safeguards of a Catholic Hall or College. If the Catholic youth were placed 'in a hall or college founded for Catholics only, under the government of a Catholic president and fellows, with Catholic discipline and instruction, and all the helps of the spiritual life—daily Mass, confession, communion, fasts and festivals—such a youth would be sustained and raised above himself, and a Catholic public opinion would be created within the walls, which would resist the contagion and infection of the surrounding intellectual and moral evils'. The remaining arguments were connected with such a projected institution. A Catholic hall 'could not fail powerfully to affect the Universities' and it would counteract 'the development of a license of opinion which is not only anti-Catholic, but anti-Christian'.

Having dealt with the chief points in favour of participation in the education offered by Oxford and Cambridge, Manning turned to examine the objections of those opposed to the idea. Such people 'neither undervalue the importance of intellectual culture, nor overrate the present intellectual standard among the youths or the professors of our Catholic colleges', but 'they are of opinion that it is the mission and the duty of the Church to provide such intellectual culture within its own unity'. They were aware that the Church in England could not immediately create a system of education possessing the maturity and extension of the ancient Universities, but they could begin 'as they first began who came to the schools of S. Frideswide'. Secondly, they were of opinion that the anti-Catholic atmosphere of Oxford and Cambridge 'cannot fail to be secretly and deeply injurious to the faith and morals of the Catholic students'. It was argued that it was not intended 'that the members of a Catholic hall at Oxford or Cambridge should live as hermits or as exiles from academical society'. The making of friendships, and the entering into relations with Protestants who will be their companions and colleagues in after-life, 'is part of the argument in favour of such a system'. This contact 'would be most dangerous to those who as yet are immature in mind and character'. Those who opposed the sending of Catholic youths to Oxford and Cambridge did so, Manning claimed, on the basis of the argument 'so elaborately and eloquently developed by Dr. Newman, in his Lectures on University Education'. Newman had urged that 'if the Catholic Faith is true, a university cannot exist externally to the Catholic pale, for it cannot teach universal knowledge, if it does not teach Catholic theology'; to blot religion out was, for Catholics, to unravel 'the web of university teaching'.[20] Seven years before

[20] See Coulson's argument in *Theology and the University*, p. 52.

Manning was writing in *The Dublin Review*, Newman declared: 'It will not satisfy me, what satisfies so many, to have two independent systems, intellectual and religious, going at once side by side, by a sort of division of labour, and only accidentally brought together. . . . I want the same roof to contain both the intellectual and the moral discipline.'[21] Newman was quite specific: 'I wish the intellect to range with the utmost freedom and religion to enjoy an equal freedom; but what I am stipulating for is, that they should be found in one and the same place, and exemplified in the same persons. I want to destroy that diversity of centres, which puts everything into confusion by creating a contrariety of influences.'[22]

Manning in 1863 could not find any justification 'for the sanguine hope that a Catholic hall would teach the colleges of Oxford and Cambridge how to live, or leaven the life and spirit of the Universities',[23] and those who were opposed to the frequentation of the Universities believed with him that the risk to a number of individuals 'is not to be weighed against the danger of committing the Church to a false position'. It would be a sad but safer alternative 'to endure the loss of any number of individuals than to place the Church in the condition it occupies in the Universities of Germany. Syncretism has borne, and will bear, its bitter fruits there as a warning to us.' The founding of a Catholic hall 'would indefinitely postpone all efforts towards founding purely Catholic colleges for higher lay education—a work absolutely needed already, and becoming every day more urgently and vitally necessary as the Catholic Church expands its own system, and multiplies its members among the middle and higher classes'. The separation of religious and secular education had been condemned in Ireland, and the Holy See had informed the Irish bishops that the basis upon which the godless colleges rested was *intrinsecè periculosa*. The question also needed to be answered 'how shall we refuse a common secular education for our poor children if we court and catch at it for the children of

[21] Newman, J. H., *Sermons Preached on Various Occasions*, 5th edn., p. 13.
[22] Ibid. See Miss Trevor's comments in *Light in Winter*, p. 110.
[23] Manning, *Miscellanies*, vol. 1, p. 53.

the rich?' Those who opposed the sending of Catholic youths to Oxford and Cambridge were particularly concerned at this time, wrote Manning, 'when the modern spirit of cultivated unbelief, in the form of criticism and philosophy, has not only entered but established itself, so as to be the predominant intellectual tendency of the more studious members of the Universities'. The only solution to the difficulties facing the Catholic body was to establish a Catholic University. Such a scheme was not utopian. 'If in times of their poverty', Manning declared, 'the vicars-apostolic could found and raise three such colleges as S. Edmund's, Oscott, and Ushaw, why should not the united Catholic Hierarchy of England found a University?' The establishment of a Catholic University in England could be achieved 'with no greater difficulty than besets all great enterprises', and it would, in turn, provide for the other chief wants of the time, a greater practical efficiency and more public experience in the laity, and a breaking down of insularity leading to a fuller appreciation of the Church's missionary role.

Manning concluded his masterly exposition of the tasks facing the Catholic body by specifying a number of dangers which his co-religionists must be prepared to face. One of these was the direct result of the absence of a Catholic literature, but another more copious and manifold was what the Germans called 'the time-spirit'. 'The first principles and maxims of Catholic education—such as submission to a teaching authority, fear of error, mistrust of our own judgments—are extinct. This spirit begins in our schools, pervades our Universities, and animates the whole of English society.' Too often Catholics of the upper classes had been prepared to swallow their religious convictions as the price of social acceptability. 'They have put off their shoes upon the threshold' of English society, 'and even, like our adventurous Captain Burton at Mecca, have entered as sound Mahometans.' Manning was firmly convinced that 'in twenty years Rationalism will inundate England', for 'it has passed through the two phases which have appeared in Germany, and it is entering upon the third. The period of Protestant dogmatism has given place to Protestant pietism, and this is now passing off into Protestant

Rationalism—the prelude of philosophical Rationalism in the educated, and rude unbelief in the people.' Dr. Colenso was a fair sample of the school of rationalistic Christianity.[24] 'There can be little question that if the majority of the Anglican clergy be against him, the great majority of the Anglican laity would be with him. His common-sense scepticism is the true Anglican layman's faith.'[25] The Universities would eventually be pervaded by a similar philosophy, and Catholics instead, therefore, of implicating themselves 'in a sinking wreck' ought to shun 'the vortex which it makes in going down'. Catholics must shift for themselves, and if it is asked where are the men, and where is the money, Manning would reply: 'Vigour creates men and coins money.'

It has for long been assumed that Manning was primarily responsible for Wiseman's growing antipathy to the national Universities. Recent writers, following E. S. Purcell, have depicted the Provost in the role of evil genius presiding over Wiseman's declining years. Purcell refers to the exertion of 'personal influence' over Wiseman, 'to persuasion', and 'at times even almost to intimidation', and he asserts that 'it is quite certain that Wiseman was favourable to Oxford, though possibly, in his last illness Manning's importunity overcame the dying Cardinal's convictions'. The key to Wiseman's attitude, however, is given by Manning himself. Writing in 1885 on 'The Office of the Church in Higher Catholic Education', Manning declared:

> There was no one who ever manifested so large and generous a sympathy with the conversions that issued from Oxford, and with members of the Anglican Communion, than the late Cardinal. His learned and powerful writings in defence of the Catholic faith were studiously directed both in matter and in manner, without sacrifice of jot or tittle of the truth, to attract and to conciliate the members of the Anglican

[24] 'The Colenso case', in which the Bishop of Cape Town deposed the controversial cleric from his see (Natal) for holding unorthodox views on Biblical inspiration, was not to reach its zenith until 1866. For over fourteen years the diocese of Natal had rival bishops, Colenso enjoying the recognition of the government and William Butler that of the Metropolitan and the Lambeth Conference.

[25] Manning, *Miscellanies*, vol. I, p. 70.

Communion and the writers of the Oxford Movement. . . . If ever, therefore, there was any one who, if it had been possible to sanction it, would have rejoiced over . . . the return of Catholic youth to the Universities which Catholic England had created, it would have been our late Cardinal. But two things forbade him: his unerring Catholic instinct, and his keen intuition of the impossibility of combining fidelity to the divine tradition of the faith with the intellectual deviations and contradictions of modern England.[26]

In his *Journal* Manning writes that Wiseman was by instinct opposed to the College plan,[27] and there is little doubt that *Essays and Reviews* and the corpus of thought they represented caused considerable alarm in Wiseman's breast. Furthermore, Wiseman's growing wariness of the talk of a Catholic College at Oxford was influenced by suspicion of the activities of Ambrose Phillipps de Lisle. The latter had been engaged since 1846 in a series of quixotic schemes for the corporate reunion of the Churches of England and Rome.[28] For some years de Lisle urged that Anglo-Catholics had a duty to remain where they were and to work within the body of the Church of England for total reunion. In the 1860s he was involved in advocating a Uniat Church for England which would adhere to an English liturgy based upon the Book of Common Prayer and would have a married clergy. In 1857 de Lisle and a number of High Church Anglicans formed the Association for Promoting the Unity of Christendom. In the articles of the Association certain assumptions were made which ultimately led to Wiseman's securing of a papal condemnation of the movement, issued after the Cardinal's death in November 1865. The assumptions were that there was truth in the claim that Roman Catholics, Greek Orthodox, and Anglicans were members of a larger body, Christ's Holy Catholic Church, that the Orders of all three Churches were equally valid, and that the Anglican clergy were sacrificing priests. Prior to the definitive and formal condemnation of 1865, Wiseman in con-

---

[26] Manning, *The Office of the Church in Higher Catholic Education*, Pastoral Letter, Easter 1885, p. 5.

[27] Manning Papers, Bayswater. Manning's *Journal*, Bk. No. 4, pp. 54 seq.

[28] See Purcell, *Life of de Lisle*, vol. 1, pp. 346 seq.

junction with the other bishops received a letter from Cardinal
Barnabo in September 1864, urging the prelates to 'use all
diligence to point out the vicious defects with which the Society
abounds, and to ward off the dangers it brings along with it'.[29]
The Association was branded a dangerous novelty. To favour it
was to support *indifferentism*. The Association was thought to
discourage 'the conversions of non-Catholics to the faith', and
to endeavour 'by means of its publications to hinder them'.[30]
De Lisle denied the imputations attributed to the movement, but
Anglicans involved in the Association did preach the futility of
individual conversion. Bishop Clifford of Clifton, de Lisle's
cousin, pointed out to him in 1864 that

of late it cannot be denied that the theory of there being three Christian
communions, the Roman, the Greek, and the Anglican, all three
branches of the true Church, but all more or less in error, as regards
minor points, has become one of the most prominent of the doctrines
advocated by the Association. I do not say that all hold it, but by far the
greater portion do, and hence the opinion was gaining ground that
Catholics who were members of the Association held this view to be
true, or at least tenable. The Church could not but condemn such a view
as heretical.[31]

Wilfrid Ward has shown that the strong Memorandum for
Propaganda drawn up in 1857, in which Wiseman indicated his
disapproval of the efforts of de Lisle to compromise him in the
questionable theological views of the members of the Association,
was drawn up in Wiseman's own hand, and 'in Wiseman's fluent
Italian, with few erasures and corrections'.[32] Wiseman had found
de Lisle's pamphlet 'On the Future Unity of Christendom' to be
'full of the grossest errors'.[33]

It needs to be borne in mind that plans which were being
formed in 1863 for the establishment of a Catholic Hall or College
at Oxford were closely bound up with de Lisle's visionary schemes

[29] Ibid. The document is given, vol. 1, pp. 387–8. The formal condemnation
of 1865 is printed *in extenso* in Appendix III of Purcell, pp. 17 seq.

[30] Ibid., p. 389.

[31] Ibid., Clifford to de Lisle, 27 Oct. 1864, pp. 402–3.

[32] Ward, W., *Life of Wiseman*, vol. 2, pp. 479 et seq.

[33] Ibid. Wiseman's report is printed *in extenso*, pp. 479–88.

for corporate reunion. Wiseman was aware of this from information supplied by de Lisle in 1863.[34] One of de Lisle's fellow enthusiasts in the reunion movement wrote in July 1863 that a Catholic Hall at Oxford 'would be the thing of all others calculated to promote kindly feelings between Anglicans and Roman Catholics', and that 'Oxford and Cambridge being the seminaries of the English clergy are the hot-beds of (anti-Catholic) prejudices', and hence 'it is there that we must dig up their roots, if we ever mean to do so'.[35] It was soon obvious to Wiseman that de Lisle was preparing to use the Oxford scheme in the larger interests of his reunion plans.

In July 1863 Edmund S. Ffoulkes, a convert to Roman Catholicism and late Fellow of Jesus College, Oxford, wrote to Bishop Thomas Grant of Southwark to ask for his support for a plan to open a Hall in Oxford. Ffoulkes, an active member of the Association for Promoting the Unity of Christendom, had de Lisle's support in the venture and Bishop Grant was thought to be sympathetic to the Universities.

Recent legislation [Ffoulkes wrote] has thrown open Oxford and Cambridge to Catholics and Dissenters . . . and as a graduate of Oxford myself, I have determined to apply to the authorities of that University for leave to open a Hall there exclusively for Catholic students. . . . It will be for them to decide how far it can be granted in the present state of the Law. . . . I will only premise, that being confined to Catholics, its staff of teachers will be as exclusively Catholic as that of Ushaw, Oscott, or Stonyhurst. Its special object will be to educate for the lay professions: but there will be no such thing known in it as what is called 'a mixed system of education'—It will prepare for the Oxford Examinations, but only just as Ushaw, Oscott, and Stonyhurst have done for those of the University of London. . . . Let me premise in the clearest manner, that I have not the slightest idea of committing any one to the success of my scheme but myself, and those who may be willing to assist me with their kind support. . . . It is a private undertaking and nothing more: and under existing circumstances I may claim full benefit of the rule 'in licitis libertas'.[36]

[34] Purcell, *Life of de Lisle*, vol. 2, pp. 3–4. [35] Ibid., p. 4.
[36] Southwark Archdiocesan Archives. Edmund S. Ffoulkes to Thomas Grant, July 1863.

A Committee was to be formed, however, from among the Catholic aristocracy to direct the venture.[37] De Lisle was to be convener, Lord Edward Howard (de Lisle's son-in-law) was to be Chairman, and Ffoulkes himself was to be Secretary. Hope-Scott was to be a member. Ecclesiastics were to be excluded from direct participation, with the exception of Newman, whose name was to be kept out of the early moves. Ffoulkes was to uphold the pretence that the scheme was merely a private venture of his own. After a year or two, the Hall having taken root, he would resign and Newman would assume 'his old quarters once more'.[38] Ffoulkes urged de Lisle to picture to himself 'what the moral effect of this would be on a place like Oxford';[39] a decisive step would be taken in the corporate reunion campaign. The Hall would cater at the outset for about a dozen well-born students and Ffoulkes hoped that England's premier Duke would be the first 'alumnus'.

Unfortunately, however, Ffoulkes made a tactical error in appealing to the sympathy of Bishop Grant, who promptly brought the issue to the attention of Wiseman and his episcopal confrères. On 8 September Ffoulkes wrote to Grant again, enclosing a circular on the projected Hall. He had heard rumours that the plan was to become the subject of episcopal discussion. He told Grant he meant to go ahead, convinced that God had called him to the work. 'London University degrees are no distinction at all in good society,' he wrote, 'on the contrary they serve but to stamp our inferiority.'[40] If the bishops were to decide on founding a Catholic University, then he would be ready to withdraw in its favour, but he urged that 'it would at least be politic to give Oxford or Cambridge a fair trial first, our laity being at present strongly prejudiced in their favour, and with a Catholic Hall, properly conducted, there could be no danger of anything like mixed education'.[41]

---

[37] See Purcell, *Life of de Lisle*, vol. 2, pp. 5 seq.   [38] Ibid.
[39] Ibid.
[40] Southwark Archdiocesan Archives. Edmund S. Ffoulkes to Thomas Grant, Nativity of B.V.M., 1863.   [41] Ibid.

II

THE CAMPAIGN FOR AN
OXFORD COLLEGE

IN 1864 the movement to establish a Catholic Hall in Oxford reached its zenith, with the issue of a number of pamphlets, a debate in the columns of the Catholic press, and the personal intervention of Newman. The most decisive note sounded in the pamphlet warfare came from the pen of 'A Catholic Layman', identified in a letter of Manning to Canon Oakeley as Peter le Page Renouf, who had been a tutor in Newman's Dublin house for aristocrats.[1] 'There are many countries', the author claimed, where ' "Catholic Universities" may live and thrive . . . they are an impossibility in countries where, as in England, the Catholic population is so small that all the demand for University education might be adequately supplied by a single College.' The author thought that there was no special danger existing at the Universities which did not exist elsewhere; 'rationalism' was a danger everywhere. This pamphlet, addressed to Newman, brought an immediate response from the Revd. Henry A. Rawes of the Oblates of St. Charles, formerly a clergyman in the Church of England and a graduate of Trinity College, Cambridge. He addressed himself directly to the Catholic Layman: 'You seem to me to have got somehow an idea into your head', he declared, 'that there is something in the eternal nature of things which makes it impossible that there can be more than two Universities in England; and makes it also impossible that those Universities can be other than Oxford or Cambridge.'[2] No mention was made of Durham University, complained Rawes, 'but from what I

[1] *University Education for English Catholics: a Letter to the Very Rev. J. H. Newman, D.D.*, by 'A Catholic Layman'.
[2] Rawes, the Revd. H. A., M.A., O.S.C.: *Cui Bono? University Education: a Letter to 'A Catholic Layman'*, p. 32.

know about it, I am certain that the education there is in every way equal to that at Oxford or Cambridge. I remember some twelve years ago that most Anglican Bishops were said to prefer candidates for Ordination from Durham to those from the two great Universities. But as to social prestige Durham does not rank with them. Consequently it is out of the question.' He wished to ask those persons 'who are so anxious for a University Education, before the Church in this land has had time to turn herself round, why do they not go to Dublin? Say it is only a provisional arrangement; why do they not go there till something can be done in England?' He declared he was certain 'that those persons who will not go to Dublin till we can get a University in England are seeking for something else than education'. They were seeking that social prestige so scathingly spoken of by Mark Pattison. The scheme for a Catholic College at Oxford was fraught with practical difficulties, and an absurd plan, thought Rawes. More than this, 'it flies right in the face of the Holy Father's decision with regard to the Queen's Colleges in Ireland'. He advanced a plea: 'Let us get a Catholic University in England. We can easily get it if we please. . . . *We need nothing but a vigorous development of our own resources.*'

Another pamphleteer in 1864 was Frederick, Canon Oakeley. An early Tractarian convert, Oakeley was a son of a former Governor of Madras. He had held a Fellowship at Balliol, where he had been a colleague of the future Archbishop Tait and a mentor of the young Matthew Arnold. Oakeley addressed his pamphlet to Bishop Ullathorne.[3] He claimed that 'any system of education which does not recognise as a first principle the necessity of guarding faith from external injury, as well as of providing for its regular sustentation, is essentially uncatholic, and, as such, ought to be avoided by all who wish to act upon the rule of the Catechism,—that we are to take more care of the soul than of the body, because Our Lord had told us, that the interests of the

---

[3] *The Question of University Education for English Catholics, considered principally in its Moral and Religious Bearings, in a Letter to the Right Rev. the Bishop of Birmingham*, by Frederick Oakeley, M.A. (Oxon.), Canon of the Metropolitan Chapter, formerly Fellow of Balliol College.

soul are incommensurate with the interests of the world'. With regard to the plan of sending younger members of the Catholic aristocracy to the existing Colleges of Oxford or Cambridge, he wrote:

> I can see nothing whatever to be said of it except in the way of condemnation, [for] there would be the thoroughly uncatholic, not to say anti-Catholic, air of the place, pressing upon the soul like a nightmare, and the general dearth of spiritual food, gradually tending to convert into a merely passive and unresisting inanition the appetite which at first yearned ineffectually for the satisfaction of its cravings, but was gradually dying away under the effects of disappointment and desuetude.

Concerning the possibility of an exclusively Catholic foundation in England, Oakeley was nervous, unless it were to be run by a single religious community. Diversity of interests would complicate matters. A Catholic College at Oxford was certainly a possibility, but the community selected to run it ought to have the reins very much in its own hands.

W. G. Ward commented on all these pamphlets and on the rejoinders of the various authors in *The Dublin Review*. In October 1864, in an article entitled 'University Education for English Catholics', he reviewed the pamphlet of the Catholic Layman. Ward felt that the author was too optimistic concerning the talent available among Catholics.

> If we could take so sanguine a view as this writer takes of the *personnel* which is now at the disposal of our Episcopate, we should humbly submit that the full time has come in which, not his scheme [for a Catholic College at Oxford], but a scheme directly inconsistent with his, might at once be started with the greatest possible advantage to English Catholics. . . . On such an hypothesis, we humbly submit that no time should be lost in at once starting either a Catholic University, or a Catholic College of Higher Studies, totally removed from Oxford or any other Protestant institution, and placed under the control of these highly and rarely gifted men.[4]

Even with a Catholic College established in Oxford, the free social intercourse of the student with powerful and influential

---

[4] *The Dublin Review* (Oct. 1864), p. 373.

Protestant intellects at the most impressionable period of his life would 'unconsciously saturate his mind with anti-Catholic notions'.

The *Dublin* also turned its attention to Oakeley's arguments. Ward had gone up to Oxford in 1830 as Commoner of Christ Church, and he took issue with Oakeley regarding the condition of that particular college. Oakeley had postulated that under-graduates mixed very little with men outside their own colleges and that Catholic students in a Catholic Hall at Oxford would do likewise. This view Ward disputed.

> Canon Oakeley mentions that when he was at Christ Church, Christ Church men mixed very little with others. But this was due to their contempt for other Colleges; and it must not be forgotten that (unless our memory deceives us) there were at Christ Church nearly 200 under-graduates—many men of conspicuous ability—from whom any indi-vidual could choose his society. This exclusiveness, moreover, did not continue. The writer of this article was at Christ Church some ten years later than Canon Oakeley, and all his chief friends belonged to other Colleges.[5]

Renouf, using a pseudonym, replied to Ward's arguments in a letter addressed to *The Tablet* on 12 November 1864, and Oakeley published a further pamphlet as his rejoinder to Ward.[6] Oakeley claimed 'he never defended the project [of an Oxford Catholic College] with anything like enthusiasm, or, indeed, otherwise than with considerable hesitation'. He maintained that with regard to social intercourse between undergraduates of differing colleges it was well known that cricket and boat-racing formed the basic staple of their conversation. Furthermore, Catholic Superiors would have to regulate the youths' intercourse with Protestant companions and 'moderate, or even interdict it in the case of those with whom it might be dangerous'.[7] Finally, Oakeley doubted whether Catholic gentlemen would be deterred from sending their sons to Oxford, however great the dangers.

---

[5] Ibid., p. 401.

[6] *Appendix to a Letter on University Education for English Catholics*, suggested by an article in *The Dublin Review*, by Very Revd. Canon Oakeley.

[7] Ibid., p. 39.

In January 1865 Ward replied to Oakeley's *Appendix*.[8] He acknowledged that Oakeley agreed with himself in thinking 'that unless that instruction which is specially Catholic occupies the paramount place in a student's intellect, imagination, and affections, those disastrous results must ensue at which he "shudders" no less than we do'. With regard to Oakeley's contention about the topics of conversation among undergraduates he remarked, 'if he is speaking of ordinary and every-day youths, we were never so absurd as to doubt this, but such a fact is altogether irrelevant to our argument. If, on the other hand, he means that when youths of keen and earnest intelligence congregate together they seldom speak except of cricket and boating, we are a good deal surprised at his opinion.' Such discipline and watchfulness over companions as Oakeley advocated was quite absurd when applied to university life. It would, wrote Ward, 'simply issue in heart-burnings, jealousies, resentments, and disaffection . . . the members of such a College would be laughing-stocks to the whole University'. With regard to the argument concerning the inevitability of Catholic youths' attending the Universities— a major part of Oakeley's hypothesis—Ward wanted to know what guarantee there was that they would attend a Catholic College if one existed. Youths 'would be far more keenly alive to the social advantages exclusively obtainable in a place like Christ Church, than to the spiritual evils of which it might be the occasion'. Ward was primarily afraid of the circumambient anti-Catholic and anti-Christian atmosphere of the Universities. 'A Catholic University or higher college in England would be the best means of supplying a confessed desideratum.'

The debate was intensified by the intervention of Newman. The story of his attempt to establish a house of the Oratory in Oxford is well known.[9] He chose the very year of Ffoulkes's projected scheme to make yet another claim in the interests of the English Catholic aristocracy. The years since his return from

[8] *The Dublin Review* (Jan. 1865), pp. 125–41.
[9] See especially Ward, W., *Life of Newman*, vol. 2, ch. XXI, pp. 47 seq.; Purcell, *Life of de Lisle*, vol. 2, pp. 7 seq.; Butler, *Life of Ullathorne*, vol. 2, ch. XIII, pp. 1 seq.

Ireland had been devoted to the establishment of the Oratory School, to provide for those aristocratic youths he had failed to attract in Dublin. It was time, however, to think again along more adventurous lines. He saw his opportunity in the obvious covetousness of the aristocracy for the social benefits of Oxford life. If he could place himself at the head of a movement which they would support, he could yet achieve, on more congenial terrain, what he had failed to do in Ireland. In August 1864 (a few months after the bishops had considered how they could discourage the attendance of Catholics at Oxford) Newman purchased five acres of land there. Hope-Scott, Bellasis, and others of a like kidney promised money; Ullathorne offered the care of the mission. Newman seemed to have a watertight plan. He was going to Oxford to establish a house of the Oratory, and he was going in obedience to his bishop to take charge of the parochial work. In reality Newman's motives were much less innocent. He was endeavouring to establish himself in Oxford, where he knew he would be on the spot should the rich Catholics get their way in the matter of higher education. We are left in no doubt as to his strategy. Writing to Hope-Scott in August 1864, Newman declared: 'No college would be set up, but the priest—i.e. the Fathers of the Oratory—would take lodgers.'[10] The lodgers would be undergraduates. He asked Hope-Scott: 'Can the Oratory, that is I, *when once* set up, without saying a word to anyone, make the Oratory a Hall?' Ullathorne, it seems, was to be tricked. 'The *Oratory* is *confessedly* out of the Bishop's jurisdiction', he wrote. Newman's defence would be '*the support of the Catholic gentry*'. The plan to establish a Hall would be '*independent* of any *Mission* plan, but it is a great point to come in under the Bishop's sanction and to be carrying out an idea of his'. Also, 'it gives us an ostensible position quite independent of the College plan', Newman declared. He added, significantly, 'It would not be worth while coming to Oxford to keep a mere lodging house,—but, being there already as Missioners it is natural to take youths into our building, and many parents would like it.' He

[10] Ward, W., *Life of Newman*, vol. 2, pp. 51–3. Newman to Hope-Scott, 29 Aug. 1864.

anticipated he would get into hot water with *Propaganda*, but he was prepared to challenge Rome as well as the English episcopate. 'The Catholic gentry alone could save me here', he warned.

By October 1864 Newman was disappointed that many of the Catholic gentry appeared 'to *prefer* sending their boys to the existing colleges',[11] and his scheme seemed impracticable. Yet, with an Oratory in Oxford, he could afford to wait. A month later he was informing a rich friend that he was going to Oxford, 'primarily and directly to take care of the Catholic youth who are beginning to go there, and are in Protestant Colleges'.[12] Nothing was calculated more to make the bishops suspicious of Newman's intentions than his determination to present them with a *fait accompli*. It had been the use of similar tactics which had led to strain in Newman's dealings with Cullen.

Bishop Grant of Southwark, friendly to Newman as he was, was particularly determined that the hierarchy should not slip into the affair without an opportunity for full discussion. In November he had already taken to task Fr. G. R. Kingdon, S.J., for encouraging Henry Stourton to go to Oxford, Kingdon's defence being that 'people who are bent on a thing very easily interpret anything that may be said as a direct encouragement of their wish'.[13] Grant urged Wiseman to act before it was too late.

Wiseman called a meeting of the episcopacy for 13 December, and meantime 'drew up with his own hand an interrogatory dealing with this question in detail'.[14] In his *Journal* Manning indicates that the questions were framed by Wiseman personally and that Wiseman was responsible for their dispatch.[15] The interrogatory was drawn up, and the episcopal meeting arranged, as a direct result of a letter received by the Cardinal Archbishop from the Cardinal Prefect of *Propaganda* on 7 November 1864. The latter had been sent in response to a request for guidance which the episcopacy had made at its Low Week meeting of that

---

[11] Ward, W., *Life of Newman*, vol. 2, Newman to Gaisford, 30 Oct. 1864, pp. 54–5.

[12] Ibid., Newman to Wetherell, 1 Nov. 1864, pp. 55–6.

[13] Southwark Archdiocesan Archives. Kingdon to Grant, 27 Nov. 1864.

[14] Manning's Pastoral Letter, Easter 1885.

[15] Manning Papers, Bayswater. Manning's *Journal*, Bk. No. 4, pp. 54 seq.

year. The Cardinal Prefect thought 'that the differences of opinion and the perplexity which had . . . arisen were such as to make it necessary that some rule should be laid down for the guidance both of the clergy and of the laity', and he declared that His Holiness desired 'that an extraordinary meeting of the Bishops should be held as soon as possible, for the purpose of seriously considering the said project (of a Catholic Hall at Oxford) and of accurately making known to the Holy See the opinions which the Bishops should severally express'.[16] The meeting was not called to deal with Newman and the Oratory project, as Newman himself was later to assert that it was. The Ffoulkes scheme provided the original stimulus of the inquiry, but the debates in the Catholic press and the growing demands of a small vocal group were the chief cause of episcopal concern. In December prayers were ordered in every diocese for light to guide the bishops in their deliberations.

Wiseman's circular was sent to a large number of clergy and laity having direct experience of university life. Newman, for his part, was received in person by Wiseman a month before the dispatch of the interrogatory, and the Oxford plan was discussed. He wrote afterwards to Ambrose St. John that Wiseman 'listened to the Oxford plan, half querulously'.[17]

Wiseman's letter was as follows:[18]

On Tuesday the 13th the Bishops will meet to discuss questions relative to the education of Catholic young men in the two English Universities. As you went through the academical course at . . . you would greatly oblige me, by furnishing me with such information as your experience may suggest, by replying, as concisely and as accurately as possible, to the following queries, referring, in your answers, to the numbers which they bear:

1. Is there anything in the English University education which it seems to you impossible, or very difficult, to give, in our Catholic Colleges, by any practicable addition to, or variation of, their present system or condition? Please state in what it consists.

[16] Manning Papers, Bayswater. 'Decisions of the Holy See and Acts of the Bishops on the Subject of Higher Catholic Education', 7 Nov. 1864.
[17] Ward, W., *Life of Wiseman*, vol. 2, p. 61. Newman to St. John, 5 Nov. 1864.
[18] Cornthwaite Papers, Leeds Diocesan Archives.

2. What would you say is the exact meaning of *scholarship* as the peculiar characteristic of University education?

3. What are the studies in which a Catholic youth going to a Protestant University would be engaged during his course in it?

4. Would he acquire a greater knowledge than he could in a College

(*a*) of modern languages, as French, Italian and German?
(*b*) of foreign literature?
(*c*) of history, geography, art and other general subjects of information?

5. Have you observed or heard on any good authority that in competitive examination, attending to proportion of numbers, the Catholics have fallen below Protestant aspirants, whether in military or administrative competition?

6. Has it similarly come under your notice that, attending to ratio of numbers, at the Bar, from the bench downwards, or in any other learned profession, persons brought up in a University have shewn a decisive superiority over those educated in Catholic establishments?

7. Putting aside all question of tone and manner, and considering the average of young men who annually go into the world from the University and of those who finish their studies exclusively among Catholics, does any superiority in solid learning and good education manifest itself in the first above the second?

8. Supposing a young Catholic, whose education had been carried in one of our Colleges to the extent professed to be taught there, were to go for three years to a Protestant University, in what respect and to what extent do you suppose that his education would be found advanced and his character better formed?

9. And more specifically, do you consider that the chances of improvement in moral and religious condition would be increased during that interval, and that the probability is that he would be found better grounded in faith, in piety, and in moral feeling at the end than he was at the beginning of that term?

10. Considering the present condition of belief in the truths of revelation among leading minds in the Universities, do you think that the intercourse natural between the learned and able men of the Universities with younger minds and inexperienced scholars, would not necessarily tend to weaken the faith in these?

11. Would it be possible, not to say expedient, to guard such impres-

sionable minds, especially where there was an ardour for learning, by weakening or destroying all confidence on the part of youth in those whom they were otherwise expected to respect and submit their judgement to?

12. Why is the demand in favour of University education according to your way of viewing it, to be limited to the laity?

13. If there be a higher, a nobler and a more useful education to be attained at a University than can possibly be given in a Catholic College unless such College is established in a Protestant University), why should the Clergy be deprived in England alone of those signal advantages?

14. Ought the principle to be admitted that the laity should be more highly educated than their clergy, considering the reproaches too readily cast on the latter for lagging in the progress of knowledge and solid attainments?

15. May it not be justly considered (1) that if no danger of loss of faith or morals exists for a layman, *a fortiori* there can be none for an ecclesiastic? (2) that the mixture of virtuous and fervent ecclesiastical scholars will sustain and encourage their former College companions?

16. Is it not true that although we treat the Universities as though great national institutions for lay education, they are no less, or perhaps in the main, the Protestant substitutes for Ecclesiastical Seminaries, and form in reality the places in which all the clergy of the Church of England are educated? Are not all the Archbishops and Bishops of England and in great measure of Ireland, all the dignitaries, certainly of England and the vast bulk of the parochial clergy of the Established Church educated there; and has not the fruit of such education been on the whole to produce a Clergy most hostile in feeling and most heterodox in doctrine in their attitude towards the Catholic Church?

17. Do you think that such being the case, it would be worthy of the Catholic Church and its pastors, believing themselves to be under the guidance of the Holy Spirit, to surrender the highest education of their children, or of their ecclesiastical students, to the teaching and guiding of such a body of men?

18. Is not the great teaching body of the Universities composed of Protestant, consequently of heretical clergymen; and do you think that the Bishops ought to advise the Holy See to commit the final training, and the finishing touch to the formation of mind and

heart of the children of God's people, to the hands of those who have publicly declared and professed to hold that belief in the most solemn and consoling doctrines, and observance of the most beautiful practices of devotion in the Church, are damnable and idolatrous?

19. Or do you think it possible for a professor or teacher holding the Holy Catholic Church in contempt, and perhaps execration, from day to day to lecture upon even indifferent topics without almost involuntarily allowing his feelings to escape from any amount of watchful guardedness, and insinuate themselves into the susceptible minds or imaginations of a few unnoticed Catholic pupils?

20. On the whole, after considering all these questions and the answers which you have no doubt conscientiously given them in the presence of God, looking at the whole state of Europe, and of England, and weighing in the balance of the Sanctuary the opinions, political, scientific, social, and moral, in conflict through the world, do you believe that should a considerable body of young Catholics receive education in Protestant Universities, that the result will be the formation of a future Catholic body more conscientious, more orthodox, more religious, more devout, and more pure than we can obtain by any other process of education? And that should the decision be now in favour of Protestant University education, our successors, and the future heads of Catholic families, will feel thankful to God, and believe that His Providence has guided and blessed the decision?

Many of the questions were ingenuous, and Wiseman in forming the interrogatory clearly indicated where he himself stood on the issue under debate. It is erroneous, however, for Coulson to maintain that Oxford was to be anathema *simply* because it was the home of the Anglican establishment.[19] Similarly, it is incorrect for Coulson to maintain that Wiseman was trying to argue, in question 14 of the interrogatory, that the clergy ought to be better educated than the laity, or that the latter should be kept in intellectual subjugation to the former.[20] As questions 12, 13, 14, and 15 show, he was anxious to ensure that the educational standards of the clergy, attacked so readily by writers of *The Rambler* school, should keep pace with those of the laity.

[19] Coulson, J., Newman's Idea of an Educated Laity, in *Theology and the University*, p. 56.   [20] Ibid., p. 54.

Bishop Grant of Southwark was appointed to act as general organizer for the arrangement and classification of the results of the inquiry, and correspondents were free to reply to any individual bishop. It is not possible to quote from all of the extant replies but a selection will indicate the major viewpoints. The most powerful reply against the frequentation of the Universities undoubtedly came from the pen of Robert Aston Coffin, Redemptorist, ex-Oratorian, and future Bishop of Southwark. Coffin, an ascetical writer of distinction, was a former Student of Christ Church. Before his conversion to Catholicism in 1845 he had been Vicar of St. Mary Magdalen's, Oxford. With characteristic thoroughness he took each of Wiseman's points in turn. A number of his arguments are quoted at length because they embody the chief feelings of those converts who were antipathetic to Oxford.

Question 1

A young man of 18 who has made good use of his time in a Catholic College will have certainly gone thro' all the necessary preparatory work and should have laid a good foundation for his future course; but after that age, up to his 21st or 22nd years, he requires, as it seems to me, a higher course of Instruction, and opportunities for the formation and development of his mind which is gained not merely from attending Professorial Lectures in the Higher Branches, but also, from a more free association and intercourse with men, both above, as well as of, his own age, who are all engaged in the same pursuit, whilst the latter are considered and treated no longer as school boys, and as entirely 'in statu pupillari'.

It seems to me that it would be possible and not very difficult to meet this want in some measure, until such time as it should please Divine Providence to give us an English Catholic University, in some of our present Colleges, as Ushaw, Oscott, or Stonyhurst, and this by providing in them for students from the age of 18 and upwards a higher education and by relaxing, in certain points, College rules and discipline necessary for boys, in the same way as is done in the Collegio Pio, so as to give them a proper sense of independence and self-control, and a certain introduction to their future life in the World.

To carry out such a plan two things seem to me to be necessary:

1st. That certain Professorships should be founded with salaries sufficient to be an encouragement for men to prepare themselves well, and in an efficient manner, for the Chairs which they may hope one day to occupy and to induce those appointed to such Chairs to continue for some time in them, and to take a real interest in the work attached to them; and

2ndly. That the students belonging to this higher department of the College, should have every opportunity given them for associating freely with the professors and Superiors, and should feel that that bar of separation between the teacher and the taught, which is perhaps necessary in a mere school or college for boys, no longer exists.

Question 9

I believe that with some few rare exceptions, the results of 3 years' residence of our young men in an English Protestant University, would be an addition year by year to the numbers of worldly, disloyal, half-hearted, Catholics who cause sorrow to the Holy See and who would perpetuate that want of simple, hearty, obedience to and respect for, Ecclesiastical Authority, from which Holy Church has at this present moment, in my humble opinion, far more to fear, than from all her open and declared enemies from without.

Question 10

I unhesitatingly say that I should consider it a grievous sin to expose, *unnecessarily*, even a talented young Catholic, and far more one of only moderate abilities, to the attractive influence, naturally speaking, of such men as Professor Jowett and Dean Stanley.

Questions 12, 13, 14

I believe that the present cry for University Education arises in reality from the false impression

1. that a young man who has not been at Oxford of Cambridge will not be able to take his place in Society, or to mix easily with his equals in after life;

2. that to have been at Oxford or Cambridge is a *necessary* part of the education of a gentleman, and

3. that those who have not been at an English University are not, and will never be, *gentlemen* and *men of the world* in the ordinary worldly acceptation of the terms.

Hence up to the present moment we have heard nothing of the advantages of such education for *candidates for the priesthood*.

A few years ago it was said that we had no School for the children of gentlemen, hence such a School had to be formed [the Oratory School] and it was then expressly stated that it was not intended for those who had a vocation (or might have, for at 12 years old, it is ordinarily difficult to speak of certain vocation) to the Priesthood.

The worldly prestige attaching to Oxford and Cambridge, and the passport which the adjuncts to one's name of '*Student of Christ Church*', '*Late of Balliol*', '*Gentleman Commoner of Oriel*' afford for entrance into good Society are not considered necessarily, or even thought of for the Clergy, who are supposed to have nothing to do but to say Mass, hear Confessions, and look after the Irish poor, and therefore nothing is said of a higher education for the Clergy.

Question 16

It was certainly true, until perhaps within the last few years, that the two Universities of Oxford and Cambridge were almost exclusively the Protestant-Church of England substitutes for Ecclesiastical Seminaries: by far the larger proportion of Ministers had been educated at them. Durham, St. Bees, and Lampeter supplied comparatively few. . . . All the Archbishops and Bishops, Deans of Cathedrals, Canons, etc. and holders of large family livings, and Squire Parsons, are Oxford or Cambridge men . . . and many have been Heads, Fellows, and Tutors of Colleges . . . and there is no doubt, unless Liberalism and Rationalism have thoroughly changed Oxford from what it was 25 years ago, that it is still, as it has ever been since the Reformation, the seminary and hot-bed of Anglicanism, of Church of England orthodoxy and Evangelicalism, the stronghold and perpetual propagation of the 'Elizabethan Tradition', and the school of false nationality, and of the absurd and narrow-minded spirit which pretends to despise and depreciate everything that is not English.

It is at Oxford that a man learns to perfection 'the gentleman heresy' and with it the adoration of national greatness and prosperity, of success, of rank and wealth, and social position, and of all that the World prizes, and with all this, he sees in the University much that is naturally beautiful, graceful, refined and attractive, and if he were so disposed will easily mistake nature for grace, and the human for the divine. . . .

Question 18

In my time, i.e. 1837–1845, the Tutors of Colleges were *all* Ministers, all the Heads of Colleges, saving two, all the Public Professors, e.g. of

Moral Philosophy, Poetry, Modern History, and most of the resident
Fellows of Colleges. . . . You cannot take a step in Oxford, without
coming across a representative and a teacher of the Anglican heresy. . . .
[To send Catholics to Oxford would] absolutely prevent this country
for generations to come, if not for ever, from having a University or
other means of Higher Education of her own.

Question 20

[My belief is that permitting Catholics to frequent the Protestant
Universities would result in] the formation of a future Catholic body
less conscientious, *less* orthodox, *less* religious, *less* devout, *less* pure
than we can obtain by keeping the education of our youth as far as
possible in our own hands.[21]

Coffin's arguments received support from others, among them
David Lewis, George Wenham, and—at this time—James Spencer Northcote. David Lewis, Newman's curate at St. Mary's
in 1843, wrote from Arundel to say that the foundation of a
Catholic Hall at Oxford would delay for a century the foundation
of a Catholic University, and that he could not conceive of a
greater calamity. 'If a hall or College be founded in Oxford,' he
pointed out, 'the discipline of the house must be either the same
with that prevailing there, or it must be more severe. In either
case the results will be nearly alike. The young men will be
tempted to "migrate" from it to the Protestant Colleges.'[22] There
would also be the social stigma of belonging to a Hall as opposed
to a College, and he feared especially the University's teaching of
Philosophy. It would be quite impossible to enforce an exceptional discipline and a bishop could only be a Visitor of the
Catholic establishment. George Wenham was converted to
Roman Catholicism in 1846, after being an Anglican army
chaplain in Ceylon. A graduate of Magdalen, he was to become
Provost of the Southwark Chapter. Wenham doubted 'whether
the Universities do so much to nourish Protestantism as they
do to develop infidelity', a view he was still to hold in 1867.[23]

---

21 Southwark Archdiocesan Archives.
22 Ibid., Lewis to Grant, 3 Dec. 1864.
23 Ibid., Wenham to Grant, 27 Sept. 1867.

Northcote advanced the suggestion that a full course of university studies should be provided at Oscott. In 1864 he was opposed to the Oxford association; rich Catholics did not want studies, they went to Oxford for Society. 'Although I should expect to see many of the old Catholic families keeping aloof from Oxford,' he wrote, 'yet I should fear that many others, and four-fifths of the converts, will be sending their sons there, and so we shall have a race of very indifferent Catholics in the next generation.'[24] Oscott, he asserted, 'was prepared to carry on its own or any other students that might offer, through the *studies* of a University course, and see whether it would *take*. If it did, the egg having been hatched, the chick might go off bye and bye and make a home for itself elsewhere, or it might, cuckoo-like, take over the College for its own, and let the College migrate.'

Dr. Todd of St. Mary's Orphanage, Greenwich, while acknowledging the risks, felt that adequate precautions could be taken. 'I do not think that there is actual danger of losing the Faith [at Oxford]', he wrote, but 'except in very rare cases, youths will become *liberalised*, and especially they will become imbued with political and social opinions incompatible with loyalty to the Holy See, and the traditions of Rome.'[25] He added 'but I do not see that this would, of necessity, be the case, if a Catholic College under able Catholic management were founded in Oxford or Cambridge'.

Richard Simpson was the chief advocate of the Hall or College plan:

If the University professors indulged in any misplaced or intruded sneers at the Catholic religion, they would be more likely to kindle the wrath than to weaken the faith of the Catholic student. To keep up his reputation as a man of honour he would be obliged to resent the insult. The '*esprit de corps*', especially of a minority in the presence of a majority, keeps persons on their good behaviour. . . . We must not regard the generality of University students as soft, flabby, impressionable lumps of unbaked dough. My experience of undergraduates is that as a class they are touchy, turbulent, obstinate, wedded to home prejudices

[24] Ibid., J. Spencer Northcote to Bishop of Southwark, n.d.
[25] Ibid., Todd to Grant, 9 Dec. 1864.

in religion, and always readier to oppose the University authorities than to be tame and passive recipients of any form impressed upon them.[26]

Fr. G. R. Kingdon, S.J., protested 'that the idea of all the young men at Oxford and Cambridge (or even any considerable portion of them) being debauched is an entire mistake. I suppose everybody speaks as he has found. I never can remember [at Cambridge] to have been put in any danger of sin by any one of my associates during five years of residence there. . . . In a word the great majority are at least gentlemen, and you can always easily cut any who are not.'[27] But hardly any of the replies which the bishops received, even if they favoured the Oxford College project, were able to do so without some misgivings, hesitations, or reservations.

It has often been asserted that the decision arrived at by the bishops at the episcopal meeting of 13 December 1864 was the work of—in Newman's words—'a small active clique'.[28] By this phrase we are meant to understand Manning, Ward, and their friends.[29] Newman's view has received support from Wilfrid Ward, Cuthbert Butler, Purcell, and Meriol Trevor.[30] We are fortunate in the survival, however, of a verbatim account of the episcopal meeting in question from the pen of Robert Cornthwaite, Bishop of Beverley. The account, recently discovered among the Bishop's papers, points to a different interpretation. The only person present at the meeting who was not a bishop was Canon Morris, Wiseman's secretary. Wiseman, ill man as he was, presided. All the diocesan bishops were present, with the exception of the sickly Bishop of Hexham, William Hogarth. Manning was not present.

Wiseman opened the meeting by declaring that they had

[26] Southwark Archdiocesan Archives, Richard Simpson to Grant, 12 Dec. 1864.
[27] Ibid., Kingdom to Grant, 27 Nov. 1864.
[28] See Newman's letter to Hope-Scott, referring to this meeting, quoted in W. Ward, *Life of Newman*, vol. 2, p. 65.
[29] Ibid., p. 64.
[30] See Ward, W. *Life of Newman*, vol. 2, pp. 64 seq.; Butler, *Life of Ullathorne*, vol. 2, pp. 9 seq.; Purcell, *Life of de Lisle*, vol. 2, pp. 7 seq.; Trevor, *Light in Winter*, pp. 356 seq.

gathered together in obedience to instructions from the Holy See. Cornthwaite writes:

His Eminence and the Bishops then mentioned that they had collected replies and information from various persons connected with the two universities. The Bishop of Birmingham read letters respecting the establishment of an Oratorian Mission at Oxford by the Very Rev. Dr. Newman. Canon Morris for His Eminence read opinion of Mr. Allies in favour of plan of a Catholic College at Oxford and of the Very Rev. Fr. Dalgairns against the plan. His Eminence stated that whilst of the opinions received by him and by others in reply to the questions annexed, were some for and some against the College plan, none, with one or two exceptions, of the writers thought it was advisable to allow our Catholic youths to belong to the existing Protestant Colleges of the Universities. The Bishop of Southwark read replies of Mr. Simpson in favour of a Catholic College and of Mr. David Lewis against it. The question was then put: 'What answer shall be sent to Rome?' and 'In what form?'[31]

The bishops were asked individually for their views. The Benedictine Bishop of Newport and Menevia, Thomas Joseph Brown, who in 1859–60 had delated Newman to Rome for unorthodoxy, was at this time opposed to the foundation of a Catholic College at Oxford. All those who had written to him agreed that 'the dangers to Faith and Morals could be very serious, although perhaps individuals would not necessarily incur the dangers'. He was afraid, however, that an absolute prohibition might be disregarded and this 'would weaken our authority'.

Brown's fellow monk, Ullathorne, declared:

At Easter was wrote as our unanimous judgment that a College could not be established, for as the law stood and still stands, the head of such a College, as member of Convocation, must sign the Thirty-Nine Articles. We added that the existing Colleges were dangerous to Faith and Morals. An Act of Parliament could not be obtained to command the University to allow the establishment of such a Catholic College as is proposed. The University would not agree to such an Act

---

[31] Leeds Diocesan Archives. Bishop Cornthwaite's account of Bishops' Meeting of 13 Dec. 1864.

and Parliament would respect its objections. [He concluded] we must give as good an education as we can in our own Colleges. . . . If a College could be established [at Oxford] it would not prevent our youths from going to the Protestant Colleges. [He was afraid, however, that greater evils might arise from any fresh prohibition], although we all are afraid of the dangers to which the youths are exposed.

Bishop Grant of Southwark thought that 'the College cannot be established for the reasons already given', and he declared that the bishops 'ought to be able to state that [they] think that the existing Colleges are dangerous, although it must be left to the Holy See to consider whether it would be safer to publish a prohibition which at the present time might lead to greater evils'. In his opinion 'the University has its privileges by Papal concession, and has forfeited them by its falling into heresy and we cannot put a College under it'.

Bishop William Turner of Salford believed that the establishment of a College at Oxford would be simply dangerous to Faith and Morals.

Bishop James Brown of Shrewsbury argued 'that the College cannot be founded without an Act of Parliament; that means to found it cannot be collected, and even if the College could be founded, it would expose our youths to dangers against Faith and Morals'. He added: 'We must try to improve our present Colleges. It is for the Holy See to consider whether there ought to be a distinct prohibition when so many are disposed to go to the present Colleges.'

Richard Roskell, Bishop of Nottingham, declared he adopted all the previous reasons. He thought 'the proposed College would be a positive scandal and would tempt Catholics to send their children to the Protestant Colleges'.

The Bishop of Liverpool, Alexander Goss, thought that 'we cannot alter our Colleges so as to meet the reasons for which our gentry wish their sons to go to the Universities', but nevertheless 'establishment of a Catholic College at Oxford ought to be discouraged, as it is against the law, and would, like Trinity College in Ireland, expose souls to the loss of Faith'. 'Whilst we and the Holy See must discourage going to the Protestant

Colleges,' he added, 'a distinct prohibition would perhaps be disobeyed at this time. We must never agree to send our youths to sit under heretical masters even for Humanity Studies.'

William Vaughan, Bishop of Plymouth, declared that 'it is impossible for Catholics to establish a College by reason of the law of the country and of the evils that would follow if it was established', but 'it is better not to issue a prohibition against going to the existing Colleges at this time as it would by some be disobeyed'. The Honourable William Joseph Hugh Clifford, Bishop of Clifton, adopted the reasons of Ullathorne, and declared 'neither the Bishops nor the Holy See can erect a College in connection with a Protestant university'. But he added:

it would be ill-advised to prohibit individuals from going to the exist-ing Colleges at this time, as the number of those going is not as large as is supposed and as the increase of converts educated in the Univer-sities tempts young men to wish to go to the Colleges where their friends have been educated and the prohibition might be thought unjust and oppressive by those who are at this hour well-disposed to obedience and much more so by persons less favourably disposed. But, trusting to the Bishop of Birmingham to take such precautions as he thinks towards lessening the evils of the system, we must discourage Catholics going to them. Our present Colleges are not a substitute for the University, but means ought to be adopted towards providing learned masters in our Colleges who could supply the want of Univer-sity education.

The Bishop of Northampton, Francis Kerril Amherst, in whose diocese Cambridge was situated, pronounced that 'the establish-ment of a Catholic College would be dangerous to Faith and Morals and would be a failure. Even if it would not be a failure, the Church in England would be committed by the establishment of such a College to a step that would be disastrous and irrevoc-able.' 'Let us discourage,' he urged, 'without issuing a prohibition that would be disregarded, Catholics going to the existing Colleges. Let us ask the Holy See to tell us what answer to give to parents disposed to send their sons to the Protestant Colleges. One of the chief reasons urged by those who send their children to the present Colleges or who wish for a Catholic College is for the sake of those very social advantages which we believe to constitute the greatest danger to youth.'

Finally, Bishop Cornthwaite of Beverley gave his own opinion. He was opposed to the College 'or anything that will place our youths in connection with Protestant teaching. A prohibition is unnecessary if the Holy See expresses unmistakably that going to the present Colleges is dangerous. Ireland, Belgium, and Germany all shew us the dread which Catholics feel of placing their youth in the existing unCatholic Universities.'

Each bishop then agreed that while they all had stated different reasons for their opposition, none of them excluded the reasons of the others.

Wiseman put a draft statement of ideas to the bishops which it was intended might provide the substance of the reply to *Propaganda*. This read:

Having deliberated seriously and each having stated his opinion after the information collected by him, the Bishops feel that the Holy See has asked the Bishops to speak and that they cannot advise the Holy See to sanction a College [at Oxford]. With only one or two exceptions all the answers given to the Cardinal and to the Bishops show that Catholics ought not to go to the existing Protestant Colleges:

1. Because the Holy See cannot admit that her own children cannot furnish a sufficient education and the Bishops feel that the comparisons made in disparagement of intellect and learning amongst the old Catholics in England are very unjust and untrue;

2. If a [Catholic] Hall were established, Catholics would still not go to it:

(*a*) Because parents seek the social prestige which the Hall could not give in their estimation;

(*b*) If we founded a Hall, the system would be one of mixed education as our youths would be tempted to go to the public classes conducted by Protestants. . . .

(*c*) Mixed education has been condemned in Ireland.

(*d*) Our own primary education is kept unmixed.

(*e*) The head of such a College would be necessarily a Protestant unless there were a special Act of Parliament.

(*f*) The jurisdiction of the Ordinary would be destroyed over this College.

(g) A few Catholic youths would be cast amongst a large Protestant and perhaps infidel majority, where their Faith and Morals would be endangered.

The bishops agreed unanimously on these points and Canon Morris left to draw up a letter to *Propaganda* embodying their opinions. The letter, approved and signed by all the bishops present at the meeting, declared '1. that the establishment of Catholic Colleges at the Universities could in no way be approved; and 2. that parents were by all means to be dissuaded from sending their sons to the Universities'.[32] An absolute prohibition was not requested.

No mention was made of Newman and his Oxford scheme. Ullathorne assured the prelates that Newman's only interest was to provide for the Mission in the city of Oxford; as such, it was purely a matter for the discretion of the Ordinary. Ullathorne informed Newman of what had progressed at the episcopal meeting. The intention was benevolent; he meant to reassure Newman that there had been no attempt on the part of the bishops to interfere with the Oratorians' assuming responsibility for the Oxford Mission. Newman passed on the information thus obtained to his rich supporters. The Catholic gentry had already been urged to make themselves heard at Rome,[33] and a lay petition, organized by Newman's supporters, was initiated. Bellasis, who had been instrumental in the foundation of the Oratory School as an exclusive establishment for the sons of the Catholic gentry, was determined that the boys of the school should continue their education at Oxford under Newman's guidance. Furthermore, he was convinced that Oxford was ready for mass conversions. 'I think Dr. Newman's going to Oxford', he writes, 'of the greatest importance, religious matters there have got into such a state that they are ripe for the sickle.'[34] Bellasis was wintering in Rome in 1864–5, and Thomas F. Wetherell, a contributor to *The Rambler* who had also been involved in the Oratory School project, made contact with him, and together

[32] Manning Papers, Bayswater. 'Decisions of the Holy See . . . etc.'
[33] Ward, W., *Life of Newman*, vol. 2, p. 65.
[34] Bellasis, Edward, *Memorials of Mr. Serjeant Bellasis, 1800–1873*, p. 154.

they presented a petition signed by many of Newman's friends
and most of the parents who had sons at the Oratory School.
Bellasis, we are told, 'spared no pains to delay, if not to hinder,
anything in the nature of a positive prohibition being issued'.[35]
The cat was out of the bag; the gentry had obviously intended to
place their sons under Newman's care in Oxford.

The manœuvre came to nothing. Lord Herries, Lord Petre,
and the Hon. Charles Langdale, disapproving of the tactics employed by the organizers of the petition, dissociated themselves
from it. They wrote to George Talbot protesting against the
document. Similarly, Roger William Vaughan, a scion of the
famous Old Catholic family of that name, published in 1865
a scathing indictment of the petitioners, entitled *University
Education and the Memorialists, by the Son of a Catholic Country
Squire.*

Newman abandoned his attempt to go to Oxford. He was
prepared to accept the Oxford Mission 'solely for the sake of the
Catholics in the Colleges', he informed Gaisford in December
1864.[36] He claimed that Ullathorne had been given to understand
this. He wrote to Sister Imelda Poole of Stone that he would not
have thought of going to Oxford 'except for the sake of Catholic
youths there',[37] and he repeated that Ullathorne had always been
cognizant of this motive. Ullathorne for his part denied that
the Oratory scheme had anything to do with the attendance of
Catholic youths at Oxford. Perhaps Newman's need for self-
justification played tricks with his memory, as it had done on his
leaving Ireland. He hinted to his correspondent[38] that the inter-
position of *Propaganda* which had led to the calling of the special
episcopal meeting had been malevolently engineered to keep him
away from Oxford. But even Bishop Hedley, destined to be one
of the prime movers in the 1880s in trying to secure a reversal of
traditional policy in regard to the Universities, was forced to
admit that 'whatever Cardinal Newman thought, it is most

---

[35] Bellasis, E., *Memorials of Mr. Serjeant Bellasis, 1800–1873*, pp. 154–5.
[36] Ward, W., *Life of Newman*, vol. 2, p. 66. Newman to Gaisford, 16 Dec. 1864.
[37] Ibid., p. 67. Newman to Sister Imelda Poole, 28 Dec. 1864.
[38] Ibid.

certain that at the time [1864], it would have been very rash on the part of the Catholic body to establish an Oxford College'.[39]

On 15 February 1865 Cardinal Wiseman died. Twelve days before his demise, however, the Cardinal Prefect of *Propaganda* had signed a document to be sent to the English episcopate, stating:

1. that the Sacred Congregation, in its general meeting of January 16th had, after mature examination, confirmed the judgment of the Bishops, made known by their letter of December 13th, as being in entire conformity with the principles which the said Congregation had always laid down; 2. that, as the incompleteness of the education received in the Catholic Colleges of England was alleged by some as a reason for desiring the establishment of Colleges at the Universities, the Bishops were exhorted by the Sacred Congregation to use every care and effort to perfect the system of education in the Colleges already existing.[40]

On 24 March 1865, while the see of Westminster was still vacant, the bishops, by means of a circular letter, informed the clergy of their declaration of 13 December 1864, and of Rome's confirmation of it:

At a meeting of the English Bishops, held yesterday [23 March 1865] at Birmingham, it was unanimously agreed that each Bishop should address to his own Clergy, for their guidance, a copy of the following document:

'The Bishops are unanimous in their disapproval of the establishing of a Catholic College at any of the Protestant Universities. And they are further of opinion that parents ought to be in every way dissuaded from sending their children to pursue their studies at such Universities.'

This judgment was expressed by the Bishops, and by our lamented Cardinal Archbishop, in the last meeting over which he presided, and in forming it they were guided by those principles which the Church has ever maintained in the matter of education.[41]

The decision to issue an *ad clerum* was the spontaneous act of the episcopacy under the temporary leadership of Ullathorne.

[39] *The Ampleforth Journal*, article by Hedley (Apr. 1898).

[40] Manning Papers, Bayswater. 'Decisions of the Holy See . . . etc.'

[41] Archives of the Archdiocese of Birmingham. Ullathorne's *ad clerum*, 24 Mar. 1865.

Rome had merely confirmed the episcopal resolutions, and had urged the bishops to do something to improve the education offered in the existing Catholic colleges. Manning could rightly claim in 1867 that he was not concerned in the original deliberations of the bishops, and that he was not involved in the failure of Newman's first effort to re-establish himself in Oxford. 'As to the question of the Oratory in Oxford,' Manning informed Oakeley, 'Newman will know that when it was proposed in the Cardinal's time it was given up on the ground that it would have the effect of encouraging young Catholics to go to Oxford. . . . I never knew the facts until after the event, and had no part in them.'[42] Manning, on his assumption of episcopal authority in 1865, was confronted with a unified policy and one confirmed by Rome.

And what of Edmund S. Ffoulkes, the man who perhaps more than anyone else had initiated the furore? He apostatized, and devoted his energies to writing a series of violently polemical pamphlets against Catholicism. The land acquired by the Oratory at Oxford was sold, because, as Newman melodramatically informed de Lisle, 'I knew that the opposition was not directed against an Oratory at Oxford as against me.'[43] The matter appeared now to be settled, and the way cleared for the episcopacy to decree constructive measures for the improvement of the higher education of English Catholics. The hush was deceptive; it was merely a lull before the storm.

[42] Purcell, *Life of Manning*, vol. 2, p. 333. Manning to Oakeley, 14 Aug. 1867.
[43] Purcell, *Life of de Lisle*, vol. 2, pp. 8–9. Newman to de Lisle, 13 Feb. 1865.

III

ARISTOCRATIC CONSPIRATORS
AND ROMAN REPRISALS

HENRY EDWARD MANNING was consecrated as the second Archbishop of Westminster on 8 June 1865, after the see had been vacant for almost three months. The first year of his episcopate was an exceptionally active one, occupied by the necessity of placing the diocese in smooth working order, following the neglect occasioned by Wiseman's indifferent health. Before the close of 1866, however, the new Archbishop found himself concerned for the first time in his official capacity with developments relating to higher education and the Oxford sanctions.

Particularly anxious to unite the diocese with him after the turbulence and acrimony which had characterized the second half of Wiseman's rule, Manning decided to convene a Diocesan Synod, the first of many such periodic gatherings during his episcopate. In this way, he felt, the priests of the diocese would be welded into a strong body, united in spirit with the Ordinary, and associated with him in government, administration, and legislation. The Synod met on 14 December 1865. Among the decrees it promulgated was one which noted that the bishops of England 'by the discretion of the Sacred Congregation of *Propaganda* in letters dated February 3rd of the present year, while the Metropolitan Church was silent and vacant, forbade the erection of Catholic Colleges in the Anglican Universities, and opposed the sending of Catholic youth to the same Universities'. It then resolved: 'We, therefore, in obedience to the authority of the Holy See, as made known recently to us on the 23rd of November last, adhere with full assent to the judgment of our brethren the Bishops of this Province, and enjoin in the Lord that all who are invested with holy orders shall endeavour by timely counsel and by all means to dissuade Catholic parents from sending their sons to the aforenamed Universities.'[1] This resolution obviated the necessity for the issue of an *ad clerum* along the lines adopted by Ullathorne and the other bishops.

Further developments took place consequent upon the private visit to England of Cardinal Reisach in 1866 and the resurrection of Newman's Oxford plan. Wilfrid Ward claims that Reisach 'came to England with a view to ascertaining the general feeling on the Oxford question'.[2] Both Abbot Butler[3] and Miss Trevor[4] concur. The latter goes further, declaring that Reisach 'was commissioned to inquire into the state of Catholic Education in England, so that he could make a personal report to *Propaganda* and the Pope'. Reisach was not involved, however, in any such work. In Rome he had cultivated a private friendship with Fr. Coffin and a personal regard for Manning. He accepted pressing invitations from the former to visit England and on this unofficial visit he was the guest of both Coffin and the Wards. Indeed, there was nothing to inquire into! Rome, in full possession of the united opinions of the episcopate, had pronounced on the matter, and its injunctions had been accepted by the episcopate. Manning had been barely a year in office and there had been no pressing renewal of demands for Oxford. *Propaganda* was familiar with the views of the gentry from the petition of the Memorialists and Reisach made no formal reports to *Propaganda*. From the account of his visit to Oscott preserved among the College archives we know that Reisach informed his hosts that 'his visit to England was purposely to study the English character'.[5] Indeed, he proved to be more interested in cricket than in education, and 'expressed almost unbounded surprise at the readiness with which all obeyed the decision of the umpires'.[6] He rather amusingly drew from the game of cricket 'a conclusion that Englishmen must naturally be submissive to authority'.[7] Reisach's friend and guide, however, was Coffin, and ever since the latter's defection from the Oratory

---

[1] Manning Papers, Bayswater. 'Decisions of the Holy See . . . etc.'
[2] Ward, W., *Life of Newman*, vol. 2, p. 122.
[3] Butler, *Life of Ullathorne*, vol. 2, pp. 14–15.
[4] Trevor, *Light in Winter*, p. 387.
[5] Oscott College. See also account of this in *Oscotian* (1888), p. 87.
[6] Ibid.   [7] Ibid.

his activities were viewed with suspicion by the Birmingham house.

Not unnaturally, Coffin wished to show his friend as many of the chief places of Catholic interest as possible. It is not surprising that Oxford should figure on the itinerary, or that Coffin should have desired Reisach to see the pulpit of St. Mary Magdalen which he had occupied so frequently, Christ Church where he had spent so many momentous days, or the spot from which the conversions of 1845 had taken place. Reisach saw the new ground which Newman had just bought 'for the chances of the future, not as connected with myself', as the latter had explained to his bishop.[8] Miss Trevor writes: 'The Cardinal (Reisach) visited several Catholic Colleges, including Oscott, only a few miles from Edgbaston; he met Ullathorne there. Not only did he not come to visit the Oratory School, not only was Newman not invited to meet him at Oscott, but Newman never even knew he was in England till the faithful Miss Bowles wrote from London excitedly asking why he did not come to see Reisach.'[9] The myth needs exploding. Manning wrote to Ullathorne asking him to bring Newman to meet Cardinal Reisach at Oscott. Ullathorne replied 'Dr. Newman is absent from Birmingham',[10] and hence Newman missed the opportunity. It is to be regretted that Ullathorne failed to inform Newman of the invitation, because the latter immediately connected the visit of Reisach, and what he considered to be a personal snub, with the plans he was meticulously re-forming for a house of the Oratory in Oxford. In view of this fact, Miss Trevor's other point answers itself. It would have been out of the question to have visited the Oratory School in the absence of Newman. Oscott, for its part, had historic traditions, was the perfect example of the seminary lay school peculiar to England, and was the scene of Wiseman's great endeavours. The Oratory School had none of these associations, and Coffin would not have been welcome there. He had,

---

[8] Ward, W., *Life of Newman*, vol. 2, pp. 123–4. Newman to Ambrose St. John, 27 Aug. 1865.

[9] Trevor, *Light in Winter*, pp. 387–8.

[10] Manning Papers, Bayswater. Ullathorne to Manning, 14 July 1866.

after all, left the Oratory on account of what he considered to be its misguided educational policy.

One month after Newman had received Ullathorne's *ad clerum* enjoining the clergy to dissuade with every means in their power the attendance of Catholic youth at the ancient Universities, he was interpreting his bishop's renewed offer of the Oxford mission as if it were 'for the sake of the Catholic youth there, who are likely to be, in the future, more numerous than they are now'.[11] He was still reluctant to acknowledge the fact that Ullathorne's offer was relating to parochial needs only. Newman, using the mission plan to disguise his real intentions, was in touch with Hope-Scott, Lord Blachford, and the aristocratic set. 'We dined with Acton yesterday,' he told Henry St. John on June 23rd, 'and after dinner came Monteith, the O'Conor Don, Mr. Maxwell, Blennerhassett, etc. On Thursday we met at Hope-Scott's all the Kerrs. At Gladstone's breakfast I met young Lady Lothian, Lord Lyttelton, General Beauregard, etc. Tomorrow we lunch with the [Frank] Wards and dine with Bellasis. On Thursday I am to dine with the Simeons to meet Mr. Chichester Fortescue, Stanley, and perhaps Gladstone. On Monday we shall breakfast with Badeley.'[12] Hope-Scott, Neville, Acton, Maxwell, Kerr, Bellasis, Badeley—these were names to conjure with. The price for their financial support was to be Newman's continuing concern for their sons at the University. A prospectus, put out by Newman in January 1867, after the sanction of *Propaganda* had been granted for a house of the Oratory in Oxford, was a carefully worded document. Ullathorne's letter, entrusting the mission to the Oratory, was given in full. Oxford was 'the only city in England of importance which has a Catholic congregation without a Catholic Church', and it was with great satisfaction that Ullathorne found Newman 'disposed to answer the call, so often made upon you, to build a Church in Oxford, with the view of ultimately establishing an Oratory there of St. Philip Neri'.[13]

---

[11] Ward, W., *Life of Newman*, vol. 2, p. 121. Newman to Pusey, 29 Apr. 1866.
[12] Ibid., p. 131. Newman to St. John, 23 June 1866.
[13] Ullathorne's letter and Newman's circular are printed *in extenso* in W. Ward, *Life of Newman*, vol. 2, pp. 131–3.

Newman, however, stressed that the Oratory was expressly created and blessed for the purpose 'of bringing Catholicity before the educated classes of society, and especially those classes which represent the traditions and the teaching of Oxford'. The Oratory, 'since many of its priests have been educated at the Universities', would have acquaintance and sympathy 'with academical habits and sentiments'. He appealed for between £8,000 and £10,000, and was buoyant with expectation. He sent Fr. Neville to Oxford in April and told him to 'have a good look at the Catholic undergraduates in Church. Tell me how many they are. Try and find out *who* they are and what they are like. Let me know where they sit in the Church, that I may picture beforehand how I shall have to stand when I preach, in order to see them naturally, and address them.'[14] He had dreams of inaugurating a new Movement—'such men as Mark Pattison may conceivably be won over. Although I am not young, I feel as full of life and thought as ever I did. It may prove to be the inauguration of a second Oxford Movement.'[15]

Then came the blow! Ullathorne, while informing Newman in December 1866 of *Propaganda*'s permission for the new House, had concealed from him the Holy Father's desire that Newman should not himself go to Oxford. The prohibition can be laid at Ullathorne's door. Basing his authority on an earlier assertion by Newman, Ullathorne had informed *Propaganda*, when asking for permission, that Newman did not intend to live in Oxford. *Propaganda*, on its part, simply embodied this fact as a condition in the Roman letter. It seemed an admirable compromise. As Newman did not intend to live in Oxford, the great power of his name would not result in encouraging Catholic youths to the University. There was no reason, on the other hand, why Newman's priests should not staff the city mission. *Propaganda*'s letter was sent directly to Ullathorne and neither Manning nor Newman knew of the condition. Cardinal Barnabo later informed Ambrose St. John of the Roman attitude. *Propaganda* had given permission for the new Oratory in order that 'the way might be tried whether it was possible to do some good to Oxford without

14 Ibid.   15 Ibid.

undoing all that had been consistently done against mixed educa-tion'.[16] The fathers of the Congregation had voted to allow the Oratory, 'on the condition that Father Newman did not go to live there', and 'it was the Pope himself who had insisted on the special condition being put in against Newman's going to live at Oxford, as his going to Oxford would give too much weight to the position of Catholics there, and inevitably encourage Catholic students to go. This the Holy Father could not make himself a party to.' Barnabo added that in all this there was nothing personal against Newman; it was simply a matter of safeguarding the policy determined upon by the English hierarchy as a body. Ullathorne had made the original error, and did not know how to communicate the decision to Newman, knowing full well that it would cause a torrent of self-pity and accusations of conspiracy. The stipulation, leaked to the press, was wrongly construed in *The Weekly Register* as impugning Newman's orthodoxy. The information coming from the Roman Correspondent of the paper subsequently led to protracted negotiations at Rome with a view to vindicating Newman's orthodoxy.

Newman was despondent. Dashed were his hopes of converting eminent men in the University; dashed were his hopes of placing himself at the head of an Oxford house having a special mission to the sons of the Catholic aristocracy. If *he* could not go to Oxford neither would any of his subjects. The whole plan must be abandoned at once. 'The money was given to *me* personally', Newman informed the Jesuit, Fr. H. Coleridge, in August 1867, 'the subscribers wanted to see *me* in Oxford (I am talking of the majority of them)—they would not give their money for an Oxford mission merely. When the *Propaganda* decided that I was not personally to be there, it would have been a misappropriation of their money to spend it merely on an Oxford Church.'[17]

Manning's defence of his own actions is unequivocal. Since he had become Archbishop, he wrote,

I have opposed the sending young Catholics to Oxford as before. I have also expressed my regret that the subject of the Oratory in

[16] Ward, W., *Life of Newman*. St. John to Newman, 30 Apr. 1867, pp. 160 seq.
[17] Ibid. Newman to Coleridge, 30 Aug. 1867.

Oxford should be renewed, and that on the reason given by Newman in one of his letters to the Bishop of Birmingham, and communicated by his desire, on the occasion, to some one of the cardinals in Rome— namely, that his going there would attract young Catholics to the University.

Nevertheless I stated that, as the subject had been again proposed to him, I thought he would have cause to complain if the permission to go to Oxford were refused; but that the permission ought to be accompanied by a renewal of the declaration against our youth frequenting the University.

As to the personal restraint of Newman's going to Oxford, I never heard or imagined such a thing until the Rescript had been for at least two months in England.[18]

George Talbot considered that 'the effect of Dr. Newman's circular [of 1867] is to imply that Rome is undecided and influenced by some transient personal cause',[19] and Bishop Brown of Newport and Menevia considered that the decision to allow Newman to open a house in Oxford implied an alteration in Roman policy.[20] Certain it is that Newman's sponsors were very angry at the destruction of *their* plans. Newman's action in returning subscriptions made them more furious. It had long been a tradition among the Old Catholic families to act in concert by means of Clubs—as in the old Cisalpine Club, for instance—to ensure the preservation of their peculiar concerns. These gatherings had frequently been Gallican in outlook and policy. The gentry had formed another such Club in the nineteenth century to demonstrate that the interests of English Catholicism were not to be identified with those of the immigrant Irish, the labouring classes, or the rising commercial and mercantile middle class. The Stafford Club held its meetings in a London hotel, and became, in the words of Percy Fitzgerald, the haunt of all kinds of religious cranks and bores, 'who talked and criticised, and were vehemently intolerant to those who would not agree with their views'.[21]

[18] Purcell, *Life of Manning*, vol. 2, pp. 333–4. Manning to Oakeley, 14 Aug. 1867.

[19] Purcell, *Life of de Lisle*, vol. 2, p. 13.

[20] Wilson, J. Anselm, *The Life of Bishop Hedley*, p. 228.

[21] Fitzgerald, P., *Fifty Years of Catholic Life and Social Progress*, vol. 2, p. 289.

The Club, formed in 1851 'to co-ordinate Catholic resistance to the "no-popery" agitation',[22] was anti-hierarchical, for Wiseman and the new hierarchy, it was felt, had been responsible for the obloquy poured upon the Catholic gentry who had been in danger of losing their places in acceptable society. Early members of the Club were John Wallis, one-time editor of *The Tablet* and notorious for his acrimony to Cardinal Cullen, and the eccentric Sir George Bowyer. Lord Edward Fitzalan Howard (guardian of the young Duke of Norfolk), the Earl of Denbigh, Lords Arundell, Camoys, Stourton, Petre, Stafford, Dormer, Clifford, and Herries were members of the exclusive establishment. On 24 April 1867 *The Guardian* was speaking scornfully of Newman's 'alliance' with this clique, and the reason for its jibe was the Address of Sympathy which declared its support for Newman in his 'trials'. The ostensible reason for the Address was the article in *The Weekly Register*, but the real motive was disappointment at the failure of the Oxford manœuvre. Indeed, in the first draft of the Address specific reference was made to the Oxford affair,[23] and this was only expunged after Lord Petre, Lord Herries, Charles Langdale, and others refused to sign it in that form. The Address informed Newman that 'every blow that touches you inflicts a wound upon the Catholic Church in this country'.[24] The reaction it caused among the episcopate and at Rome can only be fully understood when we realize that it was the Pope himself who had insisted upon Newman's personal exclusion from Oxford. The letter of the Stafford Club, therefore, took the form of an anti-papal innuendo. The letter had been framed by Monsell and Mr. Frank Ward (who had a son at Oxford and stood to benefit from Newman's ministrations). These men were closely associated with the Memorialists of 1865. They were particularly incensed against Rome, because in March 1867 *Propaganda* had written a letter to Newman ordering him to stop preparing youths for Oxford at the Oratory School. Complaints had been laid before *Propaganda* by Herbert Vaughan that Newman was actively engaged in such work, and Manning

[22] Altholz, Josef L., in *The Journal of British Studies*, vol. 4, no. 1 (1964), p. 98 n.
[23] Ward, W., *Life of Newman*, vol. 2, p. 145.   [24] Ibid., p. 143.

had proof in March 1867 that Newman was at that time coaching John Townsley's son for Oxford.[25] Newman was prepared to comply with the letter of *Propaganda*'s instruction while ignoring its spirit. He told Sir Justin Sheil that what the Oratory School must do would be 'to relinquish those who go to Oxford for a short time before they go there if I should find they need, in addition to the general instruction we give them here, any *special* preparation for the University'.[26] Manning feared 'we are slipping sideways into the whole mischief'.[27] Talbot, in spite of his indiscretions, was perceptive enough to see into the real significance of the Stafford Club's Address. 'Of course your suffragans are frightened by the address of the laity', he wrote. 'You will find yourself much in the position of Dr. Milner.'[28]

A month before the publication of the Address of the Stafford Club, Rome showed its concern at the course events had taken. An unsolicited letter was sent from *Propaganda* to the Archbishop, stating that the Holy Father wished the bishops to consider the entire issue again at their approaching annual meeting, and then 'to communicate with the *Propaganda* upon the measures to be taken for preventing Catholics from studying at Oxford'.[29] There was no question now of 'dissuasion', but of 'prevention'. Manning, as Metropolitan, was requested to communicate the message to his suffragans.

The meeting of the bishops took place at Westminster on 30 April 1867, three weeks after the challenge thrown down by the Stafford Club. Two bishops were absent in Rome reporting on the state of their dioceses, Bishop Brown of Newport and Menevia, and Bishop Cornthwaite of Beverley. The only additions to the episcopal body since the last time university education was discussed were Manning himself, who took the Chair at the meeting, and James Chadwick, the successor of William Hogarth as Bishop of Hexham and Newcastle. Four resolutions

---

[25] Manning Papers, Bayswater. Manning to Talbot, 1 Feb. 1867.

[26] Ward, W., *Life of Newman*, vol. 2, p. 136. Newman to Sheil, 22 Mar. 1867.

[27] Manning Papers, Bayswater. Manning to Talbot, 1 Feb. 1867.

[28] Ward, W., *Life of Newman*, vol. 2, pp. 146–8. Talbot to Manning, 25 Apr. 1867.

[29] Manning Papers, Bayswater. 'Decisions of the Holy See . . . etc.'

were unanimously passed, and a letter was written to *Propaganda*
urging that body 'to make known to the Clergy that the Holy See
enjoins upon all priests to carry out fully the letter of 1865'.[30]
Rome was asked 'what is to be done in the case of Ecclesiastics
being asked to prepare Catholic young men for the Universities
expressly', and what is to happen 'in the case of young men
converted during their stay at the Universities'. The bishops, in
view of the recent outburst of the Stafford Club, thought 'it is
inexpedient to publish to the Faithful the letter of 1865', and the
prelates corrected one or two errors of fact in Barnabo's letter.
The bishops also advanced the suggestion that they would wish
'by pastoral letters' to make known to the Faithful 'the grave
danger incurred by those who should enter the Universities in
spite of the admonitions of their pastors'.[31]

The letter to *Propaganda*, signed by all the prelates present at
the meeting, was dispatched to Rome on 1 May. The reply,
addressed to Manning, came on 6 August, urging the bishops to
lay down by means of Pastoral Letters 'a clear and certain rule
upon which to act in a matter, which is of the greatest gravity,
and is intimately connected with the eternal salvation of souls'.
Propaganda's Letter is one of the most significant documents on
the Universities issue, on account of the abandonment of the old
'dissuasive' element. It declared:

. . . your Grace should clearly explain in your Pastoral Letter the doctrine on avoiding the proximate occasions of mortal sin, to which occasions no one can without grievous sin expose himself, except under
the pressure of grave and adequate necessity, and unless such precautions
be taken as shall remove all proximate danger of sin. But in the present
case, where, as the Sovereign Pontiff has declared, there is an intrinsic
and most grave danger, not only for purity of morals, but especially for
the faith (which is altogether necessary for salvation), everyone must
see that it is next to impossible to find circumstances in which non-
Catholic Universities could without sin be frequented. The inconstancy
of disposition and the instability of young men, the false opinions
which are inhaled with the atmosphere in such Institutions, without

[30] Birmingham Archdiocesan Archives. MS. of 'Meeting of Bishops in Low
Week, 1867' by Ullathorne.
[31] Manning Papers, Bayswater. 'Decisions of the Holy See . . . etc.'

the antidote of a sound teaching, the very great influence which human respect and the ridicule of companions bring to bear upon young men, render their danger of falling into sin so manifest and so proximate, that in general[32] no sufficient reason can be imagined to justify Catholic youth being sent to non-Catholic Universities. Therefore in these circumstances it is left to your wisdom to use in the Pastoral Letter which will be published, such arguments of authority and of reason, so that hereafter it may be quite plain both to all Priests and lay Catholics what they ought to think and how they ought to act in this most grave duty. And I may not omit to repeat to your Grace that you should so act in concert with the other Bishops of England, that the Pastoral Letters above mentioned may be conceived with a unity of design, and may be published simultaneously.

Each prelate received a copy of Barnabo's Letter and Manning issued a circular to the bishops requesting opinions on the best way of carrying the injunctions into effect. He wrote to Ullathorne on 3 October 1867 that

from the answers of the Bishops to the circular of September and other correspondence it appears that some of our colleagues are of opinion that the Rescript of the Sacred Congregation intends each bishop to address a separate Pastoral to his flock on the subject of the Universities. But the bishops are unanimous in the judgment that the same Rescript requires a conformity of matter in the directions to be given to the clergy and faithful. Would your Lordship, therefore, oblige me by informing me whether you desire that a meeting of the bishops should take place for this purpose: or whether the same end can be attained without requiring such a meeting, and if so, by what course of proceeding.[33] [A week later he was writing again to say,] from the replies of the bishops, I find 1. that they do not consider a meeting, on the subject of the Pastorals respecting the Universities, to be necessary; 2. that they think uniformity of matter and expression will be sufficiently secured, if we all insert in our Pastorals the passage from the Rescript from the words *Amplitudo tua* to *committantur* (i.e. 'you will clearly explain in your Pastoral Letter the doctrine of the Church about avoiding the dangers of mortal sin' to 'generally, no sufficient reason can be conceived why young men should be entrusted to these Universities'), and

---

[32] *'generatim'*—according to the nature of things.
[33] Birmingham Archdiocesan Archives. Manning to Ullathorne, 3 Oct. 1867.

the sentence ['Such being the case, you in your wisdom, will so use the arguments of authority and reason in publishing the Letter, that it may be at length clearly seen, as well by all the Clergy as by the Faithful, what it is their duty to think and to do in this most grave matter'].[34]

The bishops all issued their Pastorals in the autumn or at Advent, and, apart from the inclusion of the passages indicated by Manning, each approached the subject in his own characteristic way. Cornthwaite of Beverley roundly declared:

It is a grievous sin to expose one's self to the proximate danger of grievous sin, without adequate necessity, and such precautions as may remove that danger: but in a course of studies at a Protestant University there is such danger, for incurring which, there is no adequate necessity, and against which the necessary precautions are next to impossible. The consequence is obvious, and we feel bound to state it; it would run thus: that unless (which is next to impossible) the precautions are such as to remove the imminence of the danger, to pursue a course of studies in these Universities would be grievously sinful in the sight of God.[35]

Grant of Southwark appealed to 'the history of Trinity College in Ireland' which 'tells a gloomy story of some who yielded their faith to the ridicule of their fellow-students, or who bartered their birthright for preferments and advancements'.[36]

Chadwick of Hexham and Newcastle argued 'but even suppose it were true that a Catholic became more esteemed because he had been at one of the Protestant Universities, yet this is no adequate reason for his endangering that which is more to be valued than all that the world can bestow, namely, the purity both of his morals and of his faith'.[37]

Brown of Shrewsbury drew a parallel with the education of the lower classes: 'If it be the duty of the wealthier classes of Catholics to abstain from sending their children to the Universities because they will be there exposed to such serious peril, clearly

---

[34] Birmingham Archdiocesan Archives. Manning to Ullathorne, 11 Oct. 1867.
[35] Cornthwaite Papers, Leeds. Cornthwaite's Pastoral, 10 Nov. 1867.
[36] Grant's Pastoral, 6 Aug. 1867.
[37] Chadwick's Pastoral, Oct. 1867.

there must be the same reason why persons of a lower class should exercise the same care in regard to their children.'[38]

Of particular interest, because of the author's patrician background, is the Pastoral of Bishop Clifford of Clifton. He gave a 'solemn warning' and talked of the necessity of fleeing from the dangerous occasions of sin. 'It must always be borne in mind', he wrote,

> that these institutions are essentially Protestant institutions; that therefore, even when the teaching in no way has reference to matters of doctrine, still the influence, the tone, the atmosphere of the place is necessarily Protestant. It is this that forms the chief danger of these establishments: for not only do young men frequent the Universities at an age when they are most susceptible to impressions of this kind, but they go there with a view of forming their minds and characters, and it is therefore most difficult to guard against all the dangerous impressions which may result from influences which surround young students on every side. Hence, whatever relaxation be made in the exclusiveness of the Universities, they must ever remain highly dangerous to Catholic youth.[39]

Particularly significant, too, is the Pastoral of Bishop Ullathorne, which had to be read from the Pulpit of the Oratory. Ullathorne wrote:

> Awakening to the novel sense of independence, the restless and inquisitive mind of youth is susceptible of every fresh influence, and accessible to every new idea, whilst neither his character has obtained that consistency, nor his judgment that maturity which will enable him to resist the charms that attach to novelty, or to repel the spirit of free inquiry that meets him with all its fascination on every side. . . . Surrounded and pressed upon by a crowd of sentiments, views, and theories, touching God and man, creation and redemption, religious, moral, and social principles, the products of free-thinking or of Protestant tradition, whilst his own Catholic teaching is thrown into abeyance, he will of necessity imbibe views of human science, of history, and of what concerns revelation, both hostile to his religion and driving him towards principles that are subversive of all faith. And their influence

---

[38] Brown of Shrewsbury's Pastoral, 17 Nov. 1867.
[39] Clifford's Pastoral, 22 Oct. 1867.

will be the more insidious and the less alarming to the conscience of a Catholic youth for the very reason that there is probably no formal intention of perverting his principles; and that the very urbanity and the courteous forbearance with which those principles and views are held, throw him off his guard and soothe him into security. . . . A mixed system of education is essentially a Protestant system. It is Protestant by the very exclusion of Catholic elements. . . . We see this in the god-less colleges and the mixed system of popular education in Ireland. We see it in the extreme reluctance to grant any civil advantages to the Catholic University already established by dint of so much effort and sacrifice. We see it in the efforts of Australian legislation to put down the separate system which had there so long and happily prevailed. Protestant Germany has acted like Protestant England, until the nobler Catholic minds were aroused to remedy its fatal results. And the cry for a Catholic University for German Catholic youth is the final ex-pression of that peril from which they are seeking to escape. Catholic Belgium, oppressed with the educational schemes first of its Protestant Dutch Government, and next by those of the free-thinkers within its borders, found a solution of the conflict in the re-establishment of the Catholic University of Louvain.[40]

Ullathorne's solution was obvious; a Catholic higher-education programme for England was urgently needed. Meantime, he approved the association with London University. 'But what we fear', he concluded, 'is, that it is not so much a course of studies that is sought for, as a certain social atmosphere. . . . It is precisely from this atmosphere that we would wish to shelter Catholic youth until their character and principles are formed.'

It would be tedious and repetitive to quote from all the episcopal letters issued at this time. The prelates fulfilled their task seriously and in full conformity with the injunctions of Rome.

In the Westminster diocese, the seventh Diocesan Synod, held in 1867, reinforced the papal instructions. In the fourth decree on non-Catholic Universities, priests were enjoined in the Lord 'more effectually to hinder Catholic parents from exposing their sons to the perils of non-Catholic education'.[41] Manning, writing of this period in his *Journal*, supports the arguments advanced by

40 Ullathorne's Pastoral, 13 Oct. 1867.
41 Manning Papers, Bayswater. 'Decisions of the Holy See . . . etc.'

Ullathorne and Clifford in their Pastorals. 'In truth nobody cared for higher studies', he stated. 'Certain Catholic parents wished to get their sons into English Society, and to have latch keys to Grosvenor Square. Nevertheless a great noise was made about the needs of higher studies.'[42] This view was reinforced by many converts.

In October 1867 *The Dublin Review* took up the arguments of the bishops. 'There are two classes of Catholics who may be fascinated by the prospects of an Oxford education', it asserted. One class is made up of 'the Catholic peers and landed proprietors and men of independent wealth—non-professional men'.[43] For such a class 'there is to be an undefinable influence and authority to be acquired in the county, not only in elections and magistrates' meetings, and quarter sessions, and public gatherings, but in a thousand other ways and details, in which the public, with a rational docility, yields itself to the personal action of a superior intelligence when accompanied by a high sense of duty, and an honourable spirit of *self-sacrifice*.' The aristocracy had now serious rivals for such posts: 'The wealthy manufacturer, the successful merchant, the keen-eyed speculator, introduce a new element of social power, which they double in their sons by securing to them the benefits of a liberal education.' The demand for university education had, therefore, to be viewed in the nature of a class struggle for power and influence. The higher classes would find themselves swamped 'by the growing masses of the middle class, of the mechanics, artisans and labourers, for these have learnt to think, to combine, to "strike"; they feel their strength, and the representation of the country is now in great measure in their hands.' But Oxford would provide no safeguard against the energy of the London-educated middle class and the professionally trained. Men, too, 'must now look, not to their degree and to the name of their school, but to their brains, to their perseverance, to the strength and honesty of their will'. It had to be recognized that 'the Oxford degrees possess no privilege which is not also shared by the degrees of the nine other Universities of the United

[42] Manning Papers, Bayswater. Manning's *Journal*, Bk. No. 4, pp. 54 seq.
[43] *The Dublin Review* (Oct. 1867), pp. 381 seq.

Kingdom'. Ward took up Newman's point that what might be said of the dangers of Oxford could also be alleged against entering the navy, the army, the law, medicine, or the civil service. The rejoinder was masterly. Life at Oxford 'is not a profession but an education'; Catholics are 'not obliged to be educated at Oxford', and 'there are intellectual dangers peculiar to Oxford from the fact of its being a nest of education and of literary and philosophic inquiry, which do not at all exist in any of the professions'.[44] The Catholic student at Oxford would be brought into familiar intercourse 'with the most able and influential Protestants of his own age whom England produces; and these are unanimous in regarding the maxims of the Papacy, theological, social, and political, as a synonym for everything which is narrow, retrograde, and imbecile'. The religious knowledge of the Catholic student was imperfect, and his principles not firmly rooted enough to cope with this situation.

[44] *The Dublin Review*, p. 428.

IV

THE NEED ADVANCED FOR
A CENTRAL BOARD OF EXAMINERS

THE first step was to remove grievances concerning the quality and scope of the education provided in the existing Catholic colleges. At the Low Week meeting of the hierarchy in 1868 Manning presented this issue to the assembled prelates. He narrates the story of what transpired:

> In Low Week, 1868, I brought on the subject of creating a board of examiners in obedience to the Letter of Propaganda. Nearly a whole day was spent in vain and at 5.0 p.m. I withdrew the subject. That night I drew up a Minute which is in our *Acta* for 1868, and brought it on next day. To my surprise, it was at once adopted. The scheme was to create a personal university not a local: a Board of Examiners who should test and reward the best students in our existing Colleges. This was and always has been my belief as to the way of proceeding.[1]

Manning's suggestion was intended to be but the first step towards the creation of a Catholic University. The Board of Examiners would be named jointly by the bishops and those heads of Religious Orders possessing colleges, and laymen would participate. The President of the Board would be chosen by the bishops out of three names presented by the Board. After much discussion the bishops adopted seven resolutions to be sent to the Holy See. They were as follows:

1. The Bishops fully recognize that the great extension, growth, and rise of the Catholic Church during the last twenty years in England, and still more, the present intellectual condition of the country both within the Catholic Church and without it, together with the strong desires now expressed for University Education, render it necessary

---

[1] Manning Papers, Bayswater. Manning's *Journal*, Bk. No. 4, pp. 54 seq.

that some step should be taken to provide higher studies for our
Catholic youth, from the age of 18 or 19 to 21 or 22, especially in the
upper classes of society.

2. They are also of opinion that the Catholic Colleges in England,
though they have made great advances in every respect in the last
twenty or thirty years, still need a more complete course of higher
studies, as described above. . . .

3. They believe, however, that a Catholic University will hereafter
be required to complete the higher education of England, as the centre
and head of our existing academical institutions; and though, by reason
of our present urgent needs and scanty means, they are unable to found
such a University, they are of opinion that a first step may be taken,
which in future may issue in such a University.

4. With this view they would propose to appoint a commission of
Bishops, Heads of Colleges, and other persons, selected from the existing Colleges and elsewhere, who may be most capable to obtain or to
give information on the actual state of our higher education, its quality,
extent, and needs, and to frame suggestions as to the course to be
pursued.

5. The Bishops are of opinion that among the subjects to be examined
will be the probable number of those who need such higher studies,
the relation of the London University to our Catholic education, and
whether a wholesome stimulus and a valuable direction to the higher
studies in our existing Colleges may not be given by the formation of
a body of Examiners and other officers under the united guidance of
the Hierarchy, with power to confer degrees. Besides the inducements
to study afforded by the *laurea*, burses and scholarships, and premiums
and other rewards of merit might gradually be vested in the disposal
of such a body.

6. Such an academical system, which at first would be simply personal, i.e. comprised of officers meeting only from time to time and
for their special functions, would prepare the way for a future local
foundation, when the means of purchasing land and of erecting the
necessary buildings shall be at our disposal. The Bishops believe that
the existence and operation of such a body as is here described would
powerfully attract the means necessary for its local foundation and
endowment.

7. While they are convinced that a Catholic University for England
must be a creation of the Holy See, to give it authority—and that it
must be the work of the Hierarchy in England, in order to extend its

action throughout the Church in this country—they would invite the co-operation of the Religious Orders in the scheme of Examination described above, and hereafter in founding Houses of their respective Orders in union with any future local university.

It was resolved that the above-mentioned Commission of Inquiry, who will meet in London, shall consist of—1. the Archbishop and the Bishops; 2. the Heads of Orders having Colleges of general education in England; 3. the Heads of Colleges; and 4. of other members to be elected from the clergy and laity. The Archbishop and the Bishops of Birmingham and Southwark were chosen to direct the said Commission.[2]

A number of the bishops, including Manning and Ullathorne, felt it would be well to begin with the examination of religion before proceeding to the secular curriculum of the Colleges. The Board could meet once or twice a year to discuss books, treatises for study, examinations, and examination-papers. Eventually the Holy See could be asked to grant degrees. Prizes of books, burses, and money could be allocated and the results of examinations published. Age limits would determine various categories and the decision as to who should be entered for examinations would remain with Superiors. Expenses would be met by fees. Hence 'the church having condemned the proposal that Catholics should frequent the national universities would thus give an earnest of her desire to provide for higher education by taking the first step towards university education'.[3] Nothing, meantime, was to be allowed to interfere with students' taking London University degrees; the two systems were to function together.

Bishop James Chadwick did not agree with this outline policy. The Board ought to examine in Arts and Philosophy and follow closely the model of London University. Thus the wishes of the Holy See would be more closely adhered to and there would be a more healthful incentive for the lay students. To examine Religion, Theology, and Philosophy would mean that a Board containing Religious would be examining the studies of clerical students and that was contrary to the Council of Trent.

[2] Ampleforth Archives, vol. 242, no. 7.
[3] Leeds Diocesan Archives. Cornthwaite's account of Low Week Meeting, 1868.

Fr. Herbert Vaughan, at the behest of the Archbishop, drew up a scheme for discussion. He adhered to Manning's belief that the best way to secure a university education for English Catholics was to begin with a Board of Examiners and with the examination of religious disciplines. The organization of the higher studies into one compact system, would, Vaughan asserted, 'be equivalent to a growing claim upon Government for the grant of a Charter: and although we may not in our day secure it we may lay the strong foundations of the claim which may be successfully used by those who will follow and come after us'. He considered that 'the question of establishing a University composed of Colleges actually and naturally united as the universities of Oxford and Cambridge, or those of Louvain or Rome, need not be considered on account of its extreme difficulty and for such would seem to be the result of a long course of action and of contributory circumstances, which may be witnessed in a more distant future'. A university was 'the moral and intellectual conjunction of various communities subject to a common intellectual discipline and direction in all the higher branches of learning'. He foresaw, however, that 'it would be a matter of delicacy to respect the rights of each College'. Vaughan advanced seven suggestions:

1. The bishops first agreeing to combine the higher studies and to unite their Colleges should then invite the Jesuits and Benedictines or other principal Regular Colleges to combine with them into a University Corporation; and to obtain for this the sanction of the Holy See.

2. That other smaller schools be allowed to affiliate themselves upon the principle of the London University.

3. That the form of this University Corporation should be a President and Vice-Presidents, who might consist, for instance, of the Archbishop and the Bishops having interest in the three existing Colleges and of the President of the Benedictines and the Provincial of the Jesuits or other chief Superiors representing the Colleges belonging to the Religious Orders and of the Presidents of the Colleges with or without elective voice. Some of the more distinguished of the laity might fill such offices as Chancellor and Vice-Chancellor, etc.

4. That common boards of examiners be formed by the different component Colleges of the various branches which shall compose the general curriculum of the studies.

5. That the Examinations be conducted on the principle of the London University local examinations or, if oral examination be deemed desirable, the board of examiners should for this purpose visit the different Colleges.

6. That the Holy See should be petitioned to grant the power of conferring degrees in science and letters, philosophy, law, and theology.

7. That rewards or prizes would be established in time for the successful competitors in the examinations, as these exist in the old Catholic Universities of this Kingdom.[4]

The suggestions of Bishop Chadwick found the greatest welcome among the prelates. In adopting them, however, the bishops ensured that the scheme would never get off the ground. If but Religion, Philosophy, and Theology had been proposed for examination at the beginning of the venture then only the episcopal colleges—Oscott, Ushaw, and St. Edmund's—would have been affected. Once the scheme was seen to work in practice in these establishments, it might have been less difficult to extend it first to the secular subjects in those colleges and then, perhaps, to the smaller colleges. The large colleges staffed by Religious would then have been tempted to participate. Chadwick's plan meant involving the Orders at the outset, and Benedictines, Jesuits, and Rosminians feared episcopal interference in their establishments.

Manning worked hard to get the scheme off to a good start. In 1869 he journeyed to St. Beuno's College, Tremeirchion, to confer with the Jesuit Provincial about the Board, and he urged the Society not to pronounce on the plan too early.[5] He sent the Jesuits a copy of the document drawn up by the bishops 'and approved by the Holy See' for a Board of Examiners 'to promote the higher studies of our Colleges, and in the end to form some system of the nature of a University in England'.[6] Jesuit reluctance, however, to become involved in the scheme is indicated by two developments at this time, both of which were not calculated to further cordial relations between the Society and the

---

[4] Vaughan MSS., Mill Hill, London.
[5] Farm Street Archives. Manning to Jesuit Provincial, 7 July 1869.
[6] Ibid. Manning to Jesuit Provincial, 26 July 1869.

Archbishop. The first of these was an article by Fr. G. R. Kingdon, S.J., in *The Month*, the semi-official organ of the English Province of the Society. The article, published in October 1868, was highly critical of the examinations of London University, and hinted that admission to the degrees of Oxford and Cambridge, without residence, would be a great boon to the Catholic colleges.[7] *The Dublin Review* entered the dispute and *The Month* replied in February, May, and July 1869. Fr. H. J. Coleridge, S.J., in what was but a thinly veiled attack on the Archbishop and the bishops who thought like him, roundly declared:

It is a misfortune which has had more than one bad consequence that a good deal has been written about Oxford life, in particular, by converts whose experience has been that of one large College in that University, which in certain important points is distinct in character from the rest. Invidious comparisons are always to be avoided, but it is fair to say that there is as much difference as to expensiveness, gaiety, laxity of discipline, and other kindred matters, between a very large, aristocratic, and fashionable College, and the rest, as there is between Pall Mall, Piccadilly, or the Haymarket, on the one hand, and Russell Square, or some dull though respectable nook in Bayswavia, on the other.[8]

To *The Dublin Review*, however, the real issue was not simply one of preventing Catholic youths from mixing with 'fashionable' youths at Christ Church, nor was it a fear that Catholic youths at Oxford might turn away 'from the creed of Pius to that of the Thirty-Nine Articles'. Rather such youths would be unsettled and the Catholic mind sent adrift 'to wear or pluck out its principles without putting others in their place'. The same point was emphasized by Roger Bede Vaughan in a pamphlet entitled *What Does it Profit a Man?*[9] published about this time. Have the Catholics who wish to be associated with Oxford, he asked, 'measured the spirit of the times, the freedom of thought, the irreverence of intellect, the mental pride, the impatience of authority, the independence of judgment in things the most

---

[7] *The Month* (Oct. 1868), pp. 390-2.   [8] Ibid. (July 1869), pp. 10-11.
[9] By 'The Son of a Catholic Country Squire' (London, Burns and Oates), p. 34.

sacred and august, the poison that exudes from every pore of the monster University, mixing itself in science, in literature, in society, pouring itself into the minds and the hearts, by its tenderness, its delicacy, its sensitiveness, its refinement, by its gentleness of manner, its charming address, its convincing reasoning, and embellished style—"Impia sub dulci melle venena latent" '?

The alarm, felt by the bishops at the manifestation of Liberalism in the Universities, received constant emphasis in *The Tablet* in 1869. In March the discussions on the Universities Tests Bill were extensively reported, including a number of the more extreme pronouncements, and in April the journal declared that 'no Conscience Clause could neutralise and destroy the poison of heresy, latitudinarianism, and rationalism with which the atmosphere [at Oxford] is saturated'.[10] The journal reported that the Wesleyan Methodist Conference had set up a committee to deliberate on 'whether it would be best to bolster up the Universities by building denominational Colleges, or some ten or twelve Universities, to be planted in different parts of the country', and *The Tablet* was not sorry to see 'that the movement in favour of denominational universities is awakened among the Nonconformists of England as well as among the Catholics of Ireland'.[11] The wish led to the thought that one thing remained to be done for English Catholics, too, 'the formation in England of a Catholic University as the crown and completion of our Catholic Colleges'. In September there were reports of a Catholic University to be built by the Archbishop of Cologne in Fulda.[12] What the rest of the Catholic world were doing could also be done in England. Provided that the co-operation of the Religious Orders was secured, a tentative beginning could be made. But the Jesuit attitude as portrayed in *The Month* did not augur well for the future.

The second of the developments which led to strained relations between the Society of Jesus and the Archbishop occurred in February 1869, and was concerned with the Jesuit plan to open

---

[10] *The Tablet*, 3 Apr. 1869.   [11] Ibid., 21 Aug. 1869.
[12] Ibid., 25 Sept. 1869.

a school for the well-to-do in London. Without reference to the Archbishop, the Jesuit Provincial determined to establish a school in the old Servite convent near Brompton Oratory. The Oratory protested to Manning, because it had itself for some time been contemplating provision of a school for middle-class education within its parish boundaries. Furthermore, the Jesuits failed to consider the effect of their scheme upon the other educational foundations in London, and especially upon the pioneer College of lay Catholic education in the metropolis, St. Charles's, Bayswater. A Jesuit school in Brompton would ruin the Oblates of St. Charles and frustrate the Oratorians. Manning wrote to the Jesuit Provincial on 19 February 1869, stating that 'the formation of any such work in the parish of the Oratory, and on that site, and for the service of their parish, is in my judgment so gravely at variance with the welfare of the Oratory and its Flock, and also with the highest spiritual interests of the Diocese that I trust you will not hesitate to relinquish the idea. I feel no doubt that had we been able to confer upon it before any step was taken this would have appeared to be right. And I fully confide that it will so appear to you now.'[13]

The Jesuits regarded Manning's action as one of antagonism to the Society as a whole, rather than one emanating from local diocesan interests. Their attitude is portrayed in a letter which Fr. W. Eyre, S.J., sent from Stonyhurst College to the Provincial in November 1870 bitterly ridiculing the Archbishop, who had gone to Rome for the Vatican Council. He trusted that 'at Rome they will know how to appreciate the ridiculously exaggerated ability of a man who has three hobbies, to make everyone a tee-totaller, to build a Cathedral which would cost a million when he has not a million pennies, and to govern all England when he cannot keep his own priests in order, and has not the confidence of one third of the English Catholics'.[14]

Canon Barry relates that 'for Manning in 1870, the last hour of European institutions had struck'.[15] A leading figure at the

---

[13] Farm Street Archives. Manning to Provincial, 19 Feb. 1869.
[14] Ibid. W. Eyre, S.J., to Jesuit Provincial, 22 Nov. 1870.
[15] Barry, William, p. 85.

Vatican Council, the Archbishop still found time for domestic issues. He was instrumental in 1870 in settling a number of serious disputes between the Rector of the English College in Rome and the clerical students of the College, and he was in constant touch with Gladstone throughout the year, cajoling, threatening, persuading, on behalf of the denominational schools and trying to get a fair deal for Catholic elementary education.[16] It would be too much to expect, however, that plans for the improvement of Catholic higher education should have made much progress during 1870. In effect, the rapid secularization of education in Italy, a knowledge of which was gained at first hand by the Council Fathers, made the bishops more determined than before to protect English Catholics from similar contamination. Moreover, it was not so much a question of 'protection' as a passionate belief that there existed another answer, another philosophy, and that Catholics had a duty to state it and not servilely acquiesce in current fads and theories. It was this 'missionary' aspect of the education debate which led Manning to associate himself with the leading agnostics and free-thinkers of the day in the Metaphysical Society. He had something infinitely precious to sell and he was determined to take up his stand in the heart of enemy territory. The Church's case could not go by default. The picture of what was happening in Italy frightened the bishops. 'Secular teaching is to be everywhere introduced, and that in Italy means the instruction of little boys and girls, of young men and women, in atheism and immorality at the public expense', wrote Herbert Vaughan. 'It is much the same everywhere, but in Italy it is not even at the trouble of putting on a cloak of hypocrisy, and its fruits during the last ten years may be seen in every great Italian city, in every Apennine and Umbrian village where its influence has extended.'[17]

During the absence of the bishops *The Tablet* was left to state the official Catholic viewpoint towards the Universities Tests Bill. The speeches in Parliament advocating the repeal of the Tests only convinced Catholics, the journal claimed, that they

[16] See my *Cardinal Manning*, ch. III, pp. 61 seq.
[17] *The Tablet*, 22 Oct. 1870.

'must speedily be provided with Universities of [their] own in Ireland and England, and that those Universities must have the power to confer degrees recognised by the State'.[18] It was vain to hold out to Catholics 'an empty shape of religious equality while we are practically reduced to deprive our young men of the higher educational advantages afforded by the State, unless we consent to place them amongst a crowd of non-Catholic companions under the guidance of Protestant and free-thinking professors.' The State, in fact, was preparing to offer Catholics 'a higher social standing, and a better chance of emolument', on condition that 'we entrust those children, when just rising into manhood, to companionship which we cannot conscientiously approve, and to teaching which we both dread and detest'. The only way 'to escape from this persecution and to remove the dangers of our position' was 'to have Catholic Universities of our own, with power from the State to confer degrees, and with a share of Government grants in proportion to our numbers'.

On 7 May 1870 *The Tablet* took up the complaint voiced in *The Echo* of the previous Tuesday that if the government's Bill was passed there would be nothing to prevent a Roman Catholic College from being incorporated by charter at Oxford, and nothing to prevent Archbishop Manning, as its President, from coming in rotation to be Vice-Chancellor and practical ruler of Oxford or Cambridge University. 'We beg our contemporary to pardon us for making no objection', *The Tablet* rejoined. 'It is so distinctly the determination of the Catholics of Great Britain to have, in course of time, their own distinct University, that it seems to us, whatever may be the facilities afforded by new legislation, there will still be very far from "nothing to prevent" our having a Catholic College at Oxford.'[19] In July *The Tablet*'s editorial declared unequivocally: 'Catholics have no designs upon Oxford. We should deeply deplore the progress of unbelief there, or the abolition of such respect to Christianity as is still paid in its Colleges. We pray that its dry bones may yet live, but we have no desire to reclaim (so long as England is Protestant) its dignities or its emoluments, or to associate our youth with its "alumni".'[20]

[18] *The Tablet*, 9 Apr. 1870.   [19] Ibid., 7 May 1870.   [20] Ibid., 30 July 1870.

V

A COMMISSION OF INQUIRY INTO
CATHOLIC HIGHER STUDIES

THE third item on the agenda for the Low Week meeting of the
hierarchy in 1871 was 'to consider the state of the higher and
middle-class education of Catholics in England, and the steps
necessary to be taken on that subject'.[1] The item was inserted by
the Archbishop as a direct consequence of yet another unsolicited
letter received from Cardinal Barnabo on 9 July 1870, urging
upon the prelates 'the necessity of prompt and energetic action'.[2]
Propaganda had approved the resolutions recommending the
establishment of a Board of Studies as the first preliminary
towards a Catholic University, and it was anxious to have something definite to place before the next meeting of the Congregation. The Vatican Council had been chiefly responsible for the
hiatus, but the delaying tactics of the Religious Orders had also
played a significant part. Roman accusations of episcopal dilatori-
ness, however, so incensed Bishop Goss of Liverpool that he
decided 'to call the attention of the Bishops to the irregular way
in which they are invited, both from within and without their
body, to take united action'.[3] There were other matters to be
considered, too: the policy of the hierarchy towards the new
School Boards, about to be set up under the provisions of Forster's
Act of 1870, and, above all, the attitude to be adopted towards
Oxford and Cambridge in the year when the Tests were repealed.

The changes effected by the latter were significant. 'Except for
theological degrees and Professorships, every man at Oxford was

---

[1] Birmingham Archdiocesan Archives. Agenda of the Bishops in Low Week,
1871.

[2] Southwark Archdiocesan Archives. Barnabo's letter of 9 July 1870.

[3] Birmingham Archdiocesan Archives. Agenda of the Bishops in Low Week,
1871.

to be free to take degrees and to hold office without subscribing any article or formulary of faith', writes Mallet.[4] 'He need not make any declaration of religious belief, or attend any form of public worship, or belong to any specified church or denomination. The religious services and the religious instruction of Oxford were preserved. But no person was to be compelled to attend any lecture to which he objected on religious grounds.'[5] There was to be no rush, however, on the part of Dissenters to avail themselves of the new opportunities. John Bright explained why: 'they are mainly of the middle-class, and their general impression of an Oxford education is not a favourable one. They think it costly—leading young men into extravagance and often into profligacy, and not qualifying them for commercial life.'[6] The great majority of the Roman Catholic bishops endorsed the attitude of the Dissenters. Gladstone's Act had merely loosened the stranglehold of the Established Church on the Universities; it had not revolutionized the teaching in those institutions. The objections of the hierarchy had always been against the free-thought and agnosticism which had found a welcome in the Universities rather than against their Protestant character. Even Newman by 1871 began to be disturbed at what he had heard was happening in the Universities. In a private letter to the Jesuit, Robert Whitty, he admitted 'for the last year or two' he had been 'frightened by the growing tendency in Oxford to introduce into the examinations anti-Catholic philosophy'.[7]

Manning's attitude was quite clear and was twofold. A more satisfactory professional training had to be secured for the Catholic middle class, and it had to be recognized that although the degrees of London University were open to such a class they could only be a temporary expedient. It was wrong, however, to allow the groans of a handful of wealthy Catholics, yearning for social 'acceptability', to obscure the real and vital issues.

If we except Thomas Grant, who had died while attending the Vatican Council, all the prelates present at the Low Week meeting

[4] Mallet, C. E., vol. 3, p. 332.   [5] Ibid.
[6] Herman Ausubel, in *In Hard Times: Reformers Among the Late Victorians*, pp. 205–6.   [7] Farm Street Archives. Newman to Whitty, 25 Nov. 1871.

in 1868 were also present at the meeting in 1871. They reiterated their earlier resolution regarding the setting up of a commission to find out the extent of the need for higher education and their belief in the efficacy of a Board of Examiners. 'Such an academical system,' the bishops repeated, 'which at first would be simply personal, that is, comprised of officers meeting only from time to time and for their special functions, would prepare the way for a future local foundation, when the means of purchasing land and of erecting the necessary buildings shall be at our disposal.' The co-operation of the Religious Orders was to be sought.[8] Bishop Clifford suggested to the Low Week meeting that the repeal of the Tests would create a new situation in the Universities, and he thought the episcopal policy on the Universities might be reconsidered. Finding himself in a minority of one, he later made a lone appeal to Rome, claiming that the repeal of the Tests was sufficient reason for asking the bishops to think again.[9] *Propaganda* took no action, other than to endorse the resolutions of the hierarchy and approve anew the recommendations for a Board of Examiners.

On 26 October 1871 a letter was sent out from York Place, London, to the Heads of Religious Orders and the Presidents of Schools and Colleges providing lay education. It was signed by Manning, Ullathorne, and Clifford, as delegates of the hierarchy. The letter suggested the holding of a meeting at St. Mary of the Angels, Bayswater, on the last three days of November 1871.[10]

This Conference formed itself at the house of the Oblates of St. Charles on 28 and 29 November, and all those invited attended. It resulted in the formation of a sub-commission to obtain information on four major topics: the state of Roman Catholic higher education in those Colleges providing such courses; the numbers of those wishing to have higher education; the relation of the London University to such education; and the advantages of the formation of a body of examiners, under the guidance of

---

[8] Leeds Diocesan Archives. Resolution, 1871.

[9] In Nov. 1867 Clifford put forward an elaborate scheme for a Catholic University, suggesting Prior Park as a location. His letter has been published in my *Cardinal Manning*, pp. 104–7.

[10] A copy of the letter is at Farm Street.

the bishops, with power to confer degrees. The sub-commission was also asked ' "generally" to frame suggestions'.[11] It consisted of five members, one a nominee of the bishops, one of the secular colleges, and the other three nominees of the principal Religious Orders having lay colleges. The bishops, in giving the Religious a majority of representatives, hoped to dispel antagonism to the scheme. The Religious selected were Prior J. N. Sweeney, D.D., of Bath (a Benedictine), the Revd. E. Purbrick, S.J., of Stonyhurst, and the Revd. Peter Hutton, Rosminian President of Ratcliffe. The secular colleges elected Northcote, President of Oscott, and the bishops appointed Francis Wilkinson, Rector of the Junior House at Ushaw. Of those selected, only Wilkinson, a London graduate, had been completely opposed to a connection with Oxford. Purbrick, a former Student of Christ Church, Oxford,[12] was not a free agent; he was already pledged to the view that a board of examiners discussing the studies of Jesuit Colleges must be resisted. The sub-commission was not permitted, however, to reopen the Oxford question, for the decision on attendance at the ancient Universities had already been settled.

The sub-commissioners drew up a questionnaire, the first part of which contained eight questions:

1. Have you been led, whether by your own knowledge and experience, or by the testimony of others, to think that there is at present deficient provision for the *general* liberal education (University Education or an equivalent, between the ages of 18 and 22) of young Catholic laymen of the higher classes in England?

2. Could you state briefly in what respect you consider such deficiency most marked?

3. Do you know whether your own views on this matter are shared by others? and to what extent?

4. Are you of opinion that any immediate step could be taken to supply the want?

5. How would you propose to meet the difficulty?

6. Would you be disposed to look favourably on any one or more of the following schemes:

A central board of Examiners for Catholics, more or less on the

---

[11] Southwark Archdiocesan Archives. Report of Meeting.
[12] Newsome, David, *Godliness and Good Learning* (London, 1961), pp. 20–1.

model of the University of London; the establishment of prizes for competition open to all our Catholic Colleges; the foundation of one or more separate houses of higher study such as might form the nucleus of a future Catholic University; an attempt to obtain admission, without residence, to the degree examinations of Oxford and Cambridge on terms to which Catholics could agree?

7. Do you attach much importance to the attainment of *degrees* recognised by the State? If so why?

8. Could you favour us with any suggestions as to the possibility and the way of providing special training for young Catholics who may wish to prepare for Competitive Examinations (e.g. Indian Civil Service), or to follow a course of technical instruction?[13]

The second part of the document consisted of questions to be answered by the various Colleges as institutions. These, thirty-one in number, were intended to provide a clear picture of what was already being achieved for lay students.

The first part of the interrogatory was sent to 800 clergy and laity, to 'all our friends and acquaintances, whom we had reason to believe specially interested in higher education, or specially qualified to give an opinion upon it'. Some effort was made to include members of the professional and middle classes, but these groups were thinly represented. The sub-commissioners moulded the answers they received (about 100 in all) into a consecutive narrative. There were important omissions among the names of those who received the interrogatory. Coffin, North, Rawes, R. F. Clarke, H. D. Clarke, Devas, Lane-Fox, Seager, Gilbert Talbot, George Talbot, F. S. Barff, and W. F. Anderdon did not receive copies, nor did the Oblates of St. Charles, a Congregation containing a considerable number of Oxford converts. These men, however, were known to be antipathetic to Oxford as a place for the education of Catholics, and they were thought to be supporters of the hierarchy's policy. The only Irish bishop consulted was a friend of Newman. Among the Religious Orders the Jesuits were over-represented, and only Jesuits and Benedictines were quoted in the Report. Two members of the Birmingham

---

[13] The questionnaire is in the Farm Street Archives. Quotations are from this source.

Oratory were consulted as against one from Brompton. Lady Herbert was the only woman who received a copy of the questionnaire.

In moulding the answers of the correspondents into a narrative, Fr. Purbrick weighted the General Report in favour of a reopening of the Oxford issue. So suspicious were the bishops of the literary endeavours of Purbrick that at the Low Week meeting in 1872 they requested the Archbishop to produce the original documents. Manning wrote to Purbrick to this effect on 15 April 1872, stating that the bishops 'wish to have before them such letters of reply as have been received by each of the five sub-commissioners severally'.[14] It was felt that in selecting a sentence here and a sentence there distortion might have arisen; qualifying phrases had perhaps not received their full importance. After an examination of the original evidence, the episcopal report to Rome showed that the outcome of the inquiry was by no means as clear-cut as the General Report at first sight suggested. There was never any insinuation that evidence had been suppressed or views deliberately distorted. It was simply that the way in which the sub-commission had chosen to present the Report did not permit of the full treatment which the seriousness of the problem necessitated. The Report, in fact, was a singularly superficial document, replete with questionable value-judgements. It did provide an indication, if little more than that, of the extent to which prejudices, both for and against the older Universities, had taken root among Roman Catholics.

The General Report was divided into five sections, the first dealing with questions 1, 2, and 3 of the first part of the questionnaire, the second dealing with questions 4 and 5, and the remaining three sections devoted to questions 6, 7, and 8 respectively. The second part of the questionnaire, completed by each individual College, did not figure in the sub-commissioners' General Report. This made the latter all the more inadequate. It was intended to lay the factual replies of the Colleges *in toto* before the bishops in Low Week 1872.

The first section of the General Report was concerned with an

[14] Farm Street Archives. Manning to Purbrick, 15 Apr. 1872.

investigation as to whether there was any deficiency existing in the provision of *general* liberal education for Catholic youths aged between 18 and 22 and, if so, wherein the deficiency was most marked. Correspondents had also been asked if they knew that their own views were shared by others, and if so, to what extent.

The sub-commissioners began by quoting Newman, who objected to the form in which the question had been presented.[15] 'University Education has, properly speaking, no equivalent', he had written. 'I know of no system of Liberal Education for youths between 18 and 22 excepting University Education; and for that, as regards English Catholics, there is at present not merely deficient provision, but no provision at all. . . . There is no deficiency in any respect at all, but a simple and entire blank. The want is not one of degree, but of kind. Your question then in its very form makes a cardinal assumption which I do not grant, and cannot be answered as it is.' J. E. Wallis, T. W. Allies, and Fr. Dalgairns are quoted as saying 'very much the same thing'. In a footnote the view of W. G. Ward is given that the greatest priority in his opinion was 'to prepare Catholic teachers of the highest order', and in doing so to offset any temptations to scepticism which might arise out of higher education.

The bias of the sub-commissioners became evident not only in the fact that Purbrick opened the Report with the Newman statement but in his use of emotive language when dealing with those who thought differently from himself: 'Others, however, confining their idea of University Education to a mere course of higher studies without any reference to the circumstances under which those studies are pursued, have taken no exception to the wording of our question, but have answered on behalf of the Colleges.' This kind of statement begs the issue. Correspondents had not been asked in these questions for their idea of university education, but for their views on *general liberal* education and its *present* provision in the Colleges. The use of the words 'mere course' in the statement quoted was in itself derisory.

Mgr. Weathers, Canon Moore, and R. S. Moody thought that

---

[15] Report of sub-commissioners, 1872, in Farm Street Archives. All subsequent quotations in reply to the interrogatory are taken from this source.

the supply in the Catholic colleges was already equal to the
demand for higher education: 'Our difficulty is, not to teach
boys in the Philosophy Class and above it, but to get them to
stay till they reach it.' Purbrick then interposed again, remarking
that 'although there is abundant evidence to show that this is
quite true, yet it is strange that it is not universally known'.
Fr. S. J. Hunter, S.J., a Cambridge graduate, felt that the Catholic
colleges did not publicize sufficiently the courses of higher
studies already available. They ought to publish at the end of
a year a list of examination successes. The laymen were divided
in their opinion. Mr. Frank Whitgreave is quoted to the effect
that 'Catholic gentlemen are more solidly educated than their
Protestant peers', and Mr. Justice Shee is quoted that 'there is no
such wonderful difference between the attainments of a man of
fair ability who has had time to go through the course at Ushaw
and the attainments of an Eton or Harrow, Cambridge or Oxford
man'. Ambrose Phillipps de Lisle declared that he had 'no reason
to be discontented: they [his own sons] have held their own, and
more than that, among their Protestant companions in after life,
and it would be very ungrateful in me, if I did not acknowledge
this'. The Revd. P. G. Munro, M.A. (Oxford), was of the opinion
that 'the generality of our young men are in advance of the
generality of young Protestants even when they leave Oxford,
so far as *instruction* is concerned'.

These opinions, however, were not common, the Report
stated. There were both moral and intellectual evils in the present
system. Some correspondents claimed that Catholic young men
were turned out deficient in confidence, others that they were
deficient in modesty. Allies supported the former contention and
R. S. Moody the latter. It was stated by a certain class of com-
plainants 'that many of our young men seem to start in life full of
a childish conceit about themselves, their family, their college, or
the clique to which they belong, in consequence of the narrowness
of the circle in which they have been so long kept, and that this
shows itself in a peculiar slang, and endless petty vulgarities of
manner, which would have been rubbed off if they had received
an intermediate training between school life and public life, such

as is provided in a University'. There was also a moral problem.
'At present our young men pass at once from the strictness of
school life to the complete liberty of the world, at an age when
its temptations are most seductive, and themselves wholly unprepared to meet them.' The Earl of Denbigh maintained that the
University was a miniature of the world under favourable
conditions, and F. R. Ward (one of the Memorialists of 1865)
stated that what was wanted were 'the conflicts and responsibilities
of *semi-independent* life'. The Report listed the deficiencies of
Catholic youth; they were said to be intellectually half-formed,
to have no power of *initiation*, to lack responsible and impartial
use of their mental powers, to be narrow, deficient in culture and
in the power of expressing ideas, and they were said to be ill at
ease in intellectual society. They 'allow themselves to be swallowed up in an increasing round of social frivolities, turn to
(so-called) farming, or go into Lloyd's or some other similarly
easy profession'. Others entered the army 'simply as a means of
idling away a few years, and without the least intention of
making it their profession'.

The Report painted a black picture of the intellectual condition of Catholic youth, but it was quite obvious that the sub-
commissioners were concerned only with a small number of
upper-class youths who could afford to live the kind of life they
described. It was quite a distorted image, based on false assumptions. The plea of a lack of worthwhile professional opportunity
was also particularly unsound. We know from the records of
London University and from those of the various Colleges that
many students took the London examinations precisely with the
intention of equipping themselves for professional life. If many
Catholics were, therefore, leading 'a life of indolence, if not of
vice', it was not because opportunities for professional qualification were lacking. Fr. John Morris, S.J., was probably right in
his belief that the gentry had an inbuilt financial reason for
exempting themselves 'from the tedium of study'.[16] As for
the social disabilities complained of, there was perhaps more

[16] Farm Street Archives. Manuscript notes on E. J. Purbrick's General Report,
p. 17.

substance in the claim, although the accusations were of such a nebulous and subjective kind that they defied positive verification. Fr. Morris was penetrating in his comment that 'if people will be honest, they will admit that it is precisely on account of the *social* advantages to be derived from an Oxford or Cambridge career that a large portion of our gentry desire University life'.[17] This, of course, had always been the contention of the bishops. The middle classes were in need of professional and academic training, the gentry of class acceptability and social respectability. It really seemed impossible for the bishops to be true to their ecclesiastical mission and to satisfy fully both groups.

The second section of the sub-commissioners' Report was perhaps the most significant part. It was concerned with questions 4 and 5 of the interrogatory. These asked: 'Are you of opinion that any immediate step could be taken to supply the want?' and 'How would you propose to meet the difficulty?' Newman declared he had no opinion to offer on either question. His silence could only be interpreted by the gentry as support for a reopening of the Oxford question, and by the bishops as reluctance to oppose them openly. A few of the correspondents quoted in the Report advocated the immediate establishment of a Catholic University. One of these was the Revd. R. E. Guy, O.S.B., who proposed the formation of a Joint Stock Company 'to purchase a considerable quantity of land, portions of which should be afterwards bought or rented by all our existing Colleges; each to establish its own Hall in the University for the reception of its own *Alumni*, but all united under one President'.[18] In this way would be maintained 'the spirit of the several Colleges', yet by mutual intercourse the University would be saved 'from collegiate jealousy and exaggerated *esprit de corps*'. Canon Oakeley was associated with this idea. Others suggested the Board of Examiners as a beginning. F. R. Ward postulated that

as a simple and inexpensive experiment . . . a small Academic Body— two or three learned priests—should be set down in some large provincial town, where the services of the Church are conducted with dignity,

[17] Farm Street Archives. Manuscript notes on E. J. Purbrick's General Report, p. 42.   [18] Report of the sub-commissioners.

where suitable residences for students could easily be found, and sufficient facilities exist for athletic amusements [and that] these priests
should be at liberty to employ, so long as it may be necessary, even
non-Catholic Tutors; that they should not encumber themselves by
making any provision for the boarding of the students, but leave this
entirely to the parents; that by and by, if the plan succeeds, lodging
houses and tutorial establishments might be expected to grow up, in
which the various grades of the upper classes would be brought together, and that perhaps ultimately two such centres might be formed,
one in the North, and the other in the South; but that at first there
should be only one. [He maintained that even that one would have no
chance of success,] unless all the existing Colleges consented, for the
general good, to relinquish competition.

Fr. Daniel Considine, the Jesuit Master of Novices and former
Scholar of Lincoln College, Oxford, declared: 'We have enough
[numbers] to make a good College at an existing University; but
not enough to create anything by itself, and of ourselves, worthy
of that name [of University].'

Purbrick assured the bishops that most of the correspondents
had deprecated 'any attempt to create a Catholic University in
any way whatever', and he pointed out that C. T. Redington and
J. Billington-Booth had advocated 'that young Catholics of good
family should be encouraged to enter the Protestant Colleges
of our ancient Universities in common with their Protestant
neighbours'. Lord Charles Thynne and F. A. Paley, agreeing with
this last view, did not qualify it by desiring that there must first
be an adequate supply of religious benefits available to such
students. The sub-commissioners added to this comment that
'they can hardly be aware, however, of the consequences which
have resulted from the system, so far as it has been acted upon
during the last few years'. W. H. Bliss, an assistant librarian at
the Bodleian in 1872, wrote of Oxford that 'the worldliness of
the place and its un-catholic and anticatholic life have the effect
of making Catholic undergraduates neglect their religious duties',
a view shared by another Oxford resident, H. A. Grissell. The
head of the Oratory School, Henry St. John, who hoped to see
Newman established at Oxford, and who, like Grissell, favoured

a Catholic College in that University, pointed out that, although several of his boys went to Oxford, 'one and all of them have suffered something from the deficient provision there for carrying on their religious instruction'. The Revd. J. Nary, who served the Oxford mission for over two years, 'during which time there was an average of twelve Catholic undergraduates', wrote that 'a very large proportion of these gradually gave up the practice of their religion'. The Revd. J. H. Corry, S.J., Rector of the Jesuit parish in Oxford in 1872, did not agree with Nary's estimate. The sub-commissioners reported, however, 'it cannot be denied that there is still a certain number who succumb to the temptations of the place'. Grissell, Corry, and Fr. St. John of the Oratory urged the old solution of one or two Catholic colleges at Oxford or Cambridge, 'under the care of distinguished priests or some religious body'. In order to clear themselves of the charge of exceeding their brief, the sub-commissioners added that the expression of this opinion 'was wholly unsolicited by the sub-commissioners'. Those named as being the most vocal in favour of the last-named plan were Lord Denbigh, Lord Gainsborough, Lord Clifford, Lord Howard of Glossop (all Stafford Club laymen), James Dormer, Henry Maxwell (of Scarthingwell), T. Galton, Ambrose Phillipps de Lisle, T. W. Allies, W. Heathcote, Simon Scrope (jun.), R. N. Chadwick, S. Day, G. T. Fincham, Mr. Thompson (of Mold), C. Berington, Fathers Harper, Corry, and Parkinson, S.J., and Father St. John of the Oratory. The chief arguments advanced in favour of such a College or Colleges were that the resources of Catholics seemed inadequate for the formation of a University of their own; that it was desirable that Catholic young men should be familiar with the thought prevailing at the Universities; that youths were already trained in military education, in law, and in medicine 'among very formidable sceptics and materialists'; that thus there need be no concession to the principle of mixed education; that the plan 'was proposed some years ago by the Roman Cardinals as a desirable thing'; that they did not 'apprehend greater danger to the faith and morals of our sons by their residence in Oxford or Cambridge, under the favourable circumstances we suppose, than there is in other walks of life upon which we are obliged to let them enter'; that a Catholic College would be an example for good at Oxford or Cambridge, and might even, in the words of Allies, 'draw to us many minds which are now without rest'; that to neglect the opportunities now opened to Catholics in the Universities would be 'to re-impose upon ourselves civil disabilities', especially in comparison with the Dissenting bodies; and that the material prizes available at the Universities were to be coveted.

On the other hand, equally powerful arguments were advanced against the erection of a Catholic College at either Oxford or Cambridge. Among the aristocracy, Lord Herries, Lord Petre, and the Hon. Colin Lindsay 'would on no account favour any connection with the Protestant Universities', for 'their glory has departed; they are hardly even Christian institutions'. David Lewis, Fellow of Jesus College, was entirely opposed to Oxford and Cambridge for Catholics, and he also expressed considerable doubts about the London connection. W. G. Ward feared 'the violently un-Catholic tendency' of the intellectual training and habits Catholics would encounter at Oxford, and the Superiors of Ushaw expressed their conviction that the *general* result, even of a Catholic College there, 'would be a coldness and indifference to the faith'.[19] Father Dalgairns quoted an article in the *Spectator* of 13 May 1871, showing that 'the ordinary and natural result of the present mode of teaching philosophy in Oxford is to produce "a hazy and wavering state of mind as to the ultimate truths" '. Its mode of approaching philosophical study 'is almost sure to produce a sort of intellectual vertigo in the mind of a student who has not yet obtained any sure notes, however simple, of philosophical truth'. In opposition to Dalgairns's viewpoint, it was argued that 'to be face to face with living error would give life and healthy tone to our own schools of theology and philosophy, as both professors and students would be actual combatants for truth, under the best circumstances'.

The second section of the Report lacked balance. No less than 155 lines was devoted to amplifying the views and arguments of those in favour of a Catholic College at Oxford or Cambridge;

[19] Report of the sub-commissioners.

less than a quarter of that space was allocated to the views of the opponents of the scheme, a mere thirty-four lines. W. G. Ward received but four lines and David Lewis two. Such an attempt to steam-roller through the views of the pro-Oxford party was ill calculated to impress the bishops with the impartiality of the Report.

Section C of the document was concerned with the specific proposal of the bishops to establish a central board of examiners and one or more houses of higher studies, as preliminary steps towards the evolution of a Catholic University. It also dealt with the other alternatives specified in question 6 of the interrogatory. Of the four schemes proposed, the one which referred to 'the foundation of one or more separate houses of higher study, such as might form the nucleus of a future Catholic University', seemed to interest the correspondents most of all. Certain objections were stated at the outset. There was a probability that the nucleus would not develop. The number of Catholics desiring higher education was declared to be insufficient to make the foundation worth while, although this argument could be brought with equal force against the Oxford plan. It was doubtful whether sufficient means could be collected to place a new foundation on a sure financial footing. The Earl of Gainsborough thought that a new Catholic College would lead to a dispersal of resources. Others felt that the cost of the education would be too expensive, although it was not clear why it should prove more expensive than going to Oxford. Gainsborough and the Hon. Colin Lindsay both considered that if such provision were to be made, the education provided should not be carried on under the same roof as that of young boys: 'Boys and young men ought not to be together; they should be removed at a certain age to a different scene and sphere of intellectual pursuits.' Lindsay suggested that Oscott should be developed exclusively for higher studies by dismissing its junior pupils. The same claim was put forward for other Colleges. The Revd. W. R. B. Brownlow, a convert clergyman destined to become fourth Bishop of Clifton in 1894, spoke up in favour of Old Hall. Slingsby Bethell argued for the Oratory School, and Thomas Eyre in favour of Prior Park. Such a plan would necessitate that all the Colleges should suppress their existing courses of higher studies in favour of the establishment selected. Problems of finance were also to be expected, together with the reluctance of certain Colleges to face a loss of income. Henry Stourton advocated the Philosophers' courses at Stony-hurst, and W. G. Ward declared that he was in favour of one house for the purpose rather than many. Fr. Dalgairns thought it essential 'that the staff of Professors should be drawn at least from all England' and, hence, not confined to any one religious community.

A number of correspondents, including Fr. Nary, Lord Denbigh, Mr. Wegg-Prosser, Mr. Weld-Blundell, Colonel Vaughan, Lord Petre, the Revd. J. Stevenson, David Lewis, and Mgr. Weathers, argued for the foundation of a new and distinct College of Higher Studies, and various sites were suggested for its location—Marlow, Abingdon, Tewkesbury, Upton-on-Severn, Ross, Newark, Usk, and London. Fr. Dalgairns urged that funds should be collected for such a College as the first step.

The sub-commissioners argued that the scheme for a Board of Examiners had not met with favour. The Benedictines of Rams-gate and Mgr. Patterson welcomed it, but the Jesuits, in the person of Fr. Hunter, thought it would 'destroy the liberty of the Colleges, hamper their individual action, and bring us all to one uniform system'. There were other objections. The presence of such a Board would tend to keep youths in their several Colleges too long, its examinations would be burdensome, because many young men would also be taking the London examinations, Roman degrees would not be recognized by the State, and there would be the added difficulty of recruiting suitably qualified and impartial examiners. Fear was expressed by David Lewis lest 'some one man would really become Master of the Catholic Education of England'. Lord Arundell of Wardour, on the other hand, recommended the bishops to make an appeal through the sub-commission 'to collect in the course of a year or two the sum of five or ten thousand pounds, to be invested as a foundation for valuable prizes. This would presently involve the appointment of a Board of Examiners, and the rest might follow.' Fr. Gerard Manley Hopkins, S.J., similarly urged the establishment of scholarships which should be to a place of higher education. Other correspondents favoured the idea of introducing prizes for competition. Some expressed fears lest such prizes should have a narrowing effect and advance individual rather than general proficiency.

A number of correspondents favoured an attempt to gain access without residence to the examinations of Oxford and Cambridge, for the standard of such examinations does 'not imply of necessity as great amount of learning' as those of the London University. F. R. Ward thought that the latter examinations 'press very hardly on young men who have no taste for the physical sciences'. The sub-commissioners concluded that a mere Oxford or Cambridge degree 'would not satisfy the more able and ambitious of our young men'.

The last two sections of the Report received summary treatment. The first was concerned with the importance to be attached to *degrees* recognized by the State. Newman thought that 'such degrees are only necessary in case no other stimulus exists equally powerful to attract students and to encourage study'. David Lewis considered 'there is no advantage whatever derivable from their possession', and added that 'the State takes no cognizance of them, and can neither give nor withhold anything on their account'. Others thought that London degrees had debased the coinage. On the other hand, it was maintained that such degrees were received as prima-facie proof of a liberal education, and as passports to employment and future professional success.

The final section of the Report was devoted to an examination of (*a*) *special* professional training for competitive examinations, and (*b*) technical instruction. In view of Manning's concern for middle-class education this section was of particular significance, despite its sketchy treatment. It began by stating that 'some deprecate exceedingly any work of this kind being taken up, either by any of our existing Colleges or any possible future University'. David Lewis thought it would involve a lowering of dignity, Robert Ornsby declared it would simply mean cramming, and that 'education trains the whole mind for the

general conditions of life, rather than for any particular circumstances', and others thought that education should be confined to
principles and not descend to details. Those favourably inclined
to the idea stressed that it ought to be left to those who wanted
to devote themselves to it. On the other hand, there were some
who wished to see a separate house established for such work,
'after the model of the Jesuit College in the Rue des Postes at
Paris'. Lord Clifford was one of them. Slingsby Bethell advocated
a Catholic Hall in Manchester, where students could live and
attend the scientific lectures in Owens College. Ornsby was not
opposed to a school of Engineering or Mining for Newcastle
upon Tyne. Mgr. Weathers proposed that one of the existing
Catholic colleges should be devoted to such work. Lord Denbigh
and Fr. T. Parkinson, S.J., urged that the work might well be
grafted on to that at present undertaken by the Catholic Colleges.
It was suggested that 'one particular branch of technical education'
could be attached to one school, but that not more than one should
be allowed in any school. Lord Denbigh and H. A. Grissell
thought provision could be made in the new College for Higher
Studies advocated earlier in the Report. The document concluded:
'Some special provision to supply the need seems very desirable
in order to remedy the present evil, of young men sent to live in
lodgings in London, Sheffield, Manchester, or elsewhere, under
no supervision at all, and merely attending so many lectures a
day, given at certain rooms by professional crammers.' It asked
'could the Bishop of the Diocese, or the Archbishop, license
certain houses in London, Woolwich, or wherever these young
men are wont to congregate, that so the safety of the inmates
might have at least some degree of security?'

The Report of the sub-commissioners was submitted to the
assembled bishops at the Low Week meeting in 1872. It was
accompanied by a personal statement from each of the five sub-
commissioners. Some years later Fr. Purbrick showed the Report
to Fr. John Morris, S.J., and the latter's comment was, 'how
many were invited to give any opinions at all except a few of the
aristocracy and *Oxford* converts?'[20] Although a large number had

[20] Farm Street Archives. Manuscript note.

received the questionnaire, Fr. Morris's question was apposite. The majority of opinions quoted in the Report seemed to belong to either the aristocracy and gentry or Oxford converts.

Of the five personal reports, Purbrick's proved to be the most trenchant. 'Outside of Oxford and Cambridge', he stated, 'there is in England no such thing as a real University, a *studium generale*, where all branches of a liberal education are taught to multitudes drawn from all parts of the Kingdom.'[21] In the absence of such a *studium generale* for Catholics he was convinced that 'a great work would be accomplished' if the existing provision for higher education was further developed. The institution of a Board of Examiners was anathema to him, 'no College under the charge of Religious could, even if they would, submit to a system of inspection and interference from without'. If the bishops gave a decision against residence at Oxford or Cambridge, then, he felt, 'as an alternative to London', Catholics would gain by pressing for admittance to the degree examinations of the ancient Universities. A Catholic University was chimerical. Unless 'the beginning be made by one or more Religious Orders, a staff of Professors for Literature, Science, Philosophy, and Modern Languages must be created and well paid, or modesty will degenerate into meanness'. Although he admitted that 'experience seems to prove that at least one fourth of those who have hitherto gone to Oxford have suffered much spiritual damage, if not shipwreck of the faith', he still felt that 'we want to make our young Catholics English gentlemen', and this could be done without danger if a Catholic hall or halls at the Universities were sanctioned. Of the two Universities, Cambridge might be more suitable than Oxford for this purpose, for 'there is more work done at Cambridge than at Oxford, the undergraduates are more numerous, and living, if I mistake not, generally less expensive'.

Prior Norbert Sweeney was as eager as Purbrick to forestall the Board of Examiners, and he was concerned to protect the exemptions of Downside. Consequently he strongly supported the Jesuit arguments. He admitted that 'no one can deny that

[21] Brompton Oratory Archives. Personal Report of the Revd. E. J. Purbrick, S.J., 1872.

there are great evils resulting from exposing our young men to the moral and intellectual temptations of English university life in these two great capitals of education',[22] but the whole thing needed to be seen in a wider context. Catholics were now 'in a position less favourable, not only than members of the Anglican Church, but less favourable than the Nonconformists and the Jews'. Catholics had gone to the London examinations to be on a par with Nonconformists; now a Jew and a Nonconformist were Senior Wranglers at Cambridge. He feared to advise opening a Catholic College in Oxford or Cambridge, but he thought that course of action was the only viable solution. He concluded that if the bishops still advised the Holy See to continue the prohibition, 'obedience to such a decision will bring a greater blessing than any University honours can bring'.

The remaining Religious among the sub-commissioners, Fr. Peter Hutton, declared that his natural leaning was towards the foundation of a distinct Catholic School of Higher Education 'to serve as a nucleus for a future Catholic University'.[23] With regard to the establishment of a Catholic Hall at Oxford or Cambridge, he declared: 'I feel myself incompetent to form a clear and well-defined judgment, owing to my total ignorance of the spirit and tone, as well as of the dangers and temptations of either University. . . . From what little I know, I am inclined to infer that converts who have studied at one of the large Protestant schools, Eton, Harrow, Rugby etc. can pass more safely through the ordeal than *born* Catholics.' He concluded: 'Taking all things, then, into consideration, I should be inclined to vote for the establishment of a Catholic Hall at Oxford, rather than that nothing should be done . . . always presupposing the existence or discovery of the necessary preservatives against mental and moral contagion.'

J. Spencer Northcote was less diffident. The fact which had impressed itself most firmly on his mind was that 'a large and

---

[22] Leeds Diocesan Archives. Personal Report of J. Norbert Sweeney, O.S.B., D.D., 1872.

[23] Southwark Archdiocesan Archives. Personal Report of P. Hutton, Inst. Ch., 1872.

important section of our upper classes earnestly desire that their sons should have an opportunity of leaving the school where they have passed their boyhood and youth up to the age of 17 or 18, and of meeting *in some other place*—almost all make a great point of this—a sufficient number of their equals *who have been educated elsewhere*, and there pursuing together some course of higher studies under less rigid discipline'.[24] He was inclined to think that the best way of achieving this was by a Catholic Hall in Oxford or Cambridge. Such an establishment would be 'the most powerful attraction to our young men of the upper classes', and in every other plan there would arise the inevitable rivalry of Religious versus Seculars. He supposed it to be undeniable that 'a certain number of Catholics will not willingly entrust the education of their sons to any hand but that of the Jesuits', and in Oxford the Jesuits were now responsible for the mission. It would be an easy matter to extend their presbytery and call it a Hall. Another Hall could be opened under the direction of the hierarchy and a healthy rivalry ensue. But there was a doubt which had to be faced. What 'if the Catholic Nobility, and Gentry, bearing great historical names should persist in sending their sons to be trained in the Protestant Colleges of the University, instead of entrusting them to the hands of Catholic Superiors'? It was essential to make sure of the academic allegiance of 'Howards and Stourtons, and Cliffords, and Petres and Scropes and Mostyns'. To attempt to build a separate Establishment elsewhere, *de novo*, would be expensive and wasteful in manpower. It would be preferable to develop one of the existing Colleges, if the ban on the Universities was to be upheld. To Northcote none of the existing Colleges were really suitable from the point of view of resources and locality. For such a College to succeed, it would be necessary for the others to cease to provide advanced courses, and he could not see the Jesuits at Stonyhurst being willing to fall in with that plan. Could the Jesuits be called upon to abandon their present Philosophers' courses 'in favour of an experiment in which it would not be easy to assign them any

[24] Brompton Oratory Archives. Personal Report of J. Spencer Northcote, 1872.

definite place at all'? They would only be willing to co-operate if they were given a good opening for an equivalent, 'and I can see this nowhere but in Oxford'. He agreed with the Jesuits that a College which consented that its students should submit to the examinations of a Board set up for that purpose 'must soon cease practically to maintain its own internal independence, for, in the long run, the examination necessarily determines the studies'. He had similar objections to the establishment of prizes. Entry to the examinations of Oxford, without residence, would lead to complications, and a College might find itself having to prepare students not only for Oxford but also for London examinations. He felt there were already too many Catholic colleges, but if it was decided to establish yet another, then a committee, with lay representation, ought to be set up to produce a carefully matured plan.

Fr. Wilkinson of Ushaw disagreed with his colleagues. He declared that the results of the inquiry had confirmed him 'in the conscientious conviction that to establish at Oxford or Cambridge, in the midst of a non-Catholic University, a College for the final education of the higher class of Catholics, would be most injurious to the best and highest interests of those for whom it would be provided, and would moreover fail to secure the objects which its advocates have in view'.[25] It was by no means certain that if a Catholic College were set up at Oxford it would attract Catholic youths away from Protestant colleges. What is more, 'if such a College were to consist exclusively of those students who have to live by a profession, it would not be likely to secure a high reputation, and for this reason, in addition to its comparative poverty, it would offer but small inducements to residence within its walls'. It would be impossible for a Catholic youth in a Catholic Hall at Oxford 'to escape the influence of the "genius loci", the spirit of the place which, as Dr. Newman says, "imbues and forms more or less and one by one every individual who is successively brought under its shadow" '. His objections to the Oxford plan were based on three arguments: the course of

---

[25] Brompton Oratory Archives. Personal Report of the Revd. Francis Wilkinson, B.A., 1872.

studies in the final schools, the moral and intellectual state of lecturers and tutors, and the companionship of those imbibing the principles of an 'infidel philosophy'.

The bishops, faced with conflicting evidence in the General Report, with the arguments of each of the sub-commissioners, and with the replies of the Colleges, had no easy task before them when they assembled in London for the Low Week meeting of 1872.

Part Four

KENSINGTON

I

THE BISHOPS AND 'PROPAGANDA'
1872

THE hierarchy assembled on 9 and 10 April 1872 at the Archbishop's residence. Twelve prelates were present, including the new Bishop of Southwark, James Danell. The only absentee was Alexander Goss, Bishop of Liverpool, who was seriously ill.

At the first meeting of the bishops concern was expressed on two counts—the way in which the sub-commissioners had exceeded their brief, in devoting considerable space in the *General Report* to the question of a Catholic Hall at Oxford or Cambridge, and secondly the manner in which the evidence collected had been summarized. Copies of the *General Report* had been circulated before the meeting. After examining the document, the bishops declared unanimously their opinion 'that sufficient provision for mere instruction and learning had already been made in our existing Colleges, but that a separate place for Catholic youth, in which the requirements of a transition state from the school to the world could be met, was most desirable'.[1] The bishops, with one dissentient, considered the question of a Catholic Hall at Oxford had been closed by earlier Roman decisions. The dissentient was Brown of Newport and Menevia.[2]

After lunch on the first day Ullathorne suggested the consideration of each of five possible plans. This was agreed, and the following subjects were then discussed in turn:

1. A Catholic University;
2. A separate College for Higher Studies;
3. A Board of Examiners;

[1] Leeds Diocesan Archives. *Acta* of Low Week meeting, 1872.
[2] Wilson, J. Anselm, p. 230.

4. Matriculation at the London University, and also at Oxford and Cambridge if made available for the students in the existing Colleges;

5. A Catholic College in Oxford.[3]

The greater part of the afternoon was given over to an examination of these points, and the weight of opinion was decidedly in favour of the second or third possibilities, or a combination of those and item 4. The foundation of a Catholic University was to be the ultimate aim and a long-term project. With regard to the question of a Catholic College in Oxford, Manning put the following question to the bishops at the end of the discussion: 'Whether it be expedient to found a Catholic College or Hall in the National Universities.' Bishop Clifford wished 'to explain to Rome certain altered circumstances as regards Catholics in respect to University Education at Oxford and Cambridge, before the Bishops come to any decision'. The altered circumstances he instanced were those consequent upon the repeal of the Tests. Clifford framed a formal resolution and Manning put it to the vote. Five bishops were in favour of Clifford's attempt to reopen the issue, the three Old Catholic representatives Clifford, Amherst, and Vaughan of Plymouth, and the two Browns (of Shrewsbury and of Newport and Menevia). Seven bishops voted against the amendment: Danell of Southwark, Chadwick of Hexham and Newcastle, Cornthwaite of Beverley, Roskell of Nottingham, Turner of Salford, Ullathorne, and Manning. Manning then adjourned the meeting to secure harmony.

The hierarchy met again on the following morning, Wednesday, 10 April. Bishop Brown of Shrewsbury, on behalf of the minority bishops, proposed a compromise resolution: 'That it is necessary to ascertain, as far as possible, how far it is competent for anybody, such as the Catholics or Nonconformists, to establish a separate College or Hall in the Universities, and how far such a College or Hall would be affected by the general regulations and laws of the Universities, and especially in relation to the jurisdiction of the Catholic Bishops.'[4] This was carried unanimously.

---

[3] Leeds Diocesan Archives. *Acta* of Low Week meeting, 1872, op. cit.
[4] Ibid.

Manning then proposed, on behalf of the majority bishops, 'That the Bishops report to the Holy See the steps taken in the last six months on the subject of Higher Education in conformity with the letter of *Propaganda* of February 3rd, 1865, and that they ask for rules to guide them in deciding on the course to be pursued'. This resolution was also carried unanimously. Bishop Brown of Shrewsbury requested Manning, in the name of the bishops, to obtain for them the information specified in Brown's resolution. The Archbishop agreed to do this, and, in addition, to obtain in the name of the bishops all the documentary evidence in the possession of the sub-commissioners. This evidence could then be fully examined before the Report to Rome was prepared. Finally, it was carried unanimously that 'the three bishops appointed as a Committee in Low Week, 1871, be requested to prepare the draft of such a Report [to Rome] to be laid before the Bishops at as early a time as possible'. The three prelates referred to were Manning, Clifford, and Ullathorne.

Within a week of the dispersal of the bishops Manning had written to the sub-commissioners, as requested, for the letters of reply in their possession. Clifford and Ullathorne remained in London to work with Manning on the draft of the Report to *Propaganda*. By mid June the latter had been completed and distributed to all the bishops. Unanimously approved, it was forwarded to *Propaganda* on 14 June 1872.

The document, a lengthy epistle, opened with the general statement, reiterating the episcopal resolution, that

the Bishops, assembled in their Annual Meeting in Last Low Week, after devoting a whole day to the discussion of the subject of the course to be pursued for the promotion of the Higher Studies for our Catholic Youth, unanimously resolved to lay before the Sacred Congregation of *Propaganda* a Report of the steps taken by them on that subject during the previous six months, and to request of the Holy See further instruction as to the course to be pursued. In proceeding to make that Report, they have thought it necessary to recite briefly the decisions and directions of the Holy See, hitherto communicated to them, and the steps that the Bishops have taken in obedience to the same. By this course a complete outline of the question will be submitted to the Sacred Congregation.[5]

There followed a factual account of seventeen stages in the problem effected since 1864.

The second part of the letter dealt with the reports of the sub-commissioners. It began by pointing out that 'the sub-commission were able only to report on the letters of their general correspondents'; the replies of the Colleges 'were too complicated and voluminous to admit of a synopsis' or to be studied in full by the bishops at their meeting. The question of establishing a Catholic College in the University of Oxford had not been included in the interrogatories of the sub-commission, nor had it been proposed by the bishops, but

the introduction of this question appears to have arisen from the three following causes: First, from the fact that the letter of interrogatories had been sent, obviously with the best intention, to a very large number of persons who cannot be regarded as capable of forming a judgment for the guidance of the Bishops, on the grave subject of perfecting the higher Education of our Catholic Youth.

Secondly, from the fact that the previous decisions of the Holy See, on the subject of the National Universities, appear not to be sufficiently known to many, both of the Clergy and of the Laity of this country.

Thirdly, from the fact that some appear to think that the changes made by the Act of Parliament in 1871, in the government of the University of Oxford, have rendered it advisable to re-open the question of founding a Catholic College in that place.

It was reported that five of the twelve bishops at the Low Week assembly had thought the Act of 1871 necessitated that the subject should be resubmitted to the Sacred Congregation, whereas the remaining seven considered it inadvisable to reopen the question. In view of this difference in view, the bishops were petitioning 'for direction as to the course to be pursued'.

---

[5] *Report of the Archbishop and Bishops to His Eminence the Cardinal Prefect of the Sacred Congregation of Propaganda on the Subject of Higher Catholic Education in England, June 14th, 1872.* Copy preserved in the Leeds Diocesan Archives (Cornthwaite Papers), from which the quotations here are taken.

Having stated the chief pros and cons of the debate, the Report went on to consider the standard of studies in the existing Catholic colleges. It certainly was not true 'that comparative inferiority in our studies is the reason why certain higher families in England are in favour of the education of Oxford. Their sons are already better educated than the majority of Oxford students.' It maintained that 'the closer attention of both professors and students in our Catholic Colleges, the better discipline, the more industrious habits of application which prevail in them, ensure in the majority of our students a higher average standard of intellectual formation, than is to be found in the majority of the students of the University of Oxford'.

A strong argument in the reports of the sub-commissioners was next examined. 'It is the intellectual pervasion of rationalistic and infidel philosophy', the bishops declared,

which renders Oxford emphatically dangerous to Catholic students. In the course of preparation for the Army and for the Navy, no such intellectual dangers exist. The young Cadets, in the course of their studies, would probably never come into contact with anything dangerous to their faith, beyond those ordinary temptations which, in an uncatholic country, they must meet everywhere, and even in their own homes. There is, therefore, no parallel between residence in the Military or Naval Academies, and residence in the University of Oxford.

The opinions of Mark Pattison, Pusey, Liddon, and Appleton, and the testimony given before the various Committees of Parliament, were quoted at length to prove the dangers to faith and morals to be encountered at Oxford, and the conclusion was reached that the kind of social intercourse made so much of by the gentry 'will assuredly not promote intellectual culture or habits of study, much less the formation of such moral habits as the Catholic Church implants and matures in its education of youth'. The arguments, too, that Catholic youths were on the whole awkward, lacking in polish, or uncouth, were rejected. Isolated examples could be found, of course, but these were not peculiar to Catholics. In society at large, 'even in the highest born and in the richest families', such examples were to be discovered.

The reports of the sub-commissioners had maintained that there were sufficient Catholic youths to fill a College but not enough to form a University. The numbers were estimated as being between one and two hundred. In fact, at the time the bishops were writing in 1872, there were but eight Catholics in attendance at Oxford.[6] The bishops felt that the numbers advanced by the sub-commissioners would need to be greatly reduced 'if a distinction be made between those who desire higher intellectual cultivation and those who desire what is called social advantages'.[7] Catholics could adequately provide for the higher intellectual cultivation of such a number from their own resources. The time for founding and endowing a Catholic University as such was not yet come, but whatever steps were taken now must have that ultimate aim in view. 'The foundation of a Catholic College in Oxford', on the other hand, 'would most powerfully obstruct the future foundation of a Catholic University.'

The Report concluded with a section entitled 'General Remarks'. The desire for a College in Oxford 'was originated and chiefly promoted by converts, in whom old memories and attachments appear to prevail over the discernment and the caution of their judgment'. From them it spread 'to certain Catholic families unduly attracted by the imaginary prestige of the National Universities'. It was termed an imaginary prestige because 'at the present time the number of graduates from the two Universities to be found in the learned professions of England, that is among the Judges, the Lawyers, the Physicians, the Scientific, and Literary Men, and also among the members of Parliament, is a small proportion, and that proportion is diminishing every year'. Catholics 'may freely graduate at the London University; so that no Catholic youth is at any public or professional disadvantage as compared with his fellow-countrymen'. Candidates for London degrees were trained in Catholic colleges and examined within their walls. To substitute degrees of Oxford or Cambridge, without residence, for those of London was legally impossible, and, in any case, would be 'but the first step

---

[6] *The Dublin Review* (Autumn 1939), p. 103 n.
[7] Report to *Propaganda*, 1872.

towards asking for residence in Oxford'. The abolition of the
Tests had merely rendered the studies of the University 'more
rationalistic, more infidel, and therefore, more dangerous, not
only to Catholic youth, but to all who retain any belief in
Christianity'. The bishops would have no academical jurisdiction
over an Oxford College or Hall or over its head, nor would they
be able to control 'the conduct of the students as members of the
University'. Many of the arguments and analyses of the sub-
commissioners' reports were grouped as appendices to the episcopal document.[8]

   Propaganda could be in little doubt as to the answer required.
Barnabo, writing to Manning on 19 September 1872, referred to
the fact that 'the British Parliament has lately entirely abolished
all profession of religious belief as a condition no longer to be
required of the students of the Universities',[9] and he declared that
the Sacred Congregation now believed the dangers to faith and
morals in those institutions to be immeasurably greater than ever
before. 'The Holy See cannot refrain from urging your Grace,'
the letter stated, 'and from urging also by your means your
Colleagues in the Episcopate of England, to make known to all
whom it shall concern that, not only does the Holy See perceive
no reason why it should recede from the aforementioned decision
of 1865, but that, in proportion as the reasons which called forth
that decision have increased in gravity, so much the more
necessary does it appear that that decision should be maintained.'
Copies of Barnabo's letter were distributed to the bishops.

   In 1873 Newman reissued *The Idea of a University*.[10] The reissue

---

[8] Butler in his *Life of Ullathorne*, vol. 2, p. 35, fails to realize that Ullathorne
was a member of the Committee of Three which prepared the Report to *Propaganda*. Butler gives no reference for his statement, but it becomes clear from the
context that he is unaware of the exact delineation of the parties at the episcopal
meeting in Low Week 1872. It may well have been that when he read the completed Report *as a whole* Ullathorne thought it overstated the case against an
Oxford College. But the bishop's last-minute scruples were not strong enough
for him to take positive action or to withhold his formal and explicit consent.

[9] Leeds Diocesan Archives. Letter of Cardinal Barnabo to Manning, 19 Sept.
1872.

[10] *The Idea a of University, Defined and Illustrated*, by John Henry Newman,
D.D., of the Oratory.

coincided with the Fourth Provincial Synod of Westminster in the summer of that year. The latter, the first and last Provincial Synod over which Manning presided, was held at St. Edmund's College, Ware. Newman, invited to attend, declined the invitation. One of the subjects scheduled for discussion was higher education, and in the light of this, and of the recent Roman pronouncement on the Universities, Newman's view in the introductory discourse of *The Idea* gained added significance.

Ecclesiastical authority, not argument, is the supreme rule and the appropriate guide for Catholics in matters of religion [he had written].[11] It has always the right to interfere, and sometimes, in the conflict of parties and opinions, it is called on to exercise that right. It has lately exercised it in our own instance: it has interposed in favour of a pure University system for Catholic youth, forbidding compromise or accommodation of any kind. . . . Moreover such a decision not only demands our submission, but has a claim upon our trust. It not only acts as a prohibition of any measures, but as an *ipso facto* confutation of any reasonings, inconsistent with it.

[11] *The Idea of a University*, p. 10.

II

THE FOURTH PROVINCIAL SYNOD
OF WESTMINSTER AND
JESUIT COUNTER-MOVES

THE letter from Cardinal Barnabo of 19 September 1872 instructed the bishops to deal with higher education at the Fourth Provincial Synod of Westminster, scheduled to assemble in the summer of 1873.[1] The Synod, attended by the twelve diocesan bishops of England and Wales (including two recently consecrated prelates, Vaughan of Salford and O'Reilly of Liverpool), was presided over, as papal representative, by Archbishop Manning. Three major documents associated with this gathering are particularly important. One is a joint Pastoral Letter issued by all the bishops in September 1873; the second is the Synodical Letter proper, published at the close of the proceedings in 1874, and the third, a Circular Letter issued under the authority of the bishops, and containing detailed plans for the improvement of higher studies.

The Pastoral Letter indicated the hierarchy's concern for the middle class:

Until the last quarter of a century the middle-class hardly existed in the Catholic Church in England. There were indeed in parts of the country a few families of the yeomanry still faithful, but our flock was for the most part made up of a small number of venerable and honoured Catholic families, who represent the spiritual inheritance of our forefathers, and a multitude of the poorest in the land. At this time, partly by prosperity in the commerce and industries of our country, and partly by a large accession of educated families to the Faith, a numerous

[1] Leeds Diocesan Archives. Letter of Cardinal Barnabo to Manning, 19 Sept. 1872.

middle class has been formed, for which a corresponding education must be carefully provided.[2]

The bishops acknowledged their duty 'to labour with all provident care that the higher studies of our Catholic Colleges shall be so raised and matured as to leave nothing wanting to a mature Catholic education'. Though, at this time, their Lordships recognize that they may not have the power to found a Catholic University, it is certain 'that those who come after us will be compelled to accomplish in some way this great and necessary work'. Parents were warned against allowing their children to frequent the national Universities, exposing them 'to the peril of losing either faith or morals, or perhaps both'. No parent could so expose a son 'without incurring grave sin'.

The Synodical Letter was issued almost a year after the joint Pastoral, and represented the fruits of considerable planning. It was signed by all the prelates attending the Synod, and read from the pulpit of every Church and public Oratory throughout England and Wales on 30 August 1874. The document pointed out that the hierarchy did not as yet possess any distinct College for youths from 17 to 21 or 22 years of age:

It may indeed be said, and with truth, that at some of our greater Colleges courses of more advanced literature and science are provided of which young men, may, if they will, avail themselves. But it can hardly be said that to any great extent they do so, and it is obvious that such a course does not and cannot supply the need of a College in which young men alone are received without the admixture of boys, where more advanced studies can be made, under a discipline more fitted to the age of manhood.[3]

It was proposed to form an undertaking in which all the Catholic colleges in England could, if they wished, stand in relation to a common centre, namely 'the Bishops with the aid of a Senate in

[2] *Pastoral Letter of the Archbishop and Bishops of the Province of Westminster in Provincial Council Assembled, September 20th, 1873.* Copy, St. Edmund's College, Ware.

[3] *Synodical Letter of the Archbishop and Bishops of the Provinces of Westminster Assembled, August 1874.* Copy among the Manning Papers, Bayswater.

which two-thirds shall be laymen'. This Senate would be made up of the Heads of all the Colleges, the Heads of those Religious Orders having Colleges, and representatives of both clergy and laity. The model to be followed would be that of the University of London. 'It has been so composed', the Synodical Letter declared, 'that any existing College, if it should desire at any time, may stand in relation with it and find in it a representative. It is to be hoped that hereafter the means of encouraging and elevating our general intellectual culture by uniform action may thus be found.' The independence of individual Colleges would be safeguarded. Furthermore, 'premiums and burses may be hereafter offered for proficiency in Literature, Science, and Arts, which cannot fail to stimulate the industry of students, and therefore, to raise their efficiency. Essays may be rewarded by prizes. A system of comparative examinations may be gradually created, and the results given in the form of class lists.' The details and the machinery needed for effecting these reforms would be left to the proposed Central Council or Senate.

Attention was next given to the foundation of a new College to cater exclusively for the 18–22 age-group. Basing its comments on the details of a circular letter drawn up by Manning at the behest of the bishops, the Synodical Letter declared that the proposed establishment was not to be regarded as a University:

It is strictly a College, and the first of the kind, placing itself in relation to the Council or Senate of advice. If at any future time other Colleges existing in various parts of England should desire to confederate themselves together round the same centre, preserving their own independence inviolate if they be Colleges of the Hierarchy and privileges intact if they be Colleges of Religious Orders, then an approximation would be made to the idea of an University, not, as we have before said, to be congregated in one place, but dispersed throughout England, and yet confederated round one common centre.

The new College was to be regarded as the first of many preparing for the public service at home or abroad, for the Army and the professions. The course of studies would be organized 'to enable the students to present themselves for the Civil Service and other Examinations and, when required, to obtain such degrees as confer advantages in the practice of certain professions, and which, under the present state of legislation, can be obtained by Catholics at the London University only'. The bishops estimated that the cost of the site and the cost of the preparation of lecture rooms, a theatre, and other rooms, in the house already standing on the property selected for the venture at Kensington, would be about £25,000. It was hoped that half of this sum would be collected before Christmas, and that a certain annual income would be ensured until the number of students increased and the College became self-supporting. The Synodical Letter ended:

> We appeal to you, therefore, not to give alms to educate the sons of the richer and upper classes—let no one so misconceive the breadth and importance of this work—we call on you to help us in completing a system which shall consolidate the Catholic education of England, which shall draw to a centre its present widespread and noble efforts, and add one more College of a distinct and higher kind to those already founded by the Vicars Apostolic and by the Hierarchy since its restoration.

A number of facts emerge from a study of the work of the Synod. The bishops had done all in their power to meet the wishes of the laymen, short of conceding Oxford. The direction of higher education was to be turned over to a body, a Council or Senate, in its composition two-thirds lay, which would be directly responsible to the hierarchy as a whole. The Senate, modelled on the federal pattern of London University, would be able to affiliate Catholic colleges to itself, to arrange Conferences, to set up prizes and exhibitions, to institute a team of examiners. The Colleges, for their part, would still be able to obtain London degrees for their students, but their studies would be organized upon a surer footing. The new College the prelates hoped to erect in Kensington would meet the demands of parents for a separate institution for Higher Studies.

The Kensington College was to be a creation of the hierarchy. It was not to be under the direction of the proposed Senate or to have any favoured position with that body. Its relationship with the Senate would be the same as that intended to be enjoyed by

Ushaw or Oscott or Stonyhurst. The scheme had considerable affinities with one being formed in the north of France in 1873. The Cardinal Archbishop of Cambrai, the Archbishop of Rheims, and the Bishops of Arras, Amiens, Beauvais, and Soissons had called together a group of clergymen and laymen with the intention of organizing a College of Higher Studies to serve as the nucleus of a Catholic University, once the National Assembly had persuaded itself to annul the monopoly enjoyed by the State University. The new College, meantime, would prepare its students for the degrees of the State University, just as it was intended the Kensington College should work towards those of London University.[4]

Commenting on the English hierarchy's decision, *The Tablet* in November 1873 remarked, 'what is being accomplished is being effected with as little flourish of trumpets as possible. It is desired to avoid anything like a great show on paper with few positive results.'[5] The scheme was simple, unpretentious, and practical. Invitations to become members of the Academical Senate were sent to important ecclesiastics: Newman; Monsignor Capel; the President General of the Benedictines; the Provincials of the Jesuits and Dominicans; the Presidents of Ushaw, St. Edmund's College, Oscott, and Prior Park; Canons Crookall, Toole, and Charles Teebay (of the Liverpool diocese); Fr. Dalgairns of the Oratory; and the Revd. R. G. Macmullen, a convert. To these names would be added those of the Heads of Colleges staffed by Religious, if and when they agreed to participate. The laymen invited to become members were the Duke of Norfolk, the Marquess of Bute, the Earl of Denbigh, Lord Petre, Lord Arundell of Wardour, Lord Clifford, Lord Howard of Glossop, Sir Robert Gerard, Sir George Bowyer, Sir Humphrey de Trafford, W. H. G. Bagshawe, W. A. Charlton, John Day, Basil Fitzherbert, William Ford, John Hardman, John Herbert of Llanarth, Stuart Knill, Charles Langdale, Daniel Lee, Denis F. McCarthy, St. George Mivart, John Hungerford Pollen, Richard A. Proctor, C. R. Scott-Murray, Henry Sharples, Colonel Vaughan, Aubrey de

---

[4] *The Tablet*, 27 Dec. 1873.
[5] Ibid., 29 Nov. 1873.

Vere, W. G. Ward, and Thomas Weld-Blundell.[6] The list had been compiled from suggestions made by each bishop. The Stafford Club set, the landed gentry, and the Old Catholics were well to the fore. McCarthy and de Vere, friends of Newman, had been involved in the Irish venture. Professional interests were represented by such men as Hardman and John Day. All those requested to be members of the Senate accepted the invitation, with the exception of Newman and Charles Langdale.[7] Newman's reason for refusing was that he could not take part 'in an Institution, which formally and "especially" recognises the London University'.[8] He had earlier declined Manning's invitation to be present at the Provincial Synod, on the ground of 'my total ignorance of synodal matters'.[9] By the mid 1870s Newman's attitude had marked him out as the symbol of a divisive element among English Catholics. *The Spectator* broke down the Bishops' list into classes: 'nine are members of the aristocracy, eight country gentlemen, six commercial men, and seven members of the learned professions.'[10]

As soon as Fr. Gallwey, the Jesuit Provincial, heard of the intention of the hierarchy to open a new College in London, he wrote to Manning, announcing that the Society had fixed 'on a site in the country about thirty miles from London' for a Jesuit College, but after the Synod, 'when I received your Grace's letter, Fr. General wished us to proceed no further till we understood more clearly the intentions of the Bishops'.[11] At the Low Week meeting of the hierarchy in 1874 Manning had to inform the assembled bishops that the Jesuits had appealed to Rome. The appeal lodged at *Propaganda* by the Jesuit General asserted,

(*a*) That it is not stated what part the Society are to have in the proposed College; but that it would seem that only one College is now to be established;

---

[6] Farm Street Archives. Manning's letter to Jesuit Provincial, Fr. Gallwey, 21 Nov. 1873.

[7] Leeds Diocesan Archives. *Acta* of Low Week meeting, 1874.

[8] Newman Papers, Birmingham. Newman to Manning, 24 Nov. 1873.

[9] Newman Papers, Birmingham. Copy. Newman to Manning, n.d.

[10] *The Spectator*, 6 Dec. 1873.

[11] Farm Street Archives. Gallwey to Manning, Holy Innocents (1874).

(*b*) That the Colleges to be established in the future would be under the inspection of the Hierarchy, and under the same Academical Senate;

(*c*) That of the fourteen Ecclesiastics in the Senate, only one is of the Society, although it is by the Society that at least a third of those who are receiving a liberal education in England are educated, and that the secular Colleges enumerated in the Circular do not contain so large a number of students;

(*d*) That whereas the Rectors of all the chief secular Colleges are on the list of the Senate, the Rectors of all the Jesuit Colleges are omitted;

(*e*) That, of the fourteen Ecclesiastics on the list of the Senate, only three are Religious, although it is the Religious who educate by far the larger part of those who are receiving a liberal education.

The Society petitioned:

(*a*) That the Religious may have a fair proportion in the Senate;

(*b*) That nothing be done which shall be contrary to that freedom of teaching which the Religious have always enjoyed, and which they have exercised with so much good to religion;

(*c*) That nothing may be done which shall interfere with the exemption of the Religious in their own houses.[12]

Manning's answer to the charges was approved unanimously by the bishops. It was quite simple. The hierarchy were more than willing to agree to points (*b*) and (*c*) of the Society's petition. With regard to the number of Jesuits and other Religious on the Senate, it had been agreed that the Rectors of all Colleges would be members as soon as the latter indicated their willingness to be included in the scheme. The Jesuit Colleges had not done this, hence the names of the Jesuit Rectors were omitted. The Society would be entitled to have on the Senate the Provincial and the Rector of each Jesuit College which participated. Similarly with regard to the other Religious. At the hierarchy's meeting Manning suggested that the Rector of Stonyhurst should be invited to join the Senate in his own right. This was agreed. He also put forward some further names for membership of the Senate, which were likewise approved: the Pro-Visitor of the Cassinese Benedictines (Ramsgate Abbey); the Provincial of the Rosminians; the Revd.

[12] Leeds Diocesan Archives. Cornthwaite's Papers, 14 Apr. 1874.

H. A. Rawes of the Oblates of St. Charles; Lord Stourton; T. W. Allies; F. W. Barff; S. N. Stokes; H. Sumner; J. de Lacy-Towle; and Dr. West.[13]

As soon as the Jesuits had studied the Synod's proposals, the English Provincial wrote to Fr. Alfred Weld, the Society's English Assistant in Rome. Weld, a member of an Old Catholic family, replied on 28 November 1873. The hierarchy's plan would be laid before *Propaganda*, together with a protest, in order that 'fair play be given to us'.[14] He went on: 'The first thing for you to do is to find out whether we are to be invited to take direct part in this Bishops' College or not. If we are, I think we cannot refuse, but at the same time that we fight vigorously to have our proper rights.' Weld maintained that Manning had promised the Society the Chair of Philosophy, should the undertaking grow. 'If we have fair play,' he wrote, 'there would be nothing to prevent our getting as much hand in it as we wish.' But on the other hand, if it was intended 'to make this a Secular College and not to invite Religious to take part in it, then our part is at once to open one elsewhere, and to obtain from the Holy See that our liberty of teaching and our exemption within our own walls be not interfered with'. He referred to what he called 'the hostility of the Archbishop', which would 'not always be in the way', and said that the Society, if it was asked to partake in the teaching at Kensington, would soon 'assert' its position. The letter concluded: 'If we do open a separate College, though I like Reading on account of its great convenience for railways, I am a little afraid of its being too far from London, unless you get a site very close to the station. . . . I have sometimes thought of Chertsey, which is a nice distance from London.'

Three weeks later Weld was writing to urge the Provincial to get all the Religious Orders to co-operate in signing the memorial which the Jesuit canonists in Rome were drawing up against the VIIth Decree of the Synod on the question of Higher Studies. 'It is not proposed in this memorial', he pointed out, 'to touch the

[13] Leeds Diocesan Archives. Cornthwaite's Papers. A new Circular embodying these names was issued on 9 May 1874.
[14] Farm Street Archives. Weld to Provincial, 28 Nov. 1873.

question of the University directly, as it is not very clear as yet what to ask for, and the particular thing of our representation on the Senate should be kept separate from the great question of the privileges of Religious which are involved in the other points. The University question will be affected because by stopping the Congregation of Studies (Senate and Examining Body) our liberty of opening Colleges and our independence in them will be secured.' He suggested Richmond, Surrey, as a site for a new Jesuit Hall for lay students, which would constitute an effective rival to the Bishops' College.

In August 1874 Weld declared that the printed Circular of 9 May, containing a revised list of Senate members, provided a good opportunity 'to go on with the question with Mgr. Agnozzi, Secretary of the Propaganda, who takes a very sensible view of all these questions, and is well disposed to us'.[15]

At Low Week in 1874 the bishops pressed Manning to go to Rome and place before *Propaganda* an accurate account of the intentions of the hierarchy. Before the end of the year intimations had reached England that Pius IX intended to create Manning cardinal at the Conclave of 15 March 1875. A journey would, therefore, be necessary to receive the Red Hat. By the end of October 1874 preparations were well in hand. Weld was determined, however, to forestall the Cardinal-elect. He wrote to the English Provincial from Fiesole on 26 October:

I have spoken to Fr. General about the Archbishop's journey to Rome and we have agreed that I am to go to Rome next week. I do not mean to put myself forward as the able advocate you speak of, but I can give Cardinal Franchi the history of the University and higher studies question as well as anyone: in fact no one knows as well as I do the repeated assurances of the Archbishop that we must work together in that matter. So far I see my way, but I want some more information on this subject. I should like to know what passed between Fr. Whitty and the Bishops on the subject. My impression is that they expressed a wish for him to begin it, also with Fr. Eyre and the Archbishop especially at the beginning of last year. If you could get them both to write to me what passed, their letters would be a testimony in case it were

[15] Ibid. Weld to Provincial, 16 Aug. 1874.

questioned. Fr. General told some things to Monsgr. Howard and he would hardly believe it. Another thing I must know of distinctly. Are we allowed any co-operation at all at Kensington? And if so, what? . . .

As things are now, I think we should hardly get leave for a distinct establishment in or near London. The two working against each other would so manifestly tend to destroy each other I am not quite sure that we should really wish it. There are many parents who would not like their sons to be sent to London for education, and all such would come to us if we were 20 or 30 miles away. For this reason I really think the establishment in Kensington, which is the most fashionable part of London, is a mistake, but as things are I believe the best thing would be to get leave to bring our Philosophy and Theology to Kensington and open public schools of these two branches, without asking to board any seculars but being content with those classes and the spiritual influence we would gradually acquire. I don't altogether like Kensington for our Scholastics, but I don't know the position of Capel's establishment. I suppose the Park is near: but it would ensure the success of the establishment and would unite all parties. And this I think the Propaganda would be inclined to grant, because there is no apparent objection except the fear of our influence and it corresponds so much with what they are accustomed to in Rome. But you must make up your mind clearly what you wish and what you will accept. If we had been consulted, I should have proposed such an establishment a little out of London, near Richmond or Twickenham, but as it is established in London, I think the best thing would be for us to join in the way I propose, and perhaps it will be found later that it is best to move it and it is equally likely that if we are once connected with it we may get other professorships later if we wish it. We might begin with Philosophy. There will not be time for you to answer here, so please write to me at the English College, and as soon as you can. Let me know also when the Archbp. is expected to be in Rome.[16]

Perhaps the main point emerging from the reports of the subcommission of 1872 had been that the numbers of Catholics were insufficient to staff more than one specialized College of Higher Studies. Such a College, to inspire confidence, ought to be under the direction of the hierarchy. Furthermore, the task of establishing an alternative to a Catholic Hall at Oxford had

[16] Farm Street, Archives. Weld to Provincial, 26 Oct. 1874.

been committed to the bishops by *Propaganda*. As numbers increased, it was envisaged that the Orders would found houses of their own. Fr. Weld was, however, determined to associate the claims of the Society in connection with the Kensington College with those which the Jesuits were advancing on the school question. In this way, it was thought, Rome would be convinced that there was an episcopal conspiracy at work to defraud the Society.

As early as 1867, when there was the first sign of serious talk of a Catholic University, Weld had journeyed to Rednal to elicit the help of Newman. The latter told him, without sparing the Jesuit's feelings, that there would be difficulty 'in the prospect of getting parents to send their sons to a sort of Jesuit Noviceship; and if they did, of getting the youths themselves to acquiesce in it'.[17] Newman was not enamoured of 'a Jesuit scheme', and informed Hope-Scott: 'I will have nothing to do with the plan, unless the Professors are lay.'[18] Others contacted by Weld had been equally unenthusiastic. It is not without some significance that Weld informed Cardinal Franchi in November 1874 that the Society would have nothing to do with any scheme in which they were under the direction of laymen. Writing to the Provincial on 7 November 1874 to report on his interview with Franchi, Weld declared:

As to higher studies, he asked me if Capel (the Rector of the Kensington College) would succeed. I said the thing would certainly have succeeded if we had been consulted as to the place and had been invited to take part. As things are, it is very doubtful. Very difficult to take part now even if asked on account of expense and risk. Our view was to unite our Philosophy and Theology in some place near London where it will do more good than it can now *and to unite lay classes with them*.[19] That the best thing now would be to let Capel go on, and to allow us, when we were ready, to bring our Phil. and Theol. together near London, and when Capel has had a bit of a start to give him a chance, *attach classes for lay scholars to our own*.[20] I observed that probably Manning would say that he meant this to be a secular college and meant

---

[17] Ward, W., *Life of Newman*, vol. 2, p. 196. Newman to Hope-Scott, 10 Oct. 1867. [18] Ibid., Newman to Hope-Scott, 25 Sept. 1867.
  [19] My italics. [20] My Italics.

us to have ours later. I told him (Franchi) we wanted it near London, and that we could not be under a Senate half composed of laymen.[21]

Franchi, with the diplomacy of the curial official, spoke warmly of the Society and promised to discuss the matter with Manning. Weld concluded:

> So it will be well to let me know what you resolve on for higher studies and how long you would consent to wait before moving lay philosophers. If this part of the programme is delayed a year or two it will make it much easier to get what we want.

What Weld wanted was clear—an exclusive, Jesuit-controlled College for Higher Studies, strategically placed near London to rival the hierarchy's establishment, and, by implication, to supersede it when Kensington was unable to withstand the competition. The Society had every intention of retaining in the meantime its own lay 'Philosophers' at Stonyhurst and of continuing its course of Higher Studies there. Students would not be passed on to Kensington, but would eventually be removed *en bloc* to a new Jesuit house near London. As Stonyhurst contained more than half the youths undertaking courses of higher study in Catholic colleges, this meant that Capel's College would be ruined from the outset. With the Society it was a case of all, or nothing.

By 16 November Weld was canvassing Cardinals de Lucca, Patrizzi, and Consalini, 'who are the most influential of the Propaganda'.[22] He declared 'they all expressed the same opinion of surprise that we had been excluded from the higher studies, that as we had not been asked we could not be blamed for not taking part, that what we are now doing could not be interfered with . . .'. Franchi was reported as approving of the proposal 'to transfer the Philosophy and Theology of our Scholastics to a place near London when it is convenient to us to do so, and after a little delay to transfer to the same place our lay higher studies'. Weld felt 'it was necessary to agree to some delay about this last point in order not to appear to act in opposition to Capel, about which they were all anxious, and as I had told him that a College of our

---

[21] Farm Street Archives. Weld to Provincial, 7 Nov. 1874.
[22] Ibid. Weld to Provincial, 16 Nov. 1874.

own not far from London was the best way for us to take part as things now are. They were all anxious that all should be done peacefully, and especially that Protestants should not know any differences may exist.'

But all was not as straightforward as Weld imagined. There was first of all the united body of the episcopate to cope with, and the bishops had been antagonized by the inaccuracies of the original Jesuit complaint. Their letter of explanation had preceded Manning to *Propaganda*. There was Manning's personal visit to Rome. Then there was Cardinal Franchi himself, a doubtful ally. Weld, too, was to grow increasingly cautious concerning Franchi's enthusiasm. He wrote to Gallwey:[23] 'I think we should lose no time in acting upon what we have got to keep the Cardinal [Franchi] to his good purposes. I may here say confidentially that some of Ours have not great confidence in his standing up for us.'

Fr. Eyre, S.J., in a letter to the Provincial on 6 January 1874, claimed that Manning had once asserted to him that 'we were perfectly free to set up a house of higher studies anywhere in England but that the nearer I came to him the better, as then he would see more of me'.[24] He felt that more effort could be made by the Society to develop Higher Studies in Glasgow 'than we are now doing in the wretched imitation now existing of a middle school' (St. Aloysius' College). He concluded: 'it makes me lament more than ever that we should have such a jumble as Beaumont Lodge, and such a dilapidated ruin as Stonyhurst, as our houses of Lower Studies.'

Before the year 1874 was out the Jesuits had thrown down the gauntlet in public before the bishops, and they had carried their displeasure at the formation of the new episcopal College for Higher Studies into the columns of the Catholic press. In doing so, they staked a claim on the allegiance of the laity. The occasion was provided by the publication in *The Weekly Register and Catholic Standard*, on 6 July 1874, of an editorial notice concerning the Kensington College. The first meeting of the Senate had taken place on 21 May, and small committees had been formed to assist

[23] Ibid.   [24] Ibid. Eyre to Provincial, 6 Jan. 1874.

the prelates with various aspects of the new project. These committees had held several meetings. The paragraph which aroused the ire of the Jesuits and served as the occasion for a public break with the project was as follows:

We wish to make one thing perfectly clear to our readers—it is the fact that the Catholic University College will interfere with no existing Institution in the country. Our present Colleges are what in ordinary English would be called *schools*. They are for the education of *boys*. They are of great value, and English Catholics owe them a great debt of gratitude; but the new University College begins where they end. It breaks up entirely new ground. Its students are young men. There is no clashing; there are no contending interests. On the contrary, if it pleases God to grant the new Institution the measure of success which we may humbly hope for it, [it] may prove a stimulus to the primary colleges already in existence.[25]

The editor went on to indicate clearly that in his view the Kensington venture was to be regarded as the nucleus of a Catholic University, and among the benefits which would flow from the College would be 'the emulation that will be aroused in students who may come from the different Catholic Colleges of England, on the completion of their course of school education, the kindly sympathy that will knit them together, and the friendships that will be formed'.

It was clearly implied that the Catholic colleges would feed the new institution with students. At once Fr. E. Purbrick, S.J., Rector of Stonyhurst and a member of the hierarchy's Academical Senate, wrote to disillusion the editor. He declared:

As Rector of Stonyhurst, I hope I may be allowed a space in your next number to say that in this College, besides a school for boys, there is also a College course for young men, of whom there are at present *thirty-three* between the ages of seventeen and twenty-two. In this course there is provision for preparing for the degrees of the University of London, at least up to the M.A. degree: and the higher Mathematics and Natural Sciences, Political Economy, and Mental Philosophy—all worthy, surely, of the name of Higher Studies—are also all actually

[25] *The Weekly Register and Catholic Standard*, 11 July 1874.

taught to 'Philosophers', as these young men are called. I confine myself to the simple statement of fact, and should not have thought it necessary to make the statement had I not feared that silence might be construed into a confirmation of the *Weekly Register*'s remark, and prove injurious to the College.[26]

The letter was designed to show that the Society had no intention of transferring youths from Stonyhurst to the Kensington College. The newspaper retaliated:

We do not for a moment forget the fact that there are classes of Philosophers at our existing Colleges, and that a certain number of young men continue their studies there with a success which is amply proved by the positions they take in the examinations of the London University, but these advanced studies are not the special or primary object of the Colleges in question. Their natural position in Catholic education is similar to that held by Rugby, Harrow, and Eton in Protestant education: the classes of Philosophers are rather an accident, or a provision for a special necessity, than a part of their normal plan. The new University College is *exclusively* for advanced studies, and makes no provision for the requirements of earlier education.[27]

Purbrick was fully prepared to make his challenge explicit. 'The new College is a rival of existing institutions', he wrote to the paper on 25 July.[28] 'I do not complain of the rivalry', he went on. 'If it tends to create a keen appetite amongst us for Higher Studies, it is an unmixed benefit. But rivalry there must be.' The important thing was 'that the idea of the Society of Jesus in establishing a college is precisely the reverse of that which the writer supposes. In a College of the Society, the school department is for the sake of the College proper, and not the College for the sake of the school. The school is intended as a feeder to the College. The collegiate course is normally the main thing, not an unnatural appendage or an accidental expedient to meet a special necessity.'

Nothing could be plainer. The Society would refuse to cooperate with the new College, and it would continue to use Stonyhurst and the other Jesuit Colleges as 'feeders' for its own

[26] Ibid., 18 July 1874.   [27] Ibid.   [28] Ibid., 25 July 1874.

advanced courses. Little more needed to be said. *The Weekly
Register and Catholic Standard* could only hope that the English
Jesuits would follow the example of their Irish confrères at
Clongoeswood, who had given valuable support to the establish-
ment of the Irish Catholic University at a time when Clongoes-
wood was itself preparing students for the examinations of
London University.[29] Purbrick's claims were regarded as naïve:

The majority of Stonyhurst students leave without mastering the
Higher Studies. We are surprised to hear that so many as thirty-three
young men are there at present, who may be reckoned as belonging to
her in University fashion. Young Spaniards and other foreigners are
sent by their relatives to this country on account of troubles and wars
in their own, and we suppose that Stonyhurst would be suggested by
the members of the Society abroad as the asylum for these youths; but
they at least are 'accidental', and to include them in the number given
would be an oversight on Fr. Purbrick's part.

Purbrick erred when he said that the Kensington College was a
rival to his own and to other Colleges. 'We cannot see that it is
this,' declared *The Weekly Register*, 'either in fact or in design.
The grand old Benedictine educators would not have attacked
the Jesuits with such a word, when the Society went in for a share
of the education of the world. Fr. Purbrick will pardon our
saying that his mode of advertising Stonyhurst looks a little
ungracious.' The new College was to be

a Central College, where young men might at last meet with each other,
and make their friendships, their common cause, and try their strength,
and put away effectively the things of a schoolboy. In such a place the
defects of each and all will be discovered by contrast, and rubbed off by
contact; the excellencies of each and all will be made known and shared,
and the scholar of the Jesuit and Benedictine Fathers will have a fair
chance of being finished off by that University influence which in
England unquestionably is required, and has not till now been within
their reach.

The College should receive Fr. Purbrick's welcome, 'even though
it attract some of the 33—for it is, like Stonyhurst, "ad majorem
Dei gloriam"'.

[29] *The Weekly Register and Catholic Standard*, 1 Aug. 1874.

Ushaw reacted differently from Stonyhurst. At the beginning of August 1874 the President, Dr. Robert Tate,[30] invited the Rector of the Kensington College to be present at the annual examinations then taking place before Bishop James Chadwick of Hexham and Newcastle. The Bishop, who had disliked the early plans for a Board of Examiners, was enthusiastic about Kensington and took the opportunity to identify himself in public with the scheme. The *Manchester Guardian* for 13 August reported that Chadwick seemed to go out of his way to express his satisfaction with the foundation of the University College, 'inasmuch as it is now no longer doubtful but certain that this great work has emanated from the Holy Father, is ordered by his express command, and has his fervent prayers that it may proceed, prosper, and reign'.[31] The correspondent of the paper connected the speech with the Jesuit controversy. Motives of jealousy were referred to and the Society's opposition was declared to be concerned with the fact that 'the Jesuits at Stonyhurst had long been very solicitous to be allowed to establish a college at Oxford, or failing to obtain the Papal permission for this, to found one in London'.

The Benedictines at first were more than willing to co-operate with the Kensington foundation. Prior Burchall of Ampleforth wrote to Manning in November 1873 that he felt 'as all must feel, that the importance of the projected undertaking can scarcely be overrated, and sanctioned and encouraged as it is by the Holy See, we may confidently hope that it will meet with the zealous co-operation of that class for whose benefit the College is mainly intended'.[32] He added: 'May its establishment and success, under the blessing of God, speedily justify the anticipations of your Grace and of the Hierarchy in general.' He agreed to be a member of the Academical Senate for Higher Studies, and considered the invitation 'as almost equivalent to a command'.

In November 1873, however, Weld was urging the English Provincial of the Jesuits, Fr. Peter Gallwey, to persuade the members of other Religious Orders having colleges to join with

30 Milburn, p. 280.   31 *Manchester Guardian*, 13 Aug. 1874.
32 Ampleforth Archives. R. P. Burchall to Manning, 2 (?) Nov. 1873.

the Society in its protest to Rome.[33] This could only be done by Gallwey's convincing the Benedictines in particular that the bishops were attempting to exclude Religious from any share at all in Higher Studies, and by playing upon their fears that a Board of Examiners consisting of laymen would derogate to their privileges. At the meeting of the Senate in July 1874 Gallwey sought to embarrass the assembled prelates (Ullathorne, Clifford, and Manning) by asking point-blank 'whether Religious Orders would be allowed to open Colleges in or near London, in connection with the University'.[34] The questioner attempted to associate all the Religious Orders with the Jesuit cause. Monsignor Capel replied for the bishops. He declared that at the moment this would not be possible, for other colleges of Higher Studies would prejudice the new foundation. Abbot Alcock of Ramsgate understood this meant that 'for the present, at least', no other college would be permitted in or near London. Capel's reply had been quite consistent with the intentions of the hierarchy as expressed at the Synodical meeting. But the damage was done, and a proposal was made that the deliberations of the Senate should be conducted in the absence of the bishops. The insult was intended; Manning and the other bishops withdrew. Manning wrote in his *Journal* that the attempt to take over control of the hierarchy's College could not be permitted.[35] The Senate had been created to organize Higher Studies throughout the country, to provide a forum for discussion and for the raising of funds, to consider the feasibility of setting up a Board of Examiners, to award exhibitions, prizes, and scholarships, and to be a nucleus for the ultimate establishment of a federal University on the London pattern; it had never been the intention of the bishops that the Senate should become merely the governing body of a localized institution. The Kensington College was to stand in relation to the Senate in exactly the same way and to the same extent as Ushaw, Oscott, or Stonyhurst. The governing body of the Kensington College was the hierarchy. In the absence of more

[33] Farm Street Archives. Weld to Gallwey, 28 Nov. 1873.
[34] Ampleforth Archives. J. Wilfrid M. Alcock to Prior Prest, 20 July 1874.
[35] Manning Papers, Bayswater. Manning's *Journal*, Bk. No. 4, pp. 54 seq.

pressing duties at the outset, however, the Senate had turned its attention to the new College and had set up committees to advise on studies, discipline, finance, and appointments. Manning was later to declare that 'nearly all their suggestions were adopted'.[36] But to propose that the bishops should withdraw from a full meeting of the Senate, when the hierarchy's own College was the subject under discussion, was an intolerable usurpation of authority. By Manning's diplomatic withdrawal from the meeting, and that of Ullathorne and Clifford, an open breach had been avoided. It is erroneous for Purcell to imply that, because of what he terms the 'independent line of action' adopted by the Senate, it was 'stifled . . . by a secret pillow'.[37] It was not; the Senate met regularly each year from 1874 until 1878.[38]

It is evident that after the Senate meeting in June 1874 Fr. Gallwey had come near to winning the Benedictines to his way of viewing matters. By July, Abbot Smith thought that Manning was aiming 'to make himself Pope in England',[39] and within a year the Abbot was relating with some relish that Manning was 'no longer in favour at the Vatican' because 'he has written to the Pope to persuade him to come to terms with Italy'.[40] In August 1876 the Benedictines were fully co-operating with the Jesuits in resisting the efforts of the Senate to introduce a Board of Examiners. Burchall urged, however, that Manning should not be allowed to suspect collusion. 'With regard to the Board of Examiners as proposed by Cardinal Manning and named in my last,' he wrote to Smith,

it has occurred to me that there is perhaps a better way for the Regulars to carry their point than by a formal protest. Were it known to the Cardinal that we had all made a protest, he might never forgive it. I believe the Provincial of the Jesuits takes the same view as myself.

[36] Purcell, *Life of Manning*, vol. 2, pp. 498 seq.   [37] Ibid.
[38] Leeds Diocesan Archives. *Acta* for the Low Week meetings, 1874–8. The Senate presented its report each year and suggestions for new members were always approved.
[39] Ampleforth Archives. Abbot Smith, Agent for the Benedictines in Rome, to Burchall, 9 July 1874.
[40] Ibid. Smith to Burchall, 1875, n.d.

Might not Propaganda, at our request, be induced to declare that by virtue of Religious Exemption, we are not bound to accept the Board of Examiners. We have regularly every year an Examination in all our Colleges besides the Examination every three months. It stands to reason that Regulars will take care that their Colleges are not behind in the race of education. They are *immediately* under the jurisdiction of His Holiness, and we may say that the privileges of Regulars are the rights of the Holy See.[41]

The final breach between the Jesuits and the Archbishop occurred in 1875. Gallwey drew up a long list of complaints dating from Wiseman's time. Some of them were based on supposed sayings of the Archbishop reported from private conversations. Others were concerned with what Gallwey described as 'a number of petty incidents', such as the fact that a Jesuit had not been given permission to say Mass for Lord Petre because the Archbishop was able to supply a priest for the purpose, and that, from time to time, faculties had been withheld from certain Fathers. Then came the most serious charge. Manning was not orthodox. He wished 'to deprecate the Religious State and exalt the Diocese. You will see the same spirit in his last letter to me. He is unwilling to recognise anything but the Diocese. This is not orthodoxy.' After quoting other complaints about the direction of nuns, the Provincial concluded: 'I think all this ought to be made known to the Holy Father.'

In 1889, towards the end of his long life, Manning wrote a frank account of why he thought the Society had been opposed to him. Claiming he had no anti-Jesuit prejudices and that for some Jesuits he always had a true affection, he declared:

My whole mind was in their favour until I began to see their corporate action upon the Church in Rome and in England. It is visible at this day, and it is traceable backwards in history. They see the good they do, but they do not see the good they hinder; in exalting the Society they depress the Church—They are like the low church Evangelicals in the Anglican Church who look upon their bishops as enemies of vital godliness. . . . The Society is S. Ignatius in perpetuity,

[41] Ampleforth Archives. Burchall to Smith, copy, 14 Aug. 1876.

Spanish, aristocratic, absolute, and military. . . . Ivy is beautiful upon a wall, but it pulls it down.[42]

Looking back it must have seemed to Manning that in the matter of Higher Studies the Jesuits had ruined a work which might have been of national benefit to Catholics. Even the Benedictine, Ullathorne, commented on the Society adversely, adding: 'What a thing this corporate pride is, blinding even humble men to their own discomfort.'[43]

[42] Farm Street Archives. Copy of Manning's analysis of the Society in bound volume 'Manning—Hindrances'. Copy shown by Purcell to Fr. Gallwey about 1895. Original, Bayswater. Written 19 Apr. 1889.

[43] Birmingham Archdiocesan Archives. Ullathorne to Estcourt, 10 Nov. 1878.

III

THE CATHOLIC UNIVERSITY COLLEGE
ITS ORGANIZATION AND GROWTH

'MGR. CAPEL had already shown intelligence and energy in education. He had made a beginning in Kensington and I thought him capable of beginning the College. I suggested his name for a Bishopric . . . Mgr. Capel asked to have full liberty in forming [the College].'[1] Thus wrote Manning in his *Journal*, in the section of the document in which he endeavoured 'to put on record a narrative of the movement about Higher Studies, the University College at Kensington, and its disastrous issue'. Herbert Vaughan seconded Manning's nomination of Capel, and by October 1873 the Archbishop was able to report that the proposal had widespread episcopal support. He wrote to Bishop Cornthwaite on 13 October 1873 that 'the Bishops of Newport, Birmingham, Nottingham, Clifton, Northampton, Beverley, Hexham, Southwark, Salford, Liverpool', as well as himself, 'are of opinion that Monsignor Capel is possessed of the qualities required for the founding of a College of Higher Studies'.

The Bishop of Shrewsbury [he added], does not dissent, but raises the question whether the person selected for such a work ought not to possess high classical and scientific attainments. It has been thought that such attainments are rather to be required in the Professors, and that the qualities of organization and control are to be rather required in the person who is to found and direct such a College. It is obviously so important that no time should be lost in commencing this work, that I would propose a meeting of the Bishops, either all of us or a certain number delegated for the purpose, to be held at Birmingham, on Thursday the 23rd of this month.[2]

---

[1] Manning Papers, Bayswater. Manning's *Journal*, Bk. No. 4, pp. 54 seq.
[2] Leeds Diocesan Archives. Manning to Cornthwaite, 13 Oct. 1873.

The episcopal meeting was held at Ullathorne's residence. The bishops agreed unanimously to the appointment of Capel and the latter signified his acceptance. The Rector was to be given a year to get things in working order. Capel himself owned the site for the College and was preparing to develop a Public School on it. He was willing to use the land and the property for the bishops' College, provided he was given an immediate decision. The bishops for their part signified that Capel must give up the direction of the Public School and concentrate his energies entirely on the College of Higher Studies. The appointment was to be conditional upon this point.

The Dublin Review greeted Capel's appointment with enthusiasm. It considered that 'the Bishops have found a Rector full of energy and spirit, able and large-minded, whose chief interest has long been in matters connected with education, and who is more familiar than most priests with "the exigencies and needs of the Catholics of the higher classes" '.[3] Nine months later the journal declared that 'all who have come into contact with the Rector of the new College, have been very greatly impressed by his peculiar power of adapting means to ends. Never was there a stronger instance of "the right man in the right place".'[4] *The Tablet* similarly welcomed the appointment and also the place where the new College was to be situated. The latter was wisely selected, 'not only because there is a locality there ready to hand, but also because the new College will be able to draw on all the Catholic resources of the metropolis, so as to collect a larger body of students and a more efficient professional staff'.[5]

There was, however, an unsung reason for the appointment of Capel and the selection of the Kensington site. The latter was a highly fashionable part of London, and, if the sons of the aristocracy, of Old Catholic families, of converts, could be attracted, then the middle-class youths for whom the provision was particularly made would not be slow to follow.

In 1873 Thomas John Capel had still about him the vigour of youth. He was thirty-seven years old and had enjoyed a

---

[3] *The Dublin Review* (Jan. 1874), pp. 196–7.
[4] Ibid. (Oct. 1874), pp. 469–70.   [5] *The Tablet*, 29 Nov. 1873.

well-publicized ecclesiastical career. From 1860 to 1868 he consorted with wealthy and influential Catholics, and his frequent lecture courses in Pau, Florence, and Rome had brought him to the notice of Pius IX, who advanced him to the Roman prelacy. In March 1874, five months after his appointment to Kensington, he preached four sermons in Rome at St. Andrea della Frate, which 'were very well attended in spite of the bad weather'. We are told that 'most of the Anglican and Protestant clergymen in Rome went to hear the celebrated Catholic divine, whose former sermons in St. Maria in Monte Sancto, have gained him great reputation as an exponent of Catholic faith'.[6]

But perhaps more than all this, Capel's claim to notice in England came through the part he was thought to have played in the conversion of John Patrick, third Marquess of Bute. In 1867 Capel was acting as chaplain to Charles Scott-Murray at Danesfield. In such magnificent surroundings he first met Bute, a young man already stirred towards the Catholic Church. The chaplain was thirty-one years of age, and Bute barely twenty, but a close affinity sprang up between them. One of Scott-Murray's daughters wrote that Bute was a regular visitor to the house, 'and I remember him sitting for hours talking to my mother—almost always on religious subjects—and watching her embroidering vestments for the chapel'.[7] His relationship with Capel was a close one, although the Marquess always denied that the latter 'converted' him. 'Mgr. C. performed the ceremony of reception in December 1868', Bute later told Hartwell de la Garde Grissell. 'I chose him for the purpose because, having several times met him at the Scott-Murrays' the year before, I knew him fairly well, and was pleased with his clear and simple way of explaining certain things I wished to know. I received much spiritual help from him, and yet was unable, for certain reasons, to take the final step; and I was, and am, grateful to him for this and for much else.'[8] In fact, Capel was becoming the centre of a miniature movement of aristocratic conversions. In 1867 his friends Lady

---

[6] *The Tablet*, 21 Mar. 1874. The sermons began on 10 Mar.

[7] Hunter-Blair, Rt. Revd. Sir David, Bt., O.S.B., *John Patrick, Third Marquess of Bute, K.T., 1847–1900: a Memoir*, p. 61.   [8] Ibid.

Portarlington and Lord and Lady North were received into the Roman Church. They were joined by Lords Granard and Louth and a number of Oxford men—George Akers of Oriel; William Humphrey, chaplain to the Bishop of Brechin; Richard Clarke of St. John's; George Lane-Fox of Christ Church; Hartwell de la Garde Grissell of Brasenose; Charles Stanton Devas of Balliol. Akers soon became one of Manning's Canons and was appointed Vice-President of St. Edmund's College, Ware, in 1877. Three years later he succeeded to the President's chair. Humphrey and Clarke entered the Society of Jesus. Lane-Fox, who himself failed to persevere as a Dominican, gave two sons to Fort Augustus Abbey. Grissell remained in Oxford, a distinguished antiquarian and numismatist. Devas joined Capel at Kensington.

During the summer of 1868 Capel stationed himself in the Catholic presbytery in Oxford. Bute, who was at Christ Church, wished to have him near him. A number of undergraduates made Capel's acquaintance and there were some conversions. One of the converts was Lord Braye, who told the story of how the news was received by the Dean of Christ Church. 'One day the Dean—Liddell—sent for me for a private interview. Having expressed his disapproval of my becoming a Catholic, he was inclined to attribute my change to the influence of "one man", meaning Capel.'9 The Dean hinted pretty strongly 'that his House was not the place for converts; whilst as for conversion, no one should take such a serious step before forty or forty-five years of age'. Capel's attractive and handsome appearance, his eloquence and passionate conviction, united to a friendly personality and correct social graces, made him 'a terror to the powers of Christ Church, and the powers of Christ Church were centred and summed-up in Liddell, the Dean'.10 Braye considered Capel to be a 'really gifted man'. Capel himself wrote that Pusey was in alarm at the conversions. By 31 May Liddon was peremptorily prohibiting undergraduates from making Capel's acquaintance. But Capel added: 'All those who *want* to know me, I think, already do.'11

9 Braye, Lord, *Fewness of My Days: A Life in Two Centuries*, p. 93.
10 Ibid., pp. 73–5.
11 Hunter-Blair, pp. 67–8. Capel to Mrs. Scott-Murray, 31 May 1868.

Even Liddon's curiosity got the better of him, and he asked to meet Capel. The latter wrote that the ensuing conversation was 'quite courteous, but quite unsatisfactory, for he kept shifting his ground, and slipped away like an eel from every point I raised. To me his mind seems as confused as Pusey's, which is saying much.'[12]

Capel left Oxford in December 1868; his effect there had been meteoric. Bute wrote to Mrs. Scott-Murray that Capel had enjoyed extraordinary success, but that

his health is giving way from the perpetual physical and mental toil. He is not going to return till May, when he will recommence. For the present he has received some converts, is preparing some more, has awakened a great many, and, partially at least, sanctified the congregation, and reclaimed the wandering. The mission has received an infusion of life. On Saturday night he heard confessions till 11.30 and again in the morning. They had general Communion, and renewal of baptismal vows; at 10.30 High Mass and sermon. During the afternoon he operated privately on some rationalists: in the evening they had a very long sermon, and Benediction, with an immense congregation, among whom were a vast number of Protestants, *several Dons*, and the *President of Trinity College*.[13]

Bute spent Christmas in Nice with Capel, and they were joined later by Lady Loudoun and other aristocrats for a cruise to the Holy Land in Bute's yacht *Ladybird*. A visit was paid to Rome, where Bute received the sacrament of confirmation from the hands of Pius IX. In the course of the visit to Palestine Capel was appointed Bute's private chaplain, but he was 'not to live at either of his houses, but to be ready when needed to go to him and to travel with him'. Capel added: 'I cannot but feel that this arrangement (which is entirely his own idea) will allow me to do much more good than if I were settled in any one spot. I hope it may turn to the advantage of my soul and to God's glory.'[14] By the end of 1869 Capel was back in Oxford lecturing and having a phenomenal success. He remained chaplain to Bute until

[12] Hunter-Blair, p. 68.
[13] Ibid., pp. 71–2. Bute to Mrs. Scott-Murray, 16 Dec. 1868.
[14] Ibid., p. 76. Capel to Scott-Murray, 14 May 1869.

in 1873 he hit upon the idea of establishing a Catholic Public School for the aristocracy in London.

The Marquess, along with Lord Petre, was a benefactor of the Kensington University College when Capel assumed the rectorship, and they were both associated with the Senate of Higher Studies. It is little wonder that the bishops were impressed with Capel's record, or that they thought that in securing him for the headship of the new College they were demonstrating to the gentry that the institution would have a distinct life of its own.

Care was taken not only in the selection of the Rector. The success of the College would depend in large measure upon the quality of its staff. Those still chafing under the Oxford ban would find at Kensington men of high professional calibre, possessing direct experience of accepted modes of university teaching. Manning, Capel, and a subcommittee of the Senate were chiefly responsible for the choices made. Of necessity many converts were appointed.

Frederick Settle Barff received the Chair of Chemistry. A Cambridge graduate, he had been curate at Holy Trinity, Hull, before his conversion in 1852. The author of a number of scientific works and textbooks, he was to be the propagator of the Barff process for preventing the rusting of iron pipes. Henry Danvers Clarke (1806–87) was to help with Classics. He, too, was a convert clergyman, being at one time vicar of Iping. Received into the Catholic Church in 1851, he was a graduate of Exeter College. He is not to be confused with Fr. Robert Francis Clarke, D.D., who taught Philosophy and Christian Doctrine in the College, and who was destined to succeed Capel as Rector. Edward Butler, Newman's erstwhile Professor of Mathematics in Dublin, was appointed to the Chair of Mathematics. His son, later Abbot of Downside, received his education in the College, and in the *Life of Ullathorne* gratefully acknowledges the debt he owed 'to the high quality of the instruction and formation received there'.[15] Charles Stanton Devas at twenty-seven years of age was given the professorship of Modern History and Politics. An old Etonian and student of Balliol, he had been received into

15 Butler, *Life of Ullathorne*, vol. 2, pp. 35–6.

the Catholic Church in 1869. Within a year of his appointment to Kensington he produced the outstanding pioneering work, *Labour and Capital in England from the Catholic Point of View* (1876). Devas, who had taken a First in History and in Law, was to organize the legal studies for students preparing for professional examinations in Law. The Chair of Classics was awarded to Frederick Apthorp Paley. Educated at Shrewsbury School and Cambridge, he was the grandson of the Venerable William Paley (1743–1805), author of *The Evidences of Christianity*. In appointing Paley to the Kensington chair the bishops had in mind the fact that he had not only been a tutor at Cambridge but had also worked as private tutor in a number of well-known Catholic aristocratic families— the Throckmortons, the Kenelm Digbys, and that of the Earl of Shrewsbury. Paley, a friend of Lord Braye, was a polymath of no mean achievement. Walter Croke-Robinson became Capel's Vice-Rector and Professor of Ecclesiastical History, although it took all of Manning's tact and humour to persuade Bishop Ullathorne to release the priest from Birmingham. A recent convert (1872), he was an M.A. (and later Fellow) of New College, Oxford.

The distinguished orientalist, Charles Seager, at the age of sixty-seven was appointed to the Chair of Hebrew and Comparative Philology and was also given responsibility for teaching Oriental Languages. An Anglican curate before his conversion to Catholicism in 1843, he had taken his M.A. at Magdalen Hall, Oxford, and been a Scholar of Worcester. At one time he held the office of Assistant Professor of Hebrew at Oxford under Pusey. Gordon Thompson was appointed, immediately after his conversion in 1875, to the Chair of Early English Literature and Philology. He was received into the Catholic Church in that year from his curacy at Christ Church, St. Pancras, in north-west London. An M.A. of Cambridge, he had been Scholar of Sidney Sussex College. There were, in addition to the professors, a number of 'extra-mural' teachers, including David Lewis, Howel William Lloyd (the Welsh archaeologist), a Mr. Willis for Modern English Literature, History, and Constitutional History, and a variety of instructors for Law, languages, and technical subjects.

Included among these part-time teachers was Philip Magnus, a Jew.

Perhaps the most distinguished appointment was that of St. George Jackson Mivart to the Chair of Biology. Educated at Harrow and King's College, London, he was a Fellow of the Royal Society and Fellow and Secretary of the Linnean Society. His *Genesis of Species*, published in 1871, had established him as the leading intellectual opponent of Darwin, who in subsequent editions of the *Origin of Species* showed how seriously he viewed Mivart's objections. Mivart's *Lessons in Elementary Anatomy* (1873), *Man and Apes* (1873), and *The Common Frog* (1874) reinforced his reputation as a scholar of distinction. Although he claimed to be an evolutionist, he postulated a vital disparity between organic and inorganic matter and between human reason and animal intelligence. The formation of specific characters he explained by the principle of individuation.

An institution which gathered together such a distinguished staff cannot be branded, as one recent writer has attempted to brand it, a futile scheme.[16] *The Dublin Review* had every cause to comment that 'a staff of teachers has been brought together, by the strength of which even the Protestant world confesses itself surprised, and to the great majority of whom the task of teaching is familiar'.[17] When a report began to be circulated that the Professors were not to lecture except at occasional intervals, the *Dublin* had to assure its readers that 'they will be occupied in teaching for two or three hours of every day'.

Despite the fact that barely four months had elapsed from the date of the Synodal Letter announcing to the laity the establishment of the College and the name of its Rector, Capel opened the institution in January 1875 with a complement of seventeen students. W. G. Ward had earlier commented that the students were contributed 'by almost every English Catholic College, from St. Edmund's, the oldest, down to St. George's, Croydon, which is almost the youngest'.[18] In the second year of the College's existence the numbers rose to twenty-eight, and by the third year,

---

[16] *The Clergy Review* (Nov. 1965), p. 854.
[17] *The Dublin Review* (Oct. 1874), p. 471.   [18] Ibid., p. 472.

before a series of crises occurred, they had reached almost fifty.[19] The extent of this achievement has failed to receive adequate recognition. That a new College devoted exclusively to Higher Studies could muster almost fifty students in the first three years of its functioning needs to be set alongside the record of Stony-hurst, for instance, which thirty-five years after its original affiliation to London University could only claim to be educating thirty-three students between the ages of 17 and 22.[20] Of these thirty-three some were foreign youths who could not rightly be claimed as pursuing a course of advanced or professional study at all. There was no other English Catholic College which could lay claim to be educating more secular youths in the post-17 age-group than Stonyhurst. At Downside in 1878 there were only eighty boys in the school as a whole.[21] If the autonomous Colleges in general, and Stonyhurst in particular, had been willing to forgo their individual courses for youths staying on after the normal school years, and had passed on such students to Kensington, there would have been adequate numbers and financial backing to maintain a single College devoted to Higher Education. Capel's institution would, within five years, have had numbers exceeding the hundred. It was, however, a ludicrous state of affairs to expect the Kensington College to flourish while the old divisive authority remained. At least six Colleges were in direct competition with Kensington, and they had the added advantage that they each possessed a school to act as a 'feeder' for their own higher course. For Capel to have succeeded in attracting nearly fifty students to Kensington within three years was an achievement accomplished in the teeth of Jesuit opposition. What might have developed into a great national venture was sacrificed to the benefit of sectional interest.

Manning had hoped that if Newman would not consent to joining the Senate of Higher Studies, he would at least not refuse to preach at the ceremony of inauguration of the new College, scheduled to take place at Easter 1875. The invitation was

[19] Butler, *Life of Ullathorne*, vol. 2, pp. 35–6.
[20] *The Weekly Register and Catholic Standard*, 18 July 1874.
[21] Zeller, Hubert van, *Downside By and Large*, p. 53.

conveyed by Capel. Newman replied that he was not unmindful 'of the important fact that the English Bishops, who thought residence at Oxford and Cambridge dangerous to Catholic youth, are tolerant of the course of studies pursued at the London University'.[22] He added: 'I could not preach for you without being at liberty, if I chose, to speak against any such recognition as I fear you concede to that University, an institution which has been the great champion and example of mixed education now for fifty years, and which through all that time I have on that ground shrunk from.'

At the Low Week meeting of the hierarchy in 1875 details of the finances of the College were given. The Duke of Norfolk gave £1,000 towards the purchase of the site and promised an income of £1,000 a year for the first three years. W. G. Ward donated £1,000. Mr. Lomax provided £500 towards the site and promised £250 a year for two years. The Marquess of Ripon, disciple of Tom Hughes and F. D. Maurice, and past Grand Master of the English Freemasons before his conversion in 1874, promised £300 per annum for three years. The Marquess of Bute offered £250 a year for four years. Lord Petre gave £500 towards the site.

Capel asked the bishops if he might be permitted to allow Protestant youths to attend lectures as externs if any expressed a desire to do so. Such students would not be counted as students of the College proper. The bishops concurred. At the episcopal meeting in 1875 Ullathorne raised a complaint that a student expelled from Sedgley Park School had found a place at Kensington, and he was anxious to know the standard Capel was prepared to demand of students prior to their admission. He had heard of other complaints. Capel, in answering both points, stressed that the College had barely been in session for three months. At the same meeting a report from the Senate of Higher Studies was received and approved by their Lordships.

In April 1876 the bishops indicated their anxiety that the Senate should begin its proper duties. The prelates met representatives of

---

[22] Letter given by Fr. Henry Tristram, Cong. Orat., in the winter number of *The Dublin Review* (1936), pp. 279–80.

the body at the Low Week meeting and urged them to make a beginning. Three more names for membership of the Senate were approved: The Marquess of Ripon, Professor Paley, and Fr. George Bampfield. Paley's name strengthened the Kensington contingent. Bampfield, an Oxford graduate, had preceded Oxenham into the Church. It was agreed at the episcopal meeting to write to the Senators and urge them to take action on the implementation of those parts of the Synodical decrees relating to Higher Studies. Manning accepted the responsibility of writing a letter to the Duke of Norfolk, who would then contact the remainder. The letter was sent on 28 April 1876, and by June the Duke had written to his colleagues.

Manning had declared that the bishops were again anxious to receive the advice of the Senate. He went on:

The Sacred Congregation of Propaganda, by a Rescript dated April 2nd, 1873, directed [the bishops] to form a Board of Examiners, to ascertain the state and to elevate the standard of our Higher Studies. I would therefore invite your Grace and the Senate, to consider and report to us as to the steps to be taken for the purpose of setting on foot such a Board of Examiners, and for encouraging and elevating the studies of our Catholic youth throughout England, by examinations, by prizes, by burses, and otherwise, and to make known to us the names of any persons who may be thought best fitted for the office of Examiners. . . . I need hardly remind your Grace, or request your Grace to remind the Members of the Senate, that in asking their advice, we do not in any way desire to interfere with the perfect independence of any of our existing Colleges. Their complete autonomy under their proper authorities, ecclesiastical and collegiate, is vitally necessary to their welfare.[23]

A copy of the Duke's letter was received by the Jesuit Provincial in his capacity as a member of the Senate. He decided that if the Society could not get the idea of a Board of Examiners forbidden by Rome, the next best line of attack was to influence members of the Senate to reject the scheme or refuse to implement it. The chief opponent of the Board among the secular clergy was Newman's friend, Northcote. He was in collusion with Purbrick

[23] Farm Street Archives.

in the development of the plot. They hoped to win over Allies and the Marquess of Ripon. Early in May, a fortnight after the dispatch of Manning's letter to Norfolk, a standing sub-committee set up by the Senate met in London to consider the course to be adopted in response to the wishes of the bishops. North-cote did not attend, neither did the Jesuits, but Allies was commissioned to write to the former with information of what transpired at the gathering. Allies was to win over Ripon. On 13 May 1876 Allies duly reported that the standing subcommittee had met, and that those present in addition to himself were the Duke of Norfolk, the Marquess of Ripon, Mr. H. J. Matthews, Mgr. Capel, Professor Paley, Professor Mivart, Mr. Stokes, and Canon Macmullen. He then added: 'I had previously given your documents to Lord Ripon at a meeting here on Tuesday, and he gave them me back on Wednesday, saying that he had been struck with the ability of the printed Report. I wanted particularly to let him see the inside of certain things, which he fully appre-hends.'[24] Allies then went on:

As to our meeting, I should say we felt uncertain of our own exis-tence and had the vaguest notion of the task we were invited to per-form. A certain haziness beset our efforts to get clear as to these two points. The result of two hours talk was to request our Chairman (Norfolk) to obtain for us from the Cardinal the curriculum of the existing Colleges upon which we were called upon to operate, and to ask His Eminence to let us have the Reports sent in by the five gentle-men who received and analysed the questions answered three years ago, and also the documents which shewed what was done thereupon. As to question 1. we postponed it; as to question 2. we answered 'by a Board of Examiners to be annually appointed by the Senate.' But all this stands over until we get the Cardinal's answer. A very brief note from Fr. Purbrick indicated that the Fr. Provincial had told him he could not be spared to attend. The other Superiors by a mistake of Mgr. Capel's were not invited. I called attention to the fact that no one of the Colleges save Kensington was represented there and that was represented by 4, including Stokes who has a son there. I showed the two pages of your pamphlet which you indicated. After the meeting

[24] T. W. Allies to J. Spencer Northcote, 13 May 1876. Copy in Farm Street Archives. Sent by Northcote to Purbrick.

I lent your pamphlet[25] to Mr. Matthews. I return your written documents as desired. The upshot in my mind is, so far, that the Colleges should determine what line they mean to take and pursue it in common, if possible. The wish apparently is to submit all Catholic schools of a certain rank to a yearly examination by a Catholic Board, but whether the whole school, or the highest class, remains as yet unknown. I think the independent members look with favour on this intention, but the manifold difficulties involved in it are not appreciated by any but those who have the actual management of our schools. If we could really have a permanent council of higher studies mixed of laymen and clergy, I think it would lead to good, and make the dominion of any one man[26] impossible.[27]

Northcote told Allies that the action the senators had taken would mean 'they would not be summoned again'.[28] He was to be proved wrong, for we know that the bishops received the annual report of the Senate in Low Week 1877. Northcote and Purbrick argued that 'being unable to bring the Senate to adopt his plan, his Eminence is trying to get it ordered by authority from Rome'. This assumption was untrue. Manning did not attend the meetings of the Senate, and we know from Allies's letter of 13 May 1876 that the Senate cannot be said to have been unfavourable to the idea of a Board of Examiners. Northcote urged Purbrick to fight against the proposals tooth and nail, 'not only on your own ground of exemption as Religious, but also on common grounds to all Colleges, that it will be an intolerable nuisance to the Colleges which are doing their work and have examinations enough to provide for already—that it will have a necessary tendency to bring us all to one uniform standard, etc. etc.'[29] In fact, Northcote misconceived the idea behind the establishment of the Board, as his letter of four days later indicates. At the fourth Provincial Synod of Westminster he maintained: 'The idea of this Board was that it should be a means to bring together the Colleges *with a view to* founding something that

---

[25] Probably Northcote's submission as a member of the sub-commission. He had not favoured the Board of Examiners.

[26] Northcote's fear as expressed in his submission.

[27] Farm Street Archives. Allies's letter of 13 May 1876, op. cit.

[28] Ibid. Northcote to Purbrick, 26 June 1876.   [29] Ibid.

should have a local habitation and a name—this end has been already attained at Kensington; and yet the Board is again to the front.'[30] Appendix XVII to the *Acta* of the Synod made it clear that the Board was to exist independently of Kensington. The future foundation referred to was that of a federal University to which all the Colleges, including Kensington, would be affiliated. In fact, the bishops had gone to considerable pains to stress the point. If Kensington were to develop into something greater than a College of Higher Studies, that was all to the good, but in conception it was not in itself a university nor was it intended to be one. Northcote, however, persisted in claiming 'it is perfectly clear that the Cardinal has a fixed idea on the subject, and I think equally clear that the other bishops have *no* ideas on the subject'.[31] The ideas of the bishops were clearly expressed in the *Acta* of the Synod and in the joint Pastoral which preceded the Synodical Letter; there was no reason to assume that their Lordships were not clear as to what they had debated and signed.

The spirit of disunity, fostered by such men as Purbrick and Northcote, came in for severe criticism in the following year from no less a figure than the Honourable and Reverend William Petre, son of the twelfth baron. The opposition to the hierarchy's policy on Higher Education was engineered by 'a section of earnest Catholics, mainly clerical, and representing threatened interests',[32] he maintained. Their fractious policy was directed chiefly against the Kensington College. 'To form its professional staff a number of gentlemen offered their services. They were all more than proficient, many unquestionably eminent, in all their several departments; and with such a tutorial staff we feel bound to say that the College was justified in at once laying claim to be a noble, useful, and worthy beginning to Catholic progress in higher education.' But it did not receive the necessary support. It was clear that from the outset 'undue and impatient opposition has impeded the healthiness of its growth'. Such opposition was continued 'in the face of the distinctly expressed will of the Holy

[30] Ibid. Northcote to Purbrick, 30 June 1876.   [31] Ibid.
[32] Petre, Hon. and Revd. William, *Remarks on the Present Condition of Catholic Liberal Education* (London, 1877).

See in its regard'. This presented to Petre's mind 'the strongest evidence of the anarchy and confusion which stifles our opportunities of educational reform, retards our social progress, renders a due division of labour unattainable, keeps our "prison dress" still upon us, and holds us even yet "outside the great currents of English life, and therefore powerless to affect them" '. He concluded that 'English Catholic education groans under the constant irritations of pitted commercial interests'. The bishops were aware of the determination of Purbrick and Northcote and others like-minded to secure the allegiance of such men as Lord Ripon to their own particular faction. If this could be achieved, there would be no danger of wealthy Catholics bolstering up the Kensington College by munificent gifts or financial loans. In October 1874 Bishop Vaughan of Salford asked Lady Herbert to try and see Lord Ripon 'and some of these other big converts', because he feared 'they may fall into hands that will not help them much'.[33]

Capel opened the Kensington College in January 1875, decreeing that the academic year would consist of three terms, and that there would be terminal examinations, known as 'Collections'. Fees were to be in the region of £50 per annum. Lectures were to be daily from 9 a.m. to 1 p.m., and again from 4 p.m. to 6 p.m. (except on Saturdays). We possess an accurate account of the organization of the studies of the College, as they existed at the height of its vigour, from the pen of Fr. Robert Clarke, who took over the direction of the institution as a private venture after it ceased to be a College of the hierarchy towards the end of 1878. Although Clarke may have made some slight readjustments, they could not have been serious, for he wrote his account in January 1879, barely two months after taking over direction of the College. He informed Bishop Danell of Southwark 'there has never been a day on which the usual lectures have not been given'.[34] Clarke testified that the professional mechanism of the College had continued in the same working order as under Capel,

[33] Leslie, S. (ed.), *Letters of Herbert, Cardinal Vaughan to Lady Herbert of Lea, 1867–1903*, Vaughan to Lady Herbert, 5 Oct. 1874, pp. 260–1.
[34] Southwark Archdiocesan Archives. R. F. Clarke to Danell, 27 July 1880.

'with the exception of some lectures on the side subject of ecclesiastical history, which were discontinued'. Most of the original professors were still engaged on the staff in 1878–9. From Clarke's summary, therefore, we are able to discern the way in which Capel developed the curriculum of the College:

A lecture on Christian Doctrine is given twice a week, from 9 to 10, the order followed being that of the catechism of the Council of Trent, which is the text-book employed. Care is taken to reply to popular objections of a later date. . . .

The four remaining hours from 9 to 10 are occupied by Philosophical Lectures, two on Psychology and two on Logic (at present). . . . An Elementary course of Logic will shortly be published, based on the Peripatetic Logic, and exhibiting it in its relations with the schemes of Mill, Spencer, etc. . . .

The Classical Instruction at the College aims at combining the reading of the higher authors (Plato, Aristotle, the Tragics, Cicero, Tacitus, Plautus, etc.) with an accurate grammatical knowledge and the frequent practice of prose composition. To the reading are conjoined full explanations of ancient customs and habits of thought.[35]

The last hour in the morning was given over to private tuition and special classes. Furthermore:

An acquaintance with Chemistry is now becoming daily more necessary to a thorough mastery of many of those occupations which the sons of gentlemen follow, such as engineering in its various branches, manufactures, and the arts, in the army, and at the bar, where cases continually occur in which a barrister who knows this, and kindred subjects, is able to effectually examine and cross-examine what are called 'experts'. Particular attention is given to the study of the natural sciences, and a well-appointed laboratory, capable of accommodating twenty-five students, under the care of a thorough practical chemist is daily at the service of the students. . . .

A course of Biology is available. A museum and a biological laboratory are at the service of students who intend to devote a part of their time to this science. . . .

The other courses are those of Natural Philosophy, English History, and English, French and German Language and Literature.

[35] Ibid. Document headed 'Catholic University College'.

'The Mathematical course', we are told, embraced 'Plane, Solid, Co-ordinate, Higher Geometry; Plane and Spherical Trigonometry; Arithmetic and Algebra, including Square and Cube Roots, Properties of Numbers, Quadratics, Progressions and other Series, Binomial Theorem, Logarithms, General Properties of Equations; Differential and Integral Calculus', and the instruction was conveyed partly by lecture and partly by individual teaching.

From Clarke's account it can be seen that the curriculum established at Kensington, as regards content and method, compares more than favourably with that offered to students in the advanced courses in the other Catholic colleges. No criticism has been recorded of the quality of the studies at Kensington. In 1876 Downside was particularly pleased to have reports of the excellent progress made by its former pupils in the Catholic University College.[36]

By 1877, however, serious troubles were beginning to manifest themselves. The first ripple of disquiet was heard at the Low Week meeting of the hierarchy in that year, when Bishop Bagshawe of Nottingham drew the attention of the assembled prelates to certain passages in recent publications of Professor St. George Mivart, which he declared to be unorthodox and scandalous. The writings complained of were a collection of philosophical pieces published by Mivart in 1876 under the title *Lessons from Nature as Manifested in Mind and Matter*, and also a book *Contemporary Evolution*, issued in the same year, and in essence a collection of his articles from *The Contemporary Review*. Bagshawe argued that Mivart should be requested to withdraw his views in public or that he should be asked to resign his professorship.[37] Feelings ran high and it was plain to the Cardinal that Mivart would be condemned. Manning stepped in to save his friend before Bagshawe's proposition was put to the vote. The Cardinal declared he had been in correspondence with the biologist, with a view to asking him to take an opportunity of explaining his views more fully and removing any possible misinterpretations. Thus, asserted

36 *The Downside Review*, 12, p. 102.
37 Leeds Diocesan Archives. *Acta* of 1877 meeting, which was held on 11 April.

Manning, the controversy which had arisen from the writings might be terminated. Bagshawe was not readily appeased, and Manning asked the prelates to leave the matter with himself, adding 'this course would not preclude a formal examination' of the writings if need be.[38] By this tactical move, Manning saved the professor from formal condemnation.

It was, however, a serious matter for the infant institution to have the charge of unorthodoxy hurled at one of its most distinguished and most publicized professors. Mivart's fault, as Manning realized, was little more than that of any pioneer thinker exploring virgin territory, although it can be argued that at this early date the biologist was pursuing a line of thought which would eventually lead to his dying outside the pale of the Roman Catholic Church.

In 1877 financial troubles at Kensington began to manifest themselves. It was necessary for Capel to provide salaries for the academic staff consonant with their status and qualifications. Manning tells us that the Rector 'fixed the stipends of Mr. Barff and Mr. Mivart at £600 a year, Mr. Paley at £400, Mr. Gordon Thompson at £300, Father Clarke at £200'.[39] The institution had to commence with a considerable staff if it was to achieve the recognition hoped for by the hierarchy, but the salaries awarded were perhaps over-generous for the first two years when numbers were small. To make matters worse, Capel rendered no balance sheet to either the bishops or the subcommittee of the Senate which had been advising on finances. When the hierarchy asked him to produce one in 1878 it was discovered he had kept no accurate records. It was impossible to obtain a sound statement of income, let alone of expenditure. *The Builder* for 10 November 1877 contained elaborate designs by Messrs. Goldie & Child for a chapel commissioned by Capel for the University College,[40] and soon the Rector was deep in debt. In 1877 and 1878 Manning poured £4,000 of his own money into the institution in order to keep it solvent, but it was in vain. Capel's mismanagement was due in large part to his determination to carry on the work of

[38] Ibid.   [39] Manning Papers, Bayswater. Manning's *Journal.*
[40] *The Builder*, 10 Nov. 1877. Illustration provided.

founding a Catholic Public School in London. He had promised
the bishops he would abandon the project and devote himself
entirely to the University College. But by 1877 it was discovered
he had not only been engaged in collecting funds for the School
but had drawn up plans for a College costing £50,000 and had
floated a company to get the money. He was in debt for this
venture to the tune of £28,000.[41] Capel defended his determination to continue the School project on the grounds that a Catholic
Public School in London would ensure an ever-steady supply of
students for the University College. Such a school, too, would
make certain that the University College would not cater solely
for middle-class youths. Aristocratic youths attending his school
would ultimately add a social leaven to the College of Higher
Studies, and in doing so would make the institution more
attractive to the gentry. Unfortunately, however, the School
took precedence over the College in Capel's scheme of things.
He told Lord Petre that 'the University College was as Leah, and
the school as Rachel, to him'.[42]

There were further complaints. Lord Petre, a supporter and
benefactor of the College, protested that his younger son, a
student at Kensington, had been exposed to moral danger. The
Duke of Norfolk and Petre informed Manning 'they could no
longer advise any Catholic parents to send their sons'.[43] Complaints of immorality among some of the students were conveyed
to the bishops, and evidence was submitted of Capel's lax discipline and the 'reckless irregularity' of the institution. It was not
long before the news of Capel's own liaison with a young woman
was to become widely current, and, after a local examination,
was to lead to his suspension *a divinis* and subsequently to a long
legal battle in Rome.

In 1878 the bishops set up a subcommittee of the hierarchy to
examine the condition of the College in general and the nature
of Capel's administration in particular. Manning, Clifford, and
Herbert Vaughan considered many of the complaints to be
justified, and the bishops, on receiving the reports of their
delegates, asked for Capel's resignation. Manning tells the rest of

---

[41] Manning's *Journal.*   [42] Ibid.   [43] Ibid.

the story: 'The accounts were then examined. There were no accounts, no ledgers, no books. After long delays new books, newly written up, were produced, and a claim of £6,000 advanced against the College. Mgr Capel would not produce his book of money received. The bank account gave only a partial evidence.'[44] The bishops were appalled at the debts the Rector had incurred, at his extravagance, and at his sullen reluctance to co-operate in a full investigation of the administration. The episcopal reaction was a natural reluctance to be implicated further in such a disastrous liability. Manning summed up the situation succinctly when he wrote that Capel 'has wrecked our only united work; the highest work next to the formation of the priesthood'.[45] This fact became obvious when in the summer of 1878 the Archbishop consulted the bishops about the possible reconstitution of the University College under new management. Little enthusiasm was generated and a feeling prevailed that any reconstitution would be ill advised. Ullathorne, for example, refused to suggest names for the succession to Capel, and declared that the College could not succeed without lay co-operation. In making this last statement, Ullathorne had in mind the fact that Norfolk and Petre had been alienated, and that their example would be sufficient to deter others. Ullathorne also maintained that 'a joint responsibility in all the English bishops will not work satisfactorily'.[46] Such a College 'must of necessity be local in its management'. The bishops, as a body, need only give moral support. Along with a re-examination of the policy to be pursued in regard to Kensington, it was also imperative to reconsider the function of the Senate of Higher Studies. If the bishops did not wish to be responsible any longer for the University College, and if the Religious Orders were to continue adamant in their refusal of the Board of Examiners, or, indeed, of any lay authority over the studies in their Colleges, no matter how tenuous, then there was no longer any purpose in retaining a body which possessed no functions. Manning proposed to issue a letter in 1878 concerning the changes to be effected at Kensington; it might be well, at

---

[44] Ibid. [45] Ibid.
[46] Butler, *Life of Ullathorne*, vol. 2, pp. 148–9.

the same time, to re-examine the entire episcopal policy as laid down in 1874. Ullathorne was adverse to this. The latter did not consider it prudent to publish anything about the Senate until that body had been consulted. Many laymen were feeling sore at their inability to act out the function for which they had been assembled. Ullathorne felt, too, that there ought to be some mention of the financial ruin of Kensington, 'however delicate it may be', and he asserted that the bishops had never been fully clear as to their duties and functions in regard to the College. Ullathorne, suffering from ill health at the time, was unable to present his case to the bishops in person, but Manning undertook to lay his views before the hierarchy. Ullathorne's attitude was in large part influenced by a fear that he might become financially liable for the debts incurred by Capel on behalf of the University College. This fear was to be justified in 1879. Ullathorne was to be the only bishop who sought to avoid the collective responsibility which Capel's legal advisers claimed.

In a letter which Manning sent to the bishops he referred to the quality of the students at Kensington, many of whom 'manifested a great interest in the lectures, and a true spirit of application'. He went on:

Some have passed examinations at the London University and for the army. Some have been received from almost every College in England. . . . Other students have attended the College while dwelling under the roof of their families resident in the neighbourhood. The proportion of such students to those which may be called resident has varied from one third to one half. During the whole period of four years ninety-seven students have entered. The number actually at the College at the end of last term was about twenty-eight. Of the ninety-seven students who have entered the College since its beginning, nineteen were from abroad, seventy-eight were from England and Ireland: of these, eight were from the North of England, thirteen from the South, and fifty-seven were from London.[47]

A special meeting of the bishops was held to consider the fate of the College. Ullathorne's objections were studied in his

[47] Bayswater Archives. Letter of 1878, sent out after Kensington had been open for four years.

absence. All the bishops agreed that the financial position of the College should not be made public. To do so would be tantamount to administering a death-blow to the institution, and especially after the bishops had favourably entertained the request of a number of professors to be permitted to continue the College as a local venture under diocesan auspices. The conclusions from the last four years were stated to be:

1. That the number of students who pursue higher studies for their own sake, and are likely after leaving our existing Colleges, to desire a continuance of such studies, is at this present time small, and in all probability, for a considerable time, will not amount to a sufficient number to maintain a College;

2. That the number of Catholic youth desiring higher studies, and the preliminary studies necessary for professional careers, is at this time sufficiently large to render the existence of such a College expedient, if not necessary;

3. That there will always be a number of Catholic youth living in their own homes who will desire to avail themselves of the opportunities of higher studies, whether they have a professional career before them or not;

4. That the two latter classes form at this time, and hereafter will more certainly form, a sufficient number of Catholic youth to demand and to maintain such a College.[48]

The letter issued after the close of the bishops' meeting spoke of complaints concerning discipline. These had arisen because students had lived 'in houses of residence many in number'.[49] It was to be expected that in individual cases 'unpunctuality, irregularity, and the appearance of laxity arose'. The letter was specific:

It has been alleged at times that students of University College have been seen at theatres and other places of amusement, and, in some instances, at places which, though commonly frequented, are nevertheless of a less desirable character. . . . Of graver allegations the number is small, and the instances which can be admitted as proved or provable still smaller. Excepting one case, there is no evidence that the students incriminated deteriorated during their residence at Kensington. . . .

[48] Ibid.   [49] Ibid.

When it is remembered that this extends over a period of four years, and over a number of ninety-seven youths at the most dangerous period of life, we have no hesitation in saying that the judgment given by one of the professors most experienced in the university life of England is perfectly correct, namely, that in this point the students of University College will more than bear comparison with any similar College in England.

Then came a veiled hint that there had been forces at work anxious to denigrate the College at the expense of truth. The expression, though containing no specific accusation, was nevertheless strongly worded:

We are constrained also by indubitable evidence to add that the rumours and suspicions propagated on this subject may be traced to the ordinary sources of careless but culpable inaccuracy, and in some instances to motives of a less excusable kind.

The bishops, in defending the College, pointed out that it was not intended to be a mere continuation of school life, but was designed to provide for 'a transition from youth to manhood'. It had to be kept in mind 'that we are not dealing with boys but with men. It may be said that we are hardly dealing with the state of youth, but with the state of incipient manhood.' It was proposed to carry on the College on its existing site, to have but one house of *resident* students, to place two ecclesiastics over the house of residence, and to give it the discipline of a College or Hall. It was also resolved 'to continue the schools of classical literature, mathematics, English literature and history, natural philosophy, chemistry, modern languages, scholastic and mental philosophy, and a complete course of catechetical or theological instruction; and to suspend such schools as have been but scantily attended, and which from experience are found to be seldom required'. It was added that 'in respect to the schools which will be continued, hardly any change will take place in the staff of professors'. There was, however, to be an entrance examination, and the College was to be continued under diocesan auspices.

The bishops turned their attention to the Academical Council or Senate. The latter was not destined to meet again, the bishops noting that the Religious Orders would never accept its ministrations. The prelates did, however, affirm once again their original intention in setting up the body. 'It was never for a moment intended', the letter declared, 'that such a Senate should exercise any governing power over any existing College, or should in any way interfere or pronounce judgment upon its internal management. It was simply a council to assist the bishops, and an assembly for the interchange of experience and suggestions. It must be obvious at first sight that any interference in the internal management of any College would be fatal to its independence and to its well-being; and the greatest care was therefore taken to put beyond doubt that the Senate was never intended to possess any such authority.'

IV

THE SEQUEL TO THE
KENSINGTON VENTURE

ONE of Bishop Hedley's first acts on assuming the editorship of
The Dublin Review in 1878 was to ask Manning to contribute a
new article on 'The Work and Wants of the Church in England'.
It was to be an examination of the progress made in the sixteen
years since he had first written on the topic. The Cardinal took
each of the five wants he had posited in the original article and
discussed them in turn. Seminaries had been established in five
dioceses and three others were engaged in providing them.
Middle-class schools 'now exist in almost every diocese', he
asserted, 'and in some they are already numerous'.[1] In his own
diocese there were thirteen such schools. Evidence was given of
the achievements made in the political education and practical
efficiency of the laity. A College for Foreign Missions had been
established at Mill Hill, London.

What Manning had to say on the matter of Higher Education
was of especial significance, the article appearing but a few months
after Capel's dismissal. Two things had become evident:

the one, that very few came to Kensington for the sake of higher
studies, which was the end and purpose for which the College had been
founded; the other, that for the most part the students came for the
sake of passing some examination, such as the army, or for medicine,
or for matriculation at the London University. But this last function
belongs properly to our existing Colleges, and should be accomplished
before students reach their eighteenth year. To matriculate at the
London University is obviously no part or only the lowest part, of the
work for which a College of higher studies was intended. As to both
medicine and the army, recent arrangements of the military and medical authorities require that young men destined for those professions

[1] *The Dublin Review* (Jan. 1879), pp. 57–83.

shall enter the respective Colleges and begin their technical and professional studies by seventeen or eighteen years of age. This renders the
Kensington College useless to them for it cannot receive them before
their eighteenth year, and they cannot continue in it after that age. The
experience, therefore, of the last five years has led to the belief that for
the present it will be expedient for our existing Colleges to raise their
studies as high as they are able, and to retain their students as long as
they can.

It was still possible to gain a London degree, and Manning
produced statistics to show the advance Ushaw and Stonyhurst,
in particular, had made in that direction. He ended on a prognostic
note:

The day will come when it will be seen that young men can hardly
be formed among boys, and that boys are better trained by themselves.
. . . That a College of higher studies for Catholic young men will one
day be demanded is certain. . . . While France, and Belgium, and Germany, and Ireland are forming Catholic Universities, the Church in
England, which has been revived by a miracle of grace, . . . would
remain by its own free choice a mendicant on the uncatholic intellect
of England for letters and for science. From such humiliation may God
preserve us. . . . The bishops of England have given a public pledge in
the foundation of the College at Kensington that they will await the
time when what they offered five years ago, perhaps before it was
required, shall be demanded by the fathers of our Catholic youth.

In the year following the publication of Manning's article
Capel carried the dispute concerning Kensington into the columns
of the public press. Writing in *The Daily Telegraph*, he was at
pains to point out that the 'Catholic University College was the
foundation and property of the Catholic bishops in England', and
that 'the plan of studies, the system of discipline, the scheme of
finance, were examined and approved by the bishops'.[2] He
went on:

the bishops in a joint Pastoral appealed at the outset, for £25,000 to
purchase and furnish a suitable building, and also for an annual sustentation fund, which, in the approved scheme submitted to the Senate,

[2] *The Daily Telegraph*, 13 Oct. 1880.

was put at £5,000 for the first year, to be lessened by a thousand each successive year. The College began not only without money, but with an actual yearly debt of £800 interest for the borrowed money with which it was purchased. It never crossed my mind that it was part of the rector's duty to find the money wherewith to found and support a University College. Nor would I have accepted such a post had I imagined it devolved on me to do anything of the kind. Neither Ireland, nor France, nor Belgium asked this of the rectors of the new universities. Still, as I had begun, and was anxious to see so important a work established for the Catholics of London, I did my utmost, appealed to friends for aid, lent the few thousands I possessed, laboured gratuitously, limited all expenditure to paying the modest salaries of the staff, the interest on the mortgages, and for the purchase of necessary apparatus. As the students lived either with their families or with tutors, nothing whatever was spent for food. After struggling for two years and half with want of means, though the College was steadily increasing, I resigned.

The letter ended with a plea for 'the influence, the resources, the methods and the experience of teaching communities' to be used in providing education for the middle classes.

A week later Capel wrote to the same newspaper declaring that there were reasons other than financial for the collapse of the Catholic University College. Parents were alarmed at the temptations provided in a city such as London, and 'the hearts of many yearned to see the College at Oxford or Cambridge'. Confidence was shaken on account of the alienation of the Religious Orders, and the Senate met but infrequently.[3] The want of funds was the greatest trial. 'During my two and half years' tenure of office £35,000 ought to have been contributed for the institution', he wrote, but 'only £14,000 was given from beginning to end.' Capel claimed that this fact alone disposed 'of the absurd report so industriously circulated that I, the rector, ran the College into debt'. Although the College may have been called into existence somewhat too early, he still maintained a 'similar institution must be created sooner or later'. Once again he pointed out that 'the Catholic middle-class of London, in its present state, can only

---

[3] *The Daily Telegraph*, 19 Oct. 1880.

have its need for education supplied by an Order rich in resources, strong in distinguished members, experienced in teaching, and thoroughly cognisant of the wants of our Catholic youth'.

From these two letters it becomes obvious what Capel was seeking. He was deeply in debt on account of his Public School venture, and he had lost money, too, in regard to the University College. The bishops were collectively responsible for the establishment of the University College, therefore they must each share in its debts. He knew also that the Jesuits had always been anxious to open a School in London. If he could but sell the Public School to them, he would resolve many of his problems. Furthermore the Jesuits might be willing to permit him to remain as Head of the School during his lifetime. The Jesuits would also be able to extend the establishment and develop their own Institute of Higher Studies. Such schemes had to be developed cautiously, because Capel was aware that Dr. Clarke and other professors of the University College had resolved on continuing the latter as a private diocesan venture. This the Cardinal and bishops had sanctioned. In fairness to the professors, Manning would have to prevent any possibility of a Jesuit usurpation.

Early in 1879 Capel appealed to Rome against a charge of personal immorality levelled against him. The Jesuits, as part of their policy of embarrassing the Archbishop, assisted him. In a letter dated 15 February 1879 (but not sent until the 17th) Capel wrote to the Provincial: 'I trust the evidence I have been able to produce has destroyed the abominable and false charges made against me', and he added: 'I can never forget the generous way in which the Society has come to the assistance of myself. I hope that in Rome I may at the hands of the Fathers receive like help.'[4] The consequence of Jesuit help was to be the offer of Capel's Public School. Capel wrote:

After much consideration I have determined, if it be possible, to dispose of my school and the land on which it stands subject to the condition that I go on founding and working the school till my death. The site is about 6¼ acres in extent, is freehold, and is admirably situated for the purposes of a school in the West End of London. We now have

4 Farm Street Archives. Capel to Provincial, 15 Feb. 1879.

74 boys and our prospects and connection are good. The boys are for the most part sons of army men, of doctors, of lawyers: in other words they all belong to the category of gentlemen. Our gross income from the school is about £1100 (eleven hundred pounds). On the ground we have only a wooden building capable of accommodating 150 boys, with an Iron Chapel for about the same number. One lady pledges herself to build the future Chapel giving £10,000 for this purpose. Other legacies are promised. I would, of course, do everything to enrich the future buildings as though the property were my own. For the freehold property and all that is on it, and all that may be erected on it, I ask £25,000 subject to the conditions mentioned above. Any legacies coming to the School would naturally enough go to your community. I feel strongly that unless the school go into the hands of a Teaching Order, it will after my death stand every chance of being destroyed. The present mortgages of £9,500 and £2,500 could still remain and I should only want a part of the remainder for a while. I do hope Fr. General may entertain and accept the project.[5]

In April the Provincial received a letter from J. R. Madan, Capel's agent. In this Madan declared that he had been to Rome to see Capel, who had requested him 'to ask you to grant me an interview as early as possible, in order to talk over the matter of the school'.[6] Capel had given Madan all directions about the matter. The Jesuits, however, were not disposed to accept the condition under which Capel was alone prepared to sell. Manning provides the sequel in a letter written to the Jesuit Provincial in October 1880:

I heard through three credible persons that [Capel] had sold [the land] to your late Provincial. As Mgr. Capel was under engagement to offer it to the Diocese, I wrote to ask him whether this statement was true. He answered with much warmth that he had not sold it to the Society. Within an hour I received from the late Provincial a letter telling me that Mgr. Capel had offered the land for sale to him, but that he had declined to purchase it without the consent of the Ordinary of the Diocese.[7]

5 Farm Street Archives. Capel to Provincial, 17 Feb. 1879.
6 Ibid. Madan to Provincial, 27 Apr. 1879.
7 Ibid. Manning to Provincial, 22 Oct. 1880.

By June 1879, the offer to the Jesuits having fallen through, Capel's solicitors were offering the land to Manning. The same conditions were to apply, but a threat was made that if the Archbishop did not purchase the property it would be offered to some religious community. Manning declared he could not accept the land under the conditions laid down, and he added that if the School were withdrawn from the diocese he would 'at once replace it by one of his own'.[8] A copy of Manning's answer was sent by the Archbishop's solicitors to the Jesuits, together with a letter from Vincent Harting which declared 'the S.J. has been so freely spoken of recently as intending purchasers of Mgr. Capel's school at Kensington that I feel it a duty on my part to let you know how matters now stand between that school and the Diocese'.[9]

By October 1879 Capel, bankrupt for £28,000 on the School project, agreed to sell the land to the diocese without conditions. When it became known that Manning was the purchaser, reports were circulated that the Cardinal intended to establish a School in London to rival the Jesuit establishment at Beaumont. Manning wrote to Canon Gilbert to scotch the rumours, and his letter found its way to Farm Street:

A foolish paragraph has appeared in the last number of *The World* saying that I have purchased Mgr. Capel's land for the purpose of establishing a College in rivalry with Beaumont. The writer, I fear, intended the mischief, which his words might cause, by inducing the Jesuits to believe such an intention to exist on my part. I offered to buy Mgr. Capel's land to put an end to the miseries and sins of rivalry and ill feeling which have vexed us in the last three years. It is my intention to form a school in South Kensington for boys resident in their homes: but no school or College which by possibility can be in rivalry with Beaumont. Nothing would induce me to do so unbrotherly an act. And my chief reason for offering to buy Mgr. Capel's land is to guard against any such evil towards any one. There are mischievous minds 'out' as the Americans say: and they do endless harm among us.[10]

[8] Ibid. Messrs. Harting & Sons (on Manning's behalf) to Messrs. W. & J. Gibson (for Capel), 13 June 1879, copy.
[9] Ibid. J. Vincent Harting to the Revd. A. J. Christie, S.J., 13 June 1879.
[10] Ibid. Manning to Dr. Gilbert, 1 Oct. 1879.

The school Manning was preparing to establish was for middle-class youths.

Consequent upon Capel's letter to *The Daily Telegraph*, Manning pointed out to the Jesuit Provincial that the Society's name was being used in connection with the establishment of a School in London and that it was being stated in the press that the Jesuits were prepared at a day's notice to launch £100,000 into such a scheme. The Cardinal argued:

You will not I feel sure think that I bear towards you a hostile feeling if I say in the name of my clergy, and in my own, that any such scheme would be destructive of the schools of the Diocese and therefore to the Diocese itself. For these reasons it could not be admitted. I do not for a moment imagine that you or your Fathers have any cognizance of what is passing. But I have two reasons for giving you this information. The one is that the anonymous writer in *The Daily Telegraph* of today (i.e. October 22nd, 1880) introduced the name of the Jesuits. The other is the intervention of Mgr. Capel in these proceedings.[11]

The Provincial hastened to assure the Cardinal that he had not seen the letter in question, and added:

when I did read it I was simply amused at the assurance and ignorance of the writer. I say assurance, because whoever he is, he has no right to say nor ground for believing that the Society is disposed, even, if it had the power, to do what he says; and ignorance, because the amount he names gives us credit for riches we do not possess. The idea of our being able to put down £100,000 at any time, not to say a moment's notice, is altogether ridiculous. I do not even know who the anonymous writers are, nor has there been communication of any sort with Mgr. Capel. I can safely assert that neither I nor any other member of the Society has had anything to do with any of the letters except to read them when they appeared. Whoever mentions our name does so without our inspiration or cognizance, and simply expresses his own unauthorized desires. If I entertained the intention of setting up any school in Your Eminence's Diocese, or mooting the question in any way, Your Eminence is the first person outside our Society to whom I should address myself. But I am well aware that with Your Eminence's present convictions such an application would be useless. And, however

11 Farm Street Archives. Manning to Provincial, 22 Oct. 1880.

much I may regret their existence, I should scorn to stoop to indirect means of compassing what I could not obtain by direct.[12]

At the beginning of 1879 it became known that the University College was to be reorganized in Cromwell Place and the old buildings disposed of. Capel, who sought to press the claim that he had advanced £5,521 of his own money to the College, had taken opinion of counsel and a copy of this was sent to the Cardinal and the bishops, to the Duke of Norfolk, and Lord Petre. At the Low Week meeting of the hierarchy in 1879 Manning informed the prelates that he hoped they would not be troubled with Capel's affair. Ullathorne told Canon Estcourt that 'it was whispered about among the Bishops that Mr. Harting had made Capel an offer from the Cardinal'.[13] Manning had taken legal advice, and although his counsel did not deny that Capel had been the agent of the bishops, he advised the bishops to defend themselves 'on the ground that he had kept no proper accounts, and that no Court would pass the books which he produced as authorities and admitted accounts'.[14] The Cardinal, however, maintained that he had no doubt at all that Capel had spent money of his own, and he wrote in his *Journal*: 'I therefore was resolved that he should never have the power of accusing the Episcopate and myself.' Canon Estcourt, examining for Ullathorne the opinion of Capel's counsel, felt that a distinction ought to have been made between the liability of the bishops as a body, and between the personal liability of each individual prelate. If Capel's difficulties had been caused solely by the College (and not by the Public School), and 'if he had carried it on in a business-like way, and on sound principles, we should be inclined to have more sympathy with him', he declared. Manning considered that he had a peculiar responsibility over and above that of the other bishops, because he had urged them to select Capel in the first place, although he had always thought the foundation of the College premature. 'I yielded to my colleagues,' he wrote, 'who

---

[12] Ibid. Provincial to Manning, 22 Oct. 1880, copy.
[13] Birmingham Archdiocesan Archives. Ullathorne to Estcourt, 25 May 1879.
[14] Manning Papers, Bayswater. Manning's *Journal*.

thought that people would understand nothing that was not
in concreto.'15

All the prelates, with one exception, offered to contribute to
the £4,000 for which Capel was willing to settle. Brown of
Newport and Menevia was genuinely too poor to contribute
anything. Of all the bishops, Ullathorne was most reluctant to
pay anything, although in the end he offered £100. He claimed
he had pledged only a moral support to the College, that he had
only agreed to Capel's appointment 'provided he gave up his own
school, and devoted the whole man to the work, which he never
did',16 that he did not consider himself responsible for the
temporalities or for the administration of the College, and had
told Capel so, and that he had not participated in its affairs.
Initially, Manning was willing to pay £3,000 if the other bishops
would contribute the remainder. Canon Estcourt, in offering
£100 on Ullathorne's behalf, pointed out that 'Dr. Ullathorne
perhaps stands in a different position from the other Bishops'.17
It was hoped that Capel could be induced to accept £3,000 without pressing for more. Ullathorne told Estcourt in May 1879, 'it
would not do to have an acquittal for me from Mgr. Capel, that
would be acknowledging a claim on me. I simply propose to
assist the Cardinal in paying. I suppose his (Capel's) lawyers wish
to avoid litigation between Capel and us, which would damage
him for ever, and simply want to get all they can. I suppose also
that the Cardinal wishes to avoid calling on the Bishops if he can.
Hence the hope still entertained that £3,000 will be accepted.'18
But Capel stuck out for £4,000, and this sum was eventually
received from Manning. Capel signed an acquittance to all the
bishops.19 Manning wrote: 'What I gave him fulfils, I believe,
every duty of justice, equity, and honour, and I could not rest so
long as he could lay to our charge anything at variance with these
high obligations.'20 Bishop Vaughan wrote to Lady Herbert that

15 Manning's *Journal*. Bayswater Archives.
16 Birmingham Archdiocesan Archives. Ullathorne to Estcourt, 17 Jan. 1879.
17 Ibid. Estcourt to Messrs. Arnold & Co., Solicitors, 26 May 1879.
18 Ibid. Ullathorne to Estcourt, 27 May 1879.
19 Ibid. Ullathorne to Estcourt, 28 May 1879.
20 Manning's *Journal*. Bayswater Archives.

Manning was now 'poorer than a Church mouse and drained to the last farthing by Mgr. Capel's affairs at Kensington'.[21]

The Catholic University College was carried on from 1878 to 1882 in Cromwell Place, South Kensington, before being united to St. Charles's College, Bayswater, as its department of Higher Studies. There it functioned until the death of Cardinal Vaughan in 1903. It was modestly successful while it continued its independent existence, and before it finally committed itself to the interests of but one school. In July 1880 Dr. R. F. Clarke wrote to his friend Bishop Danell to ask the latter to secure further support for the College. He pointed out that numbers were small, because of an impression that the College 'is closed, or is carried on only in name, produced partly by the Circular of Suspension in November 1878'. In fact there had never been a day on which lectures by Paley, Lloyd, Butler, Willis, Thompson, Barff, Faribault, and Clarke himself, had not been given. 'All these classes actually meet and work. They do not exist merely on paper.' It is true that the former connection had been broken up, but old defects had been remedied and a fresh start made. Clarke described the work which was being undertaken:

> With respect to studies, we have unequivocal objective proof of the improvement which has taken place. The mere number of students who pass examinations from a given College is of little value in judging of the probable benefit which will accrue to a given youth from being there: both because it does not inform us how many have been plucked, or whether the students were picked, and still more so because the students to be sent up for examination may have been prepared in special classes, on which the 'cream' of the staff, their best attention, etc., was exercised: and beside, the passed students may form only a small proportion of the total number of youths at a College. Now all examinations passed here have been passed by attendance at the ordinary courses; no students have been picked, and with our small numbers we passed two students for the first B.Sc., five for Matriculation, two for the first B.A., one for the preliminary and one for the competitive Civil Service Examination first class, and one for the preliminary law

---

[21] Leslie, S. (ed.), *Letters of Herbert, Cardinal Vaughan to Lady Herbert of Lea, 1867–1903*, p. 303, Vaughan to Lady Herbert, 28 Jan. 1879.

examination. Besides this, another student, prepared partly here and partly in private by his father, passed the Indian Civil Service Examination; and to these passes we had three plucks, all for Matriculation, the first examination at which a youth commonly presents himself. Two of these plucks were of the same person; the third was that of a youth who had then been at the College for only two months. These facts, my Lord, are objective; they are independent of our own estimate of our work; and they show that any parent who sends a son here will have him put through a course of instruction of such a nature that without cramming there is every prospect of a high public examination being passed by it. . . . At present we have students preparing for the Civil Service, the Army, the second B.A., and the LL.B. and it is our belief founded on experience of the past, that these examinations will be passed, without the disrepute and disadvantage of cramming.[22]

Despite Clarke's efforts, however, and those of the other professors, the College was never able to recover from the damage inflicted to its prestige by the ill reputation of Capel's earlier management, by the defection of Norfolk and Petre from among its sponsors, by the pecuniary trials, and by the termination of hierarchical sponsorship. Once the establishment united with St. Charles's College in 1882, as the latter's department of Higher Studies, it ceased to have national significance for English Catholics; the training it henceforward offered was limited to a purely diocesan need and a local clientele.

[22] Southwark Archdiocesan Archives. Clarke to Danell, 27 July 1880.

V

NEW LEADERS AND
RENEWED INITIATIVES

IT is not altogether unexpected that the failure of the Kensington College, and the consequent abandonment of the scheme for a federal University, should have given rise to renewed efforts either to establish a Catholic College in Oxford or to obtain permission for Catholic youths to frequent the existing Colleges of the ancient Universities. It is, therefore, significant that the matter came up for consideration yet again at an annual Low Week meeting of the hierarchy, this time in 1882. Considerable changes in the ranks of the episcopacy had taken place. Two dioceses were not represented at the gathering—Southwark, vacant for almost a year since the death of Bishop James Danell, and Hexham and Newcastle, whose diocesan James Chadwick died on 14 May 1882. Other well-known bishops had also disappeared from the scene—Thomas Joseph Brown of Newport and Menevia had died in 1880, and James Brown of Shrewsbury died seven months before the Low Week meeting of 1882. Francis Kerril Amherst, Bishop of Northampton since 1858, although still alive, had resigned his episcopal charge in 1879. Many of the old faces were, of course, still to be seen—Manning, Ullathorne, Clifford, Cornthwaite (since 1878 Bishop of Leeds), O'Reilly of Liverpool, Bagshawe of Nottingham, the two Vaughans (Plymouth and Salford). There were a number of newcomers. Perhaps the most noteworthy of these was John Cuthbert Hedley, O.S.B., who had succeeded to the see of Newport and Menevia in February 1881, at the age of 43. He was joined by Richard Lacy, who became first Bishop of the newly erected diocese of Middlesbrough in December 1879 at the age of 38, and Arthur Riddell, who at 44 years of age became third Bishop of Northampton in June 1880. Before the year 1882 was passed, three other prelates were to be raised to the bench: Robert Aston Coffin, C.SS.R., to Southwark, John William Bewick to Hexham and Newcastle, and John Vertue to the newly created see of Portsmouth.

Of the new bishops present at the meeting in 1882, two were firm opponents of the reopening of the Oxford question. Richard Lacy, an Irishman from Navan, was to be one of the longest-lived of the bishops, ruling the see of Middlesbrough until his death in 1929 at the age of 88. He proved to be one of the most determined advocates of the need for a Catholic University. Arthur Riddell was a more curious case, in view of his antecedents. A member of the Old Catholic family of Felton Park, Northumberland, and of Swinburne Castle, he was a nephew of that William Riddell who had been Vicar Apostolic of the old Northern District from 1844 until, succumbing to typhus, he died in Newcastle in 1847. Arthur Riddell's mother was Catherine Stapleton, sister of the eighth Lord Beaumont. The story is told that she took Arthur as a baby to see the saintly Curé d'Ars, Jean Vianney, who predicted the boy would one day be a bishop.[1] Throughout his episcopal life Riddell was to prove one of the most convinced opponents of the Oxford connection; he was to remain particularly firm, even after the formal removal of sanctions.

Bishop Hedley favoured a reconsideration of the University question. An Ampleforth monk, he had spent the greater part of his life teaching Philosophy and Theology at Belmont. As editor of *The Dublin Review*, he had followed the guidance of Bishop Vaughan of Salford on education matters, but he was a close friend of both Clifford and Newman. He believed the question concerning the Universities was of chief moment to, 'almost exclusively, the rich, the noble, and the leisured class'.[2] Hedley was inclined to think that, since 1875, dogmatic Anglicanism had lost its hold on the Universities. Scepticism, indifference, agnosticism, immorality there might still be, but alongside of these there was a searching for truth—even for Catholicism itself—a religious earnestness, and a growing respect for historic beliefs. He felt it

[1] An Old Alumnus, p. 143. [2] Wilson, J. Anselm, pp. 231 seq.

was time the whole problem of Catholics and the Universities should be re-examined. 'Oxford and Cambridge,' he was to write, 'instead of being a more or less homogeneous community moulding men's minds as a stream rolls smooth the pebbles in its bed, had gradually become a kind of delta or sea, with deep places and shallows, currents and backwaters, where there was doubtless plenty of danger, but where faith and Christian life had ample opportunities for flourishing undisturbed.'[3] Hedley did not consider the original policy of the hierarchy misguided, but simply thought that in the last eighteen years a new situation had arisen. Even after the removal of the ban, in Cardinal Vaughan's day, Hedley was never to be an *enthusiastic* supporter of Catholics' attending the Universities. In 1896 he warned of 'our chief rock ahead', declaring 'it is certainly not every boy that is fit to be sent to a place like Oxford or Cambridge'.[4] At the Low Week meeting in 1882, however, seeing that he was in a minority among the bishops on the Oxford question, he did not press his arguments. The bishops agreed in passing three resolutions affecting attendance at non-Catholic Universities and at Board Schools. These resolutions were that 'the principles and spirit which animate the national Universities and pervade the Board School system, and the intrinsic dangers which such institutions present to faith and morals, create a proximate occasion of mortal sin';[5] and secondly that 'the question as to what constitutes in any particular case "grave and adequate necessity" and what precautions can be deemed sufficient to "remove all proximate danger" of mortal sin, is one the solution of which appertains to the Church, and not to the private judgment of any individuals, even of the Clergy, whether secular or regular.' Such questions, it was agreed, 'must in every instance be referred to the decision of the Ordinary of the parents, or to others responsible for the parents concerned'. The third resolution declared that 'the Bishops have agreed, each in his own diocese, to instruct all members of the Clergy, both

[3] *Ampleforth Journal*. Article by Hedley, vol. 2 (1896), pp. 1 seq.
[4] Ibid.
[5] Manning Papers, Bayswater. Resolutions of the Catholic Bishops in England at their Annual Meeting held at Archbishop's House, Low Week, 1882 (May 1882).

secular and regular, that they are bound "sub gravi" not to encourage or to permit Catholics to frequent Board Schools, or to reside at the national Universities for the purposes of education'. Hedley, despite his views, issued an *ad clerum* embodying the episcopal decision. The three bishops who were to be consecrated after the Low Week meeting—Coffin, Vertue, and Bewick— were all of the majority party. Coffin, especially, was to maintain his early vigour against Oxford during the two and a half years he occupied the see of Southwark.

The resolutions of the bishops, with their consequent tightening up of regulations, impelled one or two members of the gentry to attempt a direct appeal to Pope Leo XIII. Naturally, they looked for support to Newman. The latter, who had refused to assist the hierarchy in any way in its efforts to provide a higher education for English Catholics, remarked that the bishops 'forbid, but they do not direct or create'.[6] Ullathorne's *ad clerum*, embodying the resolutions of the hierarchy and imposing an obligation *sub gravi* upon the clergy, stimulated Newman to support the efforts of those who were about to reopen the issue at the Vatican. The young and somewhat gauche convert Lord Braye was the leader of the small group, and he was ably seconded by Hartwell de la Garde Grissell. The latter, a convert and old Harrovian, was received into the Church by Manning. He was destined to endure considerable unpopularity in Oxford for his religious convictions, and once, we are told, 'was screwed up, hustled and pelted by the undergraduates of a certain College, an affair which created a great sensation and even led to questions being asked in the House'.[7]

Such men, whose loyalty to things Roman was not suspect, were more powerful when they claimed the support of Hedley and Newman. On 2 November 1882 Newman wrote a letter in response to one from Lord Braye, supporting a re-examination of the Oxford prohibition. It was intended to read it to the Pope. The euphoria of the Oxford of the mid forties still engulfed the old man of over 80, and he wrote that it was now the moment

[6] Murphy, Thomas, *The Position of the Catholic Church in England and Wales during the Last Two Centuries*, pp. 7–8, note of Lord Braye.

[7] Martindale, C. C., *Catholics at Oxford*, p. 33.

for 'the Catholic Mission in Oxford to seize an opportunity which may never come again' for 'the Undergraduates and Junior Fellows are sheep without a shepherd'; they are 'sceptics or inquirers, quite open for religious influences'.[8] It was an old man's dream, wistful and strangely pathetic. Newman felt 'the Liberals are sweeping along in triumph, without any Catholic or religious influence to stem them', and he bemoaned what he termed 'nihilism' in the Catholic body. The Pope should be urged to send a representative to England, who would be able to talk to everyone and remain a whole summer. He suggested that the first step to this end should be that some Englishman of position, 'if one or two, so much the better', should go to Rome and remain there some months to persuade the Pope of the need for such a visitor. The Englishman should speak French and Italian.

Lord Braye, Grissell, and Bishop Hedley secured an audience of the Pope on 13 April 1883.[9] Braye himself, in his autobiography, informs us of the arguments placed before the Pope. It was claimed that

only a fraction of undergraduates attended the lectures of modernists, or went near Balliol, which seemed to have acquired a rationalistic reputation; the majority of youths only cared to get a 'pass', or spent their time in sport. . . .[10] [He goes on:] I had prepared in Italian a succinct statement of the position; this I read to the Pope, who had bidden us 'be seated' around his presence. It was somewhat difficult for the English Bishop (Hedley) and myself to make the situation clear to His Holiness (as well it might be) and we had to explain that 'Queen's Colleges' were in Ireland, and that the Irish Education Question was not connected with Oxford. Finally the Holy Father expressed a determination to consult Manning when he next should see him.

Braye placed before the Pope a translation in Italian of the letter he had received from Newman, and the Pope said he would place Newman's views before Cardinal Manning.[11] Grissell then produced a long list of Oxford converts to Rome, with details of

---

[8] Murphy, pp. 7–8 n.
[9] Not 1882, as stated by Wilson. See also Ward, W., *Life of Newman*, vol. 2, pp. 486 seq.; Murphy, pp. 7–8 n.; Stockley, p. 101; and Braye, pp. 268–73.
[10] Braye, pp. 268–73.   [11] Ward, W., *Life of Newman*, vol. 2, pp. 486–7.

their Colleges. Similarly, he provided the pontiff with a list of Catholics who had studied at Oxford and matriculated there. Copies of these lists, continued up to the nineties, are to be found among the Grissell papers at St. Benet's Hall, Oxford. The lists were to be presented to the Holy Father again in 1893. They contained the names of a number of youths educated at Newman's school and prepared for Oxford in defiance of the directives of Rome and the hierarchy: Sir Charles Wolseley, Bt., Richard Towneley, Edward Sheil, Eugene Gould, Charles Thynne (son of Lord Charles Thynne), Charles T. Wild, H. L. Ashton, Henry Higgins, A. L. Saunders, Justin Sheil, F. E. Cuming, and E. G. Lamb.[12] Other Catholic schools appear to have been loyal to the hierarchy's ruling. Three names each from Beaumont, Oscott, and Woburn, and one or two from Ushaw, occur in the lists, but these span a period of over twenty years. Apart from Newman's school, there appears to have been no *organized* attempt on the part of the Colleges to defy the hierarchy. Stonyhurst seems to have been thoroughly loyal to the episcopal policy in not preparing boys for Oxford. Grissell could lay claim to about twenty-three converts from Oxford in the years from 1871 to 1882. Hedley's chief contribution to the visit was an assertion that Rome was only in possession of resolutions taken as a result of votes at meetings of the hierarchy; bishops might express their views otherwise if consulted individually and asked to give reasons for the line they adopted. This was a point which carried weight. On 17 August 1883 a letter from *Propaganda* was sent to the Cardinal Archbishop asking for two things—'the principles on which the English Bishops are agreed', and 'the separate opinions of each one of them on matters in which they disagreed, and which find no expression in resolutions arrived at by taking the votes'.[13]

If any bishop disagreed with the Oxford policy, now was his opportunity to say so in private and to write direct to Rome. The bishops were ordered by Cardinal Simeoni to communicate directly with him. They were to write privately, briefly, clearly, and candidly, and they were not to confer with their fellow

---

[12] St. Benet's Hall, Oxford. Grissell Papers.   [13] Wilson, p. 231.

bishops.[14] Hedley immediately conferred with his fellow Benedictine, Ullathorne. Here was an opportunity for the latter to urge that the University question be reopened, if he really wished for it. Ullathorne and Hedley were in touch with Clifford, and in the contacts thus made we can see an attempt to bring party pressure to bear on Rome, under the pretence of individual opinion. It did not work, because Ullathorne refused to participate in the scheme. He informed Hedley that he was 'against the Bishop of Clifton's proposition, that we, the bishops, should ask for the question to be reopened'.[15] He could see no way to provide what the laity desired, and as Oxford was in his diocese he stated in his reply to Rome 'that there are ten Catholic students in Oxford at this moment, a Frenchman, a South American, three Irish, one recently converted in the University, the rest English. They attend Mass on Sunday, and occasionally, most of them, the Sacraments. One has been in danger of losing his Faith; it is hoped he is coming right.' He added: 'I then leave the conclusions to the Holy See.' It is significant that in 1872 there were eight Catholics at Oxford; ten years later this number had increased but by two.[16]

Hedley's draft *votum* has been printed *in extenso* in Wilson's *Life* of the bishop. He felt that a tacit permission ought to be given to reside at Oxford and Cambridge, and that a strong Catholic mission should be established in each place. The problem was a class problem. Professional education was not at issue, for to obtain degrees in Law or Medicine 'there is no necessity for residence at those Universities', and indeed 'the Universities are not generally resorted to for such degrees'. Hence for Hedley, as for Newman, the whole problem concerned the social needs of a handful of titled, ennobled, or wealthy families. Hedley saw 'the rich, the noble and the leisured class' as the one on which 'depends in each generation, the social and political status of the Catholic Church in the country, and to their wealth and capabilities the Church has to look for a very great part of her material progress'. For him admission to the Universities of Oxford and Cambridge

[14] Ibid.   [15] Ibid. Letter of Ullathorne to Hedley, 5 Sept. 1883.
[16] *The Dublin Review* (Autumn 1939), p. 103 n.

was to be permitted because there the gentry would 'form friendships which endure for life', and because in the Universities they would imbibe the true tone and character of the English gentleman 'which his class easily recognise'.[17] Hedley's statements are reminiscent of the sentiments of Newman in the fifties; he was concerned with a class-structured paternalism which was fast disappearing. Hedley admitted that Oxford and Cambridge provided dangers to faith and morals, but the risk had to be taken if young men were not to be idle 'or to find themselves outside their own class in society'. Catholics must not, however, be in a Catholic House at Oxford; the students belonged 'to various ranks of the higher class' and the social distinctions had to be preserved. Like Newman, he thought that there were great opportunities for conversions at Oxford, and especially so since the death of Pusey. But Hedley, Clifford, and Vaughan of Plymouth found themselves a minority among the bishops, and the individual reports of the members of the hierarchy were overwhelmingly against reopening the question. Another papal document was to be issued in January 1885 reiterating earlier decisions.

Newman's elevation to the Cardinalate in 1879 did not effect that reconciliation between the magnates and the bishops for which Manning hoped. Newman not only allowed himself to be used by Grissell and Braye in 1882 in their efforts to get the University question reopened but he also wrote direct to Mgr. di Rende at *Propaganda* on the subject.[18] This was not only using his exalted rank in a way which was bound to bring him into conflict with the English hierarchy but it was putting himself at the head once again of a small aristocratic clique in their war with the bishops. In May 1883 Arthur Hutton of the Oratory, together with Grissell and Braye, urged Newman to press at Rome for the removal of the Oxford prohibition. Braye visited the Oratory for this intention and was aided and abetted by Hutton. Before the close of 1884, however, Hutton had left the Oratory, apostatized, and married. We learn from the letter of Hutton to

[17] *The Dublin Review* (Autumn 1939), pp. 233–4.
[18] Grissell Papers. Arthur W. Hutton of the Oratory to Grissell, 15 May 1883.

Grissell, written in May 1883, that Newman was preparing a dossier of documents on the University problem, and that Grissell was supplying him with memoranda.[19] But Newman was not prepared for an *open* breach with the hierarchy. Hutton declared that he could see that he would be very reluctant to put himself publicly at variance with the episcopacy, although there was no doubt he would help the cause at Rome.

One of the ways to defeat the hierarchy would be to urge the British government to establish diplomatic relations with the Vatican. Braye wrote that the efforts towards this end provided a strenuous venture for the English aristocracy. A view 'that this very channel of communication might facilitate a just settling of the distracting Irish Question was linked in the mind of many of us with the prospect of a decision being given as to the Oxford and Cambridge difficulty'.[20] Newman supported the plan. Meriol Trevor, in treating of this episode, writes that Braye's efforts for the establishment of diplomatic relations were 'equally unpopular with the Cardinal Archbishop—it was worldliness and nationalism all over again'.[21] She fails to appreciate the wider implications involved. The Catholic aristocracy, in general, were antagonistic to Irish national aspirations. Manning feared, with the Irish bishops, that the British government would attempt to influence Irish episcopal appointments in order to secure a docile and sub-servient prelacy. In 1881 Newman was agreeing to assist Gladstone by writing to the Pope against the Irish bishops.[22] Manning was bitterly opposed to any attempt to curb Irish social and political aspirations by means of papal condemnations. It was because of his influence at Rome that the danger was averted. On the death of Cardinal McCabe, in 1885, the government and the Catholic aristocracy intrigued at Rome through the person of an Old Catholic, George Errington, to prevent the nomination of Dr. William Walsh, President of Maynooth, to the vacant see of Dublin. Sir Charles Dilke, who strongly disapproved of the

---

[19] Ibid.   [20] Braye, pp. 275–6.
[21] Trevor, *Light in Winter*, p. 601.
[22] See Morley, J., *Life of Gladstone*, vol. 3, pp. 62, 63; and my *Cardinal Manning*, pp. 180 seq.

whole shady episode, was in constant touch with Manning, supplying him with information to enable him to counteract the manœuvres of Errington. The Errington affair nearly led to the fall of the government. Clifford, the Bishop of Clifton, and the Duke of Norfolk were urging Errington to press the candidature of Dr. Donnelly, Auxiliary of Dublin, and later they supported the government in pressing for the appointment of the Archbishop of Sydney. Manning's intervention against Errington was, however, decisive, and Walsh was consecrated in 1885. The backstairs methods employed by the government and the Catholic aristocracy merely illustrated for Manning the dangers which would constantly arise if formal diplomatic relations were established with the Vatican.[23] It was, therefore, no narrowness of view (as Miss Trevor implies) which led the Cardinal Archbishop to oppose the movement to set up such formal relations in the 1880s. Rather, it was an example of Manning's determination to ensure the total independence of the Church in England and Ireland from government control and from the dominance of any one social faction.

In Low Week 1883 the bishops again collectively expressed their resolution not to reopen the University question. Almost contemporaneously with the meeting Bishop Vaughan of Salford published an article in *The Dublin Review* scathing in its remarks about the Catholic aristocracy. Vaughan sensed danger to the Church in England from those 'who belong to the fashionable world, or who possess wealth, and are ambitious to see the worldly success of their sons',[24] and he remarked that 'the Church can always count more surely upon the fidelity of the poor than of the rich'. Vaughan declared that a few weeks previously he had addressed a letter (reproduced in *The Dublin*) to a number of bishops and leading laymen in different parts of the German Empire, 'in order to learn with some degree of accuracy the effect of the State University education upon Catholics in Germany'. He quoted extensively from the replies received, all of them unfavourable to mixed education. 'We find that strenuous efforts

---

23 McClelland, *Cardinal Manning*, p. 193.
24 *The Dublin Review* (Apr. 1883), p. 446.

have been made by Catholics in nearly every country', he declared, 'to obtain Catholic Universities—not because no Universities existed in those countries, but because, not being Catholic, they were intrinsically dangerous to Catholic life.' He instanced the examples of Belgium, Germany, France, Ireland, Canada, and the United States. In England there were wider issues at stake. 'It is hardly possible to conceive the acceptance by Catholics of education in the Protestant or rationalistic universities without a surrender of the whole principle of denominational education, which is at present the Church's main contention in every country and for every class.' Catholic young men at Oxford or Cambridge 'would probably take every possible care to avoid a Catholic College, did one exist, and Catholic society'. Manning wrote to Vaughan: 'How easily you *might have been* deceived, and how easily I might have been biased by my love of Oxford and England.'[25]

Hartwell Grissell thought the movement to gain admission to Oxford and Cambridge would benefit considerably if its leadership was seen not to be identified with the titular aristocracy. After the experience of his appeal to the Pope in 1882, he sought to show that demands for an Oxford education were not confined to the gentry. He compiled a list of Catholic graduates whose names appeared on the books in 1877 and tried to establish a small pressure group of scholars. The list is extant and contains such names as W. H. Bliss and D. Hunter-Blair of Magdalen; E. L. Lister of Brasenose; H. Grisewood, C. H. Moore, J. O'Fallon-Pope, C. T. Weld, and C. T. T. Redington of Christ Church (the last named being Treasurer of the Union in 1868 and President in 1869); R. F. Clarke and Alexander Wood of Trinity; T. A. Eaglesim and Charles Seager of Worcester; F. W. Harvey of Hertford; T. Arnold and C. H. Kennard of University College; C. S. Devas and J. W. Flanagan of Balliol; E. G. G. Wells of Merton; D. Parsons of Oriel; E. S. Grindle and J. R. Madan of Queen's; W. C. Robinson (Fellow) and R. B. Schomberg of New College; H. A. Bellingham, U. Cave-Browne-Cave, G. Dover, A. W. Hutton, W. O. Lovell, R. S. Ross-of-Bladensburg and

[25] Snead-Cox, *Life of Vaughan*, vol. 1, p. 469.

W. C. Maude of Exeter College; and J. W. W. Drew (un-attached).[26] Some of these men were, of course, not in sympathy with Grissell's aims. We know, for instance, that Bliss, Hunter-Blair, Clarke, Seager, Devas, Madan (a Mill Hill priest), Robinson, and Redington (president of *The Universe*) were adverse to the idea of Catholics attending the ancient Universities at this time. But others could be relied upon. Hutton and Eaglesim were Oratorians and closely associated with Newman; Lovell, Ross-of-Bladensburg, O'Fallon-Pope, and Dover were Jesuits; Weld had been a boy at the Oratory School; and Cave and C. H. Moore were secular priests, the latter residing in Florence. If the group as a whole could not be united to the extent of pressing for a reopening of the Oxford question, perhaps they could be per-suaded to take a more active part in the internal affairs of the University and thus show to the bishops and to Rome that Catholic influence counted for something in Oxford. Grissell had in view the formation of an association of Catholic graduates at Oxford, which in due time would also embrace Cambridge.

B. F. C. Costelloe of Balliol, who was to be Librarian at Oxford in 1877, wrote to Grissell in April 1883 to say that he did not consider Vaughan's attitude to be as intransigent as the article in *The Dublin* might at first sight indicate. After congratulating Grissell on having 'netted Bishop Hedley', he declared that he had made a frontal assault on the Bishop of Salford:

> He seemed not at all so hostile as I expected. The chief thing he opposed is a *College*. He said expressly that he would be glad to see a set of Catholic lectures there by proper people, and that he did not object to individuals going up with leave of their Bishop: and he did not even protest when I threw out the suggestion that if there were a proper scheme of lectures two or three independent boarding houses might be founded—especially a Jesuit, an Oratorian, and a Secular, as I put it. On the whole he seemed amenable to a compromise.[27]

Costelloe's statement is important in view of the events of 1893, although he was oversanguine in his interpretation of Vaughan's position. Costelloe, after visiting Lord Braye at Stamford, was to

---

[26] Grissell Papers.   [27] Ibid. Costelloe to Grissell, 30 Apr. 1883.

go to Rome to meet Newman's contact, Mgr. di Rende, and then press *Propaganda* for a re-examination of the Oxford prohibition. Meantime, Grissell had been preparing a pamphlet arguing the case for Oxford, a copy of which was to accompany Costelloe to Rome. The bishops gained an intimation that a further conspiracy was afoot from Lord Petre, who in 1882 informed the prelates of the scheme in an interview in Low Week.

In May 1882 Grissell wrote to Fr. J. W. W. Drew, an Oxford graduate and missioner at St. Edward's, Romford. Drew was to frame hypothetical questions to test the validity of those resolutions of 1882 enjoining on priests *sub gravi* not to give permission to any layman to send his son to Oxford or Cambridge, but to submit any such request to the Ordinary. Grissell was anxious to obtain an opinion from a Roman canonist that the bishops had acted uncanonically in imposing these conditions. Drew replied:

> You want me to make out a case, so I must suppose myself to be alarmed by the Resolutions just referred to. Here is a question then: 'A priest, duly alarmed by the Resolutions, is asked by one of his penitents whether it is lawful for him to send his son to the University of Oxford. Is the priest bound *sub gravi*, to forbid the penitent to send his son to the University, and is he moreover bound to refuse absolution in case the penitent sends his son'? Here is another question: 'Is a priest guilty of mortal sin if he takes upon himself to decide the question in favour of a young man being sent to Oxford, when he knows that the Bishop, if appealed to in the case, would certainly refuse permission?'

Drew instructed Grissell to add the words: 'I shall be very thankful if you will let me know the correct answers to the above questions. I hope I shall be at liberty to say on whose authority the answers are given.'[28] Grissell and Costelloe had next to find a pliable canonist who would give the desired answers, and who would make out a case whereby the bishops' directives could be placed at defiance. Meantime further steps were to be taken at Rome.

Grissell was aided in Rome by Alexander Wood, an Oxford convert. W. H. Bliss had written an article for *The Tablet* on 'Mixed Education' which strongly argued against the reopening

[28] Ibid. Drew to Grissell, 16 May 1883.

of the Oxford question, and Wood was engaged in preparing a reply for publication in *The Fortnightly*. Bliss had visited Wood in Rome in June 1883 and had strongly advised against any intrigue at *Propaganda*. But Eaglesim of the Birmingham Oratory urged Wood to go ahead, and sent him 'a long and beautiful letter' to help him with the article.[29] The idea was to have copies of the article sent to every Missionary rector in England and Wales, to all the heads of Religious houses, and to all the bishops of Germany. It was understood that Grissell, Braye, and Lord Bute would foot the bill. Bishops Clifford and Hedley were prepared, meantime, to sanction a new approach to *Propaganda*. Mgr di Rende was to be the vehicle of submission, and it was necessary for favourable statistics to be produced to ensure that everything about 'the proximate occasion' fell down. Wood secured audiences with the Pope, Cardinal Parocchi, and Cardinal Jacobini, and he made contacts with Cardinals Pitra, Bartolini, Martinelli, Fezzieri, Bilio, Franzelin, and Zigliera. This time Grissell and his associates were in earnest; nothing was to be left to chance.

Unfortunately for Grissell and his friends, however, Alexander Wood sent a copy of the Report which was being prepared for *Propaganda* to Gladstone.[30] He wished to know how the latter would view the prospect of the establishment of a Catholic Hall in Oxford. Gladstone informed Manning. Before 1884 was out the Cardinal Archbishop had a copy of the Report to *Propaganda* in his possession and the entire affair was laid before the hierarchy. The bishops, indignant at the surreptitious manœuvrings, urged the Archbishop to write to Rome on their behalf. Manning, Ullathorne, Bewick, Cornthwaite, O'Reilly, Lacy, Riddell, Bagshawe, Vertue, Vaughan of Salford, Knight, and the sickly Bishop Coffin all declared themselves against the reopening of the question and against the establishment of a Catholic College at Oxford. Clifford and Vaughan of Plymouth maintained the matter ought to be re-examined in the light of changed circumstances. Hedley agreed with Clifford, but was opposed to the

[29] Grissell Papers. Alexander Wood to Grissell, 3 June 1883.
[30] Ibid. Wood to Grissell, 7 Sept. 1885.

idea of a Catholic Hall or College. Manning wrote to *Propaganda* on 20 December 1885. Less than a month later Cardinal Simeoni, the Prefect, replied in a brief but authoritative document:

I have received your Eminence's letter of the 20th of last month, and have learnt from it with pain that by some families little account is made of the admonitions of the Holy See as to sending their sons to the Protestant Universities. The letter points out that this arises, not so much from want of good will as from their supposing that what they do is tolerated by the Holy See. To guard, therefore, the higher education of the Catholic youth of your country from this danger of perversion, I request that you will make known to the faithful that no change whatever has taken place in respect to the instructions upon this matter which were sent by my predecessor Cardinal Barnabo to the English Bishops on August 6th, 1867, and were afterwards inserted in the Provincial Synods of Westminster. For this purpose I should think it opportune to suggest to the Bishops of England to recall the said instructions to the remembrance of their flocks.[31]

Some few months were to elapse before the bishops were able to issue instructions in accordance with Simeoni's letter and before the presence in England of the new rescript was generally known to the conspirators. Meantime, in March 1885 Grissell produced with considerable aplomb the reply of a Roman canonist to the questions of conscience Fr. Drew had concocted. The timing was accidental, but it led many such as Henry Vaughan to write to Grissell in congratulation that Oxford had raised in himself a dutiful son.[32] Lady Bellingham piously wished: ' I hope I shall be able to send my son to Oxford when he is old enough. He is now four.'[33]

During 1883 and 1884 Grissell and Costelloe had spent no little time in Rome searching for an amenable canonist. They were finally able to enlist the services of a minor advocate in the Curia, who eked out a somewhat dull existence by teaching Hebrew in the Roman Seminary. His name was Carlo Menghini. On

---

[31] Translation and copy in Farm Street Archives. John, Cardinal Simeoni to Henry Edward, Cardinal Manning, 30 Jan. 1885.

[32] Grissell Papers. Henry J. Vaughan from Dudley's to Grissell, 30 Mar. 1885.

[33] Ibid., n.d.

5 March he wrote to Grissell with his opinion on the binding force of the various instructions *Propaganda* had issued to the English bishops on University education.[34] The report contained six chief points:

A. That the instructions received from Propaganda do not constitute a formal decree, but are a rule for guidance according to circumstances.

B. That the resolutions of the Bishops are more stringent than the instructions of Propaganda warrant and they consequently tend to cause embarrassment both to Clergy and Laity.

C. That even if the instructions did involve an absolute prohibition, the changed circumstances of the case would render these instructions revocable and subject to exceptions.

D. That the abolition of tests which has taken place since the first instructions were given, and the altered constitution of the Universities in favour of Catholics constitute circumstances which change the aspect of the whole question.

E. That it is also notorious, and the Bishops cannot deny it, that the great majority of Catholics who have frequented the Universities have kept the Faith; and that many conversions have taken place among their protestant fellow students. This proves that the danger of perversion is not proximate.

F. That the instructions of Propaganda fairly interpreted require merely due precautions be taken to remove any danger of perversion or sin, and these instructions are not intended to interfere with parental rights or responsibilities.

Menghini's opinions were widely circulated by Grissell and issued in pamphlet form. The arguments were specious and rested on the false assumption that Rome was not *au courant* with the changes effected at the Universities since the first condemnation of 1865. Similarly, as Menghini was aware of but one side of the question, he failed to give adequate weight to the reasons advanced by the bishops. He neglected to point out that the prohibition was reinforced in 1872 after the changes consequent upon the repeal of the Tests were announced. Menghini's case rested on one basic argument: the extent to which a decision of *Propaganda*

[34] Menghini's opinion: 'Catholics at the English Universities', Rome, 5 Mar. 1885.

in response to the united appeal of the episcopacy and promulgated by the latter was binding under sin upon the faithful. The pamphlet came in for severe treatment in the Catholic press, and especially in *The Tablet*, and 'the fallacies' upon which it rested were pointed out. Fr. G. W. Richardson of St. Augustine's, Manchester, a well-known canonist in his day, thought little attention could be given to Menghini's opinion. Writing to Grissell some twenty years later on the issue of whether or not Catholic boys could be sent to the major Protestant Public Schools, he claimed he had been studying Menghini's words concerning the Universities.

> The reperusal [he wrote], only convinces me more than ever that he would have found as great a majority of opinion on the question of law on the other side. . . . He does not say *who* is to say *when* 'that danger is excluded and the proper precautions taken'. These matters appertain *to Bishops and not to individuals* and, in case of dispute with a bishop, to the Holy See, as Canon Menghini shows in his concluding section. . . . Our Bishops (or the Holy See) are the judges of *externals* in faith and morals and . . . individuals whether Lord Bute or a king are bound to submit their judgment to such tribunals, any individual feeling to the contrary notwithstanding.[35]

In April 1885 Grissell endeavoured to enlist Jesuit support for the idea of a Catholic College in Oxford. He consulted Fr. James Henry Corry, S.J., at the Jesuit mission in Oxford. The latter was cautious. Writing to Grissell on 8 April, he declared:

> It struck me when you had gone last night that my last words on the stairs perhaps overstrain my degree of willingness for a College of Catholics in Oxford. For, after all, I think it would be a great deal better to keep away from it, and try only to increase our efficiency in regard of those matters which I take to be the ones that give rise to desire for an Oxford education on the part of some Catholic parents. These are all secondary matters in the matter of education but still are important ones and I think we could much add to what we are able to do, or rather are doing, for our young men from 18 to 22 in respect of them. I won't explain more or I shall be too long and I only want just

[35] Grissell Papers. G. W. Richardson to Grissell, 5 Sept. 1905.

to tell you what my opinion is without going into its reasons. I think therefore

(*a*) That if we were free to choose we should do best of all by keeping away from Oxford and devoting a tithe of the energy, men and money that would be required for coming to it, to the development of the existing provision in our Colleges for boys who have reached the age of 18 and 19.

(*b*) But public opinion seems to say that there is so extensive a desire in the English Catholic body for a Catholic Oxford Education as one ought not to ignore.

(*c*) Therefore the question is raised 'could a Catholic Hall or College be made to work well here, in which the young men who came to Oxford would be much better provided for than they are at present.' To this question I answer 'yes, if you have good men and good money'. I think it must be done thoroughly well and therefore expensively if done at all: it must *start life* here a *complete and perfect thing*, and not ask permission to grow into greatness from small beginnings—the only development I can allow is *increased* extent, but I demand that the very commencement consists of a college consisting of excellent classes, first class professors and excellent buildings, i.e. it must be an extensive concern at the very commencement. Of course this is difficult and costly to produce, but it is not impossible. A small and only half efficient college here would ruin itself and its cause I think, leading to the evil you told me Mgr. Capel had suggested to be a very possible one.[36]

Grissell was also in touch with Fr. Joshua Bradley, S.J., on the issue.[37] Perhaps the Jesuits could be persuaded to make a beginning in Oxford, using the mission as a nucleus. But Bradley was anxious that nothing should 'be quoted in connection with *my name*'.[38]

[36] Grissell Papers. James Henry Corry, S.J., to Grissell. 8 Apr. 1885.
[37] Ibid. A. Joshua D. Bradley, S.J. (writing from The Holy Name, Manchester, where he was supplying for Fr. Bernard Vaughan, S.J.) to Grissell, 30 Apr. 1885.
[38] Ibid. Bradley to Grissell, 15 Apr. 1885.

VI

THE LAST YEARS OF
THE PATRIARCH OF THE
SECOND SPRING

THE reaction of the bishops to Menghini's opinion was to issue statements in their respective dioceses in accordance with the letter from Cardinal Simeoni of 30 January 1885. All the prelates complied with the wishes of *Propaganda* and the matter was discussed fully at the ensuing Low Week meeting. Manning's Easter Pastoral of 1885 has been described by a somewhat unsympathetic scholar as 'a magnificent piece of powerful and moving writing, appealing from "worldly motives" to the highest principles of spirituality'.[1] In it, Manning answered Menghini's assertion that circumstances had changed by listing ten chief stages in the development of the University prohibition, and by showing that Rome had been informed of each significant change and that she had responded by reaffirming early decisions. He then turned to two of Menghini's chief points, the necessity of sending Catholic youths to Oxford and Cambridge, and the problem of 'the proximate occasion' of sin:

First, as to the necessity of sending Catholic youths to Oxford and Cambridge. No one, so far as I have hitherto heard, has ever ventured to assert this necessity, which, on the face of it, would be untrue. Half a century ago it was indeed true that no degree, recognized in the law of England, could be obtained except at Oxford and Cambridge; but it was precisely to abolish this necessity, intolerable both to Catholics and Nonconformists, that the power of conferring degrees, recognised in English Law, was extended to the London University. The occasion is therefore voluntary. Secondly, as to the removal of all proximate danger of sin. The Rescript[2] affirms 'The Sovereign Pontiff has declared,

---

[1] Evennett, Outram, in Beck, G. A. (ed.), *The English Catholics, 1850–1950*, p. 305.   [2] Of 1867.

that the mixture of Catholic youth in the non-Catholic Universities involves an intrinsic and most grave danger.' This is a sentence of universal application, relating not to Oxford and Cambridge only, but to all mixed education at all times and in all countries. This has always been the judgment and direction of the Holy See.[3]

Manning went on to outline the function of the Church in Education:

The Church cannot abdicate its office; and by its divine commission it is bound to form its own members. Their education in childhood and youth is the inalienable duty of the Church. To educate is to form the intellect, the conscience, and the will, and this formation the Church cannot, without betraying its trust, surrender to any authority upon earth. Woe be to the Church when it shall form its boys, and not its men, or when the last hand in forming its members is surrendered to non-Catholic institutions. . . . When once formed [the Catholic youth] must go forth into the atmosphere and dangers of our public life . . . into army and navy, or the Bar or Parliament; but not until their Catholic formation is complete. The Church would abdicate its pastoral office if it were to suffer the formation of its youth to pass from its own hands into the hands of teachers external to its own intellectual and Catholic unity.

It was not the mission of the Church in England

to conform itself to the varying currents of intellectual activity, philosophical and religious, which have passed and are still passing over the intelligence of the English people. For three hundred years what was thought to be the liberation of the English intelligence from the bondage of Catholic tradition has issued in what is called the progress of Modern Thought. . . . There never was a time in the last three centuries when the religious diversities of the English people were so manifold, and the intellectual deviations in the higher education of England from the traditional philosophy of the Christian world so wide or so extreme.[4]

Manning examined the nature of the intellectual and spiritual integrity which, he asserted, non-Catholics expected in Catholics, and he viewed the situation among his co-religionists in Ireland,

[3] *The Office of the Church in Higher Catholic Education* (London, Easter 1885).
[4] Ibid.

in the United States, and in Belgium and France. He hinted that sooner or later England would do well to follow the pattern of continental Catholicism and establish a Catholic University.

There was, too, another factor which the Archbishop considered would arise if Catholics frequented Oxford and Cambridge: 'The priesthood of the Church in England will be for ever formed within the intellectual unity of the Catholic Church. If the Catholic laity of England should be formed not only out of that great intellectual unity, but tossed to and fro in the subtilties and ambiguities of modern mental science, the unity which is now the strength and solidity of the revived Church in England will be lost, and the heirloom of mutual trust which now binds us together will be forfeited.'

The Pastoral Letter of 1885 was the last great considered pronouncement of the patriarch of the Second Spring. His concept of Higher Education for English Catholics was in no sense a negative one. The prohibition against the ancient Universities has to be seen as but one facet of the much greater constructive project, the preparation of English Catholics for the formation of a Catholic University. Neither was the formation of such an institution an indication of a ghetto mentality. Catholics had a positive, constructive contribution to make to the development of nineteenth-century thought, and an institution, seen to be the living embodiment of a time-honoured tradition, and transcending merely national boundaries, had something to offer in enriching the life of the country. By following a pattern adopted by Catholics in Belgium, Germany, France, Canada, the United States, and Ireland, Manning noted that English Catholicism would be more united with continental Catholicism. Thus national prejudices would be overcome. To permit the dissipation of English Catholic effort would be to lose for ever the opportunity of establishing an English Louvain or Angers. Subsequent events have proved Manning right.

The reiteration of the papal prohibition in *Propaganda*'s letter of 30 January 1885, the restatement of the hierarchy's policy at the Low Week meeting of that year, the issue of the powerful Pastoral Letter of the Cardinal Archbishop, and similar warnings from the other prelates, presented a multiple crushing blow for Grissell and his associates. Fr. Ignatius Grant, S.J., wrote to Grissell from St. Mary's-on-the-Quay, Bristol, in some alarm: 'The secret is out. You will have read the Pastoral Letter of an Eminent Person by this time—as I suppose has read many a Catholic family throughout England. . . . We are just where we were.'[5] He thought it particularly unfortunate that the question had come up before the bishops again 'now at this very moment when in various places large accessions from Ritualistic Congregations are made to the Church'. Before the year was out a quarrel had arisen among the conspirators as to which of them had been responsible for forewarning Manning of the negotiations they were conducting in Rome. Grissell traced the leak to Alexander Wood. At the beginning of September 1885 he accused Wood directly of a breach of confidence. Wood replied with restrained indignation, admitting that news of the negotiations had reached Manning and the bishops on account of his own indiscretion. He had sent a copy of the report to be submitted to *Propaganda* to Gladstone: 'This copy it was my intention to mark "in private", and it can only have been given away by Mr. Gladstone in consequence of this having been inadvertently omitted by me, or his having failed to observe it.'[6] He conceded that 'Cardinal Manning is by this time acquainted with the contents.' Beyond the official circulation of the document he had also given copies to Prince Bandini and others in Rome. 'These were Catholics: but I did not draw the line there, as I wished to learn what Gladstone and Mr. Wayte would say to the prospect of a Catholic House in Oxford.' One further attempt to reopen the Oxford question had thus been inadvertently frustrated.

For the last ten years of Manning's life the editor of *The Month* was Fr. Richard F. Clarke, S.J., an M.A. of Trinity, Oxford, who thought somewhat differently from many of his fellow Jesuits on the University issue. In *The Month* for July, August, September, and October 1885, he contributed four lengthy articles on 'Catholics at the English Universities'. In the first of these he

---

5 Grissell Papers. Grant to Grissell, 17 May 1885.
6 Ibid. Wood to Grissell, 7 Sept. 1883.

declared 'we have purposely kept silence hitherto on the important subject of the residence of English Catholics at the Protestant Universities. In spite of the repeated expression of opinion on the part of authority, men who are thoroughly loyal imagined that there was some misunderstanding of the subject, and that it could not be said to have in any sense received an ultimate and definitive settlement.'[7] He felt that 'few indeed are those who have wandered in those classic groves and joined in that happy, careless, active, merry, varied life, without falling under the spell which seems to environ it.' But, he maintained, the change which had come over Oxford during the last thirty or forty years was not a change for the better. 'The abolition of tests, the admission of all forms of Dissent, Judaism, Paganism, tend to establish that sort of truce which men are almost compelled to make who differ in first principles. . . . There is a common consent to exclude religion from their life more and more, as it has been gradually edged out from their University training.' Hence he thought that '*a priori*, the University of Oxford must necessarily decline in morals, slowly but surely, and in point of fact it has declined, and is declining still'.

Sentiments of this nature were not particularly welcome to many Jesuits, and their expression came as something of a surprise to the bishops who were unaccustomed to looking for support to the columns of *The Month*. In August Fr. Clarke continued his analysis by considering 'the special dangers' for Catholics of residence at Oxford or Cambridge. He submitted that 'the question is not whether an University is needed for Catholics, but whether a Protestant University supplies the want, and whether the mischief it is likely to do to faith and morals does not far outbalance the modicum of supervision exercised by Proctors and College officers of discipline'.[8] After declaring that 'there is no profession in the world for which the Oxford or Cambridge degree is indispensable', he proceeded to examine the nature of the Philosophy teaching imparted at Oxford. The way in which this subject was taught had always been a major argument

[7] *The Month* (July 1885), pp. 345 seq.
[8] Ibid. (Aug. 1885), pp. 459 seq.

amongst Catholics against studying there. Clarke wrote that Philosophy at Oxford consisted merely of 'a general survey of the various schools of philosophy, from the early philosophy of Greece down to the latest theory of the present day'. He wrote:

The object to be aimed at is not to impart a solid knowledge of what is true as opposed to what is false, but to introduce the student to the thousand and one systems of philosophy which have been invented by the leading philosophers of the world. He has to enter as far as he can into the spirit of each, to understand his doctrines, to be able to give an intelligent appreciation of his teaching, to point out his weak and strong points. Aristotle, indeed, is professedly the basis of Oxford teaching, but anything like a thorough knowledge, even of the central principles of Aristotelianism, is rare, and 'the philosopher' (as St. Thomas calls him) is known to the large majority through one-sided exponents, and books and essays which show no real grasp of his teaching as a consistent whole.

He maintained, too, that it was impossible to teach history or to write it without bias. 'If the Popes were not the Vicars of Christ they were errant imposters, and however carefully the non-Catholic lecturer of history may gild over and veil the imposture he attributes to them, it still remains in his mind as the basis of the claim put forward by Rome.' Furthermore, few genuine social advantages were to be gained at Oxford: 'I do not believe that there are any solid advantages gained for after-life by the mere fact of residence, apart from the intellectual cultivation of the Honour School. It may be useful in some ways: it may teach a man to find his level, it may enable him to acquire certain useful accomplishments, it may gain for him many pleasant friendships. But the advantages are rather transient and superficial, and have many countervailing disadvantages and dangers.'

In September Clarke turned to the place a Catholic College would have at Oxford.

The end of all Catholic education is the avoidance of sin and the acquirement of supernatural virtue. From first to last it has in view the future life of man, and seeks to prepare him for that life. The end of Protestant education is the performance of one's duties in life, and the acquirement of such gifts and accomplishments, such knowledge and cultivation as may best enable the young to perform these duties with success. . . . The Protestant goes to the University to find Truth, the Catholic goes thither with Truth already in his possession.[9] [He did not believe that young Catholics would attend the Catholic College:] Take one who belongs to the upper class, whose object is to make friends for afterlife and mingle in the society of his equals. I imagine that he would be a little impatient of anything that tied him to the Catholic College. His friends and equals would be at Christ Church. . . . Their society would be far more congenial than that of the Catholic College, small and rather mixed as it would necessarily be. [He concluded that] we certainly must give up the idea of residence at Oxford and Cambridge, and the sooner we give it up the better for our chance of some efficient substitute for it as well as for our loyalty to the teaching authority.

Clarke's October article was concerned with examinations, and he advanced the plea that Catholics could strive to gain entry to the matriculation and degree examinations of Oxford or Cambridge on a non-resident basis. 'When non-resident Catholics have attained again and again the highest honours in the degree examinations, when they have competed successfully for scholarships and prizes, when they have passed with distinction and proved the excellencies of their education outside the precincts of the University, common justice and equity will compel the University authorities to confer upon them the degree without residence.'[10] Mixed examinations were to be tolerated but not mixed education.

Clarke's final article, advocating a resumption of the Catholic University College scheme, was to have appeared in the November issue. It was not published, following the reception of a number of unfavourable reports from Jesuit censors to whom the article had been sent in proof by the Provincial. The latter, Fr. E. Purbrick, S.J., took office in 1885 and soon made his authority felt. In the article Clarke referred to Ushaw and Stonyhurst as 'Public Schools for boys, not University Colleges for men', and

9 *The Month* (Sept. 1885), pp. 7 seq.
10 Ibid. (Oct. 1885), p. 161.

added that the very fact of a boy's having spent his early days in such an establishment made it unsuitable for the training of his manhood. 'Nor would this objection be altogether removed,' he declared, 'if the other Catholic Colleges were to mingle their students with those of Ushaw and Stonyhurst in a common course of University studies. Those boys who still remained at their own place of education would receive only a very partial benefit, and would regard those who came from outside as intruders.' The nature of the courses provided at Stonyhurst was spoken of disparagingly, and Clarke concluded that 'it would be cruel kindness to Stonyhurst or Ushaw to raise them to the dignity of University Colleges'. The two Colleges, in any case, were remote from the metropolis. Yet, he warned that Catholics did not want to see their Colleges robbed of their students 'for some institution elsewhere, which is far away and may prove of mushroom growth, destined it may be to linger on for a few years and then disappear altogether'. This statement, an obvious reference to Kensington, was a clear indication that Clarke was not about to advocate the rejuvenation of that particular institution. 'Our Catholic University College', he wrote, 'must have a separate existence of its own, unconnected with any existing institution. It must not be a mere continuation of the training of any of our present Colleges. It must be a University College, and nothing else.' The new College ought to grow up gradually from small beginnings, and bishops, priests, and laymen ought to combine in organizing it. Care should be taken, however, to see that it did not develop into an ecclesiastical college or one in which laymen were in a minority. Neither ought it to be simply for the rich and socially powerful. 'It must be a place of study suited to many classes of men, and those who are preparing themselves for many different professions . . . young men who look to the army, medicine, law, literature, diplomacy, as their future career.'

The proposed University College ought to be established not only with the permission of the Catholic Hierarchy, but under their sanction and with their full approval. Nay, more than this; it must be subject to the Bishops as its patrons. The Cardinal Archbishop should be its President: its Vice-Presidents, the members of the episcopal body at large. . . . I imagine that a Council of eight or ten members would be the most suitable number, and that they should consist chiefly of those who have the control of our various Catholic Colleges, with a certain admixture of practical men of business and representatives of the Catholic laity. . . . I should therefore propose that the Council should consist of two Secular Priests (one of them a Bishop or Arch-bishop, who should be Chairman), two Jesuits, and two Benedictines, and in addition to these, three laymen are to be invited by each of the three educational bodies contributing to the Council. This would give a Council of nine persons, to whom would be entrusted the drawing up of constitutions for the University College, the management of its funds, its relation to the already existing Universities, and all the thousand and one details which would have to be settled before it could come into existence. Whether they would form its permanent governing body or not would be a further question which need not be decided until the College was fairly started. . . .[11]

Clarke declared that such a College would be a Catholic *University* College, not only by reason of its teaching 'but because it is to unite under itself as a common centre various houses of study, which shall bear to the central body something of the same relation that the various colleges of Oxford and Cambridge bear to the University'. The Seculars, the Jesuits, and the Benedictines would each have 'a separate House or Hall of their own, where they shall train the youth placed under their care, each according to the usages and traditions of the body to which they belong'. Professors would belong to the central authority, not to the various houses, and all students, regardless of the house to which they belonged, would attend the same course of lectures. Fr. Clarke turned his attention to a possible site for the projected institution: 'Maidenhead and Taplow, Maple-durham and Pangbourne, Goring and Marlow, and other towns and villages contiguous to them are free from all suspicion of too great a proximity to London and Oxford, and the long reaches of the Thames which stretch away from one and another of them would

[11] Farm Street Archives. Unpublished manuscript of Fr. Clarke's article for *The Month* (Nov. 1885), entitled 'Suggestions for the Foundation of a Catholic University College'.

favour alike the pursuit of manly exercise and the cultivation of a love and appreciation of the picturesque scenery which fringes the chief river of our land.' Finally, he called upon 'everyone who loves his religion to put his hand to the good work of building up a home for our Catholic youth'.

The article was examined by the Provincial. Purbrick not only disliked the line the editor of *The Month* had taken but he was concerned lest the final article should commit the Society in the event of there being a renewed attempt to establish a Catholic University College. His former connections with Stonyhurst did not make him view with equanimity critical references to that institution. Purbrick selected the unusually large number of seven Jesuits to act as censors for the article.

The reports of the censors form an interesting cross-section of Jesuit opinion. One of those who gave his views was the taciturn Fr. William Eyre. He had been on the staff of Farm Street in the sixties and had subsequently been Rector of Stonyhurst. Writing from St. Beuno's College in North Wales, he looked upon Fr. Clarke's article 'as a pretty dream, described in pleasing language', adding 'I shall be much surprised if, after our fiascos in the matter of the Irish University, and Mgr. Capel's University College in London, the Catholic body will find the sinews of war for this fresh experiment'.[12] He was not convinced by Clarke's arguments and wrote: 'If the plan ever does get from paper into stone or brick, it will be amusing to see how a Catholic University College will hang together, in which two secular priests, two or three lay Professors, one monk of St. Benedict's Order and two Jesuits, are to constitute the staff. I much fear that in the course of a generation we should have a new version of an old story, told in a very lively style, and adding some additional volumes to a certain department of Catholic literature.' Fr. F. Smith wrote from St. Beuno's that 'if the article were to be taken by itself, I should recommend its suppression, as raising too many burning questions and likely to give offence'.[13] He argued: 'Suppose at some future time the Bishops were to take up again the Kensington scheme would

---

[12] Farm Street Archives. Fr. W. Eyre, S.J., to the Provincial, 10 Oct. 1885.
[13] Ibid. Fr. F. Smith, S.J., to the Provincial, 10 Oct. 1885.

they not have a strong point in their hands with which to press us to shut up the Stonyhurst Higher Studies by appealing to the arguments on this page of our organ?' In Clarke's reference to the fact that the Colleges did not want to see themselves robbed of their students, Smith pointed out 'the Bishops will see here an allusion to Kensington of an unpleasant nature and may also find in it confirmation of their belief that the institution was ruined by our egotism'. The Rector of St. Beuno's agreed with Fr. Smith that the article compromised the Society, although he felt some proposals ought to be made, considering the promises held out in the articles that had already appeared. There was considerable difficulty in knowing what should be done:

I fear that no protest by the writer that he speaks for himself alone would be of much avail, so prevalent is the belief that all Jesuits agree about all things. The scheme seems essentially to involve some co-operation from the very first, however modest the beginnings might be: or otherwise it would seem that all that is wanted is for someone to set up a College of Higher Studies, and wait until its success induced the Jesuits to set up similar houses in his neighbourhood. Perhaps Fr. Clarke would not be content to point out that parents are not obliged to send their boys for Higher Studies to the same place where he made his Lower Studies: that they generally do so seems to show that the evils pointed out in the Article are not generally recognised as very serious. If he could point this out he might present two alternatives: either let Ushaw boys be sent to Stonyhurst and vice versa, if parents so please, the authorities of the Colleges giving fair consideration to the idea of taking up Oxford examinations in place of London; or let some one try the experiment of establishing a new place, which by its superior excellence will drain the existing institutions.[14]

Fr. Reginald Colley, who was himself to be the Jesuit Provincial from 1901 to 1904, wrote from Stonyhurst to say:

I do not feel any great dislike to Fr. Clarke's ideas: I agree with most of them—but what I cannot bring myself to believe is their feasibility. The advantage of having some sort of course of higher studies here [at Stonyhurst] seems to me to be the support the infant gets from the life and resources of the whole establishment—lectures at St. Mary's—

---

[14] Ibid. Rector of St. Beuno's to Jesuit Provincial, 10 Oct. 1885.

games, literary, museum—share in professors, large community for the professors, etc.[15]

He wrote again the following day:

> Will Catholics try again after the Kensington failure? What possibility is there of union? Supposing these difficulties got over, will any be content to make the modest start proposed? . . . There would be a poor staff, little in the way of books and scientific appliances—and above all, where are amusements to come from, cricket, football, etc.? In other words, the old Colleges are much more of that centre which Fr. Clarke asks for than the new institution would be. But I suppose all this is rather beside the question your Reverence proposes. The proposition seems to me so impracticable that I do not think its publication can do either good or harm: it is a Utopia, which we should be glad to see realized if it were possible. Perhaps it is not so unpractical as I think: in that case it would certainly be well to set the ball rolling. And even if not within reach, talking over it would not do much harm beyond perhaps turning us aside from making the best of what we have.[16]

Fr. John Gerard was to succeed Clarke as editor of *The Month* in 1893, and four years later was to be Provincial. He thought that from the point of view of the schools a separation from the Higher Studies would do more good than harm; from the point of view of Higher Studies themselves he did not think there was a great desire for university degrees, or that Catholics could provide an adequate staff of professors for a University College. But if the establishment of such a College as projected by Clarke was to lead to an increased desire for degrees, then 'the scheme has much to recommend it.'[17] On the other hand, the real difficulty was the fact 'that we have not lay Catholics enough to work on for purposes of education to do anything with success on a large scale'.

Fr. S. J. Hunter thought the publication of Clarke's article

would go far to pledge the Society to undertake the part that is assigned to it: this is, to refuse to take men for Higher Studies at Stonyhurst, and

---

[15] Farm Street Archives. Fr. R. Colley, S.J., to the Jesuit Provincial, 10 Oct. 1885.
[16] Ibid. Fr. R. Colley, S.J., to the Jesuit Provincial, 11 Oct. 1885.
[17] Ibid. Fr. J. Gerard, S.J., to the Jesuit Provincial, n.d.

to send some at least of our Juniors and Logicians to the new establishment. I cannot suppose that there is any intention to commit the Society to so serious a change; and although the publication would not technically bind Superiors, yet they would be hampered by the risk of odium, if they disappointed expectations that had in fact been raised, and threw overboard a member of the Society whose judgment on the subject would carry weight. On its merits, the scheme seems to be a repetition of the Kensington attempt, and would not be likely to have more success. The chief difference seems to be in the distance from London, and this would add much to the difficulty of securing efficient teaching.[18]

The Rickabys, John and Joseph, were representatives of the traditional Catholicism of Yorkshire among the members of the Society, and Fr. Joseph Rickaby was to be, perhaps, the most outstanding Jesuit scholar and literary figure since the restoration of the hierarchy. Of all those consulted concerning Fr. Clarke's article, Joseph Rickaby was the only one who showed enthusiasm. He wrote from St. Mary's Hall:

I have read the proof of Fr. Clarke's article for the November *Month*. I am delighted with it, and hope to see it appear as it stands. That we cannot combine school and University, neither at Stonyhurst, nor anywhere else,—that we need an University College in the South— that this University College must start small and 'grow' gradually—all this I have felt and held strongly for years. I think Fr. Clarke succeeds in showing that his plan would not deplete Stonyhurst either of boys or philosophers. . . . At the same time, I suppose the schools would have to be magnanimous enough to decline to prepare students for the degree. (I don't count St. Mary's Hall as a school, though if our own B.A. and B.Sc. could live as Religious and study in this College in the South, it were a good thing.) As for the actual place that Fr. Clarke proposes, I think it essential to begin on a small scale, not as Kensington came forth like Athena from the head of Zeus. But then the difficulty is: who will consent to be experimented upon and become students at a small institution? Stonyhurst is far more attractive than that. I suppose we must begin small and good, and be as attractive as possible in a small way.[19]

[18] Ibid. Fr. S. J. Hunter, S.J., to the Jesuit Provincial, 10 Oct. 1885.
[19] Ibid. Fr. Joseph Rickaby, S.J., to the Jesuit Provincial, 10 Oct. 1885.

Permission was not given for the article to appear, and the laity were left with the impression that the only suggestion *The Month* could offer was to work for admission to the degrees of Oxford and Cambridge without residence. If the Jesuits had shown the courage necessary to give Fr. Clarke his head, the article appearing so shortly after the renewed papal and episcopal prohibitions would have constituted a powerful argument for reopening discussions along the lines indicated. It might also have paved the way for a *rapprochement* between the Society of Jesus and the Bishops, and led to talks or perhaps joint enterprise. But if it did none of these things, it would certainly have renewed public debate, and shown once again that a considerable body of Catholics were prepared to work towards the establishment of a Catholic University College away from Oxford. As it was, Fr. Clarke had to content himself with proposing a dull and unsatisfactory scheme which appealed to nobody, and with a justification of the studies undertaken at Kensington after the latter had ceased to be the Catholic University College *per se*.[20]

The last years of Manning's episcopate were not seriously troubled with any open revival of the Oxford agitation. Grissell at Oxford and Baron Anatole von Hugel at Cambridge were quietly gathering support for their schemes, and awaiting opportunity: a new incumbent of the see of Westminster might prove more amenable to a change in ecclesiastical policy. Before that event took place the initiative was to be concentrated more and more in Cambridge rather than in Oxford, and by 1903 it was Anatole von Hugel rather than Grissell who was looked to as the leader of the party working for the removal of the Roman prohibition. The movement was given an added impetus by the fact that the permission of the Bishop of Southwark, John Butt, was secured for the nephew of the Duke of Norfolk, James Hope, later Lord Rankeillour, to attend Oxford, and by Grissell's formation at Oxford in 1888 of the Newman Society for Catholic undergraduates.

In 1888 the literary organ of Oscott College, *The Oscotian*, was piously wishing 'to each College its own praise, and may their

[20] See also the letter in *The Tablet*, 28 Aug. 1880.

tributary streams soon combine in one current, which shall bear us to the haven of our hopes—a Catholic University!'[21] A year later Grissell was writing to the Duke of Norfolk in alarm, because he had learnt that 'the Jesuits were trying to get some scheme of theirs in connection with Stonyhurst approved by Propaganda'.[22] He reported that 'it is quite certain also that they [the Jesuits] are not so interested in Oxford as they were some few years since', and he added: 'I do think one ought to try and find out what is really going on at Rome in the matter.'[23] Manning was reported to be much vexed that the subject had been aired yet again; Norfolk was doubtful about Grissell's information. And so the affair rumbled on, punctuated by intrigue, gossip, and suspicion until 1892. The Old Man of Westminster could not live for ever, and the dreams of the conspirators were all centred on Hedley, whom they hoped would succeed to the Archbishopric. In 1892 Vaughan of Salford was in his sixtieth year, and it was known that he had neither taste nor appetite for the Metropolitan office. As Manning had for years made it obvious that he hoped Vaughan would follow him, it was felt that this alone would prevent the succession of the Bishop of Salford. The only other possible candidate, von Hugel felt, was Hedley, and he was actively committed to the plans of Grissell and his associates.

Manning died from an acute attack of bronchitis on 14 January 1892, in his eighty-fourth year, seventeen months after the death of Newman. An epoch had ended. If his passing was not particularly mourned by the small group of which Grissell and his friends were members, he was genuinely missed by the poor, by the Irish, by the labouring men. And not only by these people! As Herman Ausubel has recently shown, poets such as Lionel Johnson and Aubrey de Vere, politicians such as Chamberlain and Gladstone, social reformers such as Henry George and W. T. Stead had all felt the benefit of his interest, advice, and sympathy.[24]

[21] *The Oscotian* (1888), p. 158.

[22] Grissell Papers. Grissell to Norfolk, 5 Nov. 1889.

[23] Ibid. See also Grissell Papers, Norfolk's letter to his nephew, James Hope, of 3 Nov. 1889.

[24] Ausubel, Herman, *In Hard Times: Reformers among the Late Victorians*, p. 124.

Wherever he discovered compassion for others he felt a need to reciprocate. Perhaps two quotations from widely differing sources illustrate these qualities. W. H. Mallock relates in his *Memoirs* that on a visit to Manning

we spent most of the morning discussing the ultimate difficulties, philosophical, historical and scientific, which preclude the modern mind from an assent to the philosophy of Catholicism. He displayed on this occasion a broadness and a balance, if not a profundity of thought, in which many theologians who call themselves liberals are wanting. He spoke even of militant atheists such as Huxley and Tyndal [*sic*] without any sarcastic anger or signs of moral reprobation. He spoke of their opinions, not as sins which demanded chastisement, but simply as intellectual errors which must be cured by intellectual refutation rather than by moral anathemas; and the personal relations subsisting between him and them were relations—so I have always understood—of mutual amity and respect.[25]

The other quotation is from a letter of a stevedore in *The Weekly Register*:

I went to see Cardinal Manning at eight o'clock and I must say there seems to be a kind of magnetic attraction attached to His Eminence for I could have sat with him all night talking. . . . One hour and a quarter we were in conversation.[26]

It was the quality of adaptability, of being all things to all men, that made Manning influential in the Late Victorian period, and enabled him to lead, slowly but surely, his ill-assorted and troublesome spiritual family from the sacristy into the light of the modern world.

[25] Mallock, W. H., *Memoirs*, p. 100.
[26] *The Weekly Register*, 27 Feb. 1892.

Part Five

THE REMOVAL OF THE BAN
AND THE COLONIZATION
OF THE
ENGLISH UNIVERSITIES

I

CLASSES, COTERIES, AND
FAMILY ALLIANCES

FRIEDRICH and Anatole von Hugel, sons of a distinguished Austrian diplomat, were high-souled, and high-ambitioned. They married into influential and wealthy Catholic families. Friedrich's wife was the daughter of Sidney Herbert, who had died in 1861, and of Lady Herbert of Lea. The latter, converted to Roman Catholicism in 1865, was brought into contact with Archbishop Manning largely as a result of her friendship with Florence Nightingale, one of Manning's favoured correspondents. With Herbert Vaughan Lady Herbert developed special friendship. The letters which passed between them show that Vaughan regarded her as his spiritual mother. She was the chief benefactress of Vaughan's Society for Foreign Missions, established at Mill Hill, and she aided him in many of his literary ventures. Lady Herbert's daughter, Mary, had followed her mother into the Roman Catholic Church, and Friedrich von Hugel, after his marriage to Mary, found himself at the very centre of Catholic ecclesiastical affairs.

Anatole von Hugel married Isy, daughter of William Froude the engineer, and niece of the historian James Anthony Froude and of Newman's disciple, Richard Hurrell Froude. Anatole's mother-in-law was one of Newman's converts and she idolized the Oratorian. On account of his marriage, therefore, and later as a result of his position as Director of the Museum of Archaeology and Ethnology in Cambridge, Anatole was drawn into a circle of English Catholic aristocratic life somewhat different from that in which his elder brother found himself placed. Isy, we are told, was devoted to Newman 'from her childhood',[1] and she 'kept Newman in touch with the affairs of Catholics in the University

[1] Trevor, *Light in Winter*, p. 237.

Town'.² Anatole, after his first meeting with Newman, mused 'it makes one feel how it is worthwhile to be a saint'.³ Friedrich, on the other hand, found Newman 'depressing' and 'easily affected by the pricks which at the end even flies seemed to give him'.⁴ He noted a cruel streak in the Oratorian, and pointed out to Maude Petre that he did not like 'Newman's pulverization of Kingsley in the personal parts of the *Apologia*'.⁵ Newman was, in his final judgment, 'a great cedar under which very few can shelter'.⁶ In Manning, however, Friedrich failed to see the hardness which Anatole found painful. While not uncritical of a number of Manning's social policies and public attitudes, he yet discerned deep spiritual qualities. 'How often I have been abashed and melted', he wrote, 'by the casual discovery of endless patience, tireless self-oblivion, exercised by him hiddenly, without a shadow of pretence, towards lonely, battered, and often recalcitrant and provocative souls.'⁷

With the advent of Herbert Vaughan to the see of Westminster, in April 1892, it is not surprising to discover that Anatole von Hugel rapidly became the leading figure among those Catholics pressing for a new episcopal policy towards the ancient Universities. There was considerable hope that a change would be possible. Unlike Manning, Vaughan was a cradle Catholic with no first-hand experience of the Universities. He was a member of an Old Catholic family. Above all, he could be influenced, it was thought, by Mary von Hugel. It was with a view to exploiting this situation that Wilfrid Ward and the Duke of Norfolk contacted Friedrich von Hugel in 1894, urging him to join with his brother and their friends in pressing Vaughan for a change.⁸ Their plea was successful in enlisting Friedrich's sympathy, although, unlike Anatole, he was never personally active in the campaign. Vaughan, sixty years of age, was a somewhat tired man when he assumed Metropolitan authority. He had carried the burdens of the day and had won his golden opinions. He

---

² Trevor, *Light in Winter*, p. 633.   ³ Ibid.
⁴ De la Bedoyère, *The Life of Baron von Hugel*, p. 32.   ⁵ Ibid.
⁶ Ibid.   ⁷ Ibid., p. 62.
⁸ Ibid., p. 81. Friedrich von Hugel to Wilfrid Ward, 20 July 1894.

had hoped that Rome would have selected a younger man as Manning's successor, and his appointment was made contrary to his personal desire. The years from 1892 to 1903, during which Vaughan ruled the major Catholic see, were to witness protracted struggles over the dual system in education, culminating in the Education Acts of 1897 and 1902, internecine strife resulting from an attempt to centralize seminary education, difficulties consequent upon the foundation of the Crusade of Rescue, controversy concerning the validity of Anglican Orders, resulting in the issue of the Bull *Apostolicae Curae* in 1896, problems connected with the establishment of the Catholic Truth Society, the Converts' Aid Society, and the Catholic Social Union, and a bitter quarrel with Downside concerning the singing of Divine Office in the new Cathedral of Westminster. The rule of Cardinal Vaughan at Westminster can thus be said to have been a great transitional one in the history of the Roman Church in England. It was to continue that work of reconstruction not fully completed at the death of Manning, and to prepare for the years of quiet consolidation which were to ensue in the thirty-year reign of Vaughan's successor, Francis Bourne.

The first major problem confronting the new Archbishop was the University question. Bishop Gordon Wheeler has seen in Vaughan's attitude a simple change of heart, a realization that 'the experience of thirty years had shown that Oxford and Cambridge did not present to well-trained Catholic young men the proximate occasions to the loss of faith and morals which were the grounds of objection laid down by the Holy See.'[9] Fr. McCormack has gone further in a recent biography of Vaughan, writing of an admission that 'for a quarter of a century he had been fighting the inevitable and helping to commit the Church to a short-sighted and futile policy'.[10] In an article in *The Dublin Review* McCormack declared that Vaughan, 'on coming to Westminster . . . was prepared to open up the whole matter with an unbiased mind because circumstances had changed and also

[9] Wheeler, Gordon, 'The Archdiocese of Westminster', in Beck, G. A. (ed.), *The English Catholics, 1850–1950*, p. 167.
[10] McCormack, Arthur, *Cardinal Vaughan*, p. 264.

because there was such strong feeling among lay Catholics in England that the prohibition was harmful and out of date'.[11] Such statements as these attribute to Vaughan a perspicacity which history shows he did not possess.

Vaughan's first reaction in 1893 was to rally the bishops in an effort to establish a Catholic University. He immediately consulted Bishop Hedley on the issue.[12] The reason for the precipitancy was a realization that forces were gathering for yet another assault upon ecclesiastical policy. He even contemplated immediately asking Rome 'to promulgate further mandates of exclusion',[13] as we glean from Wilfrid Ward's correspondence with Anatole von Hugel. Ward urged von Hugel to act in concert with the Duke of Norfolk in June 1894, 'in order to prevent the Cardinal getting a stringent decree which might be quite fatal'.[14] In 1893, however, Vaughan saw his worst fears assuming substantial shape in the mooting of two plans. The first concerned the organization of a summer school for Catholic teachers in an Oxford College, and it had the approval of Bishop Ilsley of Birmingham. Vaughan saw a subtle move to implicate the bishops in an Oxford project. He declared that such a plan would help to foster 'mixed education and the frequentation of non-Catholic universities by Catholic youth'.[15] The organizers of the summer school were, for the large part, Oxford men, and Vaughan's dramatic and personal intervention in 1894 led to the abandonment of the project. But Vaughan had shown his hand too early, and in using a sledgehammer to crack a walnut had made a tactical error. He had ruffled episcopal feelings and antagonized the Bishop of Birmingham.[16] Furthermore, neither the influential laity when he sounded

[11] *The Dublin Review*, v. 239, no. 506 (1965–6), p. 330.

[12] For details of this see Wilson, J. Anselm, pp. 239–40. See also the articles 'Joy in Harvest' by Mgr. William Barry, and 'The Catholic Church and Education', in *Catholic Emancipation, 1829–1929: Essays by Various Writers*, pp. 17–18, 72–3.

[13] Anatole von Hugel Papers, Fisher House, Cambridge. Wilfrid Ward to A. von Hugel, 18 June 1894, letter marked 'private'.

[14] Ibid. Wilfrid Ward to A von Hugel, n.d. [1894]. (Sometime—probably a few days—after 18 June.)

[15] See H. O. Evennett's article in Beck, G. A. (ed.), p. 307.

[16] See the account of the incident in *The Month* (Mar. 1933), and *The Tablet*, 26 May and 9 June 1894.

them, nor the bishops, were enthusiastic about another attempt to resuscitate the Kensington College or to establish a new foundation on similar lines.

The second event in 1893 which alarmed Vaughan was of greater significance than the plan for an Oxford summer school. Anatole von Hugel was determined to present an address and a gift from the Catholics in residence at Cambridge University to Pope Leo XIII, on the occasion of the Pontiff's episcopal jubilee. He intended to make the presentation in February 1893, fully attired in Cambridge academicals. Mindful of the family's friendship with Vaughan, von Hugel wished to acquaint the Archbishop of his intentions. Accordingly, he went to see Vaughan who was himself in Rome for the Jubilee. Von Hugel tells the story:

So I went to Cardinal Vaughan who was our Ecclesiastical Chief, and I began to feel a little qualm as I went along, knowing he knew nothing about the University. It was about 10 o'clock at night. He was most affectionately kind to me personally. He asked, 'What is it about?' I said, 'I have two or three questions to ask you.' I think I said 'Cambridge' or 'the University'; before I had finished the word he was up on his legs walking round and round in a fearful state of mind. I said, 'I am only asking you two questions', 'Stop a moment, stop a moment', he said; and he said 'You know what I think of you being at a University. Of course, it is allowable for you; but I am sorry, but I am sorry.' What is it?' I said, 'I have a gift for the Holy Father from the undergraduates and an Address.' 'An Address! What about?' . . . 'A book.' 'I would rather not look at it.' I said, 'I went into this thing nicely'— and things to this effect. So at last I showed him this Address. He would not read it. He said, 'Who did it?' I said: 'I had very little time and I had forgotten.' . . . He said, 'Who has looked at it?' I said, 'Bishop Hedley. I am no scholar. He had added one or two words. He said I should take it to one or two of my friends in Cambridge. So I took it to Henry Jackson, who helped me.' And I said, 'Your Eminence, of course, I have brought my gown and hood.' . . . I asked him how I was to set about it. He said, 'I will have nothing to do with it. You know how I feel about it.' The upshot was: 'You just ask Cardinal X. He knows all about it. You take it and ask him'. And I said: 'May I mention your name?' 'Yes.' I felt it was not very satisfactory; so I went back and said, 'Do put yourself into my position. It is very unpleasant to make a fool of myself.' He said: Don't talk like that to me!' I said 'I am very sorry, but can you dictate to me how I am to talk to him?' So then he laughed. He suddenly got up and he said, 'Look here. Do whatever Cardinal X says about the book. When your turn comes, kneel in front of the Holy Father, hold it—that sort of way—, but not a word.' I said: 'I beg your pardon. I do not understand.' He said, 'I will speak'. At the audience the Cardinal stood by the Holy Father's side and was almost mum. The Pope was waiting for something more, but I said nothing. The next day, Cardinal X, who certainly in those days did not favour the idea of Universities, came to me and said, 'Never mind; you behaved very well.'[17]

It is obvious from this account that Vaughan was determined to prevent von Hugel from making any public appeal to the Pope on the University question, and, by his own presence at the time of the presentation of the gift from Cambridge, effectively precluded von Hugel from doing so. For von Hugel, however, the events of February 1893 were of especial significance, for they gave birth to a brilliant strategic plan. A strong petition containing the names of sympathetic priests and Religious, as well as the names of leading members of the Catholic aristocracy and those of former students of Oxford and Cambridge, would be drawn up. No mention of past episcopal policy would be made in critical vein nor would the petition contain any charge that the Roman prohibition was unjust. The petition would be based on the fact that the condition of the ancient Universities had changed radically, and that these institutions no longer constituted that threat to the faith and morals of English Catholics which had been the original cause of episcopal concern. Such a petition for a reopening of the question, containing no recriminations, could then be presented to Cardinal Vaughan, together with a request that he should place it before the Holy Father. Provided that a strong enough petition was drawn up, Vaughan could not refuse to transmit it to Rome, all proper ecclesiastical forms and etiquette having been adhered to. He could oppose the petition at Rome, but if so, he would clearly indicate a distinct cleavage between the aspirations of the influential laity and the policy of the episcopacy.

[17] Fisher House, Cambridge. Von Hugel Papers.

Furthermore, the bishops themselves were divided on the issue. If Vaughan were to take no action at all, the laity would probably succeed with their cause at Rome. The Duke of Norfolk assumed the initiative, so much so that von Hugel feared matters might be unduly rushed. The Baron wrote to Wilfrid Ward, in July 1894, that he had hoped 'to let the thing simmer in my head a little',[18] and that he wished 'matters had gone differently and allowed the whole question to rest for a while longer, for it would have been nice if with time the Cardinal had been compelled by his own observation to modify his views'. However, he concluded, 'it's no use crying over spilt milk'. He promised to assist in securing necessary support for the petition.

The claim of the petitioners that the intellectual atmosphere of the Universities was now radically different from what it was in the 1870s and 1880s had substance in fact. Writing in *The Quarterly* in 1899, Wilfrid Ward pinpointed essential elements in the change: 'We are now witnessing a religious reaction. There is a strong tendency to fall back upon the old religious beliefs, and upon the old liturgies and formulae in which they were embodied —not indeed with the clear definite faith of early days, yet with a vague and undefined sense of their worth, and of the bareness and solitariness of an existence from which they are totally banished.'[19]

In the 1890s speculative philosophy was beginning to play an ever-decreasing role in the Oxford and Cambridge curriculum, and with this tendency much of the old argument of the corrupting influence of irresponsible theorizing was whittled away. Other factors had also to be considered. There was no longer the sharp differentiation between the various social classes of the Catholic community that had been so marked a feature of the sixties and seventies. The policy of Manning and his bishops in encouraging the growth of a strong Catholic middle class, and the way in which they had developed Catholic educational provision to meet that end, had begun to pay rich dividends. Archbishop

---

[18] Ibid. A. von Hugel to Wilfrid Ward, July (?) 1894, copy.
[19] Ward, W. 'The Ethics of Religious Conformity', in *The Quarterly Review* (Spring 1899), unsigned.

David Mathew has indicated the main constituents of this profound change:

> The professions had received a steadily increasing quota of Catholics, law and medicine attracted the sons of those clerical families which had entered the Church during the Oxford Movement; the industrial populations developed a definite commercial element and began to filter into clerical posts of responsibility in offices and banks; there began very slowly the accumulation of a Catholic element in the Civil Service. An influx from Ireland, not numerically large, but very constant, aided these changes. It was a very different condition from the earlier portion of the century when the few Catholic conveyancers were balanced by an occasional and respected physician like Sir Arnold Knight.[20]

The working classes, too, were experiencing better housing, better health, better education, and, thanks to their Irish priests, a greater understanding of their Faith. Thrift and ambition were not unknown in such circles, and it can truthfully be said that 'this generation among the workers had a profound reverence for the Mass; broad constant humour; vitality; a virile faith'.[21]

One of the factors which undoubtedly changed the social composition of the Catholic community was the development of the provincial University Colleges. In the thirty years following the accession of Manning to the see of Westminster in 1865 University institutions had been growing up in Manchester (since 1851), Newcastle (1871), Aberystwyth (1872), Leeds (1874), Bristol (1876), Sheffield (1879), Birmingham (1880), Liverpool (1881), Nottingham (1881), Cardiff (1883), Bangor (1884), and Reading (1892). Along with London and Durham, none of these institutions came under general ecclesiastical censure. By the time Vaughan took over in Westminster a steady trickle of Catholic youths was emerging from them to form the nucleus of a strong professional class.[22] This was a policy Manning had deliberately encouraged, and it was now producing the Catholic professional man, both competent and able to take his place alongside his

---

[20] Mathew, *Catholicism in England*, p. 236.   [21] Ibid., p. 237.

[22] A local prohibition against attendance at University College, Nottingham, was imposed, however, in 1882 by Bishop Bagshawe of Nottingham.

non-Catholic counterpart. The late Professor Philip Hughes testified to the effect of this policy. The growth of the provincial University Colleges not only 'increased the university population enormously', but more significantly it 'enlarged the social character of that population'.[23] The effect of the papal prohibition on the Universities of Oxford and Cambridge had been to weaken the hold of the aristocratic families and the landed gentry on the control of the Roman Catholic Church in England and to hand it over to the new growing professional classes, to the people at large.

Manning's policy had been infectious. Vaughan, when Bishop of Salford, had shown his own commitment to the ideals of professional education. Not only had he established St. Bede's College in Manchester as a great commercial central school but he had also opened in 1888 St. Bede's on the Rhine, a college established in Metternich's old palace at Bonn, to provide courses in German for his Lancashire boys. Similarly he encouraged Dr. L. C. Casartelli, the distinguished Orientalist who was Rector of St. Bede's, to prepare his boys for entry to the local University Colleges in preference to taking London external degree examinations.[24]

Vaughan saw the question of higher education as basically a class problem. 'It would be worse than folly to disguise the fact that one of the weaknesses of the Church in this country is the feebleness of the social tie by which Catholics are held together',[25] he declared in Sheffield in 1897. 'Our peoples, generally speaking, are divided into classes and coteries and avoid social intercourse with a caste-like rigidity', he observed. Higher education for the middle classes was to prove the social panacea. On 15 August 1897 Vaughan addressed a gathering of middle-class girls and urged them to take advantage of competitive examinations, for Catholics would have 'either to rise to the level of the rising waters, or to sink beneath them and disappear'.[26] His concern for middle-class

---

[23] *The Dublin Review* (Autumn 1939), p. 101.
[24] Beck, G. A. (ed.), p. 308, n. 18.   [25] *The Tablet* (Feb. 1897).
[26] Fitzgerald, Percy: *Fifty Years of Catholic Life and Social Progress*, vol. 2, pp. 396–7.

education led him to urge the Sisters of Notre Dame at Mount Pleasant, Liverpool, to bring their Training College into a closer relationship with University College, Liverpool. From December 1903 students from Mount Pleasant were permitted to attend University College, Liverpool, with a view to obtaining the Victoria University degree. The University soon granted formal associateship to the Training College.

The demand for higher education became more urgent as the close of the century drew near, and it was stimulated by the example of Catholics reaching positions of importance and honour for the first time since Emancipation. In 1894 Lord Russell of Killowen became the first Catholic since the time of James II to be appointed Lord Chief Justice of England. Vaughan's time at Westminster also saw the election of two Catholics to the office of Lord Mayor of London—Alderman de Keyser and Alderman Sir John Stuart Knill. The year 1894 saw Francis Fortescue Urquhart elected Fellow of Balliol College, Oxford, and the same University shortly afterwards conferred an honorary degree on Leo XIII's personal librarian, the celebrated Fr. Ehrle. Not many years later, in 1920, Friedrich von Hugel himself was to be honoured by Oxford with a D.D., *honoris causa*. Catholics at the turn of the century were to witness the emergence of a set of writers willing and able to lay the foundations of that Catholic literary scholarship, the absence of which had so disturbed Dr. Manning in 1864. The names of Canon Barry, Lafacdio Hearne, Frederick Rolfe (Baron Corvo), Robert Hugh Benson, Miss J. M. Stone, Mrs. Wilfrid Ward, James Britten, Lister Drummond, Mrs. Humphrey Ward, Francis Thompson, Coventry Patmore, and the Meynells, are alone sufficient to indicate the scope and intensity of that scholarship.

The chief question facing Cardinal Vaughan and the bishops in 1894, then, was whether or not the Catholic aristocracy were to be given the same opportunities to acquire a higher education as were becoming increasingly available to Catholics of the middle classes. To London and the provincial colleges they would not go. It was clear that individuals were able to get episcopal permission to attend the Universities much more easily than hitherto. We have seen that James Hope, the nephew of the Duke of Norfolk, was able to obtain leave from Bishop Butt of Southwark, and we are told that Vaughan was 'outraged' by the concession.[27] Anatole von Hugel relates an interesting story implicating the Holy Father himself in a disregard of the *Propaganda* ruling.

One of our undergraduates [he writes], went to Rome with his father and they had a private audience of the Holy Father, Leo XIII, and he began to talk to the father about the son. What was he going to do in life? The father said possibly diplomacy; that the boy had a rich and inquiring mind. If he could go to the University it would make a very great difference to his career. The Holy Father was very much for education of the right sort. He at once smiled on this youth, put his two hands on his head, blessed him, and hoped that he would be a credit to the University of Cambridge. This boy came to the University and the bishop of his diocese was absolutely rabid against it.[28]

Von Hugel adds that the Holy Father had completely forgotten the strict proviso, and he relates that he has preserved the story 'because it shows that the situation was of course absolutely ridiculous'.

By December 1894 von Hugel's task was at an end and the petition he had helped the Duke of Norfolk to organize was delivered to Cardinal Vaughan. There had been, however, a significant change of plan in the last few months. In June 1894 the Duke presided over a meeting of interested laity and proposed that, while the formal petition should be addressed to Rome, a memorandum containing the chief arguments of the petition should be addressed to the English hierarchy. This would leave the door open for the bishops to assume the initiative if they so desired. The idea met with considerable favour. The Hon. Everard Fielding and Sidney Parry (of Newman House) had been deputed to make the first draft of the petition and of the memorandum. Four hundred and forty-eight signatures were collected, including those of a number of priests and Religious. Initiating the list were the names of the heads of the chief Catholic families: the Duke of Norfolk, the Marquess of Bute, the Marquess of

---

[27] Beck, G. A. (ed.), p. 306.
[28] Fisher House, Cambridge. Von Hugel Papers.

Ripon, the Earl of Denbigh, Lord Clifford, and Lord Herries. They were followed closely by Lord Russell of Killowen (Lord Chief Justice), Admiral Walter Kerr, Anatole von Hugel, B. F. C. Costelloe, J. W. J. Glasson (Bursar of St. John's, Oxford), T. King (Fellow of Jesus, Cambridge), C. Kegan Paul, Richard Ward, and Wilfrid Ward.[29]

It was asserted at the outset of the memorandum that 'the liberty to attend the national Universities appears to us absolutely essential at the present time for the career of those Catholics who desire to take their part in the national life, whether in politics or in the great intellectual or social movements of the day'. Furthermore, there were signs that the Church 'may have, in our own day, an opportunity of influencing the educated English mind, such as she has not had in the course of the past three hundred years'. The petitioners acknowledged 'the great work which has been wrought by the many eminent men, old Catholics, who, from Cardinal Wiseman onward have borne the burden and the heat of the day in the task of rebuilding the Church in this country'. Yet they were not unmindful of the contribution made by the Oxford converts. 'Who will deny', they asked, 'that much of the respect for the Catholic Church which exists, is associated with such names as those of Manning, Coleridge, Monsell, Oakeley, Faber, Dalgairns, Morris, Ward, Hope-Scott, Allies, Wilberforce, and a large proportion of the hundreds of cultivated men whom the Oxford movement gave to the Church, and who have made their mark in almost every department of life?' They examined the objection to mixed education, accepting it in principle, while pleading for mitigations to the principle in the case of necessity:

Let us recall Pius IX's action in the case of the Falloux law[30] which Louis Veuillot opposed in the *Univers*. It was a compromise which

---

[29] A copy of the memorandum 'de libertate Universitates adeundi Catholicis Anglicis concedenda' is preserved in the Archives, Brompton Oratory, London. It is from this source that the extracts quoted are taken.

[30] The Loi Falloux was passed on 15 Mar. 1850, shortly after Louis Napoleon had dropped 'Falloux fallax' from the Cabinet. Education, henceforth, was to be organized into a 'dual system'—the State schools in the hands of the University, and the free or denominational schools which were ultimately to lead to the development of denominational university institutions.

secured for Catholic Professors a share in University teaching, but left the Universities, nevertheless, under the control of an infidel State. Veuillot opposed it on the very ground that it failed to realise the Church's principle of opposition to mixed education. But when it was passed, the French Hierarchy acquiesced in it, and Pius IX sent a special message to Montalembert to congratulate him in his share in passing the law. . . . Catholics in Germany, Austria, France, and Spain attend the national Universities without incurring censure. Many Catholics attend the State Universities in Belgium, although they have the alternative of a Catholic University already existing.[31]

The petitioners were on more shaky ground, in their efforts to convince the bishops of the need for change, when they asserted that 'even in the interest of a young man's faith, such an experience [of Oxford or Cambridge] at the age of nineteen or twenty may be the best means of gradually accustoming him to that intercourse with non-Catholics which is a necessity in after life. The possibility of choosing to some extent his own Catholic friends, and at the same time mixing freely with others, may give the desirable combination of Catholic fellowship with knowledge of the point of view of those who do not share his faith.' Baron Anatole von Hugel personally testified that 'many of our men have most favourably impressed their tutors; and their presence in the University has certainly helped to diminish the existing blindness in matters concerning the Church'. Canon Scott, the resident priest in Cambridge, claimed that the average number of Catholics in attendance at Cambridge was fifteen, and added 'whenever I have known anything unsatisfactory, this has been due to other influence than that of Cambridge. I know of no loss of faith. The proportion of those distinguished by their faith and piety and frequenting the Sacraments is, I believe, superior to what is said to be the general rule in the case of a similar number of young men living in the world under ordinary circumstances.'

Much was made of the argument that Oxford had undergone considerable change:

The present state of things in Oxford, is very different from what it was in 1864, when *Propaganda* first gave its attention to the subject. The

---

[31] Memorandum, Oratory Archives, London.

extraordinary wave of religious enthusiasm which passed over Oxford from 1833 to 1845, affecting not only those who joined the Oxford movement, but every school of thought in the University, gave place, as is well known, to a liberal reaction, which did for a time give to public opinion in Oxford something of a directly anti-religious character. . . . Since the reaction of the eighties, associated with the names of Thomas Hill Green, Canon Scott Holland, the late Mr. Aubrey Moore, Mr. Gore, and many others of equal mark, the state of things described by Mr. Pattison, and the other witness whom we have cited has quite passed away. . . . Individualism has superseded the tendency to corporate negation.

It was now possible to avoid dangerous elements in the academic curriculum:

As to the Schools, the one from which danger would be specially anticipated is the Classical Honour School, involving, as it does, a course of philosophy which might be dangerous, unless undertaken under such Catholic guidance as does not at present exist in the University. But it may be pointed out that Catholics need not choose this School. And at present it may be added, few of them have any temptation to choose it, as the classical course at Catholic schools has not hitherto been founded on the basis required at the Universities, and is, therefore, not a sufficient preparation for one desirous of taking high honours. The History Schools are not attended by such dangers in at all the same degree, the bias in the University being anything but anti-Catholic in this department. . . . Still less could danger be anticipated from the Law Schools, or the Schools of Science or Chemistry, or from the newly established English Literature School.

Snead-Cox in his biography of Vaughan informs us that by September 1894 the Cardinal was anxious for a compromise solution. He wrote to Hedley and enclosed a copy of the memorandum.[32] The hierarchy held a special meeting on 4 January 1895, and all the prelates were present, except Edmund Knight, Bishop of Shrewsbury. By a majority vote the bishops decided to petition the Holy See to the effect that attendance at Oxford and Cambridge might henceforth be tolerated, subject to adequate spiritual safeguards. The voting was close. Those in favour of

---

[32] Snead-Cox, J. G., vol. 2, pp. 81 seq.

tolerating attendance at the Universities were, in addition to the Cardinal, Edward Ilsley of Birmingham, John Cuthbert Hedley of Newport and Menevia, William Robert Brownlow of Clifton, Thomas Whiteside of Liverpool, William Vaughan of Plymouth, John Vertue of Portsmouth, and John Butt of Southwark. Brownlow was but recently appointed to Clifton—in May 1894— and was a former Anglican priest educated at Rugby and Trinity College, Cambridge. Whiteside, too, had been Bishop of Liverpool for only a short period, in his case less than five months. Vaughan of Plymouth was the Cardinal's uncle. Three of the prelates had not actively participated in the previous policy. The six bishops of the minority were Thomas W. Wilkinson of Hexham and Newcastle; William Gordon of Leeds; Richard Lacy of Middlesbrough; Arthur Riddell of Northampton; Edward G. Bagshawe of Nottingham; and John Bilsborrow, Bishop of Salford. If Knight had been fit to attend the meeting (he resigned his see in May 1895) he would most certainly have been numbered among the minority. Before the episcopal meeting was held, the minority bishops had been gathering forces to do battle. Bishop Gordon of Leeds wrote to Bishop Wilkinson in December 1894:

> I do hope that you will stand out against this pandering to the modern and worldly spirit. I would sooner cut off my right hand than help in the least degree to forward the Cardinal's scheme—Fancy our Colleges being turned into preparatory schools for these heretic and infidel making shops. Then again I cannot conceive how he can profess that we should contribute to a fund for the support of a Professor at Oxford. If the Bishops go in for this scheme I will have no hand in it. I would sooner resign than give a farthing to such a purpose. We want money for the poor Schools and we can't be called upon to give money to help aristocrats and snobs on the High Road to Hell. His Eminence is going to Rome and he will play pranks if we are not firm and united.[33]

Gordon had served for a number of years as Rector of Leeds Seminary before his elevation to the episcopacy, and was thoroughly opposed to Vaughan's plans for a central seminary based on Oscott. Wilkinson, a convert from the Church of

[33] Letter in Bishop Wilkinson's Papers, quoted in Milburn, p. 303 n. 17.

England, was a graduate of Durham and keen to foster a closer link between Ushaw and Durham University. He was a former President of Ushaw. Among the other minority bishops, Bilsborrow had also strong seminary antecedents, being for a time Rector of Upholland College, near Wigan. None of these bishops believed in the 'altered-circumstances' argument, and they resented Vaughan's later assertions that the Universities' question had been reopened by *Propaganda* at the request of the bishops, as if the prelates had been thoroughly united on the issue. They considered Vaughan had given way to the powerful pressure tactics of an exclusive social set. Their view of the influence exerted upon Vaughan was correct. When Vaughan saw Anatole von Hugel and told him that he would submit the lay petition to Rome, now that it had been endorsed by the act of the bishops, he added bitterly, 'it would be best if I took it and tore it and threw it in the fire'.[34]

In the reply of *Propaganda*, dated 17 April 1895, no mention was made of the lay petition, and the document confined itself to providing an answer to the episcopal resolutions of January. *Propaganda*'s letter, signed by the Jesuit Prefect of the Congregation, Cardinal Ledochowski, stated that the episcopal resolutions had been laid before the Congregation at the general meeting held on 26 March 1895, and that on 2 April 1895 the Pope had approved the decision of the Congregation.

The letter opened with a fervent wish that a Catholic University should be set up in England as soon as possible. As long as it was not practicable to reach that goal 'care must be taken to ensure that as far as possible Catholic youth should receive a more satisfactory higher education without detriment to faith and morals'.[35] After referring to the necessity of maintaining until now the prohibition against attendance at Oxford and Cambridge, the letter remarked that the English bishops had noticed that circumstances have changed perceptibly of late in the Universities,

---

[34] A. von Hugel Papers, private memo.

[35] Letter from the Prefect of the Congregation *de Propaganda Fide* to His Eminence Herbert, Cardinal Vaughan, Rome, 17 Apr. 1895. Copy preserved in the Farm Street Archives, from which these extracts are taken.

'and they have at the same time considered that an opportunity now offers itself for applying practical remedies so as to diminish the dangers which remain'. Hence the bishops had asked that 'the rigour of the present prohibition be moderated'. The Congregation had decided that the attendance of Catholic youths at the Universities of Oxford and Cambridge might be tolerated, subject to 'the conclusions and precautions recently proposed by the Bishops of England for the removal of the danger of lapsing from the Faith'. Among the precautions 'first importance should be attached to the requirement that regular courses of lectures on philosophical, historical, and religious subjects should be given to Catholic students by Catholic professors, with such exhaustiveness and soundness that the minds of the young men may be effectively fortified against errors'. The Congregation ordered a special committee to be set up, consisting of certain bishops, priests, and distinguished laymen, whose task it would be to collect money for the paying of stipends to these professors, and which would deal with other financial obligations. The proviso was added, however, that 'all the deliberations of a committee of this kind should be submitted for examination by the bishops, and they should not be put into practice before they are approved by them'. Catholic parents were to be warned: 'they should beware of sending their sons to be taught at the Universities without their having been instructed with a solid Catholic education and an accurate knowledge of their religion. And if a young man seems to be at all of unstable character and is not sufficiently protected against these dangers, Catholic parents should not allow him to go to Protestant Universities.' Finally, it was directed that 'Catholic young men who will frequent the Protestant Universities referred to should be required in every possible way to attend the lectures regularly which will be given in accordance with their needs as mentioned above'. Parents and bishops alike were urged to watch over this requirement 'with equal care'.

The Rescript from *Propaganda* arrived in England in time for the bishops to consider it at the annual Low Week meeting of the hierarchy. The decision had arrived much earlier than expected, and it was a sign of the anxiety of the bishops that no young man should enter the ancient Universities until adequate spiritual aids were awaiting him there, that they at once set about nominating a Council of fifteen persons to implement the directives of Rome. The Cardinal was authorized to approach those selected to serve on the Council. One of them was the old campaigner, Fr. E. Purbrick. Writing to Purbrick on 29 April 1895 Vaughan declared: 'It is proposed to call the first meeting at Archbishop's House on June 18th, when I shall briefly lay before the Council the functions which we hope it will undertake to discharge. I may mention that the persons nominated on the Council consist of 8 Ecclesiastics of whom 2 are Bishops, and of 7 Laymen.'[36] The bishops nominated were those most anxious for the change in policy—Hedley and Brownlow. Of the six clerics who agreed to serve, only one was a diocesan priest, nominated by Cardinal Vaughan as his personal representative, Canon (later Monsignor) Moyes. He was Theologian of the Westminster Chapter, and from 1892 until 1906 editor of *The Dublin Review*. There were two Jesuits, Purbrick and Fr. John Gerard; a Benedictine, Dom Aidan Gasquet of Downside; a Redemptorist, Fr. Thomas Bridgett, who was formerly a student of St. John's College, Cambridge. The clerical complement was made up by the addition of Fr. John Norris of the Birmingham Oratory. The seven lay members were the Duke of Norfolk, the Marquess of Bute, Lord Braye, Baron Anatole von Hugel, Wilfrid Ward, Charles Stanton Devas, and James F. Hope.

The document announcing *Propaganda*'s decision to the faithful was not issued until 1 August 1896, after the Council had met five times. The letter was signed by Cardinal Vaughan and all the bishops, including the recently appointed Vicar Apostolic of Wales, Francis Mostyn. It recounted the history surrounding the reopening of the Universities' question, and stated disingenuously 'the leading members of the Catholic laity, on learning that the question had been re-opened by the hierarchy, addressed to the Bishops a Memorial, which was laid by the Cardinal Archbishop before the Holy See at the same time that he presented the

[36] Farm Street Archives, London. Herbert, Cardinal Vaughan to Revd. E. Purbrick, S.J., 29 Apr. 1895.

Petition of the Bishops'.[37] The bishops went on to give details of *Propaganda*'s decision and the conditions under which the proposed toleration was to be permitted. It re-emphasized the desire of the Holy See 'that there should be a Catholic University in England', and proceeded to specify the precautionary measures which were to be undertaken. 'Although the greater part of our Catholic people will have no direct interest in University Education,' the document reads, 'yet there is amongst us a considerable class, who, whether or not they have sons at Oxford or Cambridge, will feel that, as Catholics and as members of a great country, they are deeply concerned in securing for the coming generations of Catholics the highest form of culture and the best safeguards for their faith.' The letter ended on a cautionary note:

From what has been said, however, it must not be inferred that we offer even a general encouragement to all who can afford it, to frequent the national Universities. Far from it. As we have already intimated, none should be permitted to go thither but such as have been thoroughly prepared to meet the ordeal, and are willing to conform to the conditions laid down. It will be an evil day for the Catholic community when its members make light of the dangers which beset education given in a non-Catholic atmosphere.

[37] Brompton Oratory Archives, London. *Instruction to the Parents, Superiors, and Directors of Catholic Laymen who Desire to Study in the Universities of Oxford and Cambridge by the Cardinal Archbishop and Bishops of the Province of Westminster* (1896).

II

FULFILLING THE DIRECTIVES
OF 'PROPAGANDA'

A T the first meeting of the newly created Council on 18 June 1895 it was agreed to adopt the name 'Universities' Catholic Education Board', and that a number of men with first-hand knowledge of Oxford and Cambridge should be asked to advise on ways of carrying out the Holy See's directives. Six with strong Oxford connections were selected: Mgr. Croke Robinson, Fellow of New College; the Revds. W. Strappini and J. Nicholson, S.J., of the parish of St. Aloysius, Oxford; W. J. W. Glasson, Bursar of St. John's College; F. F. Urquhart of Balliol College; and Ralph Kerr, undergraduate of Christ Church. From Cambridge there were Canon Scott, Vicar General of the Northampton Diocese and Rector of the parish of Our Lady and the English Martyrs, Cambridge; Thomas King, Fellow of Jesus College; E. Wyatt Davies, of Trinity College; and Charles Cave, also of Trinity.

A week later the second meeting was held, at which it was arranged to set up a special subcommittee 'to investigate the feasibility and desirability of establishing at Oxford or at Cambridge, or at both, a house of resident priests with a view to further the spiritual interests of Catholic members of the Universities'. Bishop Hedley was to be Chairman of the subcommittee, whose members were to be the Duke of Norfolk, Fr. John Gerard, S.J., Baron Anatole von Hugel, and James Hope. They reported on 14 November 1895, and the Board resolved 'to establish at Oxford a house distinct from the existing Mission, with at least one resident priest paid by the Board'. The priest or priests, 'as provided by the letter of the Cardinal Prefect of Propaganda', were to be nominated by the Board and were to be responsible to it. It was also resolved 'that such priest or priests give at least one religious, historical, or catechetical lecture during each term time', and that 'the house be entirely disconnected from parish and missionary work'.

By 15 January 1896 the bishops had approved the steps taken, and the Board had purchased a house (36 Beaumont Street, Oxford) on a sub-lease for seven years at a rent of £90 per annum. Canon Moyes, James Hope, and Wilfrid Ward were appointed to draw up a list 'of such ecclesiastics as might be asked to undertake the duties of "chaplain" at Oxford', and it was intended 'that for the present, there should be appointed at Oxford one resident priest (hereinafter to be designated Chaplain) at a stipend of £200 a year, exclusive of house rent, rates, taxes, repairs, and chapel maintenance'.[1]

In regard to Cambridge, however, things did not run so smoothly. There were three reasons for this: the intransigence of Bishop Riddell of Northampton, who was opposed to the entire policy; the determination of Bishop Hedley to persuade Riddell to make over the parish of Cambridge to the Benedictines; and the efforts of Anatole von Hugel to acquire the services of the latter for the Cambridge undergraduates.

Anatole von Hugel and Bishop Hedley first approached Dom Hugh Edmund Ford, Prior of Downside, with a suggestion that the Benedictines should open a small house in Cambridge if it proved to be impossible to persuade Bishop Riddell to make over the parish to them. They could care for the undergraduates by providing the necessary conferences, as well as use the foundation to enable their own monks to acquire University qualifications. The last advantage particularly appealed to Ford, although he was not at all sure of the effect the University might have upon young Religious.

In what way would these students for the priesthood or even sub-diaconate come into contact with the University life so as to be in any way benefited from it? They would work with tutors for the exams. but in what other way would they give and take impressions? [Ford questioned the Baron.] Bp. Hedley advises [he went on] that I should see how matters are arranged and work at Mansfield College. . . . Young clerics could hardly join with other undergraduates in their

---

[1] *Universities' Catholic Education Board: a Report of its Work from 1895 to 1897.*

amusements. In any literary or debating society they might. . . . Rowing I am told is quite an exercise for curates. I am fairly revolutionary, but even I feel queer at the vision of the O.S.B. eight with a light-weight prior as Cox'n.[2]

Throughout the latter part of 1895 Anatole von Hugel was engaged in collecting money to finance the Benedictine foundation. Herman Norman thought the monks would 'become a social as well as an educational centre if they become at Cambridge like they are elsewhere', and he added that he was glad that the Rector of the parish in Cambridge, Canon Scott, 'sees the matter in the same light as you do and that he thinks the Bishop [Riddell] will take a sensible view of it', especially 'now that he is beaten on the bigger question of University education for Catholics'. Norman considered the Benedictines would be 'an actual boon for the Canon which he would really welcome'.[3]

Following the receipt of this letter, von Hugel communicated with Prior Ford:

Both you and Bishop Hedley, I think, agreed that the Order were not unwilling to establish themselves here, so long as a sum could be guaranteed to them to defray the initial expenses of the new foundation. Two or three friends interested in Cambridge have occurred to me as possible helpers in this scheme, and I have already had a talk on the subject with Mr. Norman whom I think you know at any rate by name. He is very keen about the matter and promises to do all he can. I do not as yet know whether the other friends who have occurred to me will be equally willing. . . . It seems to me very desirable that I, as the representative of Cambridge on the Board, should have some definite plan to propose at the next meeting (probably in November) especially now that the arrangements as regards Oxford are so very advanced.[4]

Four days after this was written von Hugel received an unexpected inquiry from the Vice-President of St. Edmund's College, Ware, Fr. Edmond Nolan, who wrote:

of late there have been many projects formed having in view the present attitude of the Bishops towards the University Education of

---

[2] A. von Hugel Papers. Hugh Edmund Ford to A. von Hugel, 2 Oct. 1895.
[3] Ibid. Herman Norman to A. von Hugel, 15 Oct. 1895.
[4] Ibid. A. von Hugel to Prior Ford, 20 Oct. 1895.

Catholics. Naturally these are all in the direction of our men going to
Oxford and Cambridge in greater numbers. Now the question is being
discussed as to sending even our Theological Students. But of this there
seems at present many objections. It has occurred to me that a beginning
might be made, if as is sometimes arranged, a dispensation from prolonged residence could be accorded. . . . It has been suggested to me
that you would be likely to be interested in this matter and would
pardon the trouble I am giving you in asking you to advise me on the
subject.[5]

The idea presented itself to von Hugel that perhaps Nolan might
be able to provide what the Benedictines seemed hesitant about.
Bishop Riddell would certainly favour secular priests rather than
monks, and there would be no suggestion of ousting the Northampton diocesan clergy from the parish. Bishop Hedley felt,
however, that 'it would continue to be (as it were) a public
scandal to see that splendid presbytery half empty',[6] and he was
anxious to pursue the Benedictine connection. On 8 November
1895 Prior Ford wrote that Bishop Riddell would not hear of the
Benedictines' opening a house in Cambridge,[7] and he wondered
what would happen if they did so in defiance of the Bishop, and
the latter retaliated by refusing faculties. Furthermore, Ford felt
that von Hugel and Hedley were acting too precipitately. 'We
must not seem to hurry or "bustle" the Bishop',[8] he wrote. Von
Hugel was anxious to have a scheme for Cambridge fixed before
the bishops met to approve the Board's recommendation in
regard to Oxford. It was feared that any discussion by the
hierarchy would encourage Bishop Riddell to make some pronouncement of his own about Cambridge. He wrote to Hedley
on the point, adding that, if Bishop Riddell did make some
suggestion as to what should be done at Cambridge, he hoped
that Hedley would 'not compromise the Board's action in any
way'. He felt that 'to have to object to a cut and dried suggestion
of the Bishop of Northampton might land us in fresh difficulties'.[9]

[5] Ibid. Edmond Nolan to A. von Hugel, 23 Oct. 1895.
[6] Ibid. Bishop Hedley to A. von Hugel, 1 Nov. 1895.
[7] Ibid. Prior Ford to A. von Hugel, 8 Nov. 1895.
[8] Ibid. Prior Ford to A. von Hugel, 26 Nov. 1895.
[9] Ibid. A. von Hugel to Bishop Hedley, 27 Nov. 1895.

He added: 'I should like for the Board to be first in the field with a definite proposal as in the case of Oxford [which] can be laid before the Bishops in Council. And the fact of Oxford having been taken first, and the discussion of Cambridge postponed to a future meeting of the Board is itself a reason for not discussing the question now.'

The episcopal meeting was held on 28 November 1895, and the following day Bishop Hedley wrote to von Hugel to say that the latter's prognosis had indeed been true:

At the very beginning of our meeting yesterday the Bishop of Northampton took the initiative in bringing Cambridge on the topics. He spoke somewhat strongly in the sense of strengthening the Mission, and Dr. Scott. He said that he did not see that anything more was required. He added that he would welcome assistance in the shape of Lecturers such as Dr. Gasquet. He did not get very far before someone pointed out that the 'assistant' spoken of would necessarily be responsible to the 'Universities' Committee'. The Bishop of Clifton seemed anxious that the case of Cambridge should be settled, as far as the Bishops were concerned, there and then. But the sense of the meeting was in favour of waiting for a recommendation from the Universities' Committee—and with an expression of opinion from the Bishop of Nottingham that a *centre distinct from the Clergy House* would be preferable, it was agreed to adjourn Cambridge.[10]

Hedley informed the Baron: 'I have little doubt that if Downside would undertake a small "Pusey House" at Cambridge, the Bishops would welcome it. And if the Bishops authorised it, the Bishop of Northampton would be powerless, because the matter (according to the lines of Cardinal Ledochowski's letter) is taken out of the hands of the Ordinary. But I do not think that the Bishop would object.'

Hedley's reasoning seemed to convince von Hugel at first. The monastic settlement would be distinct from the Rectory and the spiritual powers of the monks restricted to members of the University. By the establishment of a Benedictine house, von Hugel felt, 'not only would the interests of our undergraduates be secured, we would have a centre of Catholic learning and study

[10] A. von Hugel Papers. Bishop Hedley to A. von Hugel, 29 Nov. 1895.

in the University that has already done so much for the encouragement of biblical and historical studies. The time is ripe for this,
and if we could secure for Cambridge some of the Benedictines
who are working on these lines, the good which they would do,
would be very far-reaching.'[11] He told Charles Cave:

> Not only do the characteristics of the Benedictines, the gentle spirit
> of the Order and the good sound work done by its members, fit the
> situation, but it is to be remembered that Cambridge is one of their old
> homes, a home where they laboured to such good purpose that the
> University virtually owes its existence to these labours. And though
> poor Cambridge is now not what it was in the days of Faith, and there
> has been time for many a generation born in unseeing heresy to run its
> course, yet the name of Benedictine still lives on in the place as some-
> thing to be respected, a dim, shadowy something, connected with
> good, and among many of the thinking set, there is a feeling of curiosity
> connected with monks: they would dearly like to see a living Benedic-
> tine.

The difficulties in the way of the scheme were now two in
number: the attitude of the Bishop of the Diocese and the want
of funds. But

> fortunately our strong feeling that a house of this kind should be kept
> quite distinct from the existing mission has helped to clear the way, for
> Bishop Riddell *insists* on the mission and the Rectory house being kept
> for his own priests (i.e., seculars of the Northampton Diocese). But, of
> course, though the proposed Benedictine house will be separate from
> the mission, it is not meant that there should be no contact between the
> two. On the contrary, Canon Scott looks forward to receiving much
> help from the fathers in Church services, preaching, etc.—an oratory
> will no doubt form part of the house, but it will be a private one, and
> in no way harm the mission.[12]

Money, however, was not forthcoming, and Cave, one of the
richest Catholics in England, declined to help substantially.

On the 12th of December Fr. Nolan wrote again from Ware
to consult von Hugel about the project of St. Edmund's men
going to Cambridge for part of their time,[13] and his letter arrived

[11] Ibid. A. von Hugel to C. J. P. Cave, 4 Dec. 1895, copy.   [12] Ibid.
[13] Ibid. Revd. Edmond Nolan to A. von Hugel, 12 Dec. 1895.

but two days before one from Gasquet, stating that 'the sum of money to be secure every year will be very difficult to obtain, I fear',[14] and ominously warning that 'our Catholic schemes have so often failed simply because we have been too ambitious'. It appeared to Gasquet that even the modest scheme adopted for Oxford was 'too magnificent to be realised'. The depressing effect of Fr. Gasquet's letter was heightened by one received the following day from Prior Ford. 'I hardly like so formal and aggressive a purpose as a copy of Pusey House', the Prior stated, and went on: 'let any men we have attend first to their own work—and then according to opportunity develop but what is best suited to the time. I don't like entering an unknown country with a fully pre-arranged plan. We don't know enough of the conditions of the game to make any hard and fast scheme. It may be Pusey House or something quite different that would best suit. . . .'[15] On receiving this communication von Hugel was angry. He could not see where 'formal and aggressive' came in, and he had never suggested 'a copy' of Pusey House. But what he did not appreciate was that Bishop Hedley, in his desire for the Benedictines to play a great role in Cambridge, had indeed put these ideas into the Prior's head. Von Hugel in a sharp reply to Ford claimed that the interests of the undergraduates must come first, and he added: '[I have] received from quite an unexpected quarter a proposal by which the object we have kept in view would possibly be very readily received.'[16]

On the last day of December 1895 von Hugel told Herman Norman that Prior Ford had created an aura of suspicion 'by his diffident, uncommunicative manner' and his reluctance 'to commit himself to anything'.[17] The last letter he had received from Ford had made him despair, 'for I thought that he did not at all realise the importance of *our side* of the question'. When threatened with Nolan and the St. Edmund's scheme, the Prior had said 'that he never meant to imply that the undergraduate

---

[14] A. von Hugel Papers. Gasquet to A. von Hugel, 14 Dec. 1895.
[15] Ibid. Prior Ford to A. von Hugel, 15 Dec. 1895.
[16] Ibid. A. von Hugel to Prior Ford, 18 Dec. 1895, copy.
[17] Ibid. A. von Hugel to Herman Norman, 31 Dec. 1895, copy.

side of the move was a matter of little consequence'. Von Hugel informed Norman of the St. Edmund's proposal:

The advantages of this new scheme are that it is eminently satisfactory to Canon Scott, and would he *thinks* (and I *hope*) possibly smooth over all difficulties with the Bishop. It has now gradually leaked out little by little, how distasteful the idea of Regulars taking over much of the Church-work here, and the undergraduates as well, really is both to the Canon and to the Bishop. . . . It is the awkward and bold proposal of Bishop Hedley to Bishop Riddell *to make over the Church to the Benedictines,* and Prior Ford's hitherto nervous, tentative manner that has given Canon Scott fears as to how smoothly matters would run should the Benedictines be mixed up with the Church and have their hands strengthened by the Board.

The seculars, the Baron knew, had some friends at their back and 'would come for their own sake quite independently of whether the undergraduates are put into their charge or not'. He added that this was what he felt the Benedictines ought to have been willing to do; 'they have literary work in hand to encourage, which is just the thing for Cambridge; and they have students and scholastics to think of whom they ought to provide with a University training'. He could not see, except on the score of funds, 'why they should cry off if the Board should settle with others to fulfil the requisite minute of Propaganda'. He concluded: 'I am bound, however, to consider the interests of the undergraduates first, and to keep an unbiased mind, and for this reason I can't do otherwise than submit this new scheme, along with our old scheme, for the due consideration of the Board.' Von Hugel, by the time this letter was dispatched, had already committed himself to present to the University a memorandum on behalf of St. Edmund's College in which the latter begged for affiliation. Affiliation reduced the period of residence by a year and conferred other senior privileges. He was convinced that among the staff St. Edmund's would send to Cambridge there would be found a priest well qualified to fulfil the requirements of the Board. Cardinal Vaughan had promised to help by getting a letter from *Propaganda* in St. Edmund's favour. At the end of December 1895 von Hugel wrote to the Duke of Norfolk about the seminary scheme. He remarked that his work had been cut out in dealing with Prior Ford, and the latter 'has also very openly hinted that the Church and parish should be theirs. . . . The way he has set about the matter makes me see the difficulties the Board might have in "directing" Regulars and the discord which would, I now fear, be the inevitable result of the first scheme, makes me somewhat tentative about it, and inclines me to consider seriously the new one in which there would be a bond of unity from which all rivalry would be eliminated.'[18] As for Bishop Hedley and his hand in the matter, von Hugel wrote, 'I cannot even yet quite gauge'. Once Ford realized he was in competition with Old Hall, however, 'he showed himself as eager in the matter as he had until then seemed listless'.

By the beginning of January von Hugel had requested Fr. Nolan to let him have in writing a statement 'to the effect that St. Edmund's would be willing to provide a good man for the work of looking after the undergraduates and that this chaplain would be willing to undertake the work as defined by the Board'.[19] Prior Ford promised to send a similar memorandum, but was so dilatory in doing so that von Hugel had to write again to remind him.[20] On the same day as the Baron sent his reminder Prior Ford wrote to von Hugel to say that he had contacted the members of the Board and that the Duke of Norfolk, Bishop Hedley, Bishop Brownlow, Lord Braye, Mr. Norman, and Mr. King, were willing to support him. He decried the Old Hall plan:

I had pictured to myself something magnificent, half the Bishops of the country combining to secure a University education for their ecclesiastical students, but I am afraid that this is far beyond what is intended. As I understand the proposal it does not mean more than having a priest resident in Cambridge with an ecclesiastical student from Old Hall staying with him while getting his degree. . . . I do not think then that we should be putting any obstacle in the way of this

[18] A. von Hugel Papers. A. von Hugel to the Duke of Norfolk, 28 Dec. 1895, copy marked 'private'.
[19] Ibid. A. von Hugel to Nolan, 6 Jan. 1896, copy.
[20] Ibid. A. von Hugel to Ford, 6 Jan. 1896, copy.

scheme by proposing to the Board to appoint Fr. Butler as the 'University Chaplain'.[21]

Von Hugel tried to disillusion the Prior by pointing out that Old Hall did not intend sending but one priest to Cambridge. They had a scheme which in due course would affect the entire seminary. Ford promised the Board that, if they appointed Fr. Butler as chaplain, the Benedictines would keep a second or even a third man in residence with him (Gasquet and/or Bishop), and they would be willing to take under their charge any ecclesiastical students from the seminaries while such students were reading for degrees.

Bishop Hedley did not at all like the way things were going. He admitted that there was much to be said in favour of the St. Edmund's plan, and he did not wish to antagonize the Cardinal, who felt that, now lay Catholics were to go to Oxford and Cambridge, ecclesiastical students should not be allowed to remain less qualified than laymen. Yet Hedley dearly wished the Benedictines settled in Cambridge. Perhaps a compromise could be reached. 'I hope that both Downside and Old Hall will settle at Cambridge',[22] he told von Hugel. But he was afraid that his fellow bishop on the Board, Dr. Brownlow, was now all in favour of Old Hall.[23] Hedley maintained that all the Committee had to do was 'to decide upon and recommend to the Bishops, some scheme for providing at Cambridge those "lectures" which are prescribed by Propaganda', and that in doing so it would naturally accept the offer 'which would be at once the most efficient and the cheapest to work'.[24] On 9 January 1896, less than a week before the meeting of the Board which was to decide the issue for Cambridge, Friedrich von Hugel wrote to his brother Anatole urging him to adopt the Benedictine offer. He had been particularly impressed by Prior Ford's nomination of Fr. Butler for

---

[21] Ibid. Ford to A. von Hugel, 6 Jan. 1896.
[22] Ibid. Bishop Hedley to A. von Hugel, 7 Jan. 1896.
[23] Ibid. Mgr. Ward of Old Hall was in touch with Brownlow on the matter—letter dated 7 Jan. 1896, and also letter from Brownlow to A. von Hugel dated 13 Jan. 1896.
[24] Ibid. Bishop Hedley to A. von Hugel, 7 Jan. 1896.

the position of chaplain. He wrote that Butler was an exemplary Religious, and added 'young still, though not too young . . . full of energy and useful activity as right open-mindedness'. He went on: 'He is a most competent scholar, an early Christian specialist; he knows a good deal too about contemporary philosophy: above all, perhaps, he understands as few do, the younger modern minds. . . .'[25] For Old Hall, Nolan suggested for appointment a Fr. Scannell, but added 'personally, I should much like to come to Cambridge, and will if it can be arranged, to study for a time'.[26] At a recent meeting of headmasters of Catholic Public Schools the sentiment had been altogether 'in favour of establishing a College for the clergy at either Oxford or Cambridge', and Nolan remarked, 'everything seems very favourable; I pray it may all come to good and do good'.

The Board met on 15 January 1896, and after some considerable debate resolved 'that a house distinct from the existing mission, with at least one resident priest paid by the Board, be established' in Cambridge.[27] The offer of St. Edmund's College to provide the chaplain was accepted, and the Reverend Edmond Nolan, Vice-President of the College, was appointed chaplain at a yearly stipend of £150. The office of chaplain was, however, to be divided from that of lecturer. The chaplain was to be primarily responsible for the spiritual well-being of the undergraduates, whereas the lecturer was to deliver a lecture on each Sunday during full term. Both priests were to apply for faculties to the Bishop of Northampton in order to hear the confessions of undergraduates. The office of lecturer was to be filled by Dom E. C. Butler, also at a stipend of £150 a year. Both appointments were to be for two years in the first instance.

Von Hugel was delighted with the compromise solution and wrote at once to Butler:

Let me congratulate you very sincerely, and ourselves very much, on your nomination to Cambridge. I, personally, had no fears about the matter, for I felt certain that you were destined for Cambridge,

---

[25] A. von Hugel Papers. Friedrich von Hugel to Anatole von Hugel, 9 Jan. 1896.   [26] Ibid. Nolan to A. von Hugel, 9 Jan. 1896.
[27] *Universities' Catholic Education Board: a Report of its Work from 1895 to 1897.*

long before the Universities' Board was ever dreamed about and I should not have rested until your coming to us was assured. . . . It has all come to a head so quickly that I can hardly yet grasp this complete change of front. To be looking up one's College friends, as I am at present doing, to get the necessary information for the affiliation to Cambridge of St. Edmund's College, and to be talking of a seminary and a house of Benedictines in Cambridge is certainly a delightful and novel experience. The decision of the Board to divide the office of Chaplain and Lecturer seems to be a very happy one; the more so as it gives a helping hand both to the Benedictines and to the Seculars and is a promise of good fellowship. I only hope you do not dislike this arrangement, for I had indirectly something to do in bringing it about. . . . I do not know if you are acquainted with Father Nolan, who has been nominated Chaplain. He seems to me an excellent man, sociable, and his social instincts and general character will make him a very pleasant and useful member of our small, but now, thank God, fast growing community.[28]

Butler expressed himself satisfied with the arrangement, and remarked that Mgr Ward, the President of St. Edmund's, had made an offer 'that pending the establishment of a Benedictine [house], which I hope we shall be able to manage before long, I should stay at their place. That of course I should like very much.'[29]

Bishop Riddell was not unfavourable to a strong house of the secular clergy in Cambridge, provided that it gave some assistance to Canon Scott. 'You may tell the Baron', he informed the Canon at the beginning of 1896, 'that you have consulted me on the subject of St. Edmund's, Old Hall, having a branch College or house at Cambridge, and that I have no objection to its being established, but I expect that it shall be subject to the Ordinary. . . .'[30] The Bishop's attitude was clearly expressed by Lady Mary von Hugel, Friedrich's wife, when she wrote to Anatole an account of a conversation with Riddell. The latter 'was frankly open about the University question, thinking it all a mistake that

[28] A. von Hugel Papers. A. von Hugel to E. C. Butler, 17 Jan. 1896, copy.
[29] Ibid. Butler to A. von Hugel, 22 Jan. 1896.
[30] Ibid. Quotation from letter of Canon Scott to A. von Hugel, 2 Jan. 1896.

Catholics should go there—as good as said the Pope had made a great mistake but it was his business to knuckle under, so he did'.[31] Herman Norman had all along felt 'there would be great disadvantages in quarrelling with the Bishop',[32] and he declared: 'I should be willing to go a long way round to avoid scaring him and still more to avoid hurting the Canon's feelings.'

It was not until after the meeting of the Board on 24 June 1896 that the hierarchy announced the decision to the faithful at large that attendance at Oxford and Cambridge would henceforth be tolerated. At the meeting on 15 January the Board had settled the provision for Cambridge, but this had not become fully operable until the hierarchy had ratified the provision at its Low Week meeting in 1896. At the June meeting there was a long discussion on the list of names for the office of chaplain at Oxford, but no decision was taken at that meeting, or, indeed, at the following two meetings of the Board on 13 October and 6 November 1896. Various priests had been contacted, but there were considerable difficulties in settling upon a suitable candidate. The reason for the delay was again a conflict between the rival claims of the secular clergy and a religious order, this time the Society of Jesus. The Duke of Norfolk had disliked the Society of Jesus and was particularly anxious that the Jesuits should not gain a monopoly in Oxford. They already cared for the parish, and he felt that a Jesuit chaplain to the undergraduates would become merely an extra curate at St. Aloysius. He was strongly supported in this viewpoint by von Hugel's counterpart in Oxford, Hartwell de la Garde Grissell. There were others, however, prepared to work equally strongly in favour of the Jesuit interest, notably Charles Stanton Devas. The latter tried to influence James Hope, Canon Moyes, and Wilfrid Ward, who had been delegated by the Board to consider suitable candidates for Oxford. He was unable to enlist Hope as an ally and Canon Moyes inclined to the views of Grissell and Norfolk. Wilfrid Ward refused to be trapped into a party alignment, and urged the adoption of a compromise solution similar to the one found

---

[31] A. von Hugel Papers. Lady Mary von Hugel to A. von Hugel, Rome, n.d. [1896].   [32] Ibid. Herman Norman to A. von Hugel, 5 Jan. 1896.

for Cambridge, but one not as favourable to the Jesuits as the Cambridge settlement had been to the Benedictines.

Grissell's candidate for the Oxford chaplaincy was an ageing secular priest of Bishop Brownlow's diocese who was himself an Oxford graduate—Canon Arthur Kennard of Cannington. The Jesuit candidate was the celebrated Fr. Joseph Rickaby.

Grissell approached the possibility of Canon Kennard's going to Oxford in January 1896, but by March of that year he was still finding it difficult to persuade the Canon of the advantages of uprooting himself for what seemed, after all, a vague and tenuous offer. Unlike Fr. Rickaby he had not the protection of a religious order behind him, and unlike Fr. Nolan at Cambridge he had not the assurance that he could return to an ecclesiastical college if things did not work out. The Canon felt he might be left in his declining years in a most insecure position. 'I have a happy and comfortable home here, and deeply rooted,' he told Grissell in March 1896, 'and to dig them all up at a moment's notice and to accept a post I know so little about as the one proposed to me at Oxford is very difficult.'[33] He did add, however, that he was prepared to consider the proposal: 'It is very kind of you to take so much interest in the possibilities of my coming to Oxford. I have written off as you advised me today to Wilfrid Ward to ask him if they would like me to take it, to let me know the full mind of the Committee on the proposed scheme. . . . I have told him that having a house to myself is a *sine qua non* and that it would be an immense help to me in my advancing years if I was allowed to say Mass at my own private Oratory instead of turning out in a damp Oxford mist.'

The negotiations with Kennard dragged on throughout the summer, during which time the supporters of the Jesuit cause were not idle. A clear impression of this activity is given in a letter sent by Charles Stanton Devas to Anatole von Hugel in October 1896, asking for the latter's support for Fr. Rickaby. He wrote: 'I have been to Oxford, become acquainted with Fr. Joseph Rickaby, made enquiries, and in particular had a conversation

[33] Hartwell de la Garde Grissell Papers. Canon Kennard to Grissell, 17 Mar. 1896.

with Urquhart who knows Fr. Rickaby well, attended his lectures some years ago at Stonyhurst, spoke most highly of them, and considered that he was admirably suited to act as the lecturer required by the Board. Besides being a theologian and a philosopher he is an accomplished Greek scholar which for Oxford is a great advantage; and his quiet retiring manner is another advantage in that critical and fastidious circle.'[34] Devas maintained there could be no real objection to the appointment, because it was proposed that Fr. Rickaby should be completely independent of the Oxford parish. The Board had already given the Benedictines a share of the work at Cambridge, and had at one time contemplated asking the Oratorians to settle in Oxford, 'nor can monopoly be alleged, for this ignores the existence of Cambridge where there are no Jesuits, and also ignores the fact that at Oxford itself there is a grand site secured for a College for secular priests with buildings on it, that a few months' work could convert into a very serviceable structure for a beginning'. Devas concluded:

> The appointment of Fr. Rickaby on grounds of convenience, economy, and avoiding all friction, seems so natural that the Board, by passing him over, will practically commit itself to a vote of non-confidence in the Jesuit Fathers—the decision will inevitably appear in this light to the Catholic world, the Oxford world, and the general public. Such a decision, I think, would be extremely calamitous at Oxford especially. I cannot also but think that you are of the same opinion; and, if so, if it falls to me to propose the appointment of Fr. Rickaby, could I count on you to second the proposal?

The Letter ended on an ominous note:

> I do not know the Duke of Norfolk well enough to write to him on such a subject; but considering that there is an impression—as far as I know with no solid grounds to support it—that he is 'opposed' to the Jesuits, the above motion would come with peculiar grace from him, and would ensure its being carried with few or no dissentients.

In writing to von Hugel, Devas had unwittingly blundered. The Baron informed the Duke and James Hope that Devas was

---

[34] A. von Hugel Papers. Charles Stanton Devas to A. von Hugel, 24 Oct. 1896.

canvassing members of the Board. At the meeting of the Board on 7 November Devas was prevented from putting his motion to the vote, on the grounds that further inquiries as to other possible candidates had not yet been fully completed. It was promised, however, that the question would be settled on 10 December. On 29 November James Hope wrote to Grissell that 'no one can feel more strongly than I the dangers of a Jesuit monopoly at Oxford, and so long as I am on the University Board I will not cease to combat that or any form of exclusive influence'.[35]

Canon Kennard had scruples about his own suitability. Bishop Brownlow, in urging him to accept the chaplaincy at Oxford if offered, had warned him that he would have to share a house 'with other priests and probably lay boarders'.[36] Kennard knew of approaches to other candidates (notably Dr. William Barry and the Revd. A. McColl), and did not want to be a mere *pis-aller*. He would be quite happy if the Board found another man, for he did not wish to start community life, at his age, with strangers. 'I *must* have the house to myself', he stressed in a letter to Grissell. The Canon required some assurance that his appointment would not be in the nature of a stop-gap. He informed Grissell:

I have other difficulties in my way. . . . For instance, suppose I desired the Catholic undergraduates from their different Colleges to assemble together in my Oratory certain evenings of the week for Instruction and Devotion. What is to prevent them refusing my invitation? I can have no real authority over them. They would say 'my College Authorities I know, the University Authorities I know, but who are you'? 'Who gave *you* any authority over me?' And what could I answer them? If my difficulties could be solved, there is nothing I should like better than to try to influence for good our young Catholics at Oxford. You must understand, my dear friend, that since I left Church House and took a house in the village I have got a small establishment on my hands—six servants—carriage—horse—dogs, etc. I have furnished and decorated the house inside—nice gardens—orchards, etc. Now I should not like to leave all this for an *unknown* future. I must

---

[35] Grissell Papers. James F. Hope to Grissell, 29 Nov. 1896.
[36] Ibid. Kennard to Grissell, 15 Nov. 1896.

know pretty clearly what I am wanted to do and how to live before I say I am ready to undertake it.

Meantime, Fr. Joseph Rickaby wrote to Lord Herries (who had helped to finance the Benedictines for Cambridge) to say that he was going to Oxford, 'where I expect to get work among the undergraduates'.[37]

Soon there was talk that the pattern of Cambridge might be followed, the office of chaplain and lecturer being divided. Kennard was happy at the idea of such a division, and he informed Wilfrid Ward that he would be willing to act as chaplain '*without a salary*, if only I get my house rent free and they can assure me of a quasi-permanency—i.e. to say that I shall not be cast adrift if I conscientiously fulfil the duties of Chaplain'.[38] He informed Grissell that 'it is a serious thing to uproot myself and belongings at my time of life after more than twenty years of residence here and I could not face it for a merely temporary work and office'. At the same time he would be very happy to find himself at Oxford again.

The Board met on 10 December 1896, and after considerable discussion it appointed Canon Kennard as chaplain at Oxford. No time limit was specified. There then followed a significant divergence from the Cambridge example. It was resolved that it should be the duty of the chaplain at Oxford to select and engage the lecturer, with the proviso that such selection must be subject to the approval of the Board and be for a period not exceeding one year. The Jesuit supporters were in this way defeated in their objectives, although the Board, in an attempt to mollify them, recommended 'that Canon Kennard be informed that the Board would welcome the engagement of Fr. Joseph Rickaby, S.J., as Lecturer for the remainder of the current academic year'.[39] Any possibility of guaranteeing the lecturership to the Society of Jesus was prevented at the meeting of the Board in April 1897, when

[37] Herries Papers. Fr. Joseph Rickaby, S.J., to Lord Herries, 27 Nov. 1896. See also letter of 14 Sept. 1896.

[38] Grissell Papers. Kennard to Grissell, 24 Nov. 1896.

[39] Brompton Oratory Archives, London. *Universities' Catholic Education Board Report*; meeting of 10 Dec. 1896.

the question of the further provision of lecturers at Oxford was considered, and it was resolved to inform the chaplain 'that the Board would approve the engagement, at his discretion, of Dom Adam Hamilton, of Buckfast Abbey, or of Fr. F. A. Gasquet, D.D., or the re-engagement of Father J. Rickaby'.[40] Canon Kennard selected Hamilton of Buckfast. Kennard, agreeing to forgo his stipend for the time being, rented a house for himself in St. Aldate's Street, facing the 'Tom' gate of Christ Church. Finances were a problem, but Kennard had private means. An appeal for funds, however, for the two chaplaincies was issued by the Board on 1 August 1896, and Cardinal Vaughan's financial secretary, Mgr. Thomas Dunn, was appointed treasurer. The Jesuits, meantime, had opened a house of studies in Oxford for members of their own order, and this was 'licensed' as a private Hall. It was made clear that the Jesuits were to have nothing to do with lay undergraduates. In 1897 the Ampleforth Benedictines (declining to join their Downside brethren in Cambridge) followed the Jesuit example in Oxford.[41]

In August 1896 the joint letter of the bishops concerning attendance at Oxford and Cambridge was read in all churches and public oratories. Reference was made to the appointment of chaplains and lecturers at both Universities, and it was asserted that 'the Lecturers or Chaplains will not only deliver careful and suitable Conferences on Sundays or at such times as may be most convenient, but will be ever on the spot, always at the service of the undergraduates, and solely devoted to the interests of our holy faith and to fatherly solicitude for the young men who will constitute their flock'.[42] The minority bishops, however, who had been in disagreement with the recent moves, also issued instructions re-emphasizing conditions governing the *Propaganda* decision. Typical of these was the one Bishop Riddell addressed to his clergy:

When this Pastoral was decided upon, there was no idea in the minds of the Bishops of clerics or ecclesiastical students going to Oxford or

---

[40] Ibid. Tenth meeting of the Board, 30 Apr. 1897.
[41] *The Dublin Review* (Winter 1936), p. 281.
[42] *Instruction to the Parents, . . . etc.,* op. cit. (1896).

Cambridge, and therefore it applies only to laymen. The Pastoral owes its origin to the action of some of our laymen who revived the question, and who alleged 'altered circumstances' as a reason for its being reconsidered. This lay action, resulting in a petition numerously signed, forced the Bishops as a body to reconsider the question of lay Catholics attending the Protestant Universities, and to seek advice from the Holy See. The result of the Bishops' action was the Rescript of April 17th, 1895. In that letter the Holy See seems to long for the establishment among us of a Catholic University; and therefore it seems to me that this should become a part of our policy, and that we, the Catholics of England, should give all the support possible to the action of the Irish Bishops endeavouring to obtain a Catholic University, not only with the view of helping our fellow-Catholic subjects, but also in the hope that such a gain obtained in Ireland may assist us in securing for ourselves in England a similar benefit. The Rescript shows plainly that the Church of God is unchangeable in her principle that Catholic youth should be under Catholic tuition and training, whether the youths are in a primary or a secondary school, or at a University. Looking at the Rescript, it is clear that the Church does not give her sanction, and does not give even her permission, to Catholic laymen to attend the Universities: she merely *tolerates* such attendance. As this is the case we may conclude that she prefers that our Catholic young men should not attend at all, for she acts in this case as in that of mixed marriages. . . . The attendance of the Catholic undergraduates at the Lectures is declared obligatory, and this *sub gravi*: hence no one should go to Oxford or Cambridge who has not the firm intention of complying with this strict obligation, laid down by the Holy See to safeguard faith, 'without which it is impossible to please God' (Hebr. xi, 6). . . . There is a class of youths who on no account can be exposed to the agnosticism of the Universities and that is such as are not of a firm, strong, and stable character. . . . All these conditions laid down by the Holy See show how careful parents, superiors, and directors should be before they countenance the attendance of any Catholic youth at the Protestant Universities. . . . Already there are Catholic families who mourn the loss of faith in one or other member; and there is reason to fear further apostasies will follow from contamination with Agnostics; we say this in consequence of the evidence of the Rev. Anthony C. Deane as given in an article in *The Nineteenth Century*, October 1895. He writes: 'The undergraduate is left to form his religious opinions for himself, and in most cases he becomes practically an agnostic.' 'Easy going agnosticism is the average undergraduate creed.' 'The prevalent attitude towards religion is, in one word, agnosticism.' The present Catholic question is, will our youths though well armed by a knowledge of principles, though of strong character, though attending the lectures provided specially for them, stand against the assaults of Protestantism, Agnosticism, and Indifferentism? Will they be proof against these errors? As the Ordinary of this Diocese in which Cambridge is situated, I shall watch carefully over such as venture to attend that University, and I hope against hope, that they may pass through the ordeal unscathed. Let this letter be read in every public Church or chapel in the Diocese, on the Sunday after that on which the joint Pastoral is read.[43]

It must have taken no little courage on the part of this episcopal descendant of one of England's Old Catholic families to send a copy of the letter to the Duke of Norfolk endorsed 'the enclosed may be useful'.[44]

The bishops of the minority party were not the only prelates anxious as to what the ultimate effect of the permission might be. Bishop Hedley was now troubled in conscience and ill at ease. Writing three months before Riddell, he pointed out 'it is not so much by Protestantism that our Catholic youth will be tempted; nor by any crude Atheism, or even scientific Agnosticism; nor by the World and the Flesh. These things have their dangers; but the deadliest danger of all is undoubtedly this—that one should find one's first questionings about the seriousness of life suggested by an earnest friend who is ready to suggest in the same breath the necessity of universal doubt.'[45] Much of what he wrote in 1896 could very well have been produced by Coffin twenty years before. Take, for instance, the following passage from the same article:

Many parents—indeed, by far the greater part—send their sons to the University solely for the purpose of at once getting them creditably through one or two troublesome years and of launching them into society which will be useful to them in after life. It is expected that they

[43] Northampton Diocesan Archives. Letter of Arthur Riddell, Bishop of Northampton to the Clergy of the Diocese, dated 18 Aug. 1896.

[44] A. von Hugel Papers. Copy by A. von Hugel of letter of Riddell to the Duke of Norfolk, dated 26 Oct. 1896.

[45] Bishop Hedley in *The Ampleforth Journal* (July 1896), Part I, pp. 1–13.

will attain a pass; as for honours, very few try for them; and even the bare pass does not seem at all essential. Hence, numbers of young men are sent up to whom the intellectual advantages of the Universities are of very little account. They form acquaintances, row, amuse themselves, and more or less keep out of mischief; and if they come away with a degree, well and good. . . . It may be said that the unintellectual lad will be saved from intellectual dangers by never studying and seldom thinking; and that such youths are often sturdy enough in their adhesion to their faith. But the danger at Oxford and Cambridge is not purely intellectual. It is that exceedingly subtle form of mental influence which arises from consorting with those you look up to and those you like. The printed books of a Spencer or a Huxley are far cleverer than the talk of the average tutor or friend, but the talk, it is certain, will leave the deeper impression. . . . No man can put his knuckle to a charged machine without getting a shock or a prick.[46]

It was hardly reassuring to Bishops Riddell, Wilkinson, Gordon, Lacy, and Bilsborrow, and those of a like mind on the Universities' issue, to find their arch-opponent now speaking in these terms. By the end of 1897 there were twenty-eight Catholic undergraduates in attendance at Oxford and thirty at Cambridge.[47] The stress in the episcopal letters of 1897 had been upon attendance at the lectures or conferences. The desire to enforce attendance on the Catholic undergraduates—in line with the Rescript of *Propaganda*—was resisted by the Universities' Catholic Education Board. Before the end of 1896 James Hope moved 'that this Council, seeing grave practical difficulties in the way of any attempt to enforce the attendance of undergraduates at Catholic lectures at the Universities, and believing that the interests of religion may in other ways be more effectually safeguarded, earnestly submits its opinion to the Hierarchy that no such attempt should be made'.[48] The motion was carried. Hope maintained he did not deny the advantage and even the necessity of establishing courses of lectures, but he felt they ought to be attended by none but willing hearers.

[46] Bishop Hedley in *The Ampleforth Journal* (July 1896), Part I, pp. 1–13.

[47] *Universities' Catholic Education Board Report*

[48] Document containing the resolution and a copy of Hope's speech in the A. von Hugel Papers. The quotations are from this source.

III

CLERICS AT THE UNIVERSITIES

THE plan to send clerical students to Oxford and Cambridge was not viewed with equanimity by Bishops Wilkinson, Riddell, Bilsborrow, Gordon, Lacy, Bagshawe, and Carroll (Bishop of Shrewsbury since 11 May 1895), and they decided to ask *Propaganda* for a clarification. In addition to the more general request, Riddell also sent a private appeal to Rome in his capacity as Ordinary of the Diocese in which Cambridge was situated. He asked:

1. Does the letter [of *Propaganda*, 1895] *merely tolerate* presence of Catholics at the Protestant Universities of Oxford and Cambridge?
2. Can it be declared that now 'the gates of the University are thrown wide open' to all Catholics?
3. Is it lawful by virtue of that letter for ecclesiastical students, clerics, priests and religious to go to the University?
4. Is it lawful, by virtue of that letter, for any Religious Order or any Catholic College to open a house at Cambridge with a view to young men attending the Universities? . . .[1]

Rome's answer arrived in June 1896, for Vaughan had by then petitioned *Propaganda* in favour of St. Edmund's College being permitted to open a daughter house in Cambridge. Cardinal Ledochowski wrote that the Holy See gave permission to the bishops, and to heads of Religious Orders, to establish houses in Oxford and Cambridge for clerics, secular and regular. But he specified that five conditions must first be fulfilled—the number must be very small; the houses must be under careful direction; those who have to watch over them must be staid ecclesiastics; the curriculum (course of studies) must be fixed by the respective

[1] Northampton Diocesan Archives. Riddell to the Cardinal Prefect of *Propaganda* (pencilled draft).

superiors, i.e. the bishops and the heads of the Orders; and the object must be to attain degrees and to pass examinations in the art of teaching. The letter bitterly disappointed the minority bishops, although they took refuge in the consolation that at least their own ecclesiastical students would not be permitted to go to such houses. It is significant that the first Cambridge priest-graduate did not appear on the staff of Ushaw until 1913,[2] following the deaths of Bishops Wilkinson, Riddell, Bilsborrow, Gordon, and Carroll, and after the resignation of Bishop Bagshawe. In 1913 only Bishop Lacy remained of the original intransigents, and he was 72 years old. The policy of the northern bishops prevented Ushaw from joining with the English Benedictines in establishing a joint ecclesiastical house of studies in Cambridge in October 1895.[3]

Bishop Riddell drew up a document marshalling the chief arguments of the minority bishops.[4] From his account we gain a clearer understanding of the prelates' anxieties. Could not the expenditure required by a sojourn at the Universities be more usefully spent on improving the studies within the existing Catholic colleges? By taking the best men out of a class 'you lower the emulation of the men you leave behind, and so weaken the general power of that class for average good'. Riddell felt that 'the collecting together of clever men from all the Colleges would be of use if they were *men* but the design is to have *boys*. We may succeed admirably in rearing a small army of Clerical Snobs. For a young fellow would be inclined to think himself somebody because he had been a residential Oxford B.A. There is a good deal of human nature even in a clever boy.' Furthermore: 'You are removing him from the Chapel of his early boyhood, from the statue of Our Lady, from his yearly ceremonies which have become part and parcel of himself, from his director who knows his heart, and you are doing this before his character is formed or his vocation is clinched, and to give him instead classics and Belles Lettres as the reason of his being. You are taking the model

---

[2] Milburn, p. 319.   [3] Ibid., pp. 302–4.
[4] Northampton Diocesan Archives. Bishop Riddell's manuscript 'Clerics at the English Universities', pp. 1 seq.

boys from the College when their influence is of most avail because it is such as these at *their* age who are the cynosure of younger students.'

Riddell questioned: 'Where are you going to send your clever men when they leave Cambridge, and who is to find the means or time for an extended course in Rome, or Louvain, to fit your budding genius to become a second Aquinas?' The English Church required 'men who understand the "needy and the poor",—practical men'. Yet 'in putting clerics in a University hot house (as you must if they are to be first and last, clerics) you are rearing plants which will be less able to bear the winds of the world, than the hardy annual of the colleges reared in the open schools'.

The advocates of the scheme expect that the young clerics would be 'as St. Gregory and St. Basil, to know only two streets, the one to the school and the other to the church, and not to know the Isis or the Cam from the New Cut. Or you let them free.—They are men of honour, you trust them *because*, I suppose, they have no human nature, your Hostel has provided antidotes! The whole situation is anomalous, unreal and dangerous in the extreme.'

Riddell's memorandum concluded with a magnificent peroration:

The status of the students will be, I suppose, somewhat like that of the Cuddesdon men at Oxford or any extra collegiate Hostel, i.e. they will be neither 'Ewen nor Dick', but just Roman Catholics permitted to live because they may. . . . Whom will you appoint the head? An old Oxford Don? His ideas would be too broad; a Martinet? He would play mischief with the place; a pious individual? The men would play mischief with him. Who is the man? If it is so hard to fix a head for Ushaw or Oscott, is your man to hand for Oxford or Cambridge? And if he dies who next, and at once? What about money and who is to find it? Not the men, they haven't got it; not the Colleges, the funds are common; not the bishops, they cannot afford it. I suppose all would enter as ducal sizars and eat off plates with the Howard coat of arms! The whole thing is degrading. Then, your boys,—*Smith* has no family means, he cannot buy his six pennyworth of cakes as he did of yore, his expenses must increase. . . . *Montgomery*'s father with the large furniture shop, determines to keep his boy in affluence, is he not at Oxford? How are you going to stop this kind of thing? *Crackswell* with brains and no money but a name, is sought after, his father lives in Yorkshire, you see he is in danger, you must return him soon to Ushaw and there is a breach for ever,—and my young gentleman joins a Religious Order! . . . Let us convince ourselves once and for all that caste has not been cast out of Catholics in England, and in your Hostel the pitch will not be hot when there is his satanic majesty to pay. . . . The Religious Orders are going to set up schools and Hostels, therefore we. I merely question why? Lastly, cui bono, we are poor Ushaw and Old Hall men, yet I fancy our average priest is more than equal to your average parson. . . .

Nevertheless, negotiations for the formal affiliation of St. Edmund's College, Ware, proceeded rapidly at Cambridge. In February 1896 the Syndicate unofficially approved of Canon Scott as protector of the College,[5] and all that was then necessary was to make regular application. By 23 March 1896 the University Council had passed an affiliation for the College, and it was supposed that fourteen days before the next Congregation, 'if there is no notice of opposition by then',[6] it could be considered settled. The next Congregation was arranged for 30 April, so on 16 April it would be possible to know whether the affiliation would be ratified or not. No appeal was lodged and the formal application took effect from 8 May. Von Hugel was jubilant: 'Now that our lay-men have been encouraged to frequent the Universities, it stands to reason that our clerics should be found there also, so that hand in hand they may from the beginning learn to fight the good fight.'[7] In effect, the affiliation was a virtual white elephant. One reason for this was that Old Hall realized it could not provide adequate teaching. Another was more fundamental. On 2 November 1896 St. Edmund's House was opened in Cambridge, largely as a gift of the Duke of Norfolk. With its opening the need for affiliation for the parent house diminished.

In September 1896 Fr. Edmond Nolan was concerned to ensure that the new Cambridge house was established on the right

[5] A. von Hugel Papers. Fr. Edmond Nolan to A. von Hugel, 1 Feb. 1896.
[6] Ibid. Bernard Ward to A. von Hugel, 23 Mar. 1896.
[7] Ibid. A. von Hugel to Mgr. Bernard Ward, 15 June 1896, copy.

footing. If the favour of the University was to be won, a Council and trustees had to be formed. In suggesting this to Anatole von Hugel, Nolan was treading on delicate ground, because, as he wrote, 'I do not know the intentions of the Duke, our generous benefactor'.[8] He pointed out, however, 'it would be a great gain and invaluable help towards our recognition (as a public hostel) if the Duke of Norfolk would be one of the trustees and also one of the Council'. He went on: 'I am sure you could easily explain to His Grace the importance of this, and in general the Council and trustees in whose names the house should stand, to find favour with the Senate, and to make it a truly Catholic and national enterprize, should be selected from a wide body, wider I mean than any College or Diocese, tho' the Diocese of West-minster and the College of St. Edmund are entitled to considera-tion as having borne the brunt of the difficulties. But it would be a pity to narrow the Council or trusteeship.'

Nolan approached Bishop Riddell in such a tactful way that he succeeded in getting him to visit the house and bless it. Riddell, however, stressed that Canon Scott should be given a place, as Vicar General, on any future Council of government. Von Hugel engaged a firm of solicitors to examine the articles of association of Cavendish College, Somerville College, Girton College, Newnham College, and the Cambridge Training College for Women, to see if they advanced any precedents to forward the claim of St. Edmund's House to be recognized as a public hostel.[9] Before St. Edmund's House was opened in November 1896, four students, all from St. Edmund's College, Ware, had taken up residence in the rectory of the parish church, and Nolan, who had registered as a student of the University (Trinity College), acted temporarily as their Superior. Nolan's position was regarded as an interim measure, because he was intended to be full-time chaplain to the Catholic lay undergraduates. In March 1897 the Revd. William Ormond Sutcliffe, a convert and a graduate of St. John's College, Cambridge, was appointed Superior of St.

[8] Ibid. Nolan to A. von Hugel, 16 Sept. 1896.
[9] Ibid. Messrs. Few and Co., London, to A. von Hugel, 29 Sept. 1896. They urged that the House be put forward as an exclusively ecclesiastical establishment.

Edmund's House. The Benedictines, too, in the person of Dom Cuthbert Butler, had arrived in Cambridge, the latter in order to assume duties as lecturer to the Catholic lay undergraduates. He followed Nolan's example and enrolled as an advanced student of Christ's College. The letters which Butler wrote back to Downside, however, thoroughly alarmed his fussy Prior. On 19 October Prior Ford, nervous as ever, wrote to von Hugel in consternation:

Fr. Butler tells me that the Old Hall students are to cycle and join in the games wearing flannels. How does this affect your feelings? What does Wyatt Davies (of Selwyn) think of it? I don't feel quite happy about it, and I used to think I was so advanced in things of this kind that I can't really help supposing that if I feel doubtful there must be good reason to doubt. It would be a misfortune if after beginning in this way, they had to withdraw. Then the question arises as to how far we may do what they do.[10] After all they are I suppose not in any way regarded as clerics, are really only boys. I am not sure that I resist the cycling so much, but the games! We are in so much fog at present it is difficult to get our bearings. We must take present soundings (of public opinion) and keep a good look out.[11]

By 19 October 1896 Cardinal Vaughan had approved a list of members for the Council of St. Edmund's House. Bishop Riddell informed the Duke of Norfolk that 'the Bishop of a Diocese should hold himself free and independent of Councils or Committees',[12] and he declined a place on the Council. He added 'it will be my place as such to be the Ecclesiastical Visitor'. Before the end of the year Articles of Association were drawn up, and the purpose of the House was clearly stated as being to educate as members of the University of Cambridge those men 'who are destined for the secular priesthood of the Catholic Church in communion with the See of Rome'.[13] Seven men were listed as

[10] The Downside Benedictines established a House of Studies in Cambridge in 1896 for their own students only. This is now known as Benet House.

[11] A. von Hugel Papers. Prior Ford to A. von Hugel, 19 Oct. 1896.

[12] Ibid. Bishop Riddell to the Duke of Norfolk, 26 Oct. 1896, copied by A. von Hugel.

[13] Archives of St. Edmund's College, Ware. Memorandum and Articles of Association of St. Edmund's House at Cambridge, 3(A).

'Subscribers'—Norfolk, Anatole von Hugel, Christopher Scott, Charles J. P. Cave, Bernard Ward, Lord Herries, and Lord Clifford. Members of the Council were to be the Founder (Norfolk), not more than six *ex-officio* members (the Bishops of Northampton, Birmingham, and Hexham and Newcastle—an attempt to involve Ushaw in the project; the President of St. Edmund's College, Ware; the Rector of the Catholic Mission in Cambridge). The ordinary members of the Council were to consist of not less than five people nor more than would make up the registered number of members for the time being. Of the members for the time being, not less than one-third but not so many as one-half were to be laymen, and the rest Catholic clerks in Holy Orders. The ordinary members were to be nine in number (Bishop Brownlow of Clifton; Bishop Bourne, Coadjutor of Southwark; Hon. and Rt. Revd. Mgr. Algernon Charles Stanley, M.A.,[14] of Rome; the Revd. John McIntyre, D.D., of Oscott; Lord Clifford of Chudleigh; Lord Herries; Anatole von Hugel; Wyatt Davies; Charles John Philip Cave of Binstead, Cambridge.) Cardinal Vaughan was named as Visitor, and the Bishop of Northampton as Ecclesiastical Superior, in which office he was joined by four other bishops (three elected by the hierarchy from among their own number, and one appointed by the Visitor from the English Province).[15]

It was vital to have a representative body or Council, such as that adopted, in order that the House might be recognized as a public hostel of the University. The Principal of the House would, of course, be the immediate ecclesiastical Superior of the students, but the Council would represent the House before the University. It was decided that ideally the Council should consist of not less than ten nor more than sixteen members. Bishop Riddell was given special recognition but not the primacy of honour. He emphasized, however, that Canon Scott, whom he had appointed Rural Dean, must carry on all functions of that office in regard

[14] Bishop of 'Emmaus', and wealthy. He contributed substantially to the foundation, although there were many calls upon his generosity (see letter of Stanley to A. von Hugel, dated 8 Nov. 1896, among the A. von Hugel Papers).

[15] Archives of St. Edmund's College, Ware. Memorandum and Articles of Association, etc.

to St. Edmund's, and that priests who might wish to exercise their ministry in the diocese must apply for faculties direct to the bishop.[16]

In spite of the addition of the Bishop of Hexham and Newcastle to the list of the members of the Council of St. Edmund's House, it became obvious in February 1897 that the northern seminary would not participate. On the other hand, Oscott was prepared to send one student as an experiment. The Catholic aristocracy were more than pleased by the way things had developed and by the overwhelming control they were to exert over the House. Florence Bishop remarked to the Baroness von Hugel that such a House 'is terribly wanted among our clergy, they are so rough, so uncultivated, so bumptious, all who are not wellbred, and there are too many such. But I fear I fail to see how it is to work among *those* men who need the Education the most.'[17] She added a pious note: 'My heart goes out so to the poor—we all have our pet hobbies.'

At the time Riddell was becoming suitably mollified, and agreeing to attend functions of the University chaplain in Cambridge,[18] opposition to the policy being followed at St. Edmund's House began to emerge from an unexpected quarter. In August 1897 Cardinal Vaughan expressed scruples about permitting his own ecclesiastical students to go to Cambridge before ordination. It was not long before all the bishops interested in the House began to adopt the policy of permitting their students to read for a Cambridge degree only after their elevation to the priesthood, that is at about 24 or 25 years of age. This policy, in vogue until recently, is an indication of episcopal dislike of any interruption in the formal order of ecclesiastical studies. In October 1897 Bishop Stanley pointed out to Anatole von Hugel how lukewarm Vaughan had become on the question of sending ecclesiastical students to Cambridge.[19] The Cardinal's caution led to the revival of an earlier plan to consider accom-

---

[16] A. von Hugel Papers. See letter of Nolan to A. von Hugel, 26 Oct. 1896.
[17] Ibid. Florence Bishop to the Baroness, 2 Mar. 1897.
[18] Ibid. Herman Norman to A. von Hugel, 19 June 1897.
[19] Ibid. Stanley to A. von Hugel, 26 Oct. 1897.

modating lay students as well as clerical students at St. Edmund's House. The Duke of Norfolk was indignant; this might be an initial step in compelling Catholic lay undergraduates to attend the Catholic House, and this in its turn would remove those social advantages which the aristocratic families were seeking in the University. There were, in addition, academic objections to the idea. Henry Jackson of Trinity pointed out four of these: 'that the lay students will lose by seclusion from the life of the university; that they will be very conscious of their loss and therefore dissatisfied; that whether they were subjected to the rules made for the candidates for Orders, or placed under special rules, the maintenance of discipline in the House will be difficult; that this change in the scheme (for it is a change) will embitter opponents and cool the good will of friends'.[20] By the end of the year concerted opposition had killed the idea. The Duke declared that to admit lay students 'would destroy the special object I have had in view'.[21] Nevertheless, he was worried at the policy of many of those bishops, counted favourable to the House, who were now insisting that clerical students should not be sent to Cambridge prior to ordination. By far the greater proportion of students studying at Ware were candidates for the Westminster and Southwark dioceses, and both Cardinal Vaughan and Bishop Francis Bourne (who succeeded to the Southwark see on 9 April 1897) were to refuse to permit their students to attend Cambridge at the usual age for undergraduates. It was a serious blow that Bourne, who at thirty-six years of age belonged to a new generation of bishops, should take this stand. Norfolk was anxious to know 'from the University and educational point of view to what extent the difference is a very serious one', and he was worried that the numbers attending would remain very low for years to come. 'Does it practically thwart the hopes we have formed for the future?' he asked von Hugel.[22]

There was, however, still the problem of formal University recognition to be faced. On 13 January 1898, in his capacity as

[20] Ibid. Henry Jackson to A. von Hugel, 13 Nov. 1897.
[21] Ibid. Norfolk to A. von Hugel, 18 Apr. 1898.
[22] Ibid. Norfolk to A. von Hugel, 21 May 1898.

Founder, Norfolk petitioned the Vice-Chancellor of Cambridge for the recognition of St. Edmund's House as a public hostel.[23] He pointed out that the establishment had been recognized under the Companies Act, 1862–90, as an Association without dividends, and possessed a licence of the Board of Trade to omit the word 'limited'. The Master and the tutor was the Revd. W. O. Sutcliffe, M.A., St. John's College, and the Dean and chaplain, the Revd. E. Nolan, Trinity College. He enclosed a copy of the Memorandum and Articles of Association, which described the work intended to be carried out by St. Edmund's House. The communication was acknowledged and the information given that 'in the absence of the Vice-Chancellor from Cambridge' the Duke's letter and papers had been passed to the Deputy Vice-Chancellor, the Master of Sidney Sussex College.

Opposition to the application was expected, but nothing like the bigotry which was aroused. Wyatt Davies had, meantime, learned from the Deputy Vice-Chancellor that 'we could disarm the greater part of the opposition by an authoritative declaration that St. Edmund's was only intended for clerics and that laymen would not be taken. He said that the Articles of Association did not make this clear.'[24] Wyatt Davies answered, 'if this was so it was because students might be admitted exceptionally who were ecclesiastics in our sense but who to Protestants would appear as laymen'. It was suggested that a letter from the Cardinal might meet all justifiable objections. Anatole von Hugel promised to try to get such a document from Vaughan. He was fully occupied, also, in helping the Jesuits of Oxford in their attempt to have Clarke's Hall placed on a more official footing with the University there. Fr. R. Clarke had begged the Baron to help, for 'we have not the advantage of the Duke of Norfolk to support our application but we are trusting to our saints in Heaven to move the University to grant our petition'.[25] In the end the Jesuit saints were to prove as little effective as the ducal coat of arms, for the foundation was not granted the status of a permanent private Hall

[23] A. von Hugel Papers. Norfolk to the Vice-Chancellor, Cambridge, 13 Jan. 1898, copy.   [24] Ibid. Wyatt Davies to A. von Hugel, 16 Feb. 1898.
[25] Ibid. R. Clarke, S.J., to A. von Hugel, 27 Feb. 1898.

for members of the Society of Jesus until 1918, the year in which the Ampleforth foundation in Oxford, St. Benet's Hall, received similar recognition.

Vaughan's letter was a disappointment. Norfolk wrote: 'I should doubt the wisdom of making the Cardinal's letter public. It so very much accentuates the "walled-up" notion of the clerical student's life that it might overshoot the mark.'[26] It had been hoped to read Vaughan's letter in the University Senate, but in the event the Baron contented himself with showing it discreetly to one or two people of influence. Anatole von Hugel feared that someone of influence among the Fellows at Cambridge might suggest that St. Edmund's House should be recognized as a private hostel rather than admitted as a public Hall. Austen Leigh of King's College thought this was a distinct possibility, but it could be answered. 'The Statute for private hostels', he wrote, 'only contemplates individuals opening their own houses for students. A company has no private house to open, and could not undertake the obligation which the Statute imposes. Of course, if the promoters of St. Edmund's chose to supply Sutcliffe with funds and start him, *he* could apply for a grace to be allowed to keep a private hostel. But there would be no security that the hostel would go on after his departure or death.'[27]

By April 1898 the opposition to the St. Edmund's proposal was growing. An example of the feeling which inspired a good deal of it can be found in one letter which von Hugel received from a colleague, F. Jenkinson. He wrote:

I want to tell you myself that I am going to vote against St. Edmund's. I have thought over it all the vacation. Of course, I do not like opposing what you have so much at heart. But it is impossible for me to do otherwise. You and I look at the world from the opposite sides of an inaccessible barrier, and even discussion is impossible. I have felt the pain of this increasingly; I care for you but detest the organization under whose banners you have to march. And whatever you may feel for me, you are bound to resent my antagonism. And I cannot help realizing that the more your Church is countenanced in its aggression in this country,

---

[26] Ibid. Norfolk to A. von Hugel, 28 Mar. 1898, marked 'private'.
[27] Ibid. A. Austen Leigh to A. von Hugel, 18 Apr. 1898.

the more weak members of our Church are tempted—not to go over, that they are welcome to do—but to compete with your elaborate functions in order to catch the vulgar. As all these things seem to me adverse to religion and devotional feeling of a real and wholesome kind, I grieve to see them and am jealous of what is at least one of the causes. I might say: if your Church could have kept quiet and been content to minister to its own community: and soon—but of course it feels it *can* fight, and that it is its duty (at least probably some feel that). And if one party fights, the other party must fight in self-defence.[28]

Other views, less temperately expressed than those of Jenkinson, were uttered. The Revd. J. Ellis MacTaggart, destined to oppose formally the Grace for the recognition of St. Edmund's House, wrote a virulent letter to the editor of the *Cambridge Anti-Popery Gazette*. The fight was really for 'the Pure Gospel for which Cranmer and Ridley offered their saintly lives'.[29] He wrote:

That the Roman Church should venture in this age of enlightenment to attempt this assault on the liberties of the University is to some a matter for surprise; but those who look at the past history of this Great Apostacy will, I think, feel that the conduct of Cardinal Vaughan and his satellites is consonant with all the traditions of Rome. What is really surprising is that, within the precincts of the University, there should be found Members of the Senate who are willing to prostrate themselves before the pretensions of an Italian Bishop.

Those of advanced Liberal views, and in the name of Liberty, were determined 'to repel the claim of the Romanist Priesthood to share in the educational advantages of our great National University'.

In the same journal a letter was addressed to the Master of Corpus Christi College by one who called himself a militant Agnostic:

The Party of Reaction, which has already done so much harm in our elementary schools, has dared to attempt to lay hands on the University. As a militant Agnostic, it has been the aspiration of my life to set bounds to the claims of those who would, if allowed, mould and cramp the intellect of the rising generation. . . . It must be a matter of rejoicing

<hr />

28 A. von Hugel Papers. F. Jenkinson to A. von Hugel, 28 Apr. 1898.
29 Rev. J. E. MacTaggart in the *Cambridge Anti-Popery Gazette* (May 1898).

to you, that at the close of a long and honourable career, you should find yourself in a position to unite with those who, like Mr. Dickinson of King's College,[30] hold that to impress on young men at an impressionable age the tenets of *any* religion is to attack freedom of opinion.[31]

Other objectors confined themselves to more specific points. Arthur Gray of Jesus College, for instance, felt that the success of the Grace for the recognition of St. Edmund's House would lead to a spate of similar applications. Some of these, he told von Hugel,

will perhaps come from educational institutions which already have the status of Affiliated Colleges. With a view to economy they may desire to retain the privileges of affiliation for the local college while making it a preparatory school attached to the Cambridge Hostel. Such a cheapening (intellectually) of the Cambridge degree would be unwise and financially would be unfair to the older Colleges which it must be remembered exclusively provide the taxation which mainly equips the University with its staff of readers, demonstrators, etc., as well as with Museums. e.g., a local affiliated science college with a Cambridge Hostel attached would get its teaching mainly provided by the University (i.e. the older Colleges) and for a merely nominal payment, while its students claimed the additional privilege of affiliation.[32]

He added that his hesitation would be removed 'if the Governing Body of St. Edmund's House or some authoritative member of it can give a public pledge that the students of the House will not be allowed to avail themselves of the privileges to which they are entitled by the affiliation of St. Edmund's College, Ware, to the University'. Everard Fielding was likewise worried. 'It is a strong argument that if once a departure is made in favour of Catholics it will be difficult to oppose any similar application to admit a hostel for the training of Nonconformist Ministers, Board school-masters, or others for whom special conditions are desirable.'[33] Mgr. Bernard Ward attempted to reassure the wavering by declaring that he did not think the privileges of affiliation would be used, other than in exceptional cases. It was unlikely that it

---

[30] G. Lowes Dickinson.

[31] *Cambridge Anti-Popery Gazette.* Letter to the Revd. the Master of Corpus Christi College, Cambridge.

[32] A. von Hugel Papers. Arthur Gray to A. von Hugel, 6 May 1898.

[33] Ibid. Everard Fielding to the Baroness, 9 May 1898.

would be considered by the College educationally sound to reduce a young man's residence in Cambridge from three to two years. He pointed out that hitherto the College had not used the privilege in a single case. What was more, if the authorities in Cambridge 'prefer to make it a general rule that all students going there should take their full three years in preparing for their degree in every case, so far as we are concerned, we should raise no objection'.[34] He added: 'The probability is that if in some isolated instance we *did* want to use the privilege, the student in question would not be one of those sent to St. Edmund's House, Cambridge; he would more probably be a layman and would go elsewhere.'

On 12 May 1898 the Senate *nonplaceted* the Grace for the recognition of St. Edmund's House by the large majority of over 200 votes, although the minority was the more influential, all the Masters of Colleges excepting two voting for the House. The Grace was formally opposed by J. R. Tanner, G. Lowes Dickinson, and J. Ellis McTaggart. 'We believe', they declared, 'that the most important advantages of a University education can be but very imperfectly realised in an institution of which the essential characteristic is religious exclusion. . . . The establishment of Selwyn was a natural, though perhaps unfortunate, compensation given to the Established Church immediately after the abolition of many of her exclusive privileges in the Colleges.' But the admission of St. Edmund's House as a public hostel 'involves the acceptance, on the part of the University, of the principle of sectarian education in its fullest extent, and is therefore a new departure'.[35]

Reactions following the defeat of the Grace were swift. Wyatt Davies declared, 'we have been soundly beaten—and of course to us who love Cambridge this is a saddening result'.[36] Robert McDonnell was profoundly 'cut up'; 'I never thought I should feel so strongly on the question personally',[37] he remarked.

[34] A. von Hugel Papers. Mgr Bernard Ward to A. von Hugel, 7 May 1898.
[35] St. Edmund's College Archives.
[36] A. von Hugel Papers. E. Wyatt Davies to Dr. Henry Jackson, 12 May 1898.
[37] Ibid. T. F. McDonnell to A. von Hugel, 12 May 1898.

Friedrich von Hugel reflected that 'narrowness and injustice are absolutely interconfessional and international'.[38] Ultra-Liberals, Nonconformists, and Conservatives had united, and the Duke of Norfolk declared 'our opponents knew they had a force of unreasoning bigotry to appeal to and they called it up. It was no chance majority which any amount of forewarning could have enabled us to avert.'[39] Many broadminded men were disgusted at the scenes of ribaldry and intolerance which had accompanied the voting. To Anatole von Hugel, Professor Henry Sidgwick remarked, 'what a "no popery" show it was',[40] and Dr. Henry Jackson of Trinity College declared,

I am sick and ashamed that the University should have shown itself so intolerant. I have been in the habit of thinking that there was an advance in such matters everywhere, and especially at Cambridge. I thought that we had all of us learnt to respect one another's beliefs and opinions; that Christians thought more of their agreements and less of their differences, and that agnostics were less aggressive. It is not so, and I am very sore accordingly. . . . I am deeply grieved at the result. . . .[41]

Catholics themselves did not take the defeat too much to heart. Wilfrid Ward dismissed the setback as merely 'a bit of downright no-popery bigotry'.[42] Bishop Brownlow of Clifton felt 'it will be a spur to the clerical undergraduates to distinguish themselves in the Schools, and gain credit in the University and so earn recognition'.[43] Mgr. Bernard Ward was sure that 'in the long run it will be for our advantage—for one thing it dispenses of the temporary difficulty of procuring more students, for I take it that at a private hostel, a small number is sufficient, and if there had been a public hostel and in a year or two people had begun to observe that there were less than ten students, there might have been unpleasantness'.[44]

[38] Bedoyère, Michael de la, p. 108.
[39] A. von Hugel Papers. The Duke of Norfolk to A. von Hugel, 14 May 1898.
[40] Ibid. Professor Henry Sidgwick to A. von Hugel, 14 May 1898.
[41] Ibid. Dr. Henry Jackson to A. von Hugel, 17 May 1898.
[42] Ibid. Wilfrid Ward to A. von Hugel, 23 May 1898.
[43] Ibid. Bp. Brownlow of Clifton to A. von Hugel, 25 May 1898.
[44] Ibid. Mgr Bernard Ward to A. von Hugel, 16 May 1898.

Henry Sidgwick advised the Baron to ask the lodging-house committee to admit the Catholic House under its auspices, as indeed the Benedictines and Jesuits in Oxford had successfully done.[45] This advice was followed and the lodging-house syndicate permitted the establishment to continue, limiting the numbers of students to four at first, but later raising this to twelve. It was necessary, of course, for the students to become members of Fitzwilliam House, the centre for non-Collegiate students, in order to qualify as members of the University. St. Edmund's House remained under the vague protection of the non-Collegiate Board and Fitzwilliam House until the end of the First World War, by which time, in a period of eighteen years, it had presented over thirty-eight candidates for degrees. All these candidates passed, thirty-five with honours and two with First Classes, and six Exhibitions were gained. Nine candidates also obtained the Certificate in the Theory and Practice of Teaching. After the War the House became an official House of Residence with some claim on Fitzwilliam House to accept its members also as members —and therefore undergraduates—of Fitzwilliam House. After this change other Colleges—and particularly Christ's College— began to accept men from the House, and such men were required to dine in College only twice a week. From the time St. Edmund's became an official House of Residence there was no longer any limit on its numbers. In October 1964 a further step was taken, when St. Edmund's House, with no opposition whatever, was brought fully under the aegis of the University as an Approved Graduate Society, while still retaining undergraduates under its roof. At present there is a Master and seven Fellows, only one of whom is a cleric.[46]

The desirability of establishing houses of study in Cambridge and Oxford rapidly became apparent to the major Religious Orders as the twentieth century progressed. Today, in addition to St. Edmund's House and Benet House, there are in Cambridge St. Bonaventure's (Friars Minor House of Studies), Rosmini House (Institute of Charity), La Salle House of Studies (De La

45 A. von Hugel Papers. Professor Henry Sidgwick to A. von Hugel, 14 May 1898.   46 The house is no longer *exclusively* for priests and clerics.

Salle Brothers), Edmund Rice House of Studies (Christian
Brothers of Ireland), and Blackfriars, the Dominican House. A
house of studies for girls—Lady Margaret House—has also been
established by the Canonesses of St. Augustine. In Oxford there
has been similar development. The Dominicans possess a house of
studies there and this is in addition to the three permanent private
halls recognized by the University. In 1918 the Jesuit establishment
(Campion Hall) was finally officially recognized, as was that of
the Ampleforth Benedictines, St. Benet's Hall. In 1957, after
forty-seven years of hard pioneering work, the Franciscan Order
(Capuchins) finally achieved recognition as a permanent private
Hall for their house—Greyfriars. But the latter has made a significant departure from the tradition of Campion Hall and St.
Benet's. It receives undergraduates for tuition in any school of
the University, and only reserves the right to give *priority* of
acceptance to members of the Franciscan Order.

In 1900 Herbert Vaughan felt his life was drawing rapidly to
its close. He had begun to be afflicted by dropsy and by a marked
deterioration in an already troublesome heart condition. He was
rarely without pain, yet in spite of the effort and the prolonged
agony he continued to govern his diocese with courage until the
final collapse occurred in March 1903. From then until his death
on 19 June, two months after his seventy-first birthday, he was
an invalid at St. Joseph's College, Mill Hill, the house of the
Congregation of missionary priests he had founded and governed.
Bishop Gordon Wheeler has seen in the passing of Vaughan 'the
end of an epoch of gigantic personalities' in the government of
the Roman Catholic Church in England,[47] and Archbishop David
Mathew has declared that Vaughan 'in fact summed up in himself
the strength of the centuries of persecution', exemplifying 'the
strong fidelity of the old squirearchy'.[48] In the first three Archbishops of Westminster the Roman Church had seen representatives of the three main strands which went to make up English
Catholic life in the nineteenth century: the exuberance of the

[47] Wheeler, Gordon, 'The Archdiocese of Westminster', in Beck, G. A. (ed.),
p. 171.
[48] Mathew, *Catholicism in England*, p. 223.

Irish personified in Wiseman, the intellectual ability and extrovert mentality of the converts personified in Manning, and the piety and caution of the Old Catholic families personified in Vaughan. Manning's policy of bringing his co-religionists into the full stream of English public life had been largely achieved. His desire to break the stranglehold retained by the Old Catholic families, and their natural allies the country gentry, upon English Catholic affairs had been sustained by Vaughan's personal efforts to pursue what he considered to be the interests of the professional classes and the poor in educational matters and in social policy. At the close of his life Vaughan wrote to Bishop Burton of Clifton: 'But, far off in the background, I see a great multitude of eager faces, I hear their voices like the sound of the waves of the sea. Who are they? They are the boys and girls in our public element-ary schools—they are the strength, the hope, the population of the future. They form the young democracy that is going to rule the country, to make or mar the future of Christianity in this land.'[49] Such a realization was indicative that Herbert Vaughan had learned the lesson his old friend and Superior had tried to teach him.

[49] McCormack, A., p. 322.

SOURCES AND BIBLIOGRAPHY

I. ARCHIVAL SOURCES

AMPLEFORTH ARCHIVES: Letters of Abbot J. W. M. Alcock, R. P. Burchall, R. W. Cooper, J. Gillow, H. E. Manning, E. A. O'Gorman, F. Rhind, Abbot B. Smith, J. N. Sweeney, W. B. Ullathorne, Jerome Vaughan, and N. Wiseman.

BAYSWATER, St. Mary of the Angels: Manning Papers.

BEVERLEY RECORD OFFICE: Everingham Papers. Herries Papers.

BIRMINGHAM ARCHDIOCESAN ARCHIVES: Ullathorne Papers.

BROMPTON ORATORY: Copies of minutes of the meetings of the Universities' Catholic Education Board. Carlo, Canon Menghini's opinion 'upon certain instructions addressed to the English Bishops by the Sacred Congregation of Propaganda', 1885.

CAMBRIDGE, Fisher House: Anatole von Hugel Papers.

CLIFTON, St. Ambrose, Leigh Woods: Clifford Papers.

FARM STREET JESUIT ARCHIVES, LONDON, W. I: Letters of T. W. Allies, T. Capel, R. F. Clarke, S.J., R. Colley, S.J., W. Eyre, S.J., P. Gallwey, S.J., J. Gerard, S.J., H. G. Giffarde, J. V. Harting, S. J. Hunter, S.J., J. R. Madan, H. E. Manning, J. Mulligan, J. H. Newman, J. S. Northcote, G. Porter, S.J., Joseph Rickaby, S.J., J. H. Scott, F. Smith, S.J., and Alfred Weld, S.J.

LEEDS DIOCESAN ARCHIVES: The Cornthwaite papers.

MILL HILL, London, N.W. 7, St. Joseph's College: Vaughan MSS.

NORTHAMPTON DIOCESAN ARCHIVES: Riddell papers.

OSCOTT COLLEGE: Records of St. Mary's College, Oscott (manuscript and printed), 1830–1900, by Henry Weedall. Also letters of Charles Newsham, E. J. Purbrick, S.J., J. Sweeney, and H. Weedall.

OXFORD, St. Benet's Hall: Hartwell de la Garde Grissell Papers.

SOUTHWARK ARCHDIOCESAN ARCHIVES: Letters of R. F. Clarke, R. A. Coffin, E. S. Ffoulkes, G. R. Kingdon, S.J., D. Lewis, the Duke of Norfolk, J. E. North, J. S. Northcote, R. Simpson, and G. Wenham.

WARE, St. Edmund's College: Documents relating to the foundation of St. Edmund's Hall, Cambridge.

II. PERIODICALS, JOURNALS, AND NEWSPAPERS

The Ampleforth Journal; The Catholic Historical Review; The Catholic Magazine; The Catholic Miscellany and Monthly Repository of Information; The Catholic School; Catholic University Gazette; The Clergy Review; The Contemporary Review; The Daily Telegraph; The Downside Review; The Dublin Review; The Edinburgh Review; The Guardian; Irish Ecclesiastical Record; Journal of British Studies; The Month; The Monthly Magazine; The Nineteenth Century; The Oscotian; The Quarterly Review; The Rambler; The Spectator; The Tablet; Thought; The Universe; The University College Cork Record; Ushaw Magazine; The Venerabile; The Weekly Orthodox Journal; The Weekly Register and Catholic Standard; The Wiseman Review.

III. PRIMARY PRINTED SOURCES

AMHERST, W. J., *The History of Catholic Emancipation* (2 vols., Kegan Paul & Trench, London, 1886).

BELLASIS, E., *Memorials of Mr. Serjeant Bellasis, 1800–1873* (Burns & Oates, London, 1893).

BUTLER, C., *The Life and Times of Bishop Ullathorne, 1806–1889* (2 vols., Burns, Oates, & Washbourne, London, 1926).

CATHOLIC BARRISTER, A, *The New Departure in Catholic Liberal Education* (Burns & Oates, London, 1878).

CATHOLIC LAYMAN, A, *University Education for English Catholics: a Letter to the Very Rev. J. H. Newman, D.D.* (Burns & Oates, London, 1864).

CHICHESTER, C. R., *Schools* (Burns & Oates, London, 1882).

DESSAIN, C. S., and BLEHL, V. F. (eds.), *The Letters and Diaries of John Henry Newman*, esp. vol. 11 (Nelson, London, 1965).

HENNESSY, J. P., *The Failure of the Queen's Colleges and Mixed Education in Ireland* (Bryce, London, 1859).

HERON, D. C., *The Constitutional History of the University of Dublin, with some account of its present condition and suggestions for improvement* (McGlashan, Dublin, 1847).

HÜBER, V. A., *The English Universities*, English trans.; ed. F. W. Newman (2 vols., Pickering, London, 1843).

Instruction to the Parents, Superiors, and Directors of Catholic Laymen who Desire to Study in the Universities of Oxford and Cambridge, by the Cardinal Archbishop and Bishops of the Province of Westminster (London, 1896).

LESLIE, S. (ed.), *Letters of Herbert, Cardinal Vaughan, to Lady Herbert of Lea, 1867–1903* (Burns Oates, London, 1942).

McDONNELL, H. H. G., and HANCOCK, W. N. H., *Report of the Case of Heron v. the Provost and Senior Fellows of Trinity College, Dublin* (Hodges & Smith, Dublin, 1846).

MacSUIBHNE, P., *Paul Cullen and his Contemporaries, with their Letters from 1820 to 1902* (3 vols. to date, Leinster Leader, Naas, 1961–3).

MANNING, H. E., *The Office of the Church in Higher Catholic Education*, Easter Pastoral Letter (London, 1885).

MORAN, P. F. (ed.), *The Pastoral Letters and Other Writings of Cardinal Cullen* (3 vols., Browne & Nolan, Dublin, 1882).

NEWMAN, J. H., *The Idea of a University* (Pickering, London, 1873 edn.; and Longmans, Green & Co., London, 1912 edn.).

OAKELEY, F., *The Question of University Education for English Catholics, Considered Principally in its Moral and Religious Bearings, in a Letter to the Right Rev. the Bishop of Birmingham* (Burns & Lambert, London, 1864).

—— *Appendix to a Letter on University Education for English Catholics, suggested by an article in 'The Dublin Review'* (Burns & Lambert, London, 1864).

OLD ALUMNUS, AN, *Records and Recollections of St. Cuthbert's College, Ushaw*, with an introductory poem (E. Butler & Son, Preston, 1889).

Pastoral Letter of the Archbishop and Bishops of the Province of Westminster in Provincial Council Assembled, September 20th, 1873.

PETRE, W., *Catholic Systems of School Discipline* (Burns & Oates, London, 1878).

—— *The Position and Prospects of Catholic Liberal Education* (Burns & Oates, London, 1878).

—— *The Problem of Catholic Liberal Education* (Burns & Oates, London, 1877).

—— *Remarks on the Present Condition of Catholic Liberal Education* (Burns & Oates, London, 1877).

PURCELL, E. S., *The Life of Cardinal Manning* (2 vols., Macmillan, London, 1896).

—— *The Life and Letters of Ambrose Phillipps de Lisle* (2 vols., Macmillan, London, 1900).

RAWES, H. A., *Cui Bono? University Education: a Letter to a Catholic Layman* (Burns & Lambert, London, 1864).

Report of the Archbishop and Bishops to His Eminence the Cardinal Prefect of the Sacred Congregation of Propaganda on the Subject of Higher Catholic Education in England, June 14th, 1872.

ROCHE, J. S., *A History of Prior Park College and its Founder Bishop Baines* (Burns & Oates, London, 1931).

SIMPSON, R., *Bishop Ullathorne and the Rambler: Reply to Criticisms Contained in 'A Letter on the Rambler and Home and Foreign Review' (by the Right Rev. Bishop Ullathorne)* (Williams & Norgate, London, 1862).

SNEAD-COX, J. G., *Life of Cardinal Vaughan* (2 vols., Burns & Oates, London, 1910).

Synodal Letter of the Archbishop and Bishops of the Province of Westminster Assembled, August, 1874.

WARD, BERNARD, *History of St. Edmund's College, Old Hall* (Kegan Paul, Trench, Trübner, & Co., London, 1893).

—— *The Dawn of the Catholic Revival in England, 1781–1803* (2 vols., Longmans, London, 1909).

—— *The Eve of Catholic Emancipation, 1803–1829* (2 vols., Longmans, London, 1911).

—— *The Sequel to Catholic Emancipation* (2 vols., Longmans, London, 1915).

WARD, MAISIE, *The Wilfrid Wards and the Transition* (2 vols., Sheed & Ward, London, 1934).

WARD, WILFRID, *William George Ward and the Catholic Revival* (Macmillan, London, 1893).

—— *The Life and Times of Cardinal Wiseman* (2 vols., Longmans, Green & Co., London, 1912).

—— *The Life of John Henry, Cardinal Newman* (2 vols., Longmans, London, 1912).

IV. SECONDARY PRINTED SOURCES

ALLIES, MARY H., *Thomas William Allies* (Burns & Oates, London, 1907).

ALTHOLZ, J., *The Liberal Catholic Movement in England* (Burns & Oates, London, 1962).

ARMYTAGE, W. H. G., *Four Hundred Years of English Education* (Cambridge University Press, 1964).

BAILEY, C., *Francis Fortescue Urquhart: a Memoir* (Macmillan, London, 1936).

BARRY, W., *Memories and Opinions* (Putnam, London, 1926).

BASSET, B., *The English Jesuits, from Campion to Martindale* (Burns & Oates, London, 1967).

BEALES, A. C. F., *Education Under Penalty* (University of London Press, 1963).

BECK, G. A. (ed.), *The English Catholics, 1850–1950* (Burns & Oates, London, 1950).

BEDOYÈRE, M. DE LA, *The Life of Baron Von Hugel* (Dent, London, 1951).

BIRT, H. N., *Downside: the History of St. Gregory's School, from its Commencement at Douay to the Present Time* (Kegan Paul, London, 1902).

BRAYE, LORD, *Fewness of My Days: A Life in Two Centuries* (Sands, London, 1927).

Catholic Emancipation, 1829–1929: Essays by Various Writers (Longmans, Green & Co., London, 1929).

CHAPMAN, R., *Father Faber* (Burns & Oates, London, 1962).

CORCORAN, T. (ed.), *Newman: Selected Discourses on Liberal Knowledge*, with an Introduction (printed for academic use in the Department of Education, University College, Dublin, 1929).

—— *O'Connell and Catholic Education: Two Papers Published in Ireland for the Centenary Year of Catholic Emancipation* (Talbot Press, Dublin, 1929).

CORNISH, F. W., *A History of the English Church in the Nineteenth Century* (2 vols., Macmillan, London, 1910).

COULSON, J. (ed.), *Theology and the University: an Ecumenical Investigation* (Darton, Longman, and Todd, London, 1964).

COX, G. V., *Recollections of Oxford* (Macmillan, London, 1868).

CRAVEN, A., *Lady Georgiana Fullerton, sa vie, ses œuvres*, préc. d'une lettre du Card. Newman (Perrin, Paris, 1888).

CULLER, A. D., *The Imperial Intellect* (Yale University Press, New Haven, Conn., 1955).

DESSAIN, C. S., *John Henry Newman* (Nelson, London, 1966).

Dictionary of National Biography (Smith, Elder & Co., London, 1908; 7 vols., Oxford University Press, 1912–61).

EVENNETT, H. O., 'The Cambridge Prelude to 1895', *The Dublin Review*, 218 (1946).

—— *The Catholic Schools of England and Wales* (Cambridge University Press, 1944).

FITZGERALD, P., *Stonyhurst Memories; or, Six Years at School* (Richard Bentley, London, 1895).

—— *Fifty Years of Catholic Life and Social Progress* (2 vols., Fisher Unwin, London, 1901).

FITZSIMONS, J. (ed.), *Manning: Anglican and Catholic* (The Catholic Book Club, London, 1951).

FOTHERGILL, B., *Nicholas Wiseman* (Faber & Faber, London, 1963).

GASQUET, ABBOT, *Lord Acton and his Circle* (London, 1906).

GERARD, J., *Stonyhurst College Centenary Record* (Marcus Ward, Belfast, 1894).

GILLOW, J., *Bibliographical Dictionary of the English Catholics, from the Breach with Rome in 1534 to the Present Time* (5 vols., Burns & Oates, London, 1885–1902).

GORMAN, W. G., *Converts to Rome: A Biographical List of the More Notable Converts to the Catholic Church in the United Kingdom During the Last Sixty Years* (Sands, London, 1910).

GREEN, V. H. H., *Oxford Common Room: A Study of Lincoln College and Mark Pattison* (Arnold, London, 1957).

GRUBER, J. W., *A Conscience in Conflict* (Columbia University Press, New York, 1960).

GWYNN, D., *Lord Shrewsbury, Pugin, and the Catholic Revival* (Hollis & Carter, London, 1946).

—— *O'Connell, Davis, and the Colleges Bill* (Cork University Press, 1948).

HICKEY, J., *Urban Catholics: Urban Catholicism in England and Wales from 1829 to the Present Day* (Geoffrey Chapman, London, 1967).

HIRST, J. (and others), *Memoirs of Lady Mary Arundell, Moses Furlong, Angelo Rinolfi, Peter Hutton, William Lockhart* (Market Weighton Press, n.d.).

HOLLAND, B., *Kenelm Henry Digby* (Longmans, Green & Co., London, 1919).

HOLLIS, C., *Newman and the Modern World* (Hollis & Carter, London, 1967).

HUNTER-BLAIR, D.D., *John Patrick, Third Marquess of Bute, K.T., 1847–1900: a Memoir* (John Murray, London, 1921).

KENNY, T., *The Political Thought of John Henry Newman* (Longmans, London, 1957).

LEETHAM, C., *Luigi Gentilli: a Sower for the Second Spring* (Burns & Oates, London, 1965).

LESLIE, S., *Henry Edward Manning: his Life and Labours* (Burns & Oates, London, 1921).

MCCLELLAND, V. A., *Cardinal Manning: his Public Life and Influence, 1865–92* (Oxford University Press, 1962).

MCCORMACK, A., *Cardinal Vaughan* (Burns & Oates, London, 1966).

MCGRATH, F., *Newman's University, Idea and Reality* (Longmans, Green & Co., London, 1951).

MCPHERSON, R. G., *Theory of Higher Education in Nineteenth-Century England* (University of Georgia Press, U.S.A., 1959).

MAITLAND, F. W., *Life and Letters of Leslie Stephen* (Duckworth, London, 1906).

MALLETT, C. E., *A History of the University of Oxford* (3 vols., Methuen, London, 1927).

MALLOCK, W. H., *Memoirs of Life and Literature* (Chapman & Hall, London, 1920).

MANNING, H. E., *Miscellanies* (3 vols., Burns & Oates, London, 1877).

MARTINDALE, C. C., *Catholics at Oxford* (Basil Blackwell, Oxford, 1925).

MATHEW, D., *Acton: the Formative Years* (Eyre & Spottiswoode, London, 1946).

—— *Catholicism in England: the Portrait of a Minority, its Culture and Tradition* (Eyre & Spottiswoode, London, 1955).

MAYNARD, T., *Orestes Brownson: Yankee, Radical, Catholic* (Macmillan, New York, 1943).

MILBURN, D., *A History of Ushaw College* (Ushaw College, Durham, 1964).

MORLEY, J., *Life of William Ewart Gladstone* (3 vols., Macmillan, London, 1903).

MORRIS, J., *Catholic England in Modern Times* (Burns & Oates, London, 1892).

MURPHY, T., *The Position of the Catholic Church in England and Wales during the Last Two Centuries* (Burns & Oates, London, 1892).

NEWMAN, B., *Cardinal Newman: a Biographical and Literary Study* (Bell, London, 1925).

NEWMAN, J. H., *Apologia pro Vita Sua* (Everyman's, Liby. edn., London, 1912).

—— *Discussions and Arguments*, 2nd edn. (London, 1873).

—— *Sermons Preached on Various Occasions*, 5th edn. (London, 1881).

NEWSOME, D., *The Parting of Friends: A Study of the Wilberforces and Henry Manning* (Murray, London, 1966).

NORMAN, E. R., *The Catholic Church and Ireland in the Age of Rebellion, 1859–1873* (Longmans, 1965).

O'FAOLÁIN, S., *Newman's Way* (Longmans, Green & Co., London, 1952).

O'REILLY, B., *Life of John MacHale, Archbishop of Tuam* (2 vols., Fr. Pustet & Co., New York and Cincinnati, 1890).

O'SHEA, J. A., *Roundabout Recollections* (Ward & Downey, London, 1892).

OXENHAM, H. N., *Short Studies in Ecclesiastical History and Biography* (Chapman & Hall, London, 1884).

PATTISON, M., *Memoirs* (Macmillan, London, 1885).

POLLEN, ANNE, *John Hungerford Pollen* (Murray, London, 1912).

ROBBINS, W., *The Newman Brothers* (Heinemann, London, 1966).

ROTHBLATT, S., *The Revolution of the Dons: Cambridge and Society in Victorian England* (Faber & Faber, London, 1968).

RYDER, H. I. D., *Essays* (Longmans, Green & Co., London, 1911).

RYLANDS, W. H., MASPERO, G., and NEVILLE, E. (eds.), *The Life and Work of Sir Peter le Page Renouf*, First Series (Leroux, Paris, 1907).

SPARROW, J., *Mark Pattison and the Idea of a University* (Cambridge University Press, 1967).

SPENCER, P., *Politics of Belief* (Faber & Faber, London, 1953).

STOCKLEY, W. F. P., *Newman, Education, and Ireland* (Sands, Edinburgh and Glasgow, n.d.).

TAYLOR, I. A., *The Cardinal Democrat: Henry Edward Manning* (Kegan Paul, London, 1908).

The Irish University Question: The Catholic Case: Selections from the Speeches and Writings of the Archbishop of Dublin—William Walsh—with a Historical Sketch of the Irish University Question (Browne & Nolan, Dublin, 1897).

TIERNEY, M. (ed.), *Daniel O'Connell: Nine Centenary Essays* (Browne & Nolan, Dublin, 1949).

—— *Struggle With Fortune* (Browne & Nolan, Dublin, 1954).

TREVOR, MERIOL, *Newman: The Pillar of the Cloud* and *Newman: Light in Winter* (Macmillan, London, 1962).

TRISTRAM, H. (ed.), *John Henry Newman: Autobiographical Writings* (Sheed & Ward, London, 1956).

Universities' Catholic Education Board: a Report of Its Work from 1895 to 1897 (privately printed, London, 1897).

University of London: Historical Record (1836–1912) (University of London Press, 1912).

VAN ZELLER, H., *Downside By and Large* (Sheed & Ward, London, 1953).

WALSH, W. J., *Trinity College and the University of Dublin* (privately printed, Dublin, 1902).

WARD, MAISIE, *The Young Mr. Newman* (Sheed & Ward, London, 1952).

WARD, W. R., *Victorian Oxford* (Cass, London, 1965).

WILSON, J. A., *The Life of Bishop Hedley* (Burns, Oates & Washbourne, London, 1930).

WISEMAN, N., *Essays on Various Subjects* (Thomas Baker, London, 1888).

—— *Recollections of the Last Four Popes* (Hurst & Blackett, London, 1858).

—— *Sermon*, preached at St. George's Cathedral, Southwark, Sunday, 27 June 1852, in behalf of the Catholic University of Ireland (T. Richardson, London, 1852).

INDEX